THE STRUGGLE FOR PAKISTAN

THE STRUGGLE
FOR PAKISTAN

A MUSLIM HOMELAND AND GLOBAL POLITICS

AYESHA JALAL

The Belknap Press of Harvard University Press

CAMBRIDGE MASSACHUSETTS   LONDON ENGLAND   2014

Library of Congress Cataloging-in-Publication Data

Jalal, Ayesha, author.
The struggle for Pakistan : a Muslim homeland and global politics /
Ayesha Jalal.
pages   cm
Includes bibliographical references and index.
ISBN 978-0-674-05289-5 (alkaline paper)
1. Pakistan—History.   2. Pakistan—Politics and government.
3. Civil-military relations—Pakistan.   4. Democracy—Pakistan.
5. Islam and politics—Pakistan.   6. Islam and state—Pakistan.
7. Geopolitics—Pakistan.   I. Title.
DS383.5.A2J338   2014
954.9104—dc23   2014006379

In memory of my father, Hamid Jalal,
for supporting my spirit of historical inquiry

CONTENTS

PREFACE

Pakistan for me is more than just a place of origin. Ever since my formative teen years in New York City, the trials and tribulations of this self-styled Muslim homeland have sparked my curiosity and led me to ask questions for which there were no easy answers. As a high school student in the cosmopolitan setting of Manhattan during the civil war in East Pakistan, I could not reconcile the narratives of Pakistan's official nationalism with daily media reports of atrocities perpetrated by the national army and its auxiliaries against the Bengali population of the eastern wing. The events of 1971, which ended with Pakistan's military defeat by India and the creation of Bangladesh, demolished the most cherished truths of official Pakistani nationalism and left a profound mark on my development as a historian.

It was as an undergraduate at Wellesley College that understanding the causes of Pakistan's recurrent spells of military rule and the uses made of Islam by the state to govern a federally disparate and inequitable nation-state became an intellectual preoccupation. I was in Rawalpindi for my summer holidays in 1977 when General Zia-ul-Haq overthrew the elected government of Zulfikar Ali Bhutto and imposed martial law in Pakistan. The Zia regime exploited the global assertion of Islam in the wake of the 1973 Arab-Israeli war and the quadrupling of oil prices to promote "Islamization" and inject public displays of Islamic piety into the national culture. The swift transformation of Pakistan in the name of Islamic ideology defined by an unpopular military dictator propelled me toward studying history, both as a methodology and as a discipline. Zia's contention that Islam was the sole reason for the country's creation prompted my inquiry into the partition of India that resulted in my doctoral work at the University of Cambridge. This work was later published in 1985 by Cambridge

University Press as *The Sole Spokesman: Jinnah, the Muslim League, and the Demand for Pakistan*.

The insights I gained from research on British decolonization led me to envisage writing a history of postcolonial Pakistan. When my attempts to gain access to government archives in Pakistan made little headway, I used the available sources to write a book on the formative first decade. *The State of Martial Rule: The Origins of Pakistan's Political Economy of Defence* (Cambridge University Press, 1990) demonstrated how the interplay of domestic regional and international factors during the Cold War resulted in the suspension of political processes and the first military intervention of 1958. The emergence of military dominance has been the most salient and enduring feature of Pakistan's postcolonial history. I always intended to extend the analytical narrative to the subsequent decades to explain the reasons for military supremacy despite the staggering loss of the eastern wing and abortive attempts at establishing the rudiments of a functioning democracy. However, I chose to give precedence to works of theory and history based on deep research in primary sources to write *Self and Sovereignty* (Routledge, 2000) and *Partisans of Allah* (Harvard University Press, 2008). It was only after revisiting partition through the life and literature of Saadat Hasan Manto in *The Pity of Partition* (Princeton University Press, 2012) that I felt the time had come to write a definitive, contemporary history of Pakistan in a changing global context.

Even as Pakistan grapples with religious extremism, regional dissidence, and a swarm of political and economic challenges, opportunities have lately arisen for Pakistan to leave the state of martial rule behind. Military regimes in particular have used Pakistan's geostrategic location at the crosshairs of competing dynamics connecting South Asia with the Middle East and Central Asia to claim a pivotal role in international affairs. But with the Cold War now over, the military's ascendancy is more of a liability than an asset in negotiating global politics. How well a nuclearized Pakistan is able to make the necessary adjustments in civil-military relations will have major implications for its internal stability as well as global peace. The presentist turn that has crept into recent scholarship on Pakistan needs to be countered with a work of historical interpretation that is attentive to key shifts at the interconnected domestic, regional, and international levels. This narrative history of Pakistan represents decades of research and thinking about a country that is all too often reduced to facile and defective descriptions without regard for either context or content.

ABBREVIATIONS

AIML	All-India Muslim League
ANP	Awami National Party
BDs	Basic Democrats
BJP	Bharatiya Janata Party
CSP	Civil Service of Pakistan
CTBT	Comprehensive Test Ban Treaty
DG	Director General
DPR	Defense of Pakistan Rules
FANA	Federally Administered Northern Areas
FATA	Federally Administered Tribal Areas
FSF	Federal Security Force
GHQ	General Headquarters
HUM	Harkat-ul-Mujahidin
IB	Intelligence Bureau
IJI	Islamic Jumhoori Ittihad
IMF	International Monetary Fund
ISI	Inter-Services Intelligence
ISPR	Inter-Services Public Relations
JUI	Jamiat-i-Ulema-i-Islam
JUI-F	Jamiat-i-Ulema-i-Islam (Fazlur Rahman)
JUP	Jamiat-i-Ulema-i-Pakistan
KPK	Khyber Pakhtunkhawa

LFO	Legal Framework Order
LOC	Line of Control
MI	Military Intelligence
MMA	Muttahida Majlis-e-Amal
MQM	Muhajir Qaumi Movement/Muttahida Qaumi Movement
MRD	Movement for the Restoration of Democracy
NAB	National Accountability Bureau
NAP	National Awami Party
NDC	National Documentation Center
NFC	National Finance Commission
NPT	Nuclear Nonproliferation Treaty
NRO	National Reconciliation Ordinance
NSC	National Security Council
NWFP	North West Frontier Province
PAEC	Pakistan Atomic Energy Commission
PCO	Provisional Constitutional Order
PEMRA	Pakistan Electronic Media Regulatory Authority
PIA	Pakistan International Airlines
PML-N	Pakistan Muslim League (Nawaz)
PML-Q	Pakistan Muslim League (Quaid-i-Azam)
PNA	Pakistan National Alliance
PPP	Pakistan People's Party
PPPP	Pakistan Peoples Party Parliamentarians
PTI	Pakistan Tehrik-i-Insaaf
PTV	Pakistan Television
RAW	Research and Analysis Wing
RCO	Revival of the Constitution of 1973 Order
RSS	Rashtriya Swayamsevak Sangh
SAARC	South Asian Association for Regional Cooperation
TNSM	Tehrik-i-Nifaz-i-Shariat-i-Muhammadi
TTP	Tehrik-i-Taliban Pakistan
UNCIP	United Nations Commission on India and Pakistan
USIS	United States Information Service

PROLOGUE

"Speak, for Your Lips Are Free"

In the late afternoon of December 27, 2007, two fateful seconds revealed the transformation of Pakistan, the world's second largest Muslim state, into an Islamic killing field. Radiant and beaming, Benazir Bhutto stood up through the sunroof of her armored white Toyota Land Cruiser to wave at the crowd gathered outside the north gate of Rawalpindi's historic Liaquat Bagh. A fifteen-year-old child assassin only ten feet away from the crawling vehicle shot her before a suicide bomb was detonated. The massive explosion killed two dozen bystanders in addition to the attacker and injured ninety-one. Just minutes earlier, the leader of the Pakistan People's Party (PPP) had given a rousing speech at an election rally here, at the garrison city's largest and most famous public ground. This former municipal park is named after Pakistan's first prime minister, Liaquat Ali Khan, who was assassinated on October 16, 1951, while addressing an audience on the expansive open green.

More than tragedy and location link these events separated by over five and a half decades. Said Akbar Babrak, an Afghan under close surveillance by Pakistani intelligence agencies, fired the fatal shot at Liaquat from a distance of a mere eighteen feet. The assassin had been sitting in a row full of policemen with a wad of money in his pocket. The police proceeded to shoot him on the spot, foreclosing the identification of a larger conspiracy. All the evidence pointed to criminal negligence and dereliction of duty on the part of the police, who had ample information about the threat to the prime minister's life. A commission of inquiry was set up before the police investigation had been completed, leading to interagency conflict. Police in the North-West Frontier Province (NWFP), where the killer resided, were at cross-purposes with the Punjab police in attempting to parry the charge that they had not done their job properly. Under the circumstances, unearthing the motivations behind the murder or apportioning responsibility for the heinous deed proved impossible.[1]

The cover-up following Liaquat's assassination pointed to the collusion of individuals in high office. No one was ever formally charged, leading to much speculation about the likely culprits. The unsolved murder case advertised the government's lack of concern for public transparency or accountability and, in time, facilitated the military's rise to dominance against the backdrop of Cold War politics. Sudden and unexplained deaths of key politicians have been a recurring feature of Pakistani history since 1951. Often the reasons have been patently evident. In 1979 General Zia-ul-Haq, a military dictator, sent a popularly elected prime minister, Zulfikar Ali Bhutto, to the gallows about a mile away from Liaquat Bagh on flimsy charges of murder, ignoring international pleas for clemency. The executioner met his nemesis when Zia died in a mysterious plane crash as his regime tottered at the brink in 1988.

It was under the watch of yet another military ruler that Benazir met the violent end she had publicly warned against, going so far as to point the finger at the regime's innermost circle.[2] Remarkably, the police had hosed down the crime scene within half an hour of Benazir's murder, to prevent rioting by PPP supporters at the blood-soaked venue. Like the government commission that investigated Liaquat's death, the special United Nations Commission invited by the PPP government to examine the evidence related to Benazir's assassination did not attempt to identify the culprits. The members of the Commission admitted that the teenage killer could not have been acting alone. But given their limited terms of reference, they confined themselves to attributing blame for her death to a colossal security failure on the part of General Pervez Musharraf's military regime. The published report of the UN Commission noted that the members were "mystified by the efforts of certain high-ranking Pakistani government authorities to obstruct access to military and intelligence sources."[3]

The veil of secrecy shrouding high-profile political assassinations in postindependence Pakistan has extended to information on the inner dynamics of its frenzied history. Forced to imbibe the truths of officialdom, many of its literate citizens have opted for the comforts of ignorance, habits of skepticism, and, most troubling of all, a contagion of belief in conspiracy theories. Instead of critical thinking marked by cautious optimism, which might be expected of a people who have weathered many storms in their country's short but eventful history, including the traumatic dismemberment of the country in 1971, a cross-section of Pakistanis today are despondent. This has much to do with growing economic disparities and the sense of alienation in regions denied their share of resources and political power during prolonged periods of military and quasi-military rule. But the chronic state of national malaise in Pakistan stems from deeper psychological sources. There have been recurrent doubts about its ability to survive and considerable angst about the artificial nature of a state carved out of the predominantly Muslim extremities of the subcontinent. In the brutally blunt metaphor of Britain's last viceroy, Lord Mountbatten, "administratively it [wa]s the difference between putting up a permanent building, a nissen hut or a tent. As far as Pakistan is concerned we are putting up a tent. We can do no more."[4] Mountbatten had fully expected this fragile tent to collapse. Pakistan has belied the wicked prophecy of the last viceroy. But instead of being replaced with a permanent building, the proverbial tent has been metaphorically transformed into a sprawling military barrack.

The rise of the military to a position of enduring dominance within Pakistan's state structure is the most salient development in the country's history and has deeply influenced its subsequent course. This phenomenon of sustained military dominance in Pakistan can be understood and explained only in the context of Cold War and post–Cold War global politics. International factors, regional rivalries, and domestic dilemmas all contributed in the first decade of independence to tilt the balance firmly in favor of the nonelected rather than elected institutions of the state. This institutional imbalance in turn distorted the center-region dynamic within Pakistan. The suppression of democratic rights during extended periods of military rule wreaked havoc on political processes and the delicate weave of Pakistani society, accentuating tensions not only between the center and the different provinces but also between the dominant Punjab and the non-Punjabi provinces. The breakaway in 1971 of the eastern wing, where a majority of the country's Muslim population lived, was simply the most dramatic manifestation of the federal challenges that have plagued Pakistan ever since its inception and the early entrenchment of military dominance.

Pakistanis have internalized the threats, imagined and real, to the political stability and security of their country. An overwhelming fear of continued chaos and violence, if not outright disintegration, has made it difficult to arrive at balanced assessments of a disturbing present in order to plan for the future as a unified and coherent nation. Regional tensions with India and the relentless collateral damage of the American-led war in Afghanistan have taken a hefty toll on the Pakistani people. More than 40,000 terror-related casualties were recorded in the decade from 2003 to 2013 while expenditure on security was triple the amount Washington paid Pakistan for military operations in Afghanistan. Spiraling security costs have forced drastic cutbacks in public spending and development expenditure, leading to the suspension of already inadequate social services. The country's negative international persona as the axis of global terror networks has proven utterly detrimental for its citizens. After the floods of 2010, the worst ever recorded, Pakistan lagged conspicuously far behind earthquake-hit Haiti in attracting international beneficence. Severe energy shortages caused by bad planning, theft, and nonpayment of bills by state institutions and influential individuals further dented a fragile economy still reeling from the global downturn of 2008. At a time of shrinking employment opportunities at home, a rising educated middle class looking for pickings abroad has struggled to compete in the international job market because of their ill-perceived national origin. Everyday struggles for survival and an ingrained anti-imperialism among large segments of the populace have fueled bitter narratives of hate and distrust for America, which is accused of hatching conspiracies with Pakistan's premier enemy India, and also with Israel, to dismember the country and seize its prized nuclear arsenal. Cutting across class, regional, and sectarian divides, Pakistanis accuse the United States of forcing a war on hapless Afghanistan. This war's spillover into Pakistan has proven disastrous for their citizens' vulnerable livelihoods. Even among those who take comfort in the fact of the nation's past survival against heavy odds, there is mounting consternation about the kind of polity Pakistan is likely to become if "Talibanization"—a loose reference to the insular ideological agendas of radical Islamic groups in the northwestern parts of the country—

is allowed to extend its tentacles southward. Pakistan is a visibly perturbed and divided nation. Its people are struggling to find an answer to the mother of all questions: what sort of a Pakistan do they want along a spectrum of choices, ranging from an orthodox, religious state to a modern, enlightened one?

The public debate on this all-important issue has been vitiated by the long shadow of military authoritarianism. Subverting the democratic aspirations of the people, the military presented itself as the final bastion against militant Islam and the terror networks of Al Qaeda. With its well-advertised nuclear capacity and reputation as the epicenter of Muslim terrorism, Pakistan is closely watched by an international community alarmed at the prospect of its lethal military arsenal falling into the hands of extremists brandishing a virulent brand of Islam. The 2014 deadline for the withdrawal of American forces from Afghanistan has aggravated long-standing tensions in the US–Pakistani relationship. American anger at Pakistan's refusal to toe their line overlooks Pakistan's long-cherished regional security concerns flowing from a contested border with Afghanistan and ingrained anxieties about India's ultimate designs that spotlight Kashmir. Breaking off ties with Pakistan and leaning more heavily on Indian monetary and military help to rebuild Afghanistan is not a realistic option for the United States. Most security experts on the region grudgingly concede that American success in Afghanistan depends on the Pakistani Army. Paradoxically, this army is the main obstacle as well as the key to peace in Afghanistan.

There are huge stakes in keeping a nuclear state riddled with political and economic problems from imploding. Since the Pakistani Army's intelligence apparatus used militants in Afghanistan and Kashmir in the 1980s and 1990s, several groups emerged after 2001 to oppose Pakistan's alliance with the United States. Some of them have shown shocking audacity by attacking sensitive Pakistani military installations. Hinting at close links between the militants and elements within the armed forces, the spate of attacks on military personnel and buildings as well as civilian targets has demoralized the citizenry at large. The only ray of hope has been the resilience shown by ordinary Pakistanis in the face of a relentless cycle of terrorism. Needing to eke out a living at all costs, they have continued with their everyday life largely unruffled by the snarling traffic jams created by the mushrooming of security checkpoints. While some

Pakistanis take solace in denying that the terrorists could be fellow Muslims, many more are coming to question the military-dominated state's uses of Islam against internal opposition and external foes. Reduced to being the citizens of a state that can provide them with neither security of life nor of property, far less social and economic opportunity, Pakistanis across a broad political spectrum are pondering the reasons for their country's perilous condition and seeking a reprieve from violence and uncertainty. This has been finding expression in myriad ways, most creatively in a robust and thriving popular culture whose artistic, literary, and musical productions have both a local and a transnational appeal. The sense of urgency gripping Pakistan's citizens is palpable, a reflection of the politicization of the personal that tends to accompany depoliticization under authoritarian and semiauthoritarian regimes. Both in private and in public, an increasing number of Pakistanis realize that as their state oscillates between religious and secular moorings, as well as military authoritarianism and democracy, they cannot at this critical moment in world history afford the luxury of making an ill-conceived choice.

Pakistan's tumultuous history exhibits a daunting combination of contradictory factors that must affect any decisions made about its future. More than six and a half decades since its establishment, Pakistan has yet to reconcile its self-proclaimed Islamic identity with the imperatives of a modern nation-state. There were stark contradictions between the claims of Muslim nationalism and the actual achievement of statehood at the moment of the British withdrawal. Carved out of the northwestern and northeastern extremities of the subcontinent as a homeland for Muslims, Pakistan today has fewer Muslims than India and almost as many as its former eastern wing, Bangladesh. In 1947, Pakistan consisted of five provinces—Balochistan, NWFP (including the federally administered tribal areas—FATA), Punjab and Sindh in the west, and East Bengal in the east. In addition to these provinces, there were ten princely states: Bahawalpur; Khairpur; the four Balochistan states of Kalat, Mehran, Makran, and Las Bela; and the four northwest frontier states of Swat, Chitral, Dir, and Amb. Sovereignty over disparate constituent units was easier to assert than achieve. The inadequacy of religion as the sole basis of national unity was demonstrated in 1971 when Pakistan lost a majority of its population in the eastern wing after a tragic civil war that led to India's military intervention and the establishment of Bangladesh.

Geography and the historic interchange of people, ideas, and material culture have had a more decisive bearing on Pakistan's remaining regions in the northwest than any unifying conception of Islam or nationalism. Stretched across territories containing the seat of one of the world's oldest civilizations centered at Mohenjodaro in Sindh and Harappa in Punjab, Pakistan has struggled to harmonize the culturally rich layers of a complex past going back several millennia with its brief and politically turbulent recent history. What is today the Islamic Republic of Pakistan was once part and parcel of a subcontinent that took its name in ancient times from the trans-Himalayan river Indus. Traveling nearly 2,000 miles southward from the highest mountain peaks in the world to the Arabian Sea, the Indus passes through terrain of breathtaking diversity in topography, climate, and culture. The lofty mountains of the northwest frontier and brown plateaus of Balochistan and northern Punjab cover 60 percent of the total area while lush green plains watered by the Indus River system in central and southern Punjab and parts of Sindh account for the rest. People inhabiting this variegated landscape comprising snow-capped mountains, temperate forests, fertile plains, and arid deserts speak a multitude of languages and take pride in their own specific cultural traditions. A shared emotive bond with the land where the Indus and its twenty tributaries flow has created a loose sense of shared history, but a history that is bitterly contested. The heroes of one region or subregion are sometimes regarded as villains in an adjoining area. Intense rivalries for political dominance matched by wide economic disparities have meant that the triumphs of one region are, not infrequently, regarded as setbacks for another. With such clashes underpinning the historical relationship among its constituent units, it has been difficult to generate a consensus on the main themes around which a national history of Pakistan ought to be framed.

Today Pakistan consists of the four provinces of Punjab, the NWFP-renamed Khyber Pakhtunkhawa (KPK), Sindh, and insurgency-ridden Balochistan as well as the turbulent northwestern tribal areas bordering Afghanistan. Ever since its creation, Pakistan has been groping for national moorings somewhere in the twilight between myth and history. This is not a novel occurrence in a newly independent state. But declining educational standards and a media oscillating between official control and rampant commercialization have facilitated the dissemination of remarkable distortions and mistruths. Extended periods of military and quasi-military rule witnessed strict curbs on the freedom of expression. Until recently, the press was muzzled and bribed into subservience. History has been reduced by official hacks to a jumble of clichés in order to expound more and more improbable versions of Pakistan's proclaimed Islamic ideology.[5] The mutilation of history by successive governments has had attenuating effects on scholarship as a whole and the study of history in particular. There has been little by way of a sustained historical debate on issues germane to the manifold crises engulfing Pakistan.

This makes the task of historical retrieval extremely difficult but also a matter of utmost importance. There has been no serious academic or political debate inside Pakistan that can match the sophistication that distinguishes the field of South Asian history. Instead, there is merely the regurgitation of official dogma on Muslim history in India. These stories derive from the "two nation theory" that slated the Muslims of India, irrespective of regional and class variations, as a homogeneous category when it came to demanding political concessions from the colonial state. Yet the large claims of Muslim nationhood articulated before 1947 were a far cry from the limited gains that came with the winning of statehood.

The displacement of history by an ill-defined Islamic ideology has been one of the main obstacles to the development of a critical historical tradition and reasoned public debate in Pakistan. Pakistanis receive schooling in ideology that aims to reinforce belief in constructed national myths. These exaggerate Muslim differences with Hindu India to justify the existence of Pakistan and, more problematically, to deny the welter of heterogeneities within the country itself. And although myths are an important dimension of the historical imagination of a people, they are meaningful only when they bear a broad resemblance to or resonate with actual history. Any history of Pakistan has to be alert to the close interplay of official ideology and popular sentiments, of myth and history, of fabricated truths and embroidered evidence. If myth is indeed a main constituent element of Pakistani history, debunking it is less meaningful than examining why it was constructed and the effects it has come to have on the attitudes of its subscribers.

For a country that was supposed to have disappeared from the map just as quickly as it appeared, Pakistan's ability to survive against all odds is an exceptional story that deserves to be told. Since 2001 Pakistan has been

portrayed in the world's media as the breeding ground of terrorist ideologies and religiously inspired violence. However, a more valid and insightful history of the country needs to reflect on the constraints and
opportunities available to a geostrategically placed nation-state that has
consistently deployed the rhetoric of enemies at its borders to deprive its
diverse people of the elementary rights of citizenship. Such a strategy adopted by the state perpetuates its survival at the risk of undermining stability and credibility. While showing how Pakistan's past molds its present, this book steers clear of an overly presentist approach in favor of a
narrative that acknowledges many possibilities at crucial turning points,
including the crossroads at which the country now stands. Resistance to
dictatorship in Pakistan's politics and culture is as old as military dominance itself. Yet it is in the contemporary moment that this perennial
theme in Pakistan's history appears to be on the verge of achieving success. This work of historical interpretation aims to reframe the contemporary debate on a much-maligned country that arouses more scorn and
fear than understanding. Along with the vexed issue of how best to meld
a commitment to Islam with the imperatives of a modern nation-state,
questions about the relationship between identity, sovereignty, and citizenship provide the main organizing threads for this history of Pakistan.
The spirit of inquiry it follows takes inspiration from the gentle but firm
resolve so poignantly invoked by Pakistan's acclaimed Urdu poet Faiz Ahmad Faiz:

> Speak, for your lips are free
> Speak, your tongue is still yours,
> Your upright body is yours.
> See how in the blacksmith's shop
> The flames are hot, the iron is red,
> Mouths of locks have begun to open,
> Each chain's skirt has spread wide.
> Speak, this little time is plenty
> Before the death of body and tongue:
> Speak, for truth is still alive—
> Speak, say whatever is to be said.[6]

FROM MINORITY TO NATION

SIX YEARS BEFORE IT APPEARED on the map of the world, Pakistan's founding father, Mohammad Ali Jinnah, denounced the Indian National Congress and right-wing Hindu organizations for hysterically treating the proposed Muslim homeland as if it was "a nightmare or some dangerous animal." "Pakistan has been there for centuries," he claimed, "it is there to-day, and it will remain till the end of the world. It was taken away from us." Jinnah saw no inconsistency in making an apparently separatist claim to territories in the northwest and northeast of India and vowing never to let Muslim minorities elsewhere in the subcontinent be "vassalised by the Hindu majority." At the same time, he emphatically rejected concerns about Pakistan's inability to ward off a potential invasion from the northwest. European powers, including "our British masters," had invaded India from the coasts. Air and not land or sea power had in any case become the decisive weapon in modern warfare. Muslims and Hindus had to "live as good neighbours" and jointly tell the world, "Hands off India, India for the Indians."[1]

With even the chief architect of Pakistan ambivalent about the link between Muslim identity and territorial sovereignty, narrating the story of the nation and its nationalism has proven deeply contentious for Pakistanis. Reconciling the imperatives of citizenship in a territorial nation-state with the supraterritorial claims of Islamic universalism based on affinity to a worldwide Muslim community was a challenging proposition. The territorial contours of the Muslim homeland would leave almost as many Muslim noncitizens inside predominantly Hindu India as there were Muslim citizens within, compounding the problems confronting

Pakistan's quest for an identity that was both Islamic and national. The quest for a homeland for India's Muslims was fundamentally different from the Zionist movement for a Jewish homeland. There was no holy hill in Punjab or Bengal, nor in Sindh, NWFP, or Balochistan, that beckoned the faithful. These were regions where Muslims happened to be in a numerical majority, sharing cultural and linguistic bonds with Hindus and Sikhs. Muslims forming a majority in these regions also shared a religious affinity with Muslims in Indian provinces where they were in a minority and a vast worldwide community of believers beyond the subcontinent.[2]

An insistence on being treated on par with India, which continued to be referred to in popular parlance and the vernacular press as Hindustan or Bharat, was a common refrain once Pakistan was created. The delicacy of the issue prompted government officials to emphasize the country's distinctiveness by substituting the lessons of recent history with the political project of the independent nation-state. This can be seen from the controversy generated over the definition of Pakistan in the fourth edition of *The Concise Oxford Dictionary*. Initially published in 1951, the shorter version of the prestigious English lexicon managed to cause offense eight years later when someone discovered that Pakistan had been defined as "a separate Moslem State in India" or, alternatively, as "Moslem autonomy" and "the independent Moslem Dominion in India." Oblivious of Jinnah's reasons for opposing the designation "India" only for territories falling under the jurisdiction of the Indian National Congress, the bearers of his mantle vented their anger at being called a part of India by banning the dictionary. Oxford University Press admitted that the definition was "tactless" but explained that the intention had been to show that Pakistan was geographically a part of the Indian subcontinent, not that it was politically a part of India. It regretted that the correction could not be made until the publication of the next edition.[3] Recognizing it as a case of overreaction, the Pakistani government lifted the ban shortly afterward. The next edition of *The Concise Oxford Dictionary* did not appear until 1964.

Even as they strove valiantly to project Pakistan's identity as an Islamic entity distinct from Hindu-dominated India, the managers of the new state found themselves entangled in a fundamental conundrum. No one was quite sure where exactly to begin tracing the origins of Pakistan. Should the history begin with the creation of the country in 1947 or extend backward in time and, if so, how far? Ideologically driven stalwarts of an Islamic Pakistan wanted to locate its genesis in the birth of Islam on the Arabian peninsula or at the very least with the Arab invasion of India's northwestern region in 712 CE. Others with a geographical and secular bent marshaled their own evidence about when the seeds of Pakistan were first sown. In the initial years after independence when those holding secular worldviews rather than Islamic ideologues were in the ascendance, official and quasi-official histories took the 1857 revolt that marked the end of Mughal sovereignty as the point of departure to begin charting the course to the creation of Pakistan.

An equally problematic, if potentially more divisive, issue related to the sacrifices made during the struggle for Pakistan. Who were the heroes and martyrs and who had to be excluded or dubbed villains and turncoats in official narrations of the nation? An intensely political enterprise that paralleled regime changes, these decisions served to reduce historical thinking, both as knowledge and as collective remembrance, to a series of bureaucratic conjuring tricks.[4] These official manipulations did not go uncontested. But the preferred medium of social dissidence and resistance was journalism and literature, rather than history. Without a well-developed tradition of either professional or lay alternative popular histories, the state's monopoly on official narrations of the nation and its nationalism largely escaped systematic challenges. At the root of Pakistan's national identity crisis has been the unresolved debate on how to square the state's self-proclaimed Islamic identity with the obligations of a modern nation-state. This has been confounded by an official history that cannot explain the gaping inconsistencies between the claims of Muslim nationalism and the actual achievement of statehood at the moment of the British withdrawal.

The Demand for Pakistan

How did India's Muslim minority get transformed into a nation and win territorial sovereignty within just seven years only to end up being divided into two hostile states? A staunch anticolonial nationalist who had devoted his life to the cause of winning freedom from the British, Jinnah in 1916 had hailed the All-India Muslim League (AIML) as a "powerful factor for the birth of United India."[5] Even as late as 1937, he was more interested in forging a political alliance with the Congress Party at the all-

India level than striking dubious deals with Muslim politicians in the Muslim-majority provinces. It was during his presidential address at the Muslim League's Lahore session in March 1940 that Jinnah first asserted that India's 90 million Muslims were not a minority but a nation. He made the claim with no reference to any Islamic convention. Instead, Jinnah took his cues from the contemporary internationalist discourse on territorial nationalism and the doctrine of self-determination. Like any other group claiming nationhood, Muslims wanted their own separate national home in the shape of autonomous states in northwestern and northeastern India, where they were in a majority. Muslim minorities in the rest of India were to be considered nationals of this Muslim homeland and their rights and privileges safeguarded in the same way as those of non-Muslims living in the Muslim territories. What was unacceptable was a spurious notion of democracy that allowed the Indian National Congress to use the brute majority of the Hindu community to impose its will on the Muslims. The political problem in India was not of an intercommunal nature as was commonly believed. It was of a distinctly international character. In accordance with international norms of self-determination, the only logical solution was to divide India into autonomous states so that no nation could try and dominate the other. This could facilitate reciprocal arrangements on behalf of minorities and mutual adjustments between Muslim India and Hindu India.

If it embodied a separatist demand, the resolution adopted by the Muslim League in Lahore was curiously ambiguous when it came to specifying the precise geographical boundaries of the Muslim states it wanted to set up in northwestern and northeastern India where Muslims were in a majority. There were other glaring inconsistencies. The League claimed to be speaking on behalf of all Indian Muslims. Yet its objective, if realized, would leave a substantial number of Muslims outside the ambit of Muslim sovereignty. A plurality of Muslim sovereignty was implicit in the resolution's use of the phrase "Independent States" even though the League's propaganda revolved around the idea of one Muslim state. There was no discussion of any future "center"—a reference to the central state apparatus—whether Muslim or all Indian. The fourth paragraph of the resolution referred to "the constitution" in the singular to safeguard the interests of both sets of minorities, Muslims in the Hindu-majority provinces as well as non-Muslims living in the Muslim-dominated areas. This implied some sort of an all-India arrangement to cover the interests of Muslims in the majority and the minority areas. Consistent with this unstated assumption was the conspicuous omission of any reference to either partition or "Pakistan."

"Pakistan" and "partition" were not unfamiliar terms. Since the late 1930s, they had been regularly bandied about in newspapers with reference to a number of Muslim schemes proposing imaginative ways of power sharing by religiously enumerated "majorities" and "minorities" in an independent India. Anxious not to be undone by the popular connotations of "Pakistan," Jinnah avoided any mention of it in the Lahore resolution. It was the Hindu press that "fathered this word upon us" he told the AIML three years later.[6] This was a telling admission from someone dubbed the architect of Pakistan. If Jinnah—the Quaid-i-Azam (great leader) as he came to be called—was initially reluctant to be associated with "Pakistan." Choudhary Rahmat Ali, a Punjabi Muslim who coined the name in 1933 while studying at the University of Cambridge in England, denied that his scheme for a Muslim state extending from the Bay of Bengal all the way to the Bosphorus had anything to do with the Muslim League's 1940 resolution. Literally, the "land of the pure," "Pakistan" is an acronym for *P*unjab, *A*fghanistan (including the NWFP), *K*ashmir, *S*indh, and Baluchi*stan*.

The lineage of Rahmat Ali's "Pakistan" scheme, though not its form or substance, is traceable to the ideas of another Punjabi Muslim—the celebrated poet and philosopher of the East, Muhammad Iqbal. In his presidential address to the AIML in December 1930, Iqbal had proposed consolidating Muslim power in the northwest of the subcontinent as the solution to the problem of power sharing in India. Unlike Rahmat Ali's scheme for a separate and sovereign "Pakistan" linked to smaller sovereign Muslim polities in the rest of India, Iqbal's Muslim state was to remain part of the subcontinental whole. Ruling out any physical division, Iqbal called "India . . . the greatest Muslim country in the world." The "centralization" of the Muslim-majority provinces of Punjab, Sindh, the NWFP, and Balochistan, whose military and police services were indispensable to British rule, would "eventually solve the problem of India as well as of Asia."[7] Far from aspiring to hold the future government of independent India to ransom, Iqbal explained, Muslims in the northwestern provinces simply wanted to live according to their own cultural traditions without fear of Hindu domination. Muslims were "ready to stake ... all for the freedom of India" if the religious and cultural autonomy of all communities was made "the basis of a permanent communal settlement." Iqbal was at pains to deny that such a Muslim state would promote religious obscurantism. Islam was not a church but a contractual state whose citizens were spiritual beings with rights and duties in society. A Muslim state in India would permit innovations in Islam unbridled by "Arabian imperialism." This would not only bring Muslims into "closer contact" with the "original spirit" of Islam but also make them more amenable to "the spirit of modern times."[8]

Iqbal's scheme ignored Muslims living in the northeast and the Hindu-majority provinces. By contrast, Rahmat Ali's expansive imagination envisaged a "Bangistan" or "Bang-i-Islamistan" based on grouping Bengal and Assam. Despite the separatist overtones of his "Pakistan" scheme, he did not fail to take account of Muslims in areas where they were in a minority. In fact, he proposed carving out half a dozen Muslim states in India, evocatively named Osmanistan, Sadiqistan, Faruqistan, Muinistan, Mappallistan, Safistan, and Nasiristan, from what was then British and princely India as well as present-day Sri Lanka.[9] These would then be consolidated into a "Pakistan Commonwealth of Nations" as the first step to the "original" Pakistan that was eventually to be integrated with Central and West Asia.[10] It does not require much perspicacity to realize that Rahmat Ali's "Pakistan" was the territorial embodiment of the nonterritorially based idea of the Muslim ummah, or community. A contradiction in terms, it represented a creative attempt to make the worldwide community of Islam relevant at a time when the idea of territorial nationalism was rapidly coming to appeal to Muslims living under direct or indirect Western colonial domination.

Most Indian Muslim politicians dismissed Rahmat Ali's scheme as impracticable, a dangerous student fantasy that was best ignored. This did not prevent the "Pakistan" idea from filtering widely and being appropriated by urban Punjabi Muslims, some of whom mistakenly conflated it with Iqbal's Muslim state. However, it was not the popularity of the scheme but the campaign against it in Hindu-owned newspapers in Punjab and the United Provinces (UP) that kept it within the public purview. Non-Muslims were not alone in opposing a Muslim state in northwestern India. During the debate on the separation of Sindh from Bombay

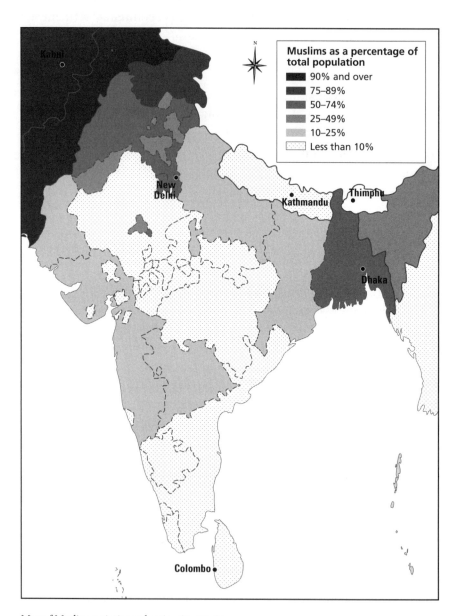

Map of Muslim-majority and -minority provinces.

Presidency, encompassing much of western and central India, the provincial Muslim leader Ghulam Hussain Hidayatullah rubbished the notion in categorical terms. For Sindhi Muslims to give up their individuality to group with their coreligionists in Punjab was nothing short of political suicide. In 1938, the Sindh Muslim League proposed dividing India into Muslim and non-Muslim states. The invocation of religious identity by Sindhi Muslims was an expression of their regional aspirations rather than an affinity with coreligionists in neighboring provinces. While sharing the Punjabi Muslim desire for strong provinces and a weak federal center, Muslims in Sindh had no intention of accepting a subordinate position in a Muslim state. Much the same sort of sentiment guided the policies of Abdul Ghaffar Khan, the leader of the Khudai Khidmatgar, or Servants of God movement in the NWFP, who advocated Pathan or Pakhtun autonomy and preferred rallying his followers under the Congress banner.

A shared religious identity was felt at the level of lived culture but rarely at the expense of the emotive affinity with local and regional cultural traditions. Despite the narratives of communitarian identity propagated in the press and publications market, being Muslim did not translate into a united political front. This is borne out by the history of Indian Muslim politics under British colonial rule. In 1909, Muslims were granted separate electorates under the Indian Councils Act known as the Morley-Minto reforms. Although separate electorates were retained in subsequent constitutional reforms in 1919 and 1935, the religious, regional, and class-based interests of Muslims clashed more often than they converged. Muslim divisions were accentuated by the nature of the British Indian political system. With the franchise restricted by educational and property qualifications, the representative institutions of the colonial state were arenas for the privileged few to experiment with the art of governing in their own interest. The lure of state patronage and the spoils of office were localized. This encouraged provincial particularisms, not the all-India perspective that was supposed to be the logical effect of Muslims being a separate political category, however dispersed geographically and diverse linguistically. Separate electorates mitigated the need for political parties with provincial and all-India orientations. Success in the colonial political system depended on rival Muslim politicians, landlords in the main, manipulating local factions as they jockeyed for position within the protected walls of specifically Muslim constituencies. So long as there was no prospect of an executive responsible to an elected legislature at the center, the significance of Muslims being an all-India political category was an asset of dubious value. It reduced Muslims to a permanent constitutional minority that lacked both unity and unanimity. Only when constitutional reforms were in the offing did Muslim politicians find the incentive to steal a glance beyond their narrow local and provincial horizons at the all-India center and articulate the distinctive communitarian interests the British believed existed.

A self-made middle-class lawyer from Bombay, Jinnah was a beneficiary of separate electorates in the central assembly. But politically he was closer to the moderate constitutional wing of the Congress represented by Gopal Krishna Gokhale and Pherozeshah Mehta than to the conservative and loyalist landlord Muslim politicians from the northwestern provinces. Making the politics of mediation his forte, Jinnah spent the better part of a long and distinguished political career trying to square the interests of Muslims in the majority and the minority provinces on the one hand and the Muslim League and the Congress on the other. His efforts to cobble together a united League and Congress anticolonial front were, more often than not, undermined by the structural contradictions inherent in the British Indian political system.

An early example of this was the Lucknow Pact, which Jinnah helped negotiate between the Congress and the Muslim League in 1916. "All thinking men," he told the Bombay Provincial Conference at Ahmedabad in October 1916, were "thoroughly convinced that the key-note of our real progress lies in the good-will, concord, harmony and cooperation between the two great sister communities." Union was "the true focus of progress" and "entirely in our hands."[11] Under the terms of the accord, Congress accepted separate electorates for Muslims in return for the Muslim League's help in forcing the British to make substantial concessions to Indians after the end of World War I. With his sights set on constitutional advance at the center, Jinnah had no qualms crafting an understanding between the two main all-India parties that entailed sacrificing the interests of Muslims in Punjab and Bengal. Congress's price for separate electorates and more representation for minority-province Muslims than merited by their population was weighted representation for non-Muslim minorities in Punjab and Bengal. Punjabi Muslims, who made up about 56 percent of the population, were given 50 percent representation. Bengali Muslims, who constituted 52.6 percent of the population, were shortchanged with just 40 percent of the seats. By contrast, Muslims in the minority provinces got more representation than their populations warranted. Muslims in Jinnah's home province of Bombay were 20 percent of the population but secured one-third of the seats in the legislature. Muslims in the UP did best; a mere 14 percent, they were allotted 30 percent of the seats in the provincial council.

Jinnah's achievement was to become the source of his political vulnerability. Muslims in Punjab and Bengal were incensed at the sellout. Hindus in the UP and Punjab, for their part, carped about Congress's pandering to Muslims. The Lucknow Pact was in line with the strategy of minority-province Muslims in the initial decades of the twentieth century to secure their own provincial interests by pointing to Muslim majorities in the northwest and the northeast of India. But in privileging all-India considerations over communitarian and provincial ones, Jinnah misjudged the tenor of politics under the 1919 reforms. The colonial policy of keeping political attentions focused on the local and provincial arenas aimed at diluting the all-India agendas of nationalist parties and politicians. Because the Montagu-Chelmsford reforms of 1919 prevented any single community from dominating the provincial legislatures, Muslim politicians had to forge alliances with members of other communities to form stable governments. With the security afforded by separate electorates, the mainly landlord politicians of the Muslim community could use their local influence to get elected without needing the assistance of political parties at either the provincial or the all-India levels. After 1920, the Congress under Mohandas Karamchand Gandhi was able to spread its tentacles in the Hindu-majority provinces by launching all-India mass movements. By contrast, the AIML created in 1906 remained little more than a paper organization, belittled and flouted by most Muslim provincial politicians. In keeping with the tenor of the constitutional reforms, alliances across community lines were forged in the UP where Muslims were in a minority and in Punjab and Bengal where they had bare majorities.

With the provincialization of politics during the 1920s, there was no effective role left for a Muslim party at the center. Muslims agitated about the future of the Ottoman caliphate following Turkey's defeat in World

War I made common cause with Gandhi. The merger of the pro-Ottoman or Khilafat agitation, as it came to be known in India, and the Gandhian-led noncooperation movements catapulted the Mahatma onto the center stage of Indian politics, pushing the AIML a shade deeper into oblivion. Jinnah disliked Gandhi's brew of religion and politics even while pro-Khilafat Muslims, such as Shaukat and Mohammad Ali, helped the Mahatma fuse Indian nationalism with Islamic universalism. Mustapha Kamal Pasha's abolition of the caliphate in 1924 left the Khilafatists in India without a cause. After the collapse of the Khilafat movement and the end of the era of Hindu–Muslim unity under Gandhi's leadership, the Muslim League was nowhere in the picture and the Congress was split down the middle. The British strategy of isolating the all-India parties from their provincial bases of support had emphatically succeeded. While the Congress was able to reassemble with relative ease, largely due to the lingering effects of the noncooperation movement, there was no all-India Muslim political party that could plausibly speak on behalf of all Muslims.

In this period of flux and reflux, Jinnah made another attempt at patching up Muslim differences by packaging their known demands into "fourteen points." The main stumbling block was the need to square the conflicting demands of Muslims in the minority and the majority provinces without undermining his own nationalist aims at the all-India center. Following the publication of the Motilal Nehru Report on the constitutional structure for independent India in 1928, Congress formally stated its preference for a strong unitary center. This was abhorrent for Muslims in provinces where they were in the majority. Jinnah's first two points asked for a federal constitution with residuary powers vested in fully autonomous provinces. There was to be adequate representation for minorities and a provision preventing a majority from being reduced to a minority or a position of equality. This was the bait Jinnah needed to restore his bona fides with Punjabi and Bengali Muslims and improve his chances of getting one-third representation for Muslims at the center. He was opposed to separate electorates because these would keep Muslims in a position of a statutory minority at the all-India level. But the political scales had tipped in favor of Punjab and Bengal, where Muslim politicians were insistent on separate electorates. So Jinnah called for their retention until Muslims voluntarily opted for joint electorates. He tried compensating for this by demanding more Muslim-dominated provinces—calling for the separation of Sindh from Bombay and pushing for constitutional advancement in the NWFP and Balochistan.

The remaining points sought to assuage Muslim worries about a Hindu-dominated center. No legislation opposed by three-fourths of the members of any particular community could be passed. Muslims were to get an adequate share of all state services. There was to be full liberty in matters to do with religion for all the communities, and Muslims were to be permitted to live in accordance with their own personal laws. In what was a deliberately outlandish demand, Muslims were to have one-third representation in ministries at the center and the provinces. Finally, no constitutional change was to be made without the concurrence of the units making up the federation. By promising Muslim provincial politicians a lot more than he believed was achievable, Jinnah was taking out insurance for his political future. With Muslims controlling nearly half of British India's provinces, the leader of a strong all-India Muslim party could try to keep a check on the majority. Congress's refusal to countenance these demands resulted in Jinnah abandoning Indian politics and settling down in England, where he hoped to exert influence on the British government's report on the future constitutional reforms.

It was not the suave Bombay lawyer but Punjab Unionists, an alliance of Muslim, Hindu, and Sikh agriculturist interests, who dominated the constitutional dialogue of the early 1930s. The Unionist construct of "Muslim interest" that was eventually incorporated in the Government of India Act of 1935 was a rude shock for minority-province Muslims, accustomed as they were to riding on the coattails of their coreligionists in the majority provinces. While advance at the center was linked to one-half of the Indian princely states voluntarily joining the all-India federation in the future, the provincial provisions were to come into effect immediately after the first elections under the new reforms. Under the Communal Award of 1932 announced by the British prime minister, Muslims in the majority provinces were allowed to retain separate electorates and were given more seats than any other community. With the new constitutional reforms ushering in full provincial autonomy, politicians in the Muslim-majority provinces could expect to control the ministries. Involving the elimination of the "official bloc"—a safeguard for minority rights—provincial autonomy heightened the insecurities of Muslims in provinces where Hindus

Mohammad Ali Jinnah with daughter Dina in London. *The White Star Photo Pvt. Ltd. Archive.*

were in the majority. The revival of the AIML in 1934 with Jinnah at the helm was a direct result of minority-province Muslim dissatisfaction with the new constitutional arrangements.

On January 4, 1934, the future Quaid-i-Azam stepped off the ship in Bombay in fighting spirit. He fired the first shot at the white paper on the future constitution, calling its federal scheme "a pure deception." The only way to stop the British from thrusting the scheme on India was for Hindus and Muslims to unite. The burning question was whether Indians could "even at this eleventh hour . . . forget the past" and muster up the strength "to resist what is being hatched both at Downing Street and Delhi." They had spent far too much time thinking about their own communities, and so Jinnah advised, "let us now concentrate upon the interests of our mother-land."[12] The theme of unity was the leitmotif of Jinnah's political stance during the run-up to the first elections under the Government of India Act of 1935. Projecting himself as an impartial mediator, he distanced himself from the bigoted and self-serving elements in both communities. He wanted to lead a progressive, organized, and united Muslim community, standing on par with other communities in the march to win India's freedom. Upon being elected president of the All-India Muslim League in March 1934, Jinnah commented that it was not going to be a "bed of roses." Muslims had to fight for safeguards without losing sight of the "wider interests of the country as a whole," which he had "always considered sacred." It was lamentable that at a most critical juncture in history, Indian Muslims were "more or less in no man's land. Make it your own land and allow no one to trespass. Think well before selecting your leader and when you have selected him, follow him. But in case you find his policy detrimental to your interests, kick him out."[13] Muslims had to repudiate the conservative elements and press the British to grant responsible government at the center, and not just in the provinces.

By the time the Government of India Act of 1935 was announced, Jinnah had far from gathered his straying flock of coreligionists. The new law extended the electorate to nearly 35 million and granted full autonomy to the British Indian provinces. Responsible government at the center was postponed until one-half of the Indian states on the basis of population voluntarily acceded to the federal union. While each of the more than 500 Indian princely states could negotiate the terms of their accession to the Indian federation, the provinces were to automatically come into the

federation. Jinnah was aware of the Muslim provinces' insistence on giving residual powers to the federating units. He also knew that the Congress aimed to vest residual powers in a strong federal center. Although
his own idea of the all-India center was closer to the Congress's, Jinnah
opted to argue the Muslim brief on constitutional grounds. Speculation is
rife about the Quaid's precise motivations in arguing the provincialists'
case despite being a centralist himself. In fact, Jinnah had long supported
the idea of an all-India federation, calling it the best solution for India's
cultural diversities. A pragmatist, he wanted a real federation, not one
based on an artificial unity. He slammed the Act of 1935 for being "thoroughly rotten" and "fundamentally bad." The princes had imposed "impossible terms," while the "iron wall" of safeguards demanded by the
British had laid a snare for unsuspecting Indians.[14] In the interests of
pragmatism and reason, which were his strong suits, Jinnah favored accepting the Communal Award and working the provincial part of the act
for what it was worth. This entailed leaving the question of the all-India
federation to future negotiations. As far as the Quaid-i-Azam was concerned, India was a British paper creation with no "flesh and blood"; "a
single administrative unit governed by the bureaucracy under the sanction of the sword."[15]

Times had changed. By the 1930s, a mere dependence on numbers was
no longer enough. Even politicians from the Muslim-minority provinces
could now see advantages in basing their demands on the fact of Muslim-
majority provinces. The right to vote remained limited to those with property and educational qualifications, making for a vote bank of a mere 35
million in a country of over 300 million. If they could persuade their coreligionists in northwestern and northeastern India of the merits of united
political action, minority-province Muslims might be able to use the cover
of their political weight at the center to wrest advantages that were denied
to them in the provincial arenas. So Jinnah and the League now stressed
that Muslims, whatever their political persuasions, should come under
the banner of a single all-India party. It was a novel claim; until then there
had been no practical need for a strong all-India Muslim party speaking
on behalf of all Indian Muslims.

The claim was rejected in the 1937 elections. Even with separate electorates, the Muslim League could poll only 4.4 percent of the total Muslim
vote cast. Barring Bengal, where it won a third of the Muslim reserved

seats, Muslims snubbed the League in the majority provinces that opted for provincial, and often nonreligious, groupings rather than for all-India parties. It did better in the minority provinces but not well enough to force a triumphant Congress to forge coalition ministries with the Muslim League. This locked out Jinnah and the League at the center and the provinces—and was evidence of the success of the British strategy of alternatively communalizing and provincializing Indian politics. Yet the provincialization of Muslim politics had not removed them as an important political category in discussions about the future of India. Congress, too, had failed to make an impact on the electoral scene in most of the Muslim-majority provinces. If the Congress high command, flush with its thumping electoral victory, was now waiting to storm British India's unitary center, it would somehow have to rein in the Muslim provinces. Such pressure as the Congress brought to bear on the Muslim provinces might conceivably force them to seek the League's mediation at the center, enabling it to bring them under its wing.

If it could emulate Congress's example in the Hindu-majority provinces and bring the Muslim-majority provinces under its sway, the League would be able to influence the negotiations to determine the constitutional future of independent India. Together with the apprehensions of Muslims in the minority provinces, this gave Jinnah the basis for a strategy designed to win an equitable share of power for Muslims at the level of all-India political arrangements. Any strategy for divided and disorganized Muslims had to make a break with the past. What Muslims needed above all was to overcome the limitations of being a minority. One way to resolve the dilemma was to assert that Muslims were not a minority but a nation entitled to being treated on par with the Hindus.

There were some vague historical antecedents to the claim. In the late nineteenth century, the educationist and social reformer Sayyid Ahmad Khan had spoken of Muslims as a *qaum*, a term loosely translated as "nation" but which more accurately means a community. As he explained, by *qaum* he meant the inhabitants of a country, regardless of internal diversities. Being Hindu or Muslim was an entirely personal matter. Muslims had come to consider India as their homeland after living cheek by jowl with Hindus for centuries: "the blood of both have changed, the colour of both have become similar. . . . We mixed with each other so much that we produced a new language—Urdu, which was neither our language nor theirs." A year before the formation of the Congress, he commented that "Hindus and Mussalmans are words of religious significance[;] otherwise Hindus, Mussalmans and Christians who live in this country constitute one nation." In his opinion, "all men are one"; he did "not like religion, community or group to be identified with a nation."[16] Despite such clear statements, Sayyid Ahmad Khan has come to be seen as the founding father of the "two nation" theory according to which Muslims were always a distinctive community that had resisted assimilation into the Indian environment. This historical distortion, significantly in vogue on both sides of the 1947 divide, flows from Sayyid Ahmad's resolute opposition to Muslim participation in the Congress and efforts to convince the British to treat Muslims on the basis of their political significance rather than their numbers.

While the genealogy of the "two nation" theory is at best suspect, Jinnah's need to invoke the idea of Muslim distinctiveness was also based on political and not religious opposition to the Congress. He had been incensed by Jawaharlal Nehru's invitation to the Muslim League after the 1937 elections to disband and join the Congress that took office in eight out of eleven British Indian provinces by 1938. Adding insult to injury, Nehru announced at the time that he had looked at the "so-called communal question through the telescope" and found nothing.[17] Seeing through the Congress game was one thing; finding a suitable antidote was quite another matter for a leader and a party whose main constituents had repudiated them at the polls. Fortunately for Jinnah, Muslim politicians in the majority provinces were wary of the implications of a Congress-dominated center in the future. Unwilling to see their provincial autonomy curtailed in any way, the premiers of Punjab and Bengal—Sikander Hayat Khan and Fazlul Huq, respectively—agreed in 1937 to accept the Muslim League leader as their spokesman at the all-India level so long as he did not interfere in their provincial affairs.

During the late 1930s, several imaginatively conceived Muslim proposals were floated on how power might be shared between religiously enumerated "majorities" and "minorities" in an independent India. In staking a claim for a share of power for Muslims on grounds of their religiously informed identities, these schemes in their different ways challenged Congress's right to indivisible sovereignty. Yet they did so without altogether rejecting some kind of identification with India. If even Iqbal's and Rahmat

Ali's schemes did not envisage a complete break with the rest of India, out-right secession was not an option for Muslims in the minority provinces. Most of the schemes penned by Muslims in these provinces considered themselves to be a nation-in-minority that belonged to the larger nation inhabiting "Pakistan" and Bengal. If Muslims in the Hindu-majority provinces were seen as belonging to a larger nation in northwestern India, religious minorities in "Pakistan" and Bengal were expected to derive comfort from the common nationality they shared with coreligionists dominating the non-Muslim state. But the notion of reciprocal safeguards could work only if Muslims and non-Muslims remained part of a larger Indian whole, albeit one dramatically reconceptualized.[18]

Muslim Regionalism and the All-India Muslim League

The outbreak of World War II in September 1939 provided an opportunity to test the political salience of contending ideas about a homeland for India's Muslims. Britain's viceroy, Lord Linlithgow, declared war on Germany without consulting Indian opinion and put a moratorium on all constitutional advance. Thoroughly affronted and unable to extract an acceptable price for cooperation in the war, Congress resigned from eight provincial governments in protest. This offered Jinnah an opening to restore his credentials as an all-India politician. Accusing the Congress ministries in the provinces of perpetrating atrocities against Muslims, he called on the Muslim League to observe a "day of deliverance." The decision of the scheduled caste leader B. R. Ambedkar to heed the League's call was a shot in the arm for Jinnah, already delighted at being asked to come to the viceregal lodge on the same footing with Gandhi. Looking for a pretext to justify postponing constitutional advance at the center for the duration of the war, the viceroy asked Jinnah for the League's "constructive policy."

Any such policy had to square the conflicting interests of Muslims in the majority and the minority provinces. Only by bringing the combined weight of the Muslim provinces to bear on discussions at the all-India level could the League expect to have a say in the future constitutional arrangements. Making the best of a poor hand, Jinnah made ambiguity and vagueness the better part of valor. Needing the Muslim-majority provinces more than they needed him, he made sure that the League's demand offered them more provincial autonomy than they already enjoyed under the Act of 1935. Without making any reference to a center, the Lahore resolution of March 1940 called for the grouping of provinces in northwestern and northeastern India into "Independent States in which the constituent units . . . [would be] autonomous and sovereign." This suggested that the "Independent States" would not just be federal in form but would have something close to a confederal structure. Averse to such an outcome, Jinnah inserted a provision under which sovereignty of not just the constituent units but possibly also the "Independent States" would be something for the future. The League's working committee was entrusted with the task of preparing a scheme that would lead to the "assumption *finally* by the respective regions of all the powers such as defence, external affairs, communications, customs and such matters as may be necessary." Until that unspecified moment, the regions had to support Jinnah at the center, giving him maximum room to maneuver in negotiations with both Congress and the British.

The disjunction between his all-India vision and the regional perspectives of his Muslim constituents continued to haunt Jinnah in the remaining years of the Raj. He tried papering over these cracks for the duration of the war by insisting that the principle of Pakistan, the territorial embodiment of the Muslim claim to nationhood, had to be conceded before settling the shape and powers of the all-India center. Implicit in this line of argument was that any transfer of power to Indians would entail the dissolution of the unitary center created by the British. Any renegotiated all-India center—unitary, federal, or confederal—had to be based on the agreement of all the constituents units, including the Muslim-majority provinces and the princely states. Once the British and the Congress accepted the principle of Pakistan, Jinnah was willing to negotiate its future relationship with the rest of India. This could be in the nature of a confederation between the predominantly Muslim and Hindu areas or based on treaty arrangements on matters of common interest between two essentially sovereign states—Pakistan (representing the Muslim-majority provinces) and Hindustan (representing the Hindu-majority provinces).

In either case, Jinnah wanted something close to parity with the Congress at the all-India level because Muslims as a nation had a right to an equal share of power with the Hindus. If it was to cover the interests of Muslims in both the majority and the minority provinces, "Pakistan" had to remain part of an all-India whole. In keeping with that aim, Jinnah made it a point to always speak of Pakistan and Hindustan and not Pakistan and India. "We are not enemies of the Congress," he told a group of Punjabi Muslim and Hindu students in August 1944, though we disagree on certain issues. "If we must have a separate State," he continued, "that will not mean we shall have nothing to do with each other." He had no doubt that "both Hindus and Muslims will be happy when Pakistan is established" as it was in their best interest. They would never "allow anybody, whether he is Afghan or Pathan, to dominate us" because "India is for Indians." It would be "foolish of the Hindus, and vice versa," not to come to the defense of Pakistan if it were invaded by any outside power.[19]

Such a vision was at odds with the humdrum of everyday politics. Leading a party whose main bases of support were in the Muslim-minority provinces rather than in the provinces demanded for Pakistan, Jinnah, the constitutionalist, with an eye on the all-India stage, was on the horns of a dilemma. Much has been made of the transformation of this secular and Westernized lawyer after 1940. Yet Jinnah's recourse to Islam was a product of political necessity—the need to win the support of a community that was a distinctive category in official and popular parlance but with no prior history of organizing on a single platform. He could not dilate on his real political objectives because what could rouse Muslims in the minority provinces would put off Muslims where they were in a majority. A populist program to mobilize the Muslim rural masses was out of the question. It would infuriate the landed men who called the shots in provincial politics. This is where recourse to Islam made sense to a politician and a party with neither a populist past nor a populist present. Both politician and party needed to steal the populist march on their rivals.

It was his manipulation not of religion but of politics that enabled Jinnah to steer the course for the League. By scrutinizing every word of the Lahore resolution, he managed to create a semblance of support for the Muslim League by raising the expectations of majority-province politicians. "Pakistan" for them was security not just against a Congress-dominated center but much more. It epitomized their aspirations for regional self-determination even if cast in the mold of religious communitarianism. What was good for Muslims as an all-India community was not always perceived to be in the best interest of Muslims in the regions. So if tensions between central and regional imperatives threatened to undermine Jinnah and the Muslim League's cause, the delicate balance between Muslim communitarian and Muslim regional interests was an even bigger source for concern.

This was exemplified by Punjab and Bengal, two provinces whose undivided territories and non-Muslim populations the League claimed for Pakistan. The only way to realistically make a bid for the incorporation of these provinces into Pakistan was by promising equal rights of citizenship and other safeguards for non-Muslims living in them. But diluting the Muslim slant of the League's demand and entertaining regionally specific matters ran the risk of eroding its appeal for minority-province Muslims. Looking for the broadest level of Muslim support with which to stop the Congress's march to power at the center, Jinnah was unwilling to be drawn into the knotty details of safeguards for non-Muslim minorities in Muslim provinces until the all-India picture had been clarified. Yet continued Muslim domination of undivided Punjab and Bengal was contingent on keeping political equations with the non-Muslims in good order. In choosing to wait for Congress and the British to concede the League's demands at the center before negotiating with non-Muslims in these two provinces, Jinnah laid the basis for a deadly contradiction. It proved to be the undoing of his strategy to deploy the demand for a Pakistan to cover the interests of all Indian Muslims, not only in the majority provinces but also in provinces where they were in a minority.

The contradiction was apparent to the more perceptive analysts. A claim to the whole of Punjab and Bengal based on Muslim self-determination could not be upheld if it meant denying that right to the non-Muslims of these provinces. The first person to raise this was Stafford Cripps, the British Labor Party leader, who came to India as London's emissary in the spring of 1942. With Japan knocking on India's doors after its sweep through Southeast Asia in early 1942, the American president Franklin Roosevelt and the Chinese leader Chiang Kai-shek prevailed on the British prime minister Winston Churchill to make one more attempt to get Congress to cooperate in the war effort. The Cripps Mission made no headway on its short-term objective of securing Congress participation in the viceroy's executive council. However, its long-term plans for independent India put the finger on the principal contradiction in the League's demand. The Congress's contention that Indian freedom ought not to be delayed in the absence of Hindu–Muslim unity was conceded. Congress could have the strong center it wanted so long as it recognized the right of the provinces to opt out of the Indian union and achieve independent dominion status.

The less insightful interpreted the Cripps local option of granting provinces the right to remain independent as meeting the demand for a "Pakistan." But the concession to opt out of the Indian union was made to provinces and not communities. With bare majorities, Muslim politicians in Punjab and Bengal could expect to exercise the right successfully only by coming to terms with the non-Muslims. Better placed to use the local option to seek independent dominion status within the British empire, politicians in Sindh and the NWFP were now even less likely than before to pay heed to Jinnah and the League at the center. All this would leave Muslims in the minority provinces to their own devices, precisely what the vague but specifically Muslim demand for a "Pakistan" was calculated to prevent. The failure of the Cripps Mission spared the Muslim League from the embarrassment of seeing its main constituents abandon all-India purposes for their own regionally construed concerns.

In 1944, the old Congress hand from Madras, C. R. Rajagopalachari, picked up where Cripps had left off by proposing a "Pakistan" consisting of the Muslim-majority districts of Punjab and Bengal. The "Pakistan" on offer would have to still share defense, communications, and commerce with the rest of India. Jinnah, too, envisaged some sort of common arrangements with Hindustan. But these had to be based on parity with the Congress, not abject dependency. So even though the territorial dimensions of Pakistan in 1947 closely approximated those conceived by Rajagopalachari, Jinnah trashed them as "offering a shadow and a husk—a maimed, mutilated and moth-eaten Pakistan" and pretending to have "met our Pakistan scheme and Muslim demand."[20]

Brushing aside Congress's moves was easier than keeping a handle on his wayward Muslim constituents. Jinnah's insistence on being the sole spokesman of India's Muslims was intended to keep a modicum of discipline in his camp. It was a losing proposition. The balance of power now lay with the provinces and not their all-India spokesman. Unable to alter political realities in the Muslim provinces, Jinnah had to rest content with the appearance rather than the substance of support in the formal arenas of politics. His uneasy alliance with the Unionists in Punjab was bitterly opposed by Muslim Leaguers who wanted the party to be on a stronger organizational footing in the province. In Bengal, Sindh, and the NWFP, Jinnah preferred to see the League shunting in and out of office rather than focus on the more difficult task of building the party organization. Given the disconnect between the League's party machinery and popular sentiments for "Pakistan," which did come to appeal to Muslims in majority and minority provinces during the remaining years of the war, Jinnah avoided tackling issues that might expose the fragility of his support base in the Muslim provinces. There was a contradiction between the Muslim claim for undivided Punjab and Bengal and the need to reassure their non-Muslim minorities that their rights would be adequately safeguarded. All he could do was to invoke the principle of reciprocity in the Lahore resolution and assert that minorities would be protected in "Pakistan" and the same treatment expected for Muslims in the Hindu-majority provinces.

The League's organizational weaknesses in the provinces demanded for a "Pakistan" meant that Jinnah could not risk losing the backing of Muslims in the minority provinces. At various stages in the movement for "Pakistan," he reminded the League of the sacrifices of minority-province Muslims that could never be forgotten. He also urged Muslims in the Hindu provinces to show magnanimity and not hinder the struggle for emancipation and freedom being fought by their coreligionists in the majority provinces. When the time came to strike the right bargain with Congress and the British, "Pakistan" was the "surest guarantee for the fair treatment of the minorities."[21] Leaguers in the Muslim-minority provinces took comfort in the assurance and, like their counterparts in the majority provinces, interpreted "Pakistan" as consistent with a confederation with Hindustan. The British reforms commissioner H. V. Hodson confirmed that "Pakistan" was effectively a revolt against minority status and that, far from aiming to divide India, it was a bid for a share of power in an independent India.[22]

If a Muslim state carved out of the northwest and the northeast was not inconsistent with a confederal arrangement covering the whole of the subcontinent, why was India partitioned in 1947? A plausible answer to this question requires shedding the presumption of a linear progression from the assertion of nationhood to the achievement of statehood. After 1940 there was no retracting of the League claim that Indian Muslims were a nation entitled to equal treatment with Hindus in all future constitutional negotiations. However, the demand for a separate sovereign state was kept open for negotiation as late as the summer of 1946. The real dilemma facing Jinnah and the League was how to cover the interests of all Muslims in the absence of a neat equation between populations and territory. There were nearly as many Muslims living in the rest of India as those residing in provinces claimed for Pakistan. With the Muslim nation straddling both "Pakistan" and "Hindustan," their boundaries had to be permeable. This was the primary reason for Jinnah's and the League's stubborn insistence on getting undivided Punjab and Bengal for Pakistan without reassuring non-Muslim minorities of their citizenship rights. The reasons for the ambivalences in the Lahore resolution can be comprehended only by underscoring the difference between a purely separatist demand and one angling for an equitable power-sharing arrangement at the subcontinental level between two disproportionate nations. Looking to challenge Congress's bid for power at the center based on the notion of monolithic sovereignty introduced by the British, Jinnah and the League came forward with a scheme that drew on the idea of shared sovereignty. Such a conception of sovereignty was in line with the subcontinent's long history of creative power-sharing arrangements among its diverse peoples and regions. Distinguishing between a "nation" and "state" and a partition of India as opposed to a partition of the two main Muslim-majority provinces helps to unravel the contradictory dynamics underpinning the demand for a "Pakistan."

Jinnah avoided discussing the more awkward aspects of the League's scheme while the war lasted. Once it was over, his tactics presented the biggest impediment to the British negotiating a deal with the Congress at the center. Before the 1945–46 elections, the governors of Punjab, Bengal, and Assam advised New Delhi and London to assure the non-Muslims of their provinces that they would not be bundled into a predominantly Muslim state against their will. But no authoritative statement was made prior to the elections. Jinnah took a rickety League into the elections on the vague but emotive slogan of "Pakistan" whose precise territories were as hazy as its ideological orientation was bitterly contested. Pro-Congress ulema represented by organizations like the Jamiat-ul-Ulema-i-Hind and the Majlis-i-Ahrar advocated a composite Indian nationalism in one breath and sharia-based personal laws for Muslims in the next. The paradox of this nonsecular vision being perfectly compatible with Congress's inclusionary nationalism is yet another example of the many possible combinations of religious and secular politics in India. No less paradoxical was the support for a "Pakistan" by Muslims who were ideologically of either the communist or the socialist ilk. The participation of such ungodly people in the campaign for "Pakistan" lent starch to the claim of pro-Congress ulema that the League was a "secular" charade and that Jinnah was not the Quaid-i-Azam or the great leader, as his followers called him, but the Kafir-i-Azam or the preeminent leader of the infidels. In this highly charged atmosphere, Muslims for and against the League used Islamic rhetoric to take down one another. Some of the attacks were patently offensive, embittering not only intra- but also intercommunitarian relations in the Muslim-majority provinces. The implications of the religious overtones of the electoral propaganda for the fragile communitarian balance of Punjab and Bengal were detrimental for Jinnah's purposes at the center.

These concerns were offset by the dramatic reversal of fortunes for the Muslim League. Stunned by voter apathy in 1937, the League found itself crowned with spectacular success in the 1945–46 elections. It not only made a clean sweep of the Muslim seats to the central assembly but also polled 75 percent of the Muslim vote cast in the provincial assembly elections. Jinnah predictably hailed the election results as an endorsement of the League's claim for parity with the Congress at the center and a "Pakistan" consisting of the two main Muslim-majority provinces. But the Muslim electorate in Punjab and Bengal were not told that voting for "Pakistan" could mean a partition of their domains on the basis of religious self-determination. This would have strained the League's hastily concluded alliances with many local politicians in Punjab and Bengal who were under the misconception that a vote for "Pakistan" would guarantee their dominance over these undivided provinces.

As it was, the Muslim League's electoral success did not translate easily into solid gains at the governmental level. Though it emerged as the largest single bloc in the Punjab assembly, the political arithmetic prevented the League from forming a ministry on its own. Neither the numerically depleted Unionists nor the Sikhs and the Congress were prepared to help the Punjab Muslim League take office. The governor called on the Unionist premier Khizar Hayat Tiwana to once again form the government, which he did with the help of the Panthic Sikhs and the Congress. Being kept out of office in a province Jinnah had called the cornerstone of "Pakistan" was not the only insult the League suffered so soon after its electrifying success. While managing to slot in a shaky ministry in Sindh, the Muslim League had to face the ignominy of seeing a Congress government take office in the Pathan heartland of the NWFP. Bengal was the only province where there was a Muslim League ministry but one that saw provincial advantages in keeping open the possibility of a coalition government with the Congress. So even with the groundswell of Muslim support for "Pakistan," a risky course awaited Jinnah before he could secure parity with the Congress at the center. Needing the Muslim provinces to take a seat at the negotiating table with Congress and the British, Jinnah had chosen not to rock the boat by enforcing too strict a disciplinary regime on their mainly landlord politicians. Although helping him gain a toehold in these provinces in the short term, this strategy was to narrow his options considerably when the time came for the final negotiations. Fissiparous tendencies and intense rivalries within the Muslim camp gave Congress's high command ample opportunities to erect roadblocks to further progress. With the NWFP already in the Congress's pocket, there was nothing to prevent it from striking deals with politicians in the Muslim-majority provinces. And it could do so with crushing effect now that the British, with an eye to the endgame, were no longer willing to smile on Jinnah's tactics. But having puffed up the League leader for their wartime objectives, neither New Delhi nor London could afford to wholly ignore his "Pakistan" demand.

In the spring of 1946, the Labor government decided to send out a cabinet delegation to determine how power was to be transferred in India. After meetings with a cross-section of Indian leaders and opinion makers, the Cabinet Mission proposed a three-tier federal constitutional framework that came close to giving Jinnah what he both wanted and needed. There was to be compulsory grouping of provinces at the second tier and an all-India federal center confined only to defense, foreign affairs, and communications. The grouping of provinces gave the League a virtual center, which it could use to control the Muslim provinces prior to bringing their weight to bear at the all-India level. This was all the more important because the mission's plan did not guarantee the Muslim provinces parity with the Congress provinces at the center. The alternative to this arrangement was a sovereign "Pakistan" minus the Hindu-majority districts of eastern Punjab and western Bengal, including Calcutta.

On June 6, 1946, Jinnah sprung a surprise on his followers and detractors alike when he persuaded a closed session of the AIML council to reject a sovereign "Pakistan" and accept the Cabinet Mission's proposal for a federated India. He won the day by arguing that the struggle for a "Pakistan" would continue even after the Muslim provinces joined the union. All residuary powers of the federation except for three subjects would be vested at the group level. The grouping of Muslim political power would allow the League to press its case in a federal constituent assembly. If worse came to worst, the Muslim provinces could opt out of the union within a ten-year period. This was the second time in two years that Jinnah had turned down the offer of a "Pakistan" based on a partition of Punjab and Bengal. But Congress had no intention of honoring grouping of provinces, which Gandhi thought was much worse than partition. Nehru, for his part, was strongly opposed to a weak federal center and saw no justification for grouping. Upon taking over as Congress president from Maulana Abul Kalam Azad, Nehru declared on July 11, 1946, that provincial grouping might not last, effectively negating Congress's acceptance of the Cabinet Mission's plan. As far as Nehru was concerned, real authority had to vest in the federal center and not the group legislatures as the League had demanded.

Grouping of provinces for Jinnah was the crux of the matter. Indication that Congress intended to break grouping by exploiting Muslim divisions persuaded him that the mission's plan was not a secure basis for a settlement. A sovereign "Pakistan" alone could give the League a center to prevent Muslim politicians from crossing the floor and joining the Congress if the political weather vane so demanded. But a sovereign "Pakistan" had to include undivided Punjab and Bengal if it was to negotiate safeguards for Muslims in Hindustan or secure a substantial share of the all-India center's assets, including the army. Jinnah was riled at not being asked to form the interim government despite the League satisfying the condition of accepting the mission's long-term proposals. Suspicious of the Congress and unsure about British impartiality, he not only advised the League to revert to its original demand of March 1940 but, in a move that was uncharacteristic of his political style, sanctioned a "direct action" movement to achieve "Pakistan" through unconstitutional means if necessary. Jinnah's willingness to adopt agitational methods was not a call to violence. Despite his calm counsels for peace and quiet introspection, di-

rect action day on August 16, 1947, turned Calcutta, the capital of a province where a League ministry was in power, into a city of the dead. For five
days the manipulators of Calcutta's underworld and bands of thugs, both
Hindu and Muslim, carried out horrific acts of cold-blooded murder, ar-
son, and pillage, leaving about 4000 dead and 15,000 wounded.

There was a general outcry against Jinnah and the Muslim League.
Pressed by London to make a conciliatory gesture and prevent further
outbreaks of violence, the viceroy Lord Wavell invited the Congress to
form the interim government despite its reservations about the grouping
clause. Seeing the world collapse around him, Jinnah promptly instructed
the League to take its place in the interim government alongside the Congress on terms that he had previously refused to countenance. Worse
shocks were on the way. On February 20, 1947, the British prime minister
Clement Attlee announced that power would be transferred by June 1948
and virtually accepted that the Cabinet Mission's plan was a dead letter.
But instead of mentioning "Pakistan," London revived the Cripps offer by
stating its willingness to transfer power to existing provincial governments if no agreement was possible at the center. Several Muslim politicians in Sindh and the NWFP interpreted Attlee's statement as a precursor to their independence. Privileging Muslim provincialism rather than
Muslim communitarianism was tantamount to pulling the rug from
under Jinnah's feet. What was more, by setting a deadline for the termination of their rule, the British had paved the way for a deal with the Congress that could secure their long-term economic and strategic interests in
South Asia.

Jinnah continued hoping that the British would not divide Punjab and
Bengal. Even before the last viceroy, Lord Mountbatten, arrived in India,
Congress had taken the first step to cut the Pakistan demand down to
size. On March 8, 1947, the Congress led by Nehru formally called for the
partition of Punjab and indicated that a similar fate may await Bengal.
This proved to be a fait accompli for the new viceroy, eager to strike a
common chord with the Congress in order to create the conditions for
Britain's honorable exit while keeping India in the British Commonwealth. Brushing aside Jinnah's arguments that it was a grave error to
equate the principle of "Pakistan" with the partition of Punjab and Bengal, Mountbatten accused Jinnah of megalomania bordering on lunacy.
Once Congress had stated its price for agreeing to dominion status and

staying in the Commonwealth—an early eviction of the League from the interim government and a final settlement based on the creation of a "Pakistan" shorn of eastern Punjab and western Bengal—the viceroy advanced the date for the transfer of power to August 1947. Congress's change of heart required abandoning two of its oldest and most sacred principles— the unity of India and full independence. But the advantages of the compromise far outweighed the disadvantages. By accepting dominion status and inviting Mountbatten to remain as governor-general, Congress got around the difficulty posed by the lapse of British paramountcy over the Indian princely states, which occupied nearly 40 percent of India's territory. Moreover, by cutting its losses and effectively demanding partition, Congress could rid itself of Jinnah and the League and settle down to ruling three-fourths of India according to its unfettered will.

In the end, instead of an equitable power-sharing arrangement between the Muslim provinces and Hindustan, Jinnah was offered an unenviable choice—an undivided India with no assurance of the Muslim share of power at the center or a sovereign "Pakistan" devoid of the non-Muslim-majority districts of Punjab and Bengal. While his preoccupations with the all-India arrangements had sunk the prospect of a power-sharing arrangement that might have saved Punjab from being rent in twain, there were some prospects of Bengal remaining united. Bengal without Calcutta, Jinnah quipped, was like asking a man to live without his heart. He sanctioned efforts to keep Bengal united and independent, noting that it would be on good relations with "Pakistan." Toward that end, he demanded a corridor linking the two independent Muslim-majority states. The Congress high command nipped the plan for a united and independent Bengal in the bud. If he had been confident of keeping his straying flock of supporters together inside the all-India constituent assembly, Jinnah might conceivably have tried giving the Cabinet Mission's plan a trial run. This could have prevented the division of the two main Muslim-majority provinces and allowed him to use their political weight, not to mention that of the non-Muslim minorities, to negotiate safeguards for all Indian Muslims.

The fundamental structural contradiction in the British Indian political system between all-India concerns and regional dynamics ultimately defeated Jinnah. Against the backdrop of mounting tensions along lines of religious community and brutal acts of violence in different parts of India, which his detractors unfairly blamed on him, he was in no position to extract any concessions from the Congress. Bluntly told by the viceroy that his recalcitrance could lose him the Pakistan that was on offer, Jinnah reluctantly acquiesced in Mountbatten's plan for a partition involving an agonizing dismemberment of Punjab and Bengal. Partition as it came about did not entail the division of India into two "successor" states, Pakistan and Hindustan. Congress inherited British India's unitary center. Pakistan consisted of the Muslim-majority provinces shorn of eastern Punjab and western Bengal (including Calcutta)—the "mutilated and moth-eaten" state that Jinnah had rejected in 1944 and again in 1946. A Pakistan without its non-Muslim minorities in Punjab and Bengal was in no position to negotiate safeguards for Muslims in the rest of India. Congress insisted on partition as a final settlement, arguing that the Muslim areas were to be seen as "contracting out" of the "Union of India." This put an end to the Indian Muslim "nation" using the grant of independent statehood to its collective advantage. Moreover, if "Pakistan" collapsed under the weight of its own contradictions, its constituent units would have to re-turn to the Indian union singly, not re-create it on the basis of two sovereign states. Jinnah's decision to become the governor-general of the new state was intended to forestall such a development. But with millions dislocated as a result of partition and the killings of hundreds of thousands of innocent men, women, and children that followed in its wake, the prospects of Pakistan surviving the trauma of its bloodstained birth looked extremely bleak. Cast against its will into the role of the "seceding" state, and with Muslim provincialism rather than the presumed unities of a common religion providing a major driving force for its creation, Pakistan's first priority was to create a viable central authority over two geographically separated territories that until then had been governed from New Delhi.

TRUNCATED STATE, DIVIDED NATION

RELIGION IS OFTEN THOUGHT to have been the main impetus behind the creation of Pakistan. The historical evidence militates against such certitude. The demand for Pakistan was intended to get an equitable, if not equal, share of power for Indian Muslims in an independent India. What instead emerged, to use the words of the founder of Pakistan, was a "truncated . . . moth-eaten and mutilated state." If their claim to nationhood had been conceded, Muslims as a "nation" were divided into two mutually hostile states. Religion as political identity did play a part in the outcome but not, as is believed, by conceding the right of self-determination to Muslims qua Muslims. In keeping with the Cripps offer of 1942, the right to opt out of the Indian union was given to provinces, not to communities.

Since the principle of self-determination was extended on a territorial basis, Congress opted to cut its losses by letting areas with a Muslim preponderance split off from the Indian union. According to the terms set by Mountbatten for ratifying partition, a minority vote of non-Muslim legislators prevailed over the majority opinion of Muslim legislators of Punjab and Bengal to keep their provinces undivided. If partition ended up stripping Muslims of their dominance in undivided Punjab and Bengal, it sundered the Muslim nation on whose behalf the AIML had raised the demand for a Pakistan. These paradoxical results of the recourse to religion as the basis of politics are inexplicable without accounting for the crucial interplay between politics in the regions and the center in late colonial India.

Once Pakistan came into being, the place of religion in state ideology was a question that had to be faced squarely in this Muslim homeland. A divided nation with a truncated state had to ponder the rights of minorities that remained in its midst even after the great exodus of 1947. Even more challenging was the task of reconciling different interpretations of Islam as well as the regional, cultural, and linguistic diversities that underlay the shared bond of Islam. A vibrant debate on the tenor of the relationship between Islam and the state played itself out in the constituent assembly as well as the more informal arenas of political discourse during the first decade of postindependence Pakistan.

Imperfect Dawn

A singular emphasis on religion obscures the drama of human emotions as communities turning into nations crossed the threshold from colonial subjection to freedom amid rivers of blood. In the famous words of the Urdu poet Faiz Ahmad Faiz, this was not the dawn for which he and his comrades had set out seeking refuge for their troubled hearts. The atmosphere may have been festive and the leaders might claim to have reached the goal, but their calming words were no cure for the pain of severance. Yet the poet's hope for an alternative dawn had not died. His mind and spirit were still free: "Let us go on, our goal is not reached yet."[1]

Hope was poor recompense for those who lost dear ones and saw their properties and livelihoods destroyed. Stories of individual trauma caused by divided families, disrupted friendships, and lost spatial moorings are among the most popular genres of writings on partition. Carrying the cumulative burdens of partition individually and collectively, these personal remembrances are invariably colored by subsequent developments and have to be read in the context of when they were written. Most partition narratives frame the violence in communitarian terms even when they invoke the spirit of humanism. Yet the agonizing pain of dislocation and the loss of loved ones were not always easy to explain in terms of religion, particularly for those who considered religion as a matter of personal faith based on inner spirituality and human ethics. The worst violence in 1947 occurred in rural Punjab. Unprecedented in scale, it was also qualitatively different from incidents of Hindu–Muslim conflict that had taken place in earlier decades, mostly in towns. Banded individuals, often drawn from the ranks of demobilized soldiers, targeted erstwhile neighbors belonging to another religious community. Yet rather than religion per se, the fight was over *zar* (wealth), *zameen* (land), and *zan* (women) highly prized by Punjab's patriarchal agrarian society. The trauma of separating at close quarters left psychological wounds that would take decades to heal.[2]

The Urdu short story writer Saadat Hasan Manto, who lived through the cataclysmic events of 1947, has left a riveting account of the psychodrama of partition as it played out in the lives of ordinary people. A witness to the troubled times, Manto kept his ears close to the ground, making his literary corpus a treasure trove for historians looking for insights into the human dimension of partition. What he saw of the *batwara,* the vernacular term he used to refer to partition, convinced him that it was not religious zealotry or piety but human greed and man's astonishing capacity for bestiality that had brought the subcontinent to such a sorry pass. A social renegade who mostly wrote on ethically challenging issues through a probing exploration of human psychology, Manto was a humanist who could not suffer bigots. In his irreverent self-epitaph, Manto wondered whether he was a greater short-story writer than God. In story after story, he captures the snapping of old bonds of friendship and the melting away of love and shared cultures in a milieu infected with the rhetoric of "Muslim" and "Hindu" animosity. He left the politics of the murderous frenzy that soaked the subcontinent in blood at the moment of the British withdrawal to latter-day historians. His forte lay in cutting through the communitarian morass of the period to lay bare the ugly but

Refugees. *The White Star Photo Pvt. Ltd. Archive.*

still strangely hopeful glimpses of human nature as ordinary individuals reacted to the rupture of partitioned lands and lives.

Based in Bombay at the time of partition, Manto wove together the personal and the impersonal in ways that elude historians. His partition short stories lift the veil over the human misery caused by the arbitrary drawing of boundaries that the bravado of national independence casts into the shade.[3] In "Toba Tek Singh," Manto questions the sanity of those who partitioned India by spotlighting lunatics in a mental asylum in Lahore after the two states had decided to exchange all inmates on the basis of religion. One inmate becomes so overwrought that he climbs up a tree and, after a two-hour-long soliloquy on the politics of partition, announces his wish to live in the tree. Upon finding out that his beloved hometown, Toba Tek Singh, is in Pakistan, a Sikh inmate refuses to be transferred to India and dies standing in no-man's-land.

If place affiliations could be stronger than the bonds of religion, the temptation to take advantage of the weak and the vulnerable, regardless of community, was amply in evidence. In "Khul Do," (Open It) a distraught Muslim father desperately looking for his kidnapped daughter eventually finds her, only to discover that the young Muslim men who had helped him locate her had also raped the girl. The story punctures the facile attribution of religious motives to the violence unleashed on members of other communities. So does the poignant yarn "Parhiya Kalima" (Recite the Muslim Confessional), which underlines why all the killings at the time of partition cannot be ascribed to religious zeal. Caught by the police holding the knife he used to kill his former mistress's Hindu lover, the murderer speaking as a true believer confesses his crime. It was a crime of passion, he insists, and not one motivated by Pakistan. It was Manto's bone-chilling story "Thanda Gosht" (Cold Meat), however, that so rattled the sensibilities of the Pakistani authorities that they booked him on charges of obscenity. The story is about a Sikh who carries off a young Muslim girl after killing six of her family members. When he reaches the canal near the train tracks, he places the girl under some bushes and forces himself on her, only to discover that she had been dead all along.[4]

In writing such graphic descriptions of the atrocities perpetrated in the name of religion and nation, Manto does not pass moral judgments on the actions of the murderers. Accepting the gruesome reality of partition at face value, he sought to find rare pearls of humanity in the man-made sea of blood, a hint of remorse felt deeply or a reflection of tears shed by murderers. Manto wanted to blow the whistle on the fraudulent self-righteousness of those around him. There were unforgettable scenes. "Muslims were very happy because they had got Pakistan. Where was Pakistan? What was it? They had no idea. But they were happy because after a long time they had a reason to be happy." The gangsters of Rampur were carousing, smoking cigarettes, and chewing on betel leaves. After days of bloodletting, there was remarkably no violence on August 14, 1947, in Bombay. People were busy celebrating the winning of freedom. "Nobody was thinking about freedom, how it was achieved and what changes it would bring in their lives." There were slogans of "Pakistan Zindabad" (Long live Pakistan) on one side and 'Hindustan Zindabad' (Long live Hindustan) on the other."[5] The obverse of these celebratory catchphrases was a barrage of denunciatory ones, most popular of which was "Pakistan Murdabad" and "Hindustan Murdabad"—death to Pakistan and Hindustan. These provided cover for all manner of human outrages, including dousing people with petrol and setting them alight.

The dizzying range of challenges that came with freedom turned the question of Pakistan's survival into a national preoccupation. There was endless chatter about sinister Hindu and British plots to nip the incipient state in the bud. The old and new inhabitants wondered whether Pakistan would reunite with India. There was also the possibility of the whole subcontinent becoming Pakistan or vanishing along with India from the map of the world one day.[6] Amid the haze of uncertainty surrounding the future location of places, establishing ownership of space was an immediate priority. The exodus of non-Muslims from the western parts of Punjab generated a boom in real estate. For all its manifold woes, Pakistan ended up with twice as many evacuee properties than Muslim migrants abandoned in India, creating a deep vested interest in the acquisition of evacuee properties by those with political connections. The distractions of property allotments dulled enthusiasm for the boons of freedom among those left to watch the spectacle from the sidelines. It was only a matter of time before the venality and matching inefficiencies of the politicians became a pretext for the derailment of the political process by the army projecting itself as the sole guarantor of Pakistan's survival.

Amid general confusion and misunderstanding about the rationale for its creation, the catchphrase "Pakistan Zindabad" gave solace to agitated minds and served as an ultimate badge of legitimacy in the land of the pure. As the first slogan of patriotism, it was readily adopted by the citizenry but was soon accompanied by more ideologically driven slogans, like "What is the meaning of Pakistan? *La ilaha ilallah*—there is no God but God." Slogans are significant not only in what they reveal about the psyche of a people but also in all that they disguise. The simple statement "long live Pakistan" celebrated the ideal of a homeland where Muslims expected to realize their aspirations and live according to their own cultural mores. For the mainly Urdu-speaking migrants from India who abandoned home and hearth to make their futures in a predominantly non-Urdu speaking country, Pakistan was the land of opportunity. Better educated than most of their coreligionists in western Pakistan, they expected to get the best jobs. Some of these *muhajirs,* as the refugees from India came to be known, had sensibly moved their money before partition in the hope of starting up new businesses in both wings of the country. The idea of material gain encapsulated in "Pakistan Zindabad" was a stretch removed from the other more loaded slogan, defining its meaning in vague Islamic terms. But for all their claims dressed up in religious terminology, the protagonists of an Islamic state too had their sights on power and pelf in the Muslim El Dorado. Although no one denied the Muslim character of Pakistan, there was a vast difference between those who interpreted it as, first and foremost, a land of opportunity and others who saw it as the perfect laboratory for their versions of Islam.

The Westernized urban classes had a universal disdain for mullahs and the "mullahcracy." Living in their newly acquired posh bungalows and enjoying membership privileges in clubs previously the exclusive preserve of the British, these English-educated classes ridiculed obscurantist mullahs and flaunted their modernity. Ballroom dancing was a rage among the social elite and cocktail parties a common practice. Using inherited or adopted Urdu cultural idioms and practices in their everyday lives, these pioneers of a postcolonial Pakistani modernity aimed at creating a secular national ethos. But in equating class privileges with modernity, they neglected to account for the woes of the underprivileged, reduced to living in low-cost housing or shantytowns, those for whom the land of opportunity had proven to be a barren wasteland of dreams. With widening social and economic disparities along class and regional lines, the cry of religion held out attractions for the urban poor only insofar as it offered a

miraculous escape from the wretchedness of daily existence. Resentful of
the rich and powerful, the subordinate social strata were not necessarily
enamored of the Islam propagated by mullahs whom many associated
with platefuls of *halwa* (sweetmeats) and a pocket full of alms. But there
were a handful of Western-educated Muslim advocates of an Islamic state
in the administrative bureaucracy and the newspaper industry who saw
advantages in promoting a religious ideology among the masses.

So long as Jinnah and Liaquat Ali Khan remained at the helm, the ideologues of an Islamic state in Pakistan had to rest content with symbolic
gestures. As a politician who knew the importance of playing to the gal-
lery, Jinnah made references to Islam that were compatible with his secular and democratic vision of a Pakistan with opportunities for all, regardless of caste, community, or creed. In one of the more memorable
contemporary recollections of Mohammad Ali Jinnah on the eve of partition, Beverley Nichols described the lanky and stylishly dressed barrister
as the "most important man in Asia." Looking every bit like a gentleman
of Spain, of the old diplomatic school, the monocle-wearing leader of the
AIML held a pivotal place in the future of India. "If Gandhi goes, there is
always Nehru, or Rajagopalachari, or Patel or a dozen others. But if Jinnah goes, who is there?" Without Jinnah to steer the course, the Muslim
League was a potentially explosive force that "might run completely off
the rails, and charge through India with fire and slaughter"; it might even
"start another war." As long as Jinnah was around, nothing disastrous was
likely to happen and so, Nichols quipped, "a great deal hangs on the grey
silk cord of that monocle."[7]

The state that this monocle-wearing leader got was very different from
the one he had sought. A string of thorny issues have dogged representations of Pakistani history ever since its appearance on the global scene as
a homeland for Indian Muslims. An anomaly among modern nation-
states, Pakistan as it emerged in 1947 was separated by a thousand miles of
Indian territory into a western and an eastern wing that had nothing in
common except the bond of Islam. In the western wing, linguistic and
cultural differences were partially offset by geographical contiguity and a
mutual dependence on the Indus. The association between its two far-
flung wings, however, was more a product of historical contingency than
of genuine empathy. The need to use the past for purposes of national integration was felt at the very outset, but the methods used to represent

Mohammad Ali Jinnah. *Jack Wilkes, Time and Life Pictures, Getty Images.*

history had consequences that were to prove inimical for the unity of the country.

The immediate challenge was to establish Pakistan's distinctiveness in the community of nations. This was complicated by India's inheritance of British India's international personality, which effectively cast Pakistan into the role of a seceding state. As the founding father of Pakistan, Jinnah had foreseen the problem and strongly objected to the Hindu-majority areas being allowed to use the designation "India" after the Muslim-majority areas had formed a separate state of Pakistan. But even he had to make a virtue out of necessity. As he put it poignantly a few months after partition:

> A vigorous propaganda has been going on from the moment that the division was agreed upon and the two States were created that Pakistan is only a truncated Pakistan, that it is merely a temporary madness on the part of the Muslim League that has brought about this "secession," that Pakistan will have to come into the Union as a penitent, repentant, erring son and that the "two nation theory" is responsible for all that has taken place . . . Pakistan will never surrender and never agree in any shape or form to any constitutional union between the two sovereign States with one common centre. Pakistan has come to stay and will stay.[8]

While warning against attempts to bring about "a forced union" between the two countries, Jinnah made it plain that Pakistan was "always ready to come to an understanding or enter into agreements with Hindustan as two independent, equal, sovereign States" in the same way as "we may have our alliances, friendships and agreements with any other foreign nation."[9]

A seasoned constitutionalist, Jinnah was dead set against autocracy, whether of the civilian or of the khaki variety, substituting the rule of law. "Pakistan is now a sovereign State, absolute and unfettered, and the Government of Pakistan is in the hands of the people," he told a gathering of civil servants in February 1948. As servants of a state that was "starting from scratch," they had "a terrific burden" on their shoulders, which he likened to a "sacred trust." Until the constituent assembly had completed framing the constitution, the governor-general continued, "our present provisional constitution based on the fundamental principles of democracy not bureaucracy or autocracy or dictatorship, must be worked."[10]

The reality on the ground was far removed from such high-minded rhetoric. An eyewitness to the violence in Lahore recalled how rich and influential Muslims helped lowly gangsters in the old city to attack their Hindu and Sikh neighbors and dishonor their women at knife's point. The local police assisted by providing canisters of petrol to the looters and looking the other way as non-Muslim homes and shops were burned down and robbed.[11] Non-Muslim neighborhoods were set on fire and emptied of the inhabitants and their belongings, ostensibly as revenge for similar attacks on Muslims in India. One participant in the great migration recalled how most non-Muslim majority areas of the city lay desolate. "You could get into any unoccupied house that you liked" and be assured of all the domestic comforts as "their non-Muslim owners had fled and left everything behind." The world had suddenly changed. One could only dream of the days when Hindu women walked to the riverbank at sunrise to offer prayers. There were some non-Muslims for whom separation from Lahore, the magical city of gardens, was unbearable. One old Hindu woman in the Gwalmandi neighborhood of the inner city yelled out from her first floor window: "I am never going to leave Lahore. People say we are going to be killed, but I am staying right here. I will not abandon my home."[12]

Such resolve was rare. Appeals from the political leadership failed to put a stop to the wanton grab for other people's property and unpardonable dishonoring of women. The counterpoint of communitarian triumphalism and hatred proved deadly, scarring individual and collective psyches on both sides of the historic divide. Brutalized memories of 1947 have reinforced the contrasting yet mutually clinging nationalisms of Pakistan and India and made it difficult to explain the human tragedy of partition by anything other than religious motivation. If religion had any role in the human atrocities of partition, it was mostly as profanity and not, as is often assumed, an expression of deeply held faith. This was all the more reason why the violence and despoliation had to be given religious justification.

While Islamic Pakistan used religion to justify its creation as a separate state, secular India attributed the division to the religious "communalism" of the Muslim League. The claims and counterclaims of Indian and

Pakistani nationalism have drawn legitimacy from the brutalized memories of millions who witnessed the dehumanizing scenes of their loved ones being put to the sword and their property pilfered merely because they happened to belong to a specific religious community. The interplay of official nationalisms and emotionally charged popular narratives of partition created a haze of myth and sentiment, making it difficult to fathom why India was partitioned along lines of religion for the first time in its millennia-old history.

Narratives from the Pakistani side of the divide for the most part adduced the "two-nation" theory to explain why in the process of dismantling their Raj the British chose to divide India. Although variants of this theory span a wide spectrum, all attribute partition to Muslims being a distinctive community that had resisted assimilation into the Indian environment. Apart from glossing over the long history of Muslim interactions with non-Muslims, the theory cannot explain why of the nearly 100 million Muslims in 1947, close to 40 million were left to their own devices in mainly Hindu India. On the Indian side, the dominant nationalist narratives tended to revolve around variations on the classic "divide and rule" theory. On this view, the British were responsible for tearing asunder two communities that history and tradition had joined. By countering Indian nationalism with Muslim communalism, the colonial rulers are believed to have manipulated religion for their own ends.

Neither the "two-nation" theory nor invocations of "divide and rule" provide coherent answers to why the subcontinent was split along apparently religious lines at the moment of the British withdrawal. Instead they have entangled the postcolonial nationalist narratives of both Pakistan and India in a series of paradoxes. Pakistani nationalism's reliance on the "two-nation" theory ended up conflating the external contours of Muslim identity with the inner domain of personal faith in Islam. In a mirror image, Indian nationalism's reliance on a sharp opposition between secularism and religious communalism blurred the distinction between religion as social demarcator of difference and religion as lived faith. The result of this confusion has been a misconception of the precise role of religion in the two countries. If Islamic Pakistan made too much of religion in its nationalist narratives, secular India underplayed religion's salience in the official annals of its nationalism. An overemphasis on religion by Pakistan and its purported erasure by India has had important consequences for their self-representations and mutual relations in the postindependence period.

Retrospectively constructed nationalist ideologies are no substitute for history. It was mainly religion as identity, not the dream of an Islamic theocracy, which had spurred the AIML to demand the creation of Pakistan in March 1940. When in December 1943 Jinnah's friend and associate, Nawab Bahadar Yar Jang, tried committing the Muslim League to a state based on Quranic principles, the Quaid-i-Azam demurred, noting that the representatives of the people would decide the future constitution of Pakistan. Although some Leaguers may have been concerned about matters of personal piety, religion as faith was not the principal driving force behind the politics of difference in late colonial India. The main impediments to evolving a framework for a united India were not disputes over issues of religious doctrine but power-sharing arrangements between members of different religious communities at the all-India level as well as in key regions like Punjab and Bengal. By making an ideology of its secular claims and refusing to go beyond the framework of the liberal paradigm to accommodate Muslim political aspirations, the Congress dealt a decisive blow to the very unity that was sanctified in its vision of an inclusionary Indian nationalism. Adopting the colonial state's policy of privatizing religion, secular India undertook to guarantee the religiously informed cultural identities of its Muslim citizens, albeit one that was strictly limited to the precepts of the sharia as defined by the ulema.

As for Pakistan, the crystallization of Muslim hopes and distinctive culture, reconciling the claims of nationhood with the winning of sovereign statehood proved impossible. The territorial contours of the Muslim homeland ensured that there were nearly as many Muslim noncitizens outside as there were Muslim citizens within. The contradiction was not addressed, far less resolved, and has been one of the principal fault lines in Pakistan's quest for an identity that is Islamic yet also national. Proclaiming Islam as the sole basis of nationality, the architects of Pakistan had no qualms severing all ties with coreligionists in India whose geographical location denied them citizenship rights in a Muslim state created on the basis of a nonterritorially defined Muslim nation.

With doubts about its ability to survive being expressed both within and outside its freshly drawn boundaries, Pakistan's insecurities were given full play in fashioning the nation's history. Using the "two-nation" theory as their crutch, state-sponsored historians wrote histories for schools and colleges as well as for more general consumption that high-lighted the tyranny of the Hindu community in order to justify the cre-ation of Pakistan. A secondary purpose of this attack was to undermine the influence of the Hindu community in the eastern wing. Estimated to be nearly 25 percent of the population, Hindus in East Bengal were prominent in business and a major component of the Bengali intelligen-tsia on account of their leading role in the teaching profession and re-gional literary circles. The early insistence on Urdu as the official language of Pakistan was not unconnected with fears of a Bengali Hindu conspir-acy to undermine the new state by retaining linguistic and cultural con-nections with India.

An anti-Indian and anti-Hindu stance in state-supported historical re-constructions was considered necessary for national self-preservation. However, in the initial decades of independence, the state's commitment to Islam was delicately balanced with a determination to preserve the sec-ular ethos of its main institutions, notably the civil bureaucracy and the military. Successive ruling configurations paid lip service to the state's Is-lamic identity without wholly succumbing to pressure from self-styled guardians of religion. Appropriate steps were taken not to ruffle the senti-ments of the religious divines unduly. These included pledges to base the educational system on Pakistan's Islamic ideology, vaguely defined, but one that was deemed to be consistent with the state's pro-Western foreign policy and project of modernization. It followed that the self-styled reli-gious leaders, mullahs as they were referred to derogatively, could not be permitted to dictate the terms of the state-controlled curriculum.

An Islamic State?

There had been strident opposition to the Muslim League's movement by several of the most vocal proponents of an Islamic state in Pakistan. A former journalist and independent scholar, Abul Ala Mawdudi was fore-most among those who alleged that the demand for "Pakistan" was insuffi-ciently Islamic to warrant support from Muslim believers. In 1941, Mawdudi had founded the right-wing Jamaat-i-Islami, which was ideologically linked with the Muslim Brotherhood in Egypt. His contention that Muslims would be better off in undivided India than in a separate state of their own drew on the fantasy of fostering mass conversions of Hindus to Islam. A critic of pro-Congress Muslim clerics and the Muslim League leadership, Mawdudi set forth a definition of Muslims that excluded the majority of the faithful from the Islamic community. After moving to Lahore to escape the violence in eastern Punjab, Mawdudi joined hands with other Islamist parties that had also opposed the Muslim League's movement to orchestrate a virulent campaign to convert Pakistan into an Islamic state. The rank opportunism of these religio-political parties, combined with their relentless criticism of the immoral lifestyles of its Westernized ruling elites, was one reason for the state keeping them at arm's length. Another was Jinnah's explicit statement of intent on the role of religion in the new state. Speaking extempore, he told the first meeting of the constituent assembly on August 11, 1947, that if Pakistan wanted to count for something in the international comity of nations, it would have to rise above the angularities of sect and community:

> You are free; you are free to go to your temples. You are free to go to your mosques or to any other places of worship in this State of Pakistan. You may belong to any religion or caste or creed—that has nothing to do with the business of the State. . . . We are starting with this fundamental principle that we are all citizens and equal citizens of the State . . . and you will find that in course of time Hindus would cease to be Hindus and Muslims would cease to be Muslims, not in the religious sense, because that is the personal faith of each individual, but in the political sense as citizens of the State.[13]

The speech stung the budding ideologues of the new state. Steps were taken at their behest to ensure that the governor-general, by now a dying man, was never allowed to speak again without a prepared script. An unrepentant Jinnah never retracted his position. In an interview to Reuters, he referred to his speech in the constituent assembly, noting how he had "repeatedly made it clear" that "minorities in Pakistan would be treated as our citizens"; they would "enjoy all the rights and privileges that any other community gets" with "a sense of security and confidence" in the new state.[14] On February 3, 1948, he told a gathering of Parsis in Karachi that Pakistan intended to stand by its promise to accord "equal treatment to all its nationals irrespective of their caste and creed." Embodying the aspirations of a nation that found itself in a minority in India, Pakistan could "not be unmindful of the minorities within its own borders." Later in a speech to the people of the United States of America, Jinnah declared:

> Pakistan is not going to be a theocratic State—to be ruled by priests with a divine mission. We have many non-Muslims—Hindus, Christians, and Parsis—but they are all Pakistanis. They will enjoy the same rights and privileges as any other citizens and will play their rightful part in the affairs of Pakistan.[15]

Jinnah's early death in September 1948 robbed Pakistan of a much-needed steadying hand at the helm during an uncertain and perilous time. With Jinnah no longer around to read the riot act, constitutional propriety and strict adherence to the rule of law were early casualties of the withering struggle between the newly created center and the provinces. Instead of a settled matter that was made part of an honored constitutional document, there is bitter disagreement on the principles and practice of minority rights in Pakistan more than six decades after its establishment. So although there is no denying the centrality of Mohammad Ali Jinnah's iconographic location in Pakistani national consciousness, the gaping chasm between the nationalist icon and the savvy political practitioner cannot escape historical scrutiny. Left to an adoring following in Pakistan and equally impassioned detractors in India, the clear-headed lawyer who never missed a cue has been reduced to a jumble of contradictions that mostly cancel each other out. Jinnah's demonization in the Indian nationalist pantheon as the communal monster who divided mother India contrasts with his positive representation in Pakistan as a revered son of Islam, even an esteemed religious leader (maulana), who strove to safeguard Muslim interests in India. Misleading representations of one of modern South Asia's leading politicians might not have withstood the test of history for as long as they have if they did not serve the nationalist self-projections of both India and Pakistan.

Nations need heroes, and Pakistanis have a right to be proud of their greatest hero. But popular memories too need to be informed by some historical context. Fed on improbable myths and the limitations of the "great men" approach to history, Pakistanis have been constrained from engaging in an informed and open debate on whether their country merits being called Jinnah's Pakistan. Is Jinnah at all relevant to the current Pakistani predicament? Brought up on state-sponsored national yarns about the past, Pakistanis are at a loss over how to settle matters of national identity and the nature of the state—democratic or authoritarian, secular or Islamic. The dismay, confusion, and disenchantment enveloping the hapless citizenry are reason enough to return to the drawing boards of history to assess Jinnah's contemporary relevance. "Other men are lenses through which we read our own minds," Ralph Waldo Emerson once said, but the great man is one who "inhabits a higher sphere of thought" and "keep[s] a vigilant eye on many sources of error."[16] Though I am skeptical of approaches to history restricted to studies of great men, it is difficult to disagree with Emerson, an ardent expositor of biography, that we can learn more from those who were truly great than from those making a mockery of being great in our own times.

After the death of the founding father in September 1948, Pakistan under its first prime minister, Liaquat Ali Khan, became more vulnerable to pressures from the so-called religious lobby to enforce the sharia. Playing on Islamic sentiments was a powerful weapon in the armory of religio-political groupings like the Jamaat-i-Islami and the Majlis-i-Ahrar to acquire legitimacy in a state whose formation they had vehemently opposed. The leadership of the new state was in no mood to be dictated to by mullahs known for their anti-Pakistan postures. When it came to burnishing their Islamic badges, they could draw on Muhammad Iqbal's scathing view of the religious preachers of Islam. "Why are the mullahs of this era the disgrace of Muslims?" the poetic visionary of Pakistan asked. Religion was too important to be left to men with half-baked knowledge of Islam:

Oh Muslim, ask your own heart, don't ask the mullah
Why has the sacred sanctuary been emptied of God's men.[17]

Leaving matters of state in the hands of such ignoramuses was out of the question. In Iqbal's view, the only purpose of the state in Islam was to establish a "spiritual democracy" by implementing the principles of equality, solidarity, and freedom that constituted the essence of the Quranic message. It was in "this sense alone that the State in Islam is a theocracy, not in the sense that it was headed by a representative of God on earth who can always screen his despotic will behind his supposed infallibil-ity."[18] Taking his cue from Iqbal, the Quaid-i-Azam had urged the members of the constituent assembly to frame the future constitution of Pakistan on the Islamic principles of democracy, equality, justice, and fair play for all. "What reason is there for anyone to fear democracy, equality, freedom . . . [as] the highest standard of integrity and on the basis of fair play and jus-tice for everybody?" he had asked.[19]

On March 7, 1949, while presenting the Objectives Resolution to Parlia-ment, Prime Minister Liaquat Ali Khan gave the clearest indication of where the balance lay between the would-be ideologues of Islam and those guarding the inner sanctuaries of state power. The Objectives Resolution, which served as the preamble to Pakistani constitutions until it was made part of the constitution in 1985, ruled out the notion of an Islamic state as a religious theocracy. Heeding the words of the founder, the resolution described Pakistan as a "sovereign, independent state" in which power was to be exercised by the chosen representatives of the people and not the guardians of religion. The Islamic principles of democracy, freedom, equality, tolerance, and social justice for all, including the non-Muslim minorities, were to be the pillars of the state. At the same time, the state undertook to ensure that its Muslim citizens lived their individual and collective lives in accordance with the teachings of Islam. Maulana Shab-bir Ahmad Usmani, the leading religious scholar at the time and a prod-uct of the religious seminary of Deoband in India, supported the Objec-tives Resolution and argued that there was no scope for rule by the clergy in Islam. At the same time, he welcomed the resolution's acknowledgment of God's sovereignty over the universe and its promise to base the state on the teachings of Islam.

A commitment to uphold the Islamic way of life, however defined, po-tentially contradicted promises to the minorities assuring them freedom to practice their religions and develop their cultures. The country's first prime minister himself laid the basis for a measure of ambiguity by pro-claiming Pakistan as a "laboratory" for an Islamic social order, on the one hand, while also, on the other, calling for "a truly liberal Government" that would permit the "greatest amount of freedom" to all its citizens. An early indication of the lip service paid to religion for purposes of political expediency, it should not be confused with a lowering of defenses against the self-proclaimed guardians of Islam that was to become characteristic of the Pakistani leadership after the 1970s. Liaquat Ali Khan let it be known in no uncertain terms that the malicious propaganda of the so-called religious leaders against the right of non-Muslims to equal citizenship would not be permitted.

The Objectives Resolution's nods in the direction of theology were sufficient to embolden the religious lobby to periodically hold the state accountable to its professed commitment to ushering in an Islamic social order. Even as the frontiers of the moral state eluded its most vocal proponents, the ambition was kept alive through well rehearsed and poignant attacks on the perceived immorality and un-Islamic lifestyles of the country's ruling elites, civil as well as military. This in turn built up pressure for public displays of Islamic rectitude, however hypocritically and unconvincingly, ultimately taking the form of an obsessive concern with guarding the Islamic frontiers of Pakistan's ideology against enemies within as well as without. With form replacing substance as the basis for Pakistan's Islamic identity, there was always opportunity for the self-appointed religious ideologues to carp and complain about the state's failure to govern according to the pristine principles of Islam.

Neither religion nor religiosity was much in evidence in the early years of the new Muslim homeland. It was the pursuit of material advancement and plenty of opportunities for those who were unscrupulously greedy that kept things ticking. On Independence Day in 1950, Manto, who had left Bombay to join his family in Lahore, saw a man taking home a tree he had cut. When Manto stopped and asked him, "what are you doing, you have no right to do this," the man replied: "This is Pakistan, this is our property." One day he found a man pulling out bricks from the pavement outside his house. When he said, "brother, don't do this, it is most unfair," the man replied, "This is Pakistan, who are you to stop me?" The privilege of ownership bent the ruling elite's sense of propriety completely out of shape. In a metaphorical sense, all Pakistanis wanted a share of the spoils of division—a privilege available only to a select few. The callousness of the rich and powerful elite of Pakistan, lording it over a destitute and illiterate majority, was to become a proverbial truth in this much-vaunted Muslim homeland. But its roots are traceable to the battles for social space that tore apart the historic ties between communities of religion. A psychology of looting and disregard for the rule of law took hold of the ruling coterie in Pakistan early on. The initial gold mine was the allotment of properties abandoned by Hindus and Sikhs in Punjab and, subsequently, also in Sindh. Senior civil bureaucrats in cahoots with prominent Muslim League politicians had the pick of the field but did not fail to pass on some of the lesser goods as favors to those with contacts. Individual citizens with little or no influence had to settle for whatever was left over, which in most cases was very modest. Justice and fair play through rule of law had been the main connotation of the slogan "Pakistan Zindabad," certainly as popularized by Jinnah. The great constitutionalist could not have conceived that the country he had established would honor his legacy by turning law into an instrument of denial for the unprivileged and a tool to be manipulated for personal ends.

Pakistan's new government proved incapable of giving the citizenry an elemental sense of confidence in its ability to look after their well-being. A less tangible casualty of partition was the loss of etiquette and a frantic rush to make the most of a twisted and ineffectual system of law. With the rulers and the administrative bureaucracy blatantly on the take, the ruled soon realized that now that freedom had been won, justice and fair play meant taking care of one's own self-interest. Instead of breaking with the colonial past, the citizens of independent Pakistan, individually and collectively, opted to chip away at colonial laws that had been hastily adapted to serve as the country's legal framework until a new constitution could be framed. In the postpartition moral world, there was more scope for advancement through devious dealings than there was in working hard for an honest morsel of bread. With social ethics at a severe discount, it was only natural to seek ultimate refuge in Islam, albeit an Islam that was more of a showpiece than a genuine blueprint for justice and fair play as the enthusiasts of Pakistan had been led to believe.

This was the opening religio-political groups seized to claim authenticity for their own brand of Islam, bristling with exclusivist, chauvinistic, and misogynist social values. An early indication of just how significant a space had been conceded to the self-appointed guardians of Islam by the Objectives Resolution was the agitation in 1953 to ostracize the heterodox Ahmadis from the pale of the Muslim community. Ahmadis were accused of violating a fundamental tenet of Islam by portraying their spiritual leader, Mirza Ghulam Ahmad, as a prophet. The anti-Ahmadi movement turned violent and resulted in the first ever imposition of martial law in Pakistan. It was spearheaded by the same elements that had been most vocal in denouncing the demand for Pakistan and abusing the Muslim League's preeminent leader. According to the 1954 inquiry commission set up to investigate the causes of the disturbances, whose findings are known as the Munir Report, the passage of the Objectives Resolution in the constituent assembly had led the ulema and the people of Pakistan to believe that "any demand . . . on religious grounds would not only be conceded but warmly welcomed by the people at the helm of affairs of the State."[20] Most of the ulema questioned by the commission said that declaring the Ahmadis non-Muslims had become imperative after the Objectives Resolution, which left no room for doubt that Pakistan was created solely in the name of Islam. It followed that the state had an obligation to define who was a Muslim and who was not.

The main target of the agitators' wrath was Pakistan's distinguished Ahmadi foreign minister, Chaudhry Muhammad Zafrullah Khan, whom they accused of being a British agent. To disguise the political nature of the movement, the agitators couched their demands in theological terms. Not to have done so ran the risk of being charged with political opportunism given that the most prominent names in the anti-Ahmadi movement had until recently either supported the Congress's ideal of secular nationalism or publicly opposed the creation of Pakistan. There were other practical issues stemming from the demand to expel the Ahmadis from the Muslim community. As the commission tartly noted, no two religious divines could agree on the definition of a Muslim. If the members of the commission tried imposing a definition of their own, the ulema would unanimously declare them to have gone outside the pale of Islam. Adopting the definition of any one religious scholar entailed becoming an infidel in the eyes of all the others.[21]

In the absence of any agreed definition of a Muslim, calls for an Islamic state were a rhetorical device aimed at gaining political mileage rather than creating a workable blueprint for Pakistan. Religious divines in the forefront of the anti-Ahmadi agitation, such as Mawdudi of the Jamaat-i-Islami, maintained that non-Muslims were not entitled to equal rights of citizenship in an Islamic state. Laying down a precise definition of a true believer was a dangerous game of brinkmanship. This was why before the 1937 elections Jinnah had refused to endorse the demand to ostracize Ahmadis from the Muslim community. With the establishment of Pakistan, there was even more reason to reject the faulty logic of the anti-Ahmadi agitators. Even if they could not match his constitutionalist vision, the last thing Jinnah's successors needed was to inject an exclusionary strain into the narratives of the nation at a time when the main challenge facing Pakistan as a modern nation-state was to extend equal rights of citizenship to all its inhabitants.

Given the uncertain benefits of recourse to religion, Pakistan came to be ruled less by ideology than by an institution. Bereft of a central state apparatus and confronted with severe administrative dislocations in the most populous provinces of Bengal and Punjab, Pakistan's political leaders relied heavily in the first instance on a quickly reassembled bureaucracy. However, it was another nonelected institution of state—the military—that would soon turn civil servants into junior partners in the firm that ran Pakistan. The territories in the western wing of Pakistan had been the chief recruiting grounds for Britain's Indian Army. Punjabi Muslims and Pathans had figured prominently since the late nineteenth century in colonial officialdom's spurious anthropological theory about martial races. Yet the conversion of Pakistan into a state of martial rule was not preordained. The military's rise to dominance as early as the 1950s can be understood only in the context of the regional and global challenges of the Cold War.

THREE

A SPRAWLING MILITARY BARRACK

A MUCH-SOUGHT-AFTER HOMELAND where Muslims expected to realize their democratic aspirations, Pakistan has been ruled by the military for more than half of its existence. The dominance of the military, the army in particular, and the senior echelons of the civil bureaucracy over Parliament and elected bodies at the provincial and the local levels of society came to be registered within a few years of independence. How was this dominance of a nonelected institution achieved in such a short span of time? The answer to this all-important question is to be sought in the context of a regional rivalry with India and the international imperatives of Cold War politics. Pakistan's domestic dilemmas owed less to the intrinsic cultural diversity and geographical peculiarity of the country and more to the ways in which institutional imbalances exacerbated center–region tensions. The supremacy of the nonelected over the elected institutions not only survived the tentative experiment in parliamentary democracy during the first decade, and the military dispensation after 1958, but also persisted following the breakup of Pakistan in 1971.

The emerging structural imbalance within the state in the first decade was given constitutional legitimacy by a judiciary forced into subservience by an all-powerful executive. This resulted in a centralized state structure, federal in form and unitary in substance, whose military authoritarian character was at odds with the tenor of politics in the regions. These structural asymmetries have been singularly responsible for the failings and distortions of the Pakistani political system—a lack of democratic institutions, inadequate mechanisms for public accountability, a

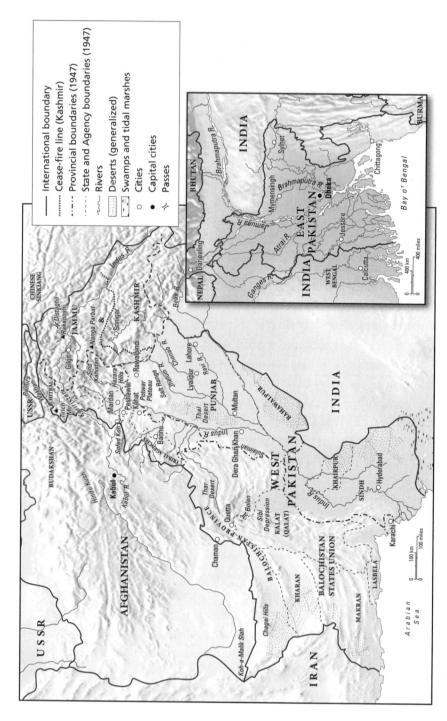

Map of Pakistan, 1947.

Legend

- International boundary
- Cease-fire line (Kashmir)
- Provincial boundaries (1947)
- State and Agency boundaries (1947)
- Rivers
- Deserts (generalized)
- Swamps and tidal marshes
- ○ Cities
- ● Capital cities
- Passes

Main map labels:

USSR · CHINESE SINKIANG · AFGHANISTAN · BUDAKHSHAN · Hindu Kush · Pamirs · Mintaka P. · CHITRAL · Lowari P. · Tirich Mir · K. Distaghil · Rakaposhi · Gilgit · Nanga Parbat · JAMMU · Sind · Kohistan · Hazara Hills · Mardan · Peshawar · Kohat · Potwar Plateau · Rawalpindi · KASHMIR · Srinagar · & · Salt Range · Jhelum R. · Chenab R. · Indus R. · Beas R. · Ravi R. · Lahore · Lyallpur · PUNJAB · Thal Desert · Multan · BAHAWALPUR · Sofed Koh · TRIBAL AGENCIES · Bannu · Kabul · Kabul R. · Koh-a-Malik Siah · Chagai Hills · Chaman · BALOCHISTAN PROVINCE · Quetta · Bolan · KALAT (QALAT) · Sibi Depression · Sulaiman R. · Dera Ghazi Khan · Thar Desert · Indus R. · WEST PAKISTAN · KHAIRPUR · SINDH · Hyderabad · INDIA · KHARAN · MAKRAN · BALOCHISTAN STATES UNION · LASBELA · Karachi · Arabian Sea · IRAN

Scale: 0 – 100 km / 0 – 100 miles

Inset map labels:

INDIA · BHUTAN · Brahmaputra R. · Sylhet · Mymensingh · Jamuna R. · Brahmaputra R. · Dhaka · Chittagong · BURMA · EAST PAKISTAN · Atrai R. · Jessore · NEPAL · Darjeeling · Ganges R. · WEST BENGAL · Calcutta · INDIA · Bay of Bengal

Scale: 0 – 400 miles

compromised media, inequitable distribution of resources, and a chronic tussle between the center and the provinces.

The uneasy symbiosis between a military authoritarian state and democratic political processes is often attributed to the artificial nature of the country and the lack of a neat fit between social identities at the base and the arbitrary frontiers drawn by the departing colonial masters. There is some truth in this assertion. Partition severed economic and social links, destroying the political, ecological, and demographic balance it had taken the subcontinent hundreds of years to forge. Yet India with far greater social diversities was able to recover from the shock of partition to lay the foundations of a constitutional democracy. With a legacy of many of the same structural and ideational features of the colonial state as its counterpart, Pakistan was unable to build viable institutions that could sustain the elementary processes of a participatory democracy. What it did not inherit was the unitary center of the British Raj. Nevertheless, it quickly went in the direction of centralization under the auspices of the military and the bureaucracy.

The reasons for the different trajectories taken by the two states that replaced the British Raj in India cannot be captured by mechanically chanting the mantra of "Army, America, and Allah" as the only explanatory variables needed to understand Pakistan.[1] The context of the Cold War and the military alliance with America after 1954 undoubtedly facilitated the army's rise to a commanding position, and Allah's will was invoked to lend a semblance of legitimacy to this unpopular alliance. But at each step in Pakistan's history, there has been the fourth "A" of the *awam*, literally the people, who have borne the brunt of Pakistan's early lapse into military authoritarianism. Reinscribing the democratic struggle waged by Pakistan's diverse and disparate regional peoples against authoritarianism is vital to fully grasp the political implications of military rule. Only by restoring historical perspective on this crucial dynamic is it possible to appreciate why, instead of creating the constitutional democracy its founding father had always hoped it would be, Pakistan ended up becoming a state of martial rule with little scope for the exercise of the peoples' sovereign will.

The common misconception that religion was the only driving force in the making of Pakistan distracts attention from the monumental difficulties faced in creating a new state amid violence and mayhem. Congress with an organizational network covering much of British India inherited the colonial state's unitary central apparatus in New Delhi. Forced against its will into the role of a seceding state, Pakistan had to set up a wholly new central government in order to impose its sovereign writ over provinces where the Muslim League's party machinery was either nonexistent or poorly organized. Initially, Jinnah's constitutional powers as governor-general were the only basis for the independent exercise of central authority in Pakistan.[2] There was no separate army to underwrite the sovereignty of the new state. Until March 1948, the commander-in-chief General Claude Auchinleck retained administrative control of the Indian defense forces. By the time Pakistan acquired one-third of the defense forces of undivided India, hostilities over Kashmir had foreclosed the possibility of getting its matching share of the military equipment. A country with a notional sovereignty now had a military with no firepower. The search for a viable defense against India was to trump several pressing internal matters.

Paranoia about Pakistan's ability to survive fanned a state-sponsored narrative of security that painted Hindu India as the archenemy acting in utter disregard of its large Muslim population. Kashmir and fears of India manipulating the flow of river waters to Pakistan's disadvantage provided a popular rallying cry against Hindu conspiracies. Against the backdrop of the Cold War and the rise of the United States of America as a global power, the Indian threat and irritations with Afghanistan's irredentist claims on its territory combined with the mammoth challenges flowing from partition to lay the basis of Pakistan's unique insecurity complex. An acute sense of threat from India molded critical policy decisions, including on Kashmir, and saw the army becoming a key player in shaping the destiny of the country. There was nothing inevitable about this outcome even if the odds were heavily stacked against the votaries of a democratic Pakistan.

Postcolonial Transition and the Rise of Military Dominance

Both India and Pakistan started their independent career with the authoritarian trappings of the colonial state whose rhetoric of democracy and development they adopted as the emblems of their legitimacy. A quintessential example of bureaucratic authoritarianism, the British Indian state's espousal of democracy aimed at no more than creating representative institutions where a privileged few could experiment with the art of governing in their own interest. Representative government of a very limited sort was a far cry from substantive democracy. Colonial development plans attempted to do no more than construct an infrastructure most suited to the preservation and promotion of privilege.[3] Any concept of citizenship emerging from a legacy of bureaucratic authoritarianism and skewed ideas of democracy and development could hardly avoid the distortions and misfortunes of the colonial era—the more so because, in addition to bequeathing nonelective institutions of state, British colonialism left behind a peculiar notion of majorities and minorities defined by religious enumeration. This effectively vitiated the prospects of democracy and the achievement of equal citizenship from the very outset.

As it was, late colonial and postcolonial nationalism made inclusionary claims that wished away the very fact of cultural difference. Those who refused to subscribe to the dominant idioms of this inclusionary nationalism ran the risk of being branded "communal" and marginalized, if not altogether excluded, from the legitimate boundaries of a unified and homogeneous nation-state. The postcolonial state, however, needed to strike a significantly different note than its colonial predecessor in one important respect. Modern nation-states make singular claims to allegiance by promising a life of dignity and freedom from want to all their citizens. Only by striking the right balance between the nonelected institutions inherited from the colonial era and their own democratically elected institutions could the nation-states of postindependence South Asia honor the contractual bond between state and citizen—unflinching loyalty in exchange for security of life and property as well as economic betterment. The challenge was a formidable one because the bureaucracy and police inherited from the colonial state were so enmeshed in society that their day-to-day operations, instead of being impersonalized and rule bound, tended to be more personalized and informal. This made the centralization of state authority susceptible to appropriation for localized and private ends to the grave detriment of both effective governance and participatory democracy.

Before the die was cast in 1947, the British Joint Chiefs of Staff had warned that the strategic defense of Pakistan, containing the two main land frontiers of the subcontinent in the northwest and the northeast, could not be considered separately from Hindustan. They questioned the wisdom of carving out a state from the northwestern and northeastern parts of the subcontinent that would have to pay the same amount for its defense as undivided India with far fewer economic resources at its disposal. With Afghanistan unreconciled to the Durand Line of 1893 as the international frontier, Pakistan would have to keep the unruly tribal areas in the northwest at bay and find a way to defend its far-flung eastern wing. To add to the problem, the areas constituting Pakistan had neither the industrial nor the military facilities for their defense. The bulk of the industrial and defense structure of British India was located in Hindustan. Even if it could foot the defense bill, Pakistan's northwestern provinces would lack strategic depth against a military incursion from Afghanistan, Iran, or the Soviet Union without the willing and active cooperation of Hindustan. If it tried constructing the requisite military infrastructure for its strategic defense with its meager resources, Pakistan would end up "ruining itself." The manpower needed for external and internal defense would necessitate a massive recruitment drive, followed by an extensive building program to accommodate the army in peacetime. A separate defense for Pakistan was "economically wasteful and quite impracticable." Special perks and privileges would have to be given to serving military personnel and pensions would have to be paid to those who retired, the cumulative cost of which would be financially draining and politically destabilizing.[4]

These ominous words were sidelined in the flurry of political maneuverings that attended the partition of India. With the benefit of hindsight, the British Joint Chiefs of Staff can be seen to have pinpointed the fundamental fault line that has informed Pakistan's historical trajectory as an independent and sovereign state. With 17.5 percent of the financial assets and 30 percent of the defense forces of undivided India, Pakistan was ill equipped to square its defense costs with its resource base. Accounting for 23 percent of undivided India's territory and 18 percent of the population, Pakistan was overwhelmingly agricultural, with less than 10 percent of the industrial base in the subcontinent and just a little over 7 percent of the employment facilities. In a comparison that clinches the difference between them, the per capita revenue of the Indian provinces was 40 percent more than that of the Pakistani provinces. The difficulties posed by the strategic and economic consequences of partition were compounded by the influx of millions of refugees and the need to establish a center over two wings separated by a thousand miles of Indian territory. Pakistan started its independent career with just Rs.200 million in the kitty, while the monthly cost of maintaining the defense forces was between Rs.35 to Rs.50 million. This was higher than what it had cost to defend undivided India. It was only by expanding the administrative capacities of the state and taking the politically fraught step of extracting a larger share of provincial resources that the new Pakistani center could hope to meet its defense expenditure. The only other option was to solicit foreign aid, a step that would undermine the sovereignty of a state that had yet to exert its independent identity in the international arena.

Once the Kashmir dispute with India reared its head in October 1947, defense expenditure became a crushing burden. After the outbreak of hostilities, India refused to release Pakistan's share of the military stores or the remaining financial assets. With less than 10 percent of the military stores of undivided India at its disposal, Pakistan had to procure essential war materials by drawing on its proportion of the foreign exchange reserves withheld by the British. Facing financial bankruptcy within months of its creation, Pakistan had to plead for foreign assistance at the capitals of the international system, London and Washington in particular. Britain's postwar troubles made it an unlikely benefactor. So Pakistan looked toward Washington for help to tide over its immediate monetary embarrassments and, in due course, to secure American military aid to try and raise a viable shield of defense against India. These efforts on the international front were matched by attempts to maximize the center's domestic revenues by plumbing deeper into provincial resources.

The conflict over Kashmir reflected Pakistani apprehensions about being denied their share of the river waters of the Indus Basin by India. Whatever the emotive claims of religious affinity with Kashmiri Muslims, it was effectively water insecurity that drove a barely armed Pakistan to make the incorporation of Kashmir one of its main strategic goals. An elusive military objective, it was given a religious flavor when the Mehsud and Mohmand tribes of the northwest were enlisted to raid Kashmir on October 22, 1947. Pathan tribesmen were roused to wage "jihad" against the Hindu Dogra rulers for oppressing Muslims in Poonch. The treatment the tribesmen meted out to their coreligionists by looting properties and creating havoc is a corrective to any blanket privileging of their religious impulse. Involving notoriously wayward tribesmen in pursuit of military objectives in Kashmir was a hardheaded calculation with grave risks for both external and internal security. Four days after the tribal invasion of Kashmir, Maharaja Hari Singh agreed to the state's accession to India, a move Pakistan challenged as illegal. There was now a prospect of the tribesmen running amok in Pakistan if the Indian Army defeated the "Azad" or free forces resisting the Dogra rulers in Kashmir. The prospect of another stream of refugees from southwest Kashmir threatened a breakdown of the administrative machinery and ensuing anarchy that the army was ill equipped to control. War with India was the last thing the Pakistan Army wanted. But the unenviable choice facing the political leadership was to either submit to the state collapsing under the burden of refugees or go down fighting a hopeless war with India.

Upon hearing of Kashmir's accession to India, Jinnah in a rush of anger ordered the newly appointed British commander-in-chief General Douglas Gracey to send in the army. India had withheld Pakistan's share of the cash balances and refused to divide the military stores. There was a mere $100,000 in the state treasury, and Gracey estimated that Pakistan had stocks of ammunition to last for five hours.[5] General Auchinleck had to rush to Karachi to confirm that sending in Pakistani Army regulars into Kashmir would be tantamount to performing hara-kiri. India would see it as a violation of its territory. In the event of a war, India could easily overrun Pakistan's fragile defenses and carve out a comfortable niche for itself in Kashmir. To avert a potential Indian attack across the newly delimited international border, the Pakistani leadership surreptitiously arranged for the arming and transportation of Pathan tribesmen to Kashmir. An undeclared war in Kashmir had the added advantage of weaning away the frontier tribesmen from Afghanistan with the temptation of a steady flow of arms and money. The strategy misfired, and India was able to tighten its grip on a princely state that Pakistan considered as its jugular. All the western rivers of the Indus flowed into Pakistan from Kashmir. Once India claimed exclusive use of the eastern river waters, the territorial importance of Kashmir became further magnified for the defense planners. Making a virtue out of weakness, the military planners opted to retain a ready pool of armed militias in the northwestern tribal areas to use if and when needed to foil both India's and Afghanistan's designs. This laid the basis for an unshakable connection between Kashmir and Afghanistan in Pakistani strategic thinking.

Jinnah recognized the delicacy of the situation on the frontier given a disputed border with Afghanistan and a pro-Congress government in the NWFP. Six weeks before partition he had assured the tribesmen that the new government would continue paying them allowances and honor all their existing agreements with the British after August 15, 1947. In an additional display of goodwill toward the tribesmen, Pakistani troops were withdrawn from Waziristan after they pledged loyalty to the new state in return for the continuation of the status quo under the British. Jinnah made it plain that the new frontier policy was designed to "eliminate all suspicion in the brotherhood of Islam, of which the tribes and the Government of Pakistan were both members."[6] Using the religious bond for strategic ends signaled a clear departure from the colonial rulers who had to intermittently utilize their troops to check tribal infractions. As late as the 1930s and early 1940s, several divisions of the British Indian Army were fighting a full-scale war in Waziristan. In April 1948, at an unparalleled joint jirga, or assembly, of Afridi, Mehsud, Mohmand, and Wazir tribesmen held under a marquee at Government House in Peshawar, Jinnah acknowledged the positive role of the tribes in the establishment of Pakistan. The withdrawal of forces from the tribal areas was a "concrete and definite gesture that we treat you with absolute confidence." Pakistan had "no desire to interfere unduly with your internal freedom, but wants to help you to become self-reliant and self-sufficient."[7] Pacifying the northwestern tribesmen who had given the British Indian Army a run for its money was among one of the few achievements of the new state.

Under the Anglo-Afghan treaty of 1921, the main burden of rights and obligations in relation to the autonomous northwestern tribal areas had fallen on Pakistan and to a lesser extent also on India. New Delhi had no interest in dabbling in the affairs of the tribes or accepting responsibility for the defense of the northwestern frontier. This was a matter of regret for the British who thought both dominions should assume their respective responsibilities under the Anglo-Afghan treaty in order to "secure the independence and stability of Afghanistan as a buffer State between the Commonwealth and the U.S.S.R."[8] There was little chance of the two states agreeing to disagree, far less of cooperating in the pursuit of any common goal. Prime Minister Nehru's government was standing up for its old colleague, Khan Abdul Ghaffar Khan, the leader of the Khudai Khidmatgars (literally servants of God), also known as the Red Shirts, having let him down badly at the time of partition. Both Ghaffar Khan and his brother Dr. Khan Sahib were in favor of Kabul's campaign to establish "Pakhtunistan," a state based on Afghanistan's merger with the NWFP and the Pathan-majority areas of Balochistan. This was a prickly thorn in the side of a Pakistani government absorbed by the unrealistic objective of taking Kashmir from India.

Any prospect of the two dominions arriving at an accommodation over Kashmir was dashed by the presence of Pakistani-backed raiders in what India claimed as its sovereign territory. In a radio broadcast on November 2, 1947, Nehru promised a plebiscite to determine the verdict of the Kashmiri people on the question of accession to India or Pakistan. He changed his mind upon learning of the Pakistani-backed invaders whom he described as a "scourge." In taking "police action" against the "barbarities" of these "freebooters," India was not endangering the peace of Pakistan or anyone else. If Pakistan cut the supply routes of the raiders and stopped them from using its territory, India was prepared to let the Kashmiri people decide their own fate in a plebiscite held under the auspices of the United Nations (UN).[9] Bewildered and dismayed by the deteriorating situation in Kashmir, Prime Minister Liaquat Ali Khan claimed that the raiders were "sons of the soil" fighting for their freedom. He dismissed Sheikh Abdullah, the foremost leader of Kashmiri Muslims, as "a paid agent of Congress" with no following except among "gangsters . . . purchased with Congress money." India was using the raiders as a pretext for its permanent occupation of Kashmir. Those opposing accession to India were being quashed by the Indian military in unison with banded groups of armed Sikhs and the Rashtriya Swayamsevak Sangh (RSS), the militant wing of the Hindu right. Fighting had to stop and all forces withdrawn before a free plebiscite could be held under an impartial administration.[10] In a message to Nehru, Liaquat proposed taking the Kashmir issue to the UN.[11]

Expecting the international community to pronounce Pakistan an aggressor, India on January 1, 1948, referred the Kashmir dispute to the UN. A United Nations Commission on India and Pakistan (UNCIP) was set up, albeit to no avail when it came to controlling the rapidly changing military realities on the ground. Despite their appetite for worldly goods belonging to others, the tribesmen while avoiding pitched battles put up stiff resistance against the Indian forces in some areas, facilitating the eventual takeover of one-third of the state of Jammu and Kashmir by the

"Azad" forces loyal to Pakistan. In March 1948, New Delhi was confronted with the grim situation of the Indian Army failing to seal up all the entry points into Kashmir and having "to contend indefinitely with a situation similar to that with which the British had to deal on the Frontier."[12] In the summer, Pakistan moved its regular army to Jammu and Kashmir, rejecting New Delhi's charges of aggression on the grounds that the state's accession to India was fraudulent. India was accused of secretly financing the redoubtable Faqir of Ipi, who had battled the British in the final decades of the Raj, to pin down pro-Pakistani forces from his base in North Waziristan and join Abdul Ghaffar Khan to establish Pakhtunistan.[13]

New Delhi's official circles were gripped by fears of a Pakistani thrust into Kashmir in August 1948. They responded by consolidating their positions in Jammu and Kashmir with reinforcements and sending in the air force to bomb Gilgit, complicating an already very complex political and military situation on the ground. Gilgit-Baltistan had acceded to Pakistan on November 15, 1947, after a revolt by the British-trained Gilgit Scouts against the Maharaja of Kashmir.[14] Ignoring the subtleties of competing sovereign claims along the northwestern rim of their Indian empire, the British for purely strategic reasons had placed the princely states of Chitral, Dir, and Gilgit-Baltistan under Dogra suzerainty. The rulers of these predominantly Muslim states reacted to Kashmir's accession to India by opting for Pakistan. But the contested nature of Jammu and Kashmir cast their constitutional status into question. Neither the rulers nor the people of these northwestern states had any desire to join India. This was a welcome relief for a desperately overextended Pakistani government that in October 1947 was at its wits' end on how to pursue its Kashmir policy. A year later, Pakistan's military position had improved considerably, thanks to the Pathan tribesmen and the rulers of the northwestern princely states. Fighting between the two sides left India in control of two-thirds of the state and the Pakistan-backed "Azad" forces with the rest.

In January 1949, the UN-negotiated cease-fire gave Pakistan further breathing space to rectify its defense inadequacies. There was no letup in the Kashmir rhetoric on the home front or the ceaseless diplomatic prate to mobilize international opinion. If a single-issue foreign policy was potentially a wasting asset, a resource-starved Pakistan could endeavor to bring Kashmir into its fold only at great peril to its delicately balanced internal political configuration. The search for resources gave added impetus to administrative centralization, enabling senior civil servants to influence key national decisions, often without the critical input of the politicians. Pakistan's first crop of leaders at the center consisted mainly of migrants from India with limited or no real bases of support in the provinces. Suspicious of their provincial counterparts, émigré politicians at the center focused on consolidating state authority rather than building the Muslim League into a popularly based national party. In February 1948, the Pakistan Muslim League was formally separated from the All-India Muslim League, and a politician from Uttar Pradesh (UP), Chaudhry Khaliquzzaman, became president. The central party selected office bearers of the provincial Leagues. Membership rolls and internal elections were doctored to keep opposition factions out of the running. The one concession to popular sentiment by the central League leaders was to make belligerent statements against India for permitting the systematic genocide of its Muslim minorities and a solemn vow to gain control over Kashmir by all possible means. The Pakistani political leadership's Kashmir rhetoric worked to the advantage of the civil bureaucracy and the army with dire consequences for center–province relations. Except in Punjab and the NWFP, the central government's Kashmir policy had little support in Sindh or Balochistan and even less in East Bengal. Instead of serving the people, civil servants and their allies in the army hoisted the political leaders with their Kashmir petard to become the veritable masters of the manor through autocratic and unconstitutional means.

Jinnah has not been spared the blame for this unhappy turn of events. He is charged with perpetuating the "viceregal system"—the executive tyranny exercised by representatives of the British crown in India.[15] Those who question the Quaid's democratic credentials maintain that he not only arrogated the power to overrule his cabinet but also acquired similar leverage in relation to the legislative assembly that simultaneously acted as the constitution-making body. Jinnah's most objectionable actions as governor-general included the summary dismissal of the Congress ministry in the NWFP. Equally notorious was his high-handed treatment of the state of Kalat, whose ruler was made to accede to Pakistan on threat of punitive military action. But arguably the most questionable of all was his insensitive handling of the Bengalis whom he bluntly told to accept Urdu as the state language in the interest of national unity. Jinnah was a stickler for constitutional propriety and a proponent of democratic norms and procedures, and thus his actions have to be seen in proper context. Quizzed on his decision to take control of Balochistan in his capacity as governor-general, he replied that things would proceed more smoothly that way. "But it does not mean that I am in favour of dictatorship," he quickly explained.[16] Anxious not to oblige detractors who predicted Pakistan's early collapse, the Quaid-i-Azam made decisions he thought necessary to establish state sovereignty and preserve national unity. It is another matter that the initial steps taken to promote state formation were not counterbalanced later with an adherence to constitutional methods that the father of the nation advocated and for the most part practiced.

Jinnah's death on September 11, 1948, was a setback for the political arms of the state and a body blow for the constitutional future of Pakistan. Despite failing health from excessive smoking, he kept a hectic schedule until April 1948, when he caught a chill in Peshawar. He never recovered. His last summer was spent in the cool and serene juniper-laden environs of Ziarat, near Quetta. By late August, he had been stricken by pneumonia. On the day of his death, he was flown back to Karachi on a stretcher and transferred to a military ambulance that traveled a few paces before breaking down. In an astonishing bungling of protocol, which led to wild speculations about Prime Minister Liaquat Ali Khan's bona fides, it took two hours for a replacement ambulance to be sent, by which time the oppressive humidity and swarm of flies had exhausted Jinnah. He died in dignity soon after arriving at his official residence. His absence left an indelible imprint on the future course of Pakistan, something he had always feared but could do little to prevent.

Even during Jinnah's lifetime, the provincial Muslim Leagues had been turned into the personal fiefdoms of influential landlord politicians. The central leadership to advance their own political interests readily exploited rivalries among provincial politicians. The organizational infirmities of the Muslim League coupled with the imperatives of a financially strapped and insecure central government resulted in policies that paid little heed to the democratic impulse in the regions. If constitution making got stalled in the early 1950s by the strident demands of the self-appointed representatives of Islam, it risked derailment because of the clashing interests of a Punjabi-dominated center and the demographic fact of a Bengali majority. Taking a leaf out of the Muslim League's pre-1947 history, West Pakistani civil bureaucrats and their allies among the

Jinnah decorating an army officer at Dhaka during his visit to East Pakistan in March 1948 with General Commanding Officer Ayub Khan looking on. *The White Star Photo Pvt. Ltd. Archive.*

landed and business classes wanted separate electorates for Hindus in the eastern wing. Once this was rejected out of hand, the only way of dealing with the problem of an overall Bengali preponderance was to insist on parity with the eastern wing. The deliberate distortion of political processes and the eventual derailment of democracy flowed in large measure from the refusal of the military bureaucratic alliance in West Pakistan to come to terms with the implications of a Bengali majority.

Yet for all the roadblocks vitiating its march toward becoming a parliamentary democracy, there was nothing inescapable about the collapse of political processes in Pakistan. In the immediate aftermath of partition, neither the elected nor nonelected institutions had a clear advantage over the other. Pakistan's civil bureaucracy and military, far from being "overdeveloped" in relation to society, were desperately short of skilled manpower and the requisite institutional infrastructure.[17] After the initiation of hostilities with India over Kashmir, more resources were allocated for defense rather than for development at a time when the political process had yet to be clearly defined. In complete disregard to the popular pulse, the need to raise revenues for the center meant that priority was given to administrative reorganization and expansion rather than to building of a party-based political system reflecting Pakistan's linguistic and cultural diversities. The shifting balance of power from the political to the administrative arms of the state was to have dire implications for relations between the center and the provinces as well as between Punjab and the non-Punjabi provinces.

The diversion of provincial resources into the defense effort pitted politicians at the provincial and local levels against centrally appointed civil bureaucrats. Punjabis from the middle and upper economic strata had been the main beneficiaries of the recruitment policies of the colonial state and dominated the military and the central civil services. Despite similarities in their socioeconomic and educational backgrounds, which encouraged the increasing socialization of these institutions through intermarriages among the big landlord families, there was a constant tussle for power between state bureaucrats and Punjab's landlord politicians for the dominant say in matters of policy. There were instances of tactical collusion. The scramble for evacuee property is a case in point. Throwing all pretenses to honesty and fair play out of the window, senior civil servants overseeing the allotment of properties abandoned by Hindus and Sikhs connived with unscrupulous politicians to reserve the choicest plums on both the urban and rural landscape for themselves or their next of kin through fraudulent claims and illegal possession. The rest of the evacuee property was parceled out to those who had contacts or could bribe their way to the corridors of power. Those with neither money nor influence—a majority of the destitute refugees—had to settle for the crumbs and, in some cases, for nothing at all. The first phase of the grab syndrome in Pakistan assumed scandalous proportions. But while becoming a part of collective memory, it has never been fully probed and recorded. The race for easy pickings in the newly created country was matched by the absence of rudimentary norms of accountability, setting a pattern for public service with far-reaching implications for the future.

With such high stakes to play for, the struggle for political office acquired added intensity, straining relations between politicians and civil servants deputed to carry out the center's tasks in the provinces. Punjab's chief minister, Nawab Iftikhar Hussain Khan of Mamdot, better known as Mamdot in keeping with the practice of naming people after their place of origin, claimed large tracts of agricultural acreage as compensation for the land he had left behind in the eastern part of the divided province. So he shot down the reformist proposal of his left-leaning minister for refugee rehabilitation, Mian Iftikharuddin, to settle the refugees on a permanent basis on both evacuee property and excess land belonging to bigger landlords. Iftikharuddin resigned, leaving Mamdot with a free hand to allot evacuee properties to friends and relatives. He refused to cooperate with the centrally appointed Pakistan and West Punjab Refugee and Rehabilitation Council and instead accused the center of meddling in provincial affairs.[18] But it was his feud with the Oxford-educated provincial finance minister Mian Mumtaz Daultana that created the first wrinkle on the post-1947 Punjabi political scene. Though sharing a common landed background, Daultana was progressive compared with Mamdot, who was supported by conservative Punjabi landlords and ideologues using religion and nationalism for their own personal ends. When the center backed the chief minister, there was a hue and cry over this unwarranted interference, forcing Daultana to resign. Mamdot and his henchmen forced the central government on the back foot with demands for a much larger outlay of funds for refugee rehabilitation in Punjab than the daunting costs of the defense procurement effort permitted.

This underlined the relative strength of the provinces, Punjab in particular, vis-à-vis a central government that, apart from being barely in the saddle, was dominated by émigré politicians. To rein in this troublesome province, the new governor-general, Khwaja Nazimuddin, instructed Sir Francis Mudie, the British governor of Punjab, in January 1949 to take over the provincial administration under Section 92a of the 1935 Government of India Act. The action backfired. Punjabis accused Prime Minister Liaquat Ali Khan of being partial to emigrants from India and riding roughshod over their provincial interests. There were bitter complaints about the underrepresentation of Punjabis in the Pakistan Muslim League Council and the constituent assembly. Punjabi civil servants carped about being elbowed out by Urdu speakers for top jobs at the federal center and the provincial government. If this was careerism parading in the colors of provincialism, when Punjabi traders were denied import and export licenses, their resulting wrath made for a persecution complex that threatened to scuttle the ship of state before it had set sail.

Seething grievances in the non-Punjabi provinces made the center's position extremely precarious, forcing increased reliance on the civil services. In the eastern wing, there was almost universal condemnation of the entire gamut of central policies, political, economic, and cultural. Bengalis were dead against the center's Urdu-only language policy. They complained of being ruled by an unpopular and incompetent provincial government and were resentful of the free rein given to West Pakistani bureaucrats who arrogantly lorded it over them. Sindhis were bitter at the loss of their provincial capital, Karachi, to the center and complained of feeling more physically colonized than ever before. An influential segment of Pathans could not bring themselves to respect a center that had dismissed their elected government and were offended at being placed under its handpicked man, Abdul Qayum Khan, who ruled the province with an iron hand. Balochis for their part never forgave the center for using military force to secure the accession of Kalat state and remained unreconciled to their incorporation into Pakistan.

Liaquat Ali Khan wanted to delay constitution making until elections had been held in all the provinces. The existing constituent assembly had been elected in 1945–46, and so renewing the mandate from the people had its merits. But the apparently democratic thrust of this policy belied a darker underside. Elections were not meant to be a reference to the people so much as a ruse enabling the center to use the civil bureaucracy to weed out the contentious and bring the cooperative to the fore. This was a variant of the center's policy of disqualifying provincial politicians from contesting elections on charges of corruption under the Public Representatives Disqualification Order of 1949. The sham of a provincial election in Punjab in March 1951 exposed the central government to a fresh barrage of accusations and, worse still, intrigues. The center actively plotted to rig the first ever election held in Pakistan under universal adult franchise. Liaquat Ali moved bag and baggage to Punjab to personally supervise the elections. The Muslim League swept the polls, defeating an opposition alliance that included Mamdot's faction of the League and the right-wing Jamaat-i-Islami. Though Daultana got slotted in as chief minister, it was a pyrrhic victory. The apparent stability provided by a strong League ministry could not dissipate the storms that were brewing just below the placid surface of Punjabi politics.

Kashmir was a burning political issue. It was not uncommon for the chauvinistic sections of the press to blame British officers serving in the Pakistan Army for losing Kashmir to India. There were demands for the removal of foreign personnel from the military and the appointment of Pakistanis to top decision-making positions. Adding to Liaquat's share of headaches was the rising graph of discontentment within the army itself. Rapid promotions through the ranks fanned political ambitions among the officer corps, some bordering on the delusional. In September 1948, in a wittily entitled speech, "Pip fever, or why we can't all start as Brigadiers," the prime minister tried dampening expectations while massaging the egos of the officers.[19] He was responding to demands for the rapid nationalization of the Pakistan Army, which contained over 400 British officers, including the post of commander-in-chief. The more circumspect advised against hastening the pace any further, fearful of the dangers that a predominantly Punjabi army could pose for the unity of the federation in the event of a military intervention. Looking to compensate for his lack of a political base in Punjab, Liaquat Ali opted to expedite the process of nationalizing the army. With the Kashmir issue hanging fire, British officers made sure that only the tried and trusted were promoted to the top jobs at General Headquarters (GHQ). The preferred Anglo-American resolution of the problem was to partition Kashmir along the Chenab River. This would leave the bulk of the disputed territory in Indian hands, with Pakistan settling for about one-third of the former princely state.

Senior Pakistani Army officers agreed with their British mentors that this was the only realistic solution to the problem. This was anathema for Liaquat. Any compromise on Kashmir would make his position at the center untenable at a time when provincial resentments against his government were on the rise. He was not unaware of the rumblings in the junior ranks of the army for a more resolute military stance against India. It was to tackle these worrisome tendencies that the British and the Americans took such an unusually keen interest in the appointment of the first Pakistani commander-in-chief. Two of the main contenders for the job, Major General Iftikhar Khan and Major General Sher Khan, were killed in a mysterious plane crash in late 1949. Both were flying to Britain to receive advanced training for the position. Although Iftikhar Khan had an edge, Sher Khan had earned the nom de plume of "General Tariq" for his successful exploits in Kashmir. Their deaths cleared the way for the Anglo-American choice—the Sandhurst-trained Mohammad Ayub Khan. To bag the most coveted office in the army at the age of forty-two after only twenty-two years of service was no small feat. Ayub's stint as the highest-ranking Pakistani officer in the ineffectual Punjab Boundary Force had raised several eyebrows. Backed by senior British Army officers, he was posted to East Bengal as general officer commanding of the Fourth Infantry division responsible for the defense of the entire eastern wing. On returning to West Pakistan in late 1949, Ayub was rewarded for his services. He served as adjutant general and also briefly as deputy commander-in-chief. Ayub's pro-Western outlook, moderate views, and fair complexion, which made him look more British than the British, confirmed his selection as commander-in-chief in January 1951.

Two months later, the new chief of the general staff, Major General Akbar Khan, a popular veteran of the Kashmir war, was arrested along with ten other senior military officers and four civilians for conspiring to overthrow the government. Harboring illusions of grandeur and indignant at being overlooked for the top position, Akbar Khan led the chorus against British officers for forcing a cease-fire in Kashmir. He was known to be openly scornful of the politicians whom he blasted for incompetence, indecision, and corruption. Others shared the sentiment. What made Akbar the principal culprit in the alleged coup to establish a military dictatorship along the lines of Syria was his belief in "revolution" and the establishment of a government willing and able to redress the mounting grievances of the people.[20] With the help of his ambitious and well-connected wife, Nasim Shahnawaz, he made contact with several leftists associated with the Communist Party of Pakistan. This included the pre-eminent Urdu poet and intellectual Faiz Ahmad Faiz, who was then editor of the *Pakistan Times,* which was owned by the former Muslim Leaguer and Communist sympathizer Mian Iftikharuddin. With the central government cracking down on their cadres, members of the Communist Party were eager to help bring it down. Akbar had agreed to give the communists a freer hand. He also undertook to align his military dictatorship with Moscow and cut off the ties of dependency with London. To win the loyalty of the more hot-blooded of the junior officers in the army, he promised a quick resolution of the Kashmir dispute. Akbar's flashy and conspicuous lifestyle proved to be his undoing. His activities were closely monitored by the intelligence agencies. The central government knew what was brewing six months prior to it being made public.

The conspirators evidently did not pose a serious enough danger to merit immediate exposure. There were doubts even at the time whether a subversive movement had ripened into a full-blown conspiracy. Some suspected an Anglo-American plot to expunge patriotic officers from the army who in their frustration over Kashmir wanted a pro-Soviet tilt. The official point of view has been that the "Rawalpindi Conspiracy," as the foiled coup attempt came to be known, aimed at establishing a tyrannical military dictatorship with communist backing. What is undeniable is that the failure of the coup was a golden opportunity for the new commander-in-chief to consolidate his position within the army. Together with the pro-British secretary of defense Major General Iskander Mirza, Ayub Khan purged the army of any remaining anti-Western elements. Faiz Ahmad Faiz's involvement in the "conspiracy" made all left-wing intellectuals suspect in the eyes of the intelligence agencies. Sentenced to four years of imprisonment, Faiz responded to the state's hospitality by composing some of the finest resistance poetry to have ever come out of Pakistan. He roused the people, exhorting them to march on against oppressors who lived in glass houses, pretending they were messiahs. If the fortunes of the tyrants were soaring today, their overlordship would soon come to an end. Pillagers and looters could neither hide nor empty the nation of its manifold riches, which belonged to the hungry and distressed people of the land.[21]

These scarcely veiled threats only strengthened the resolve of the rulers. The gagging of the press and the hounding of the intelligentsia were accompanied by systematic efforts to free the army's GHQ in Rawalpindi from the control of the political leadership in Karachi and, in due course, to shift the balance decisively against the politicians. These moves on the domestic front were paralleled by a growing American interest in harnessing Pakistan's military potential in defense of US strategic interests in the oil-rich Persia/Iraq sector. India under Jawaharlal Nehru was seen to be angling for hegemony in Asia. This cut against the grain of the US Cold War policy of containing the Soviet Union. So the US State Department made light of British warnings against any deal with Pakistan that left India out in the cold. An alliance with Pakistan would give the Americans military bases in the Indian Ocean, a crucial strategic move at a juncture when British prestige in West Asia was at an all-time low. But Washington was unwilling to pay the price demanded by the Pakistani political leadership—a territorial guarantee and assistance in pressing India to give way on Kashmir. The Americans had a better chance of swaying military and civil officials who, in an effort to gain some leverage, deliberately let out that the prime minister was toying with the idea of declaring Pakistan's neutrality in the Cold War unless the Western powers helped resolve the Kashmir issue. Its strategic location gave Pakistan some bargaining power. The American military attaché in Karachi noted that the loss of Pakistan's airfields and army "might be the balancing weight between victory or defeat at the hands of the USSR."[22]

Starting with a dismissive attitude toward Karachi's requests for financial and military assistance in 1947 and moving to a lukewarm approach by 1949, the Americans were leaning toward Pakistan by the time of the Korean War in the summer of 1950. The British were being forced to retreat in Iran and Egypt amid a surge in popular nationalism that the Soviets seemed eager to exploit. Pakistan's inclusion in a defense alliance covering the Middle East was considered vital to secure Western strategic interests in the region. Irritated by Britain's India-centered policy despite Nehru's stubborn refusal to budge from his policy of neutrality, Washington was ready to strike out on its own in South Asia. Liaquat Ali Khan had made a positive impression during his first official tour of the United States in May 1950. The trip was to have taken place after Liaquat's visit to Moscow. Pro-American civil bureaucrats-turned-politicians such as the finance minister, Malik Ghulam Mohammad, made sure that the prime minister altered his plans and went first to Washington instead. The implications of this last-minute change were far-reaching. Popular opinion in Pakistan was for a balanced if not completely neutral foreign policy. Liaquat was noncommittal on forming a military alliance with the Anglo-American bloc unless he could extract something substantive, particularly in resolving the Kashmir dispute. Neither the British nor the Americans were prepared to go so far as to upset their equation with India.

Displeased with Washington's response, Liaquat overruled his cabinet and the bureaucracy on the question of sending Pakistani troops to Korea. This put paid to the finance minister's hopes of replenishing a depleted treasury with American money. An incensed Ghulam Mohammad told the prime minister to govern or get out and rebuked the cabinet for being slow on the uptake. Unfazed, Liaquat directed Parliament to pass a resolution condemning North Korean aggression and, for good measure, earmarked 5,000 tons of wheat instead of troops. The ultimate responsibility for pushing Pakistan squarely into the Western camp without a firm guarantee on Kashmir or sustained military and economic assistance rests squarely with senior civil and military officials. The ringleaders, Finance Minister Ghulam Mohammad, Defense Secretary Iskander Mirza, and Commander-in-Chief General Ayub Khan, would have liked to have struck a better bargain. But Washington's objective of containing communism was at odds with the Pakistani interest in using the security alliance to acquire military equipment it could use against India. A relationship built on divergent interests was unavoidably rocky from the outset. Ghulam Mohammad accused the Americans of short-changing Pakistan. He noted that there was much heart burning in Pakistan about Washington's kind eye for India, "similar to that of a prospective bride who observes her suitor spending very large sums of money on a mistress . . . while she herself can look forward to not more than a token maintenance in the event of marriage."[23] The Americans were sanguine about getting their way; Pakistan needed financial and military aid for its Kashmir cause and was in no position to burn its bridges with the West.

Facing a huge Indian military buildup on its western borders in the summer of 1951 after tensions between the two neighbors over Hindu–Muslim clashes in East Bengal in 1950, Pakistan urgently needed military equipment. Its hopes of averting a war depended on the Security Council

Liaquat Ali Khan and Mrs. Rana Liaquat Ali Khan. *The White Star Photo Pvt. Ltd. Archive.*

adopting the UN mediator Dr. Frank Graham's report calling for a de-militarization of both Indian- and Pakistani-held Kashmir, followed by a plebiscite. The civil servants in the central cabinet favored accepting the report. It took a showdown with the prime minister to secure his approval. Liaquat was not averse to Graham's recommendations. A populist politi-cian, he was reluctant to make any concessions that he might live to regret. In July 1951, at a massive rally in Karachi held in response to the Indian threat, Liaquat vowed to defend the integrity of Pakistan and, in a show of his determination, clenched his fist for almost three minutes as the crowd chanted feverishly in support. Misled by official propaganda to overesti-mate Pakistan's military capabilities, the gesture was seen as endorsing a war to settle scores with India or at the very least a sign that the govern-ment was hardening its stance.

Neither the central government nor GHQ had any intention of going to war. Once it became clear that the Americans were not minded to offer anything on Kashmir, Liaquat Ali began exploring other options. This in-cluded the threat of a pro-Moscow policy and a coordinated Pakistan–Iran–Egyptian policy on the Middle East. A reshuffle of the central cabinet to throw out the more obstreperous among the pro-Western heavyweights was widely rumored. Challenged on several fronts domestically, Liaquat needed to claim success on Kashmir for his political survival. He was en-raged by the delayed presentation of Graham's report to the Security Council, suspecting an American hand as many in Pakistan saw the UN as an agency of the United States. When the American ambassador Avra Warren inquired about Pakistan's contribution to the defense of the Mid-dle East, the prime minister was extremely "cagey" and insistent that Kashmir remained the preeminent issue for his government.[24]

Four days later, on October 16, 1951, Liaquat Ali Khan was assassinated while addressing a public rally in Rawalpindi's Company Bagh. The mur-der of Pakistan's first prime minister heralded the imminent derailment of the political process and the onset of a brutal political culture of assas-sinations, sustained by the state's direct or indirect complicity. Pakistani intelligence had unearthed a plot against Liaquat's life in early 1950. Or-ders were issued to keep suspicious characters at least thirty yards away from the prime minister. The fatal shots were fired from eighteen feet of where the prime minister stood. The assassin, Syed Akbar, was an Afghan national under surveillance by Pakistani intelligence. When he pulled the trigger, Akbar was sitting in a row of policemen with 2,000 rupees in his pocket—a substantial sum in those days. He was immediately shot dead by a policeman. The investigation into the murder revealed little, hinting at a cover-up. This fanned speculations of a conspiracy involving top individuals in the civil, military, and political fraternity. Those known to be pro-British were among the key suspects. But all the main beneficiaries of the postassassination political configuration were deemed to be complicitous in one way or the other. Circumstantial evidence suggests that British intelligence may have been aware that something was afoot even if they were not directly involved in the plot to kill the prime minister.[25]

Liaquat Ali Khan's eviction from the national scene removed the last hurdle in the way of a successful Punjabi backlash against the preeminence of Urdu speakers at the federal center. It was also a major step toward eliminating the remaining pockets of resistance to Pakistan joining an American-backed security arrangement in the Middle East. There was nevertheless consternation in Washington concerning the likely fallout of the tragedy. According to an assessment by the Central Intelligence Agency (CIA), Liaquat's death had left Pakistan without "a firm guiding hand." None of his likely successors had the caliber and political vision to guide the fledgling country through the quagmire of economic and political problems. Internal instability combined with external pressure from India, the CIA's spy doctors feared, could cause Pakistan to collapse.[26] The disaster was averted, but to the detriment of establishing a stable constitutional democracy. In one of the first of the curious maneuvers that would come to characterize Pakistani successions, Nazimuddin passed the mantle of governor-general to Ghulam Mohammad and became prime minister instead. The move had the full backing of both Mirza and Ayub.

The Washington Connection

The next few years saw frenzied behind-the-scenes activity to seal the military deal with America. Ayub Khan, who had been recommended for the Legion of Merit by the American ambassador, was at the forefront of the negotiations. Focused on building up the army, the commander-in-chief did not bother consulting the central cabinet, far less seek parliamentary approval, before making a series of pledges to Washington. These included a guarantee that Pakistan would not use American military equipment against India except in self-defense. In a startling disregard of the political ramifications, the commander-in-chief was willing to let the United States build bases in Pakistan in return for military aid. As Ayub explained, he had simply told the politicians that they "must make up their mind to go whole-heartedly with the West." The Pakistan Army would "take no nonsense from the politicians," nor would it allow them or "the public to ruin the country." If there was any attempt to destabilize the government, Ayub warned, he would "immediately declare martial law and take charge of the situation," and the "army will do what I tell it to do." Conversations with senior army officers confirmed the claim, leaving American diplomats in Pakistan with the "distinct impression" that the Pakistan Army was "definitely ready to take control should Civil Government break down."[27]

Pakistan's first military intervention in 1958 was preceded by a phase of military-bureaucratic dominance that is traceable to 1951. Dispensing with the need for a nationally organized party with popular bases of support, civil and military officials such as Mirza and Ayub focused on nurturing their ties with Washington. The administrative machinery was manipulated and a culture of patronage instituted that was detrimental to center–province relations. These moves laid the foundations of what was to become a thriving political economy of defense. But the compulsion for the military takeover suggests that the power and privilege that civil bureaucrats, army officers, and their allies among the dominant social classes came to enjoy after 1951 were not immune from being challenged by politicians with provincial bases of support. The failure of the "parliamentary system" in Pakistan is often attributed to the "power vacuum" created by a fractious and corrupt provincial leadership at the helm of political parties lacking in popular support. A clear distinction between phases of dominance and actual intervention by the military suggests why weaknesses of political parties alone cannot account for the army high command's decision in 1958 to directly wield state authority. A more convincing explanation for Pakistan's first military coup has to consider the ways in which the dominance of the nonelected over the elected institutions could still be contested by an incipient democratic political process. In other words, the imperatives of the army were set under siege by the aspirations of the *awam*.

Privileging the center's agenda at the expense of the regions created malfunctions in the political system. But even a warped political process threatened the exercise of state authority by a determined band of civil and military officials in West Pakistan. Contemptuous of all politicians, they were especially wary of a Bengali majority in any future federal constitution. If permitted to secure their rightful place in the governance of the country, Bengali politicians could join their disaffected counterparts in the non-Punjabi provinces to force a change in Pakistan's Kashmir-focused and pro-American foreign policy. This seemed uncomfortably close to realization with the appearance of the constituent assembly's Basic Principles Committee Report in late 1952. Known as the Nazimuddin Report, it bore the hallmark of the new prime minister's Bengali orientation. A scion of the Nawab of Dhaka's aristocratic family, Nazimuddin was not popular among Bengalis, who derided him as a servant of the West Pakistan center.[28] In January 1952, Nazimuddin told an audience in Dhaka that Urdu would have to be the official language of Pakistan. There were howls of protest by the Awami League led by Hussain Shaheed Suhrawardy and various student groups. Police fired on a protest rally called by students on February 21, 1952, in defiance of the ban on public meetings. Four students died, and several were injured. This sealed the fate of the East Bengal Muslim League. The day became etched in Bengali popular consciousness as "Martyrs Day," the ultimate symbol of their resistance to the West Pakistani–based central government.

Missing the point, the Punjabi governor of the eastern wing, Feroz Khan Noon, had visions of converting Bengalis to Urdu by playing on their religious sentiments. He convinced himself that the agitation against Urdu was limited to government employees. "If Bengali were written in the Arabic script—85% of the words being common between Urdu and Arabic if properly pronounced," Noon fantasized, "soon a new and richer language will emerge which may be called 'Pakistani.' "[29] Ironically enough, the idea of educating Bengali children to write their mother tongue in Arabic was the brainchild of the minister of education at the center, Fazlur Rahman, who was himself a Bengali. Rahman thought this was better than the blanket introduction of Urdu and that such a change would "strengthen national unity and solidarity" between the two wings. Furthermore, it would "cut off East Bengal from West Bengal and put an end to the disruptive activity . . . carried on in the name of the common culture of the two Bengals" that appealed to the youth and intelligentsia of the province.[30] Misled into believing that a plebiscite would result in a 95 percent vote in favor of Urdu, Governor Noon used his discretionary funds to print a propaganda pamphlet on the language issue entitled "The Battle for Pakistan."[31]

Prime Minister Nazimuddin could ill afford to join this battle. Dependent on Bengali support, he was not prepared to let the West Pakistani cabal diddle the eastern province out of its share of power and influence in the new state. Confronting innumerable domestic challenges, including a hostile cabinet, and unsure of his base of support in the eastern wing, Nazimuddin saw his ultimate refuge in playing the Islamic card. Daultana as chief minister of Punjab was manipulating the anti-Ahmadi agitation to wangle his way into prime ministerial office. So Nazimuddin went a step further to placate the self-styled representatives of Islam. He was not only willing to consider the demands of the ulema to declare the Ahmadis non-Muslims, but he agreed to give the clerics a greater say in the affairs of the state. A board of five ulema was to advise the head of state on whether a law was repugnant to Islam. This was abhorrent enough to the die-hard secularists who controlled the central government, but they considered the Nazimuddin Report's recommendations for the future political structure to be nothing short of catastrophic. West Pakistani military and bureaucratic officials and their political allies in Punjab were insistent on parity between the two wings. The constitutional committee's report accepted the principle. However, parity between the two wings was possible only when the two houses of Parliament met jointly. The lower house with most of the powers of the federation was to have a Bengali majority while the upper house was to consist of nine separate West Pakistani units. Nazimuddin's formula for a solution of the two main problems in constitution making threatened to undo all the spadework by General Ayub Khan and his civilian cohorts in Washington. Amid mounting financial difficulties and a food shortage hovering on a restive political landscape, an unrepresentative and desperate central government decided to hitch its wagons to the star-spangled banner of American imperialism.

Associating the country with an Anglo-American bloc widely accused of perfidy in Palestine and increasingly also in Iran and Egypt went against the grain of popular sentiments in Pakistan. Even an apolitical individual such as Manto was drawn into questioning the wisdom of signing a military agreement with the United States. In a series of nine letters to "Uncle Sam" composed between December 1951 and April 1954, the Pakistani nephew directed the choicest barbs at his factitious foreign uncle. Fiercely independent minded, he wrote the letters after being given 300 rupees by an official of the American consulate in Lahore to write for its local publication. Struggling to eke out a living in a country that had yet to strike course, Manto took the money, noting that he was poor like the rest of his country but not ignorant like most of it. Americans needed to look into their own hearts, unless they had been taken out by one of their brilliant surgeons, to realize why Pakistan was so poverty stricken despite an abundance of imported Packards and Buicks. But those who drove such cars were not of the country. Pakistan was a country of poor people like the author and those who were poorer still.[32] American military aid was clearly not for the betterment of these people. Manto was convinced that the sole purpose of the aid was to arm the mullahs, who were the best antidote to Russian communism. He could "visualize the mullahs, their hair trimmed with American scissors . . . their pajamas stitched by American machines in strict conformity with the Sharia" sitting on prayer rugs made in America.[33]

The unpopularity of US assistance only strengthened the official disdain for intellectuals and populist politicians who seemed oblivious of the grave economic situation in the country. Shrinkage in world demand for jute and cotton had left the national economy reeling with reserves dipping dangerously close to the absolute limit needed to back the rupee. Two years of near drought had reversed Pakistan's enviable position as one of the few food surplus countries in Asia, forcing it to import 1.5 million tons of food grains with the help of an American loan of $150 million.[34] Under the circumstances, the cynical machinations that spawned the anti-Ahmadi agitation in early 1953 seemed to justify the senior civil bureaucracy and military's lowly estimation of politicians. But it was the imposition of martial law in Lahore after the failure of the civil administration to control the situation that inflated the egos of the top military brass. Dismayed by the political uses of religion by politicians, people hailed the firm and effective handling of the situation by the military. Senior military officials contemplating intervention could always draw on the positive public response to the first martial law in Pakistan's history. Needing decisive action on the international front, an emboldened army high command pressed the governor-general to do the needful. Nothing could now save

Nazimuddin. With the active connivance of senior civil officials and the commander-in-chief, Ghulam Mohammad sacked the prime minister and four cabinet ministers in April 1953. It was the first constitutional coup in Pakistan's history and one whose skillful execution delayed the need for direct military intervention. Mohammad Ali Bogra, Pakistan's "vigorous, youthful, and boyishly pro-American" ambassador in Washington, was selected to replace the colorless Nazimuddin. A little-known political figure from the backwaters of eastern Bengal, the new prime minister was expected to "steer Pakistan into full cooperation with the United States."[35]

With elections in East Bengal on the anvil, Bogra was destined to fail both the Islamic and the federal test. His proposals for the future constitution gave the religious ideologues undue importance. However, the role of religion in the state was for the moment secondary to the thorny issue of how power was to be shared between the two wings of the country. Here Bogra showed ingenuity and also, as a Bengali, sensitivity toward feelings in the eastern wing on the language issue. Bengali was given official status alongside Urdu, but English was to continue to be used for official purposes for the next two decades. There was no comfort for Bengalis in Bogra's formula, making all vital issues subject to a majority vote of the two houses of Parliament meeting together. A majority had to include at least 30 percent of the representatives from each wing. The arrangement aimed at reassuring Punjabis that the eastern wing would not outvote them. However, there was nothing to prevent 30 percent of the East Bengal representatives from voting against bills dealing with defense, foreign policy, and industrial development.

No amount of political jugglery could get around the difficulties posed by the numerical preponderance of the eastern wing. In April 1954, a United Front of half a dozen parties led by Suhrawardy's Awami League and Fazlul Huq's Krishak Sramik (Peasants and Workers) Party trounced the Muslim League in provincial elections in East Bengal. The scale of the defeat would have been appreciably greater if women voters in the rural areas had not shied away from the polling stations. A voting turnout of 65 percent was nevertheless impressive. The roll of the political dice had turned decisively against the West Pakistani–dominated establishment, weakening Bogra's already shaky grip on power. By no means a monolithic entity with common interests, the term *establishment* in the Pakistani context has been best defined by a latter-day insider as "a tendency, a certain outlook—socially conservative and protective of vested interests, favorable to authoritarian methods, contemptuous of the idea of democracy, and impatient with the restraints of the rule of law."[36] Alarmed by the Bengali rebuff, Governor-General Ghulam Mohammad overturned the democratic mandate by dismissing the United Front ministry headed by Fazlul Huq and appointing Major General Iskander Mirza as the governor of East Bengal.

Bengalis were not alone in feeling mowed down by a small group of power-hungry men who enjoyed the backing of the army and America. Steps to forcibly assimilate the princely states of Bahawalpur and Khairpur and merge West Pakistan into one unit by amalgamating the provinces in the western wing accompanied these overtly authoritarian signs. In addition to solving the problem of parity, the elimination of provincial boundaries in the west would diminish the chances of non-Punjabi provinces, or even disillusioned Punjabi politicians, closing ranks with Bengalis and restricting the center's autonomy in decision making. Signs of this were already in evidence. In September 1954, non-Punjabis banded together in the Muslim League's assembly party to reject the proposals for a unification of the western wing. Punjabi politicians now had to weigh the costs of opposing a center where the nonelected institutions of the state were calling the shots. A constitutional device to offset the Bengali majority in the eastern wing, the one-unit move was implemented mainly through unconstitutional methods. Non-Punjabi politicians had to fall into line or face the center's ire. The appointment of the pro-Congress Dr. Khan Sahib as chief minister of West Pakistan in October 1955 was designed to placate the Pathans and take the sting out of Afghanistan's "Pakhtunistan" propaganda. It proved to be a good decision, especially in light of the everyday inconveniences of the Pathans who now needed to refer matters to the provincial headquarters at Lahore. Sindh and Balochistan remained unreconciled to an administrative centralization that privileged Punjabis.

Opposition to the one-unit scheme was inconvenient for Ayub, Mirza, and Ghulam Mohammad at a time when small amounts of American military assistance had started arriving. Although the $25 million aid package was well below Ayub's expectations, it was better than nothing. There was a clear realization, however, that an open alliance with America could jeopardize Pakistan's relations with the Soviet Union and China. In order to alleviate the political fallout of the decision, domestically as well as internationally, Pakistan signed a pact with Turkey before formally aligning itself with the United States in 1954. This was accompanied shortly after by Pakistan becoming a member of two American-sponsored security pacts—the Southeast Asian Treaty Organization (SEATO) in 1954 and the Baghdad Pact in 1955. The latter marked the triumph of John Foster Dulles's "northern tier" concept of using pro-US regimes in Turkey, Iraq, Iran, and Pakistan to contain Soviet communism over British ideas of centering Middle East defense around UK-controlled bases in the region. Iraq's anti-Western coup in 1958 necessitated the renaming of the Baghdad Pact as the Central Treaty Organization (CENTO).[37]

Rumblings of protest against Pakistan's alliance with America threatened to disrupt the flow of military aid. So political processes had to be derailed by a ring of senior army and civil officials operating within the constraints of constructing and consolidating a state in a difficult regional and international setting. Tensions with India combined with international pressures to influence domestic politics and economy, distorting relations between the center and the provinces in particular and the dialectic between state construction and political processes in general. The carefully cultivated nexus between the top echelons of the military and the civil bureaucracy in Pakistan and the centers of the international system in London and Washington was of tremendous significance in this context.

A major constitutional crisis reared its head in September 1954 when a group of politicians in the constituent assembly tried clipping the governor-general's powers to dismiss a cabinet that in theory was responsible to Parliament. This would have spelled the end of Ghulam Mohammad, who after being paralyzed by a stroke could neither think nor speak clearly and was confined to a wheelchair.[38] But with senior civil and military officials willing to do his bidding, the governor-general was able to secure the support of provincial politicians like Daultana in Punjab and M. A. Khuhro in Sindh, sections of the business community in Karachi, as well as the chief justice of Pakistan. With the recently concluded mutual defense assistance agreements on his mind, Ghulam Mohammad raised the specter of martial law with Bogra and dismissed the constituent assembly on October 24, 1954. This was just a few days after the assembly had agreed on a constitutional document after years of incessant bickering. Foreshadowing a decisive shift in the balance of power from elected to nonelected institutions, a mentally and physically unfit Ghulam Mohammed mocked parliamentary practice by appointing a "cabinet of talents" that included General Ayub Khan as defense minister and Iskander Mirza as interior minister with the doyen of the civil bureaucracy, Chaudhri Mohammad Ali, retaining the all-important finance portfolio. Once the non-Punjabi provinces in the west had been summarily bundled into an unwanted union with Punjab in October 1955, only an act of God could prevent Pakistan from tying the proverbial knot with Washington. That the marriage was doomed to fail was less significant than the dowry it would fetch in the form of badly needed military equipment. Having bartered away Pakistan's sovereignty in exchange for a military arsenal that was just a fraction better than the World War II hardware possessed by the defense forces, the coterie of civil and military officials led by Ayub, Mirza, and Ghulam Mohammad were naturally eager to protect their own interests.

The self-serving exercise of central authority by a small faction claiming to be protecting the national interest of Pakistan did not go unopposed. Maulvi Tamizuddin Khan, the Bengali president of the constituent assembly, led the charge by filing a petition in the Sindh High Court challenging the dismissal of the constituent assembly. He is said to have escaped the heavy police cordon placed around his house by wearing a burka—the tentlike garment with tiny meshed peepholes that covers the whole body. If true, this symbol of women's oppression has to be credited with playing a significant role in the early resistance against authoritarianism. The Sindh High Court unanimously upheld Tamizuddin's plea challenging the governor-general's dismissal of the constituent assembly. As a sovereign body established to frame a constitution, the assembly could not be dissolved before the completion of its task. The federal government's contention that all bills passed by the constituent assembly without the assent of the governor-general were invalid was also shot down. In the opinion of the Sindh High Court, the constituent assembly had the sovereign authority to amend and repeal laws and frame a new constitution. Most annoyingly for the authoritarian clique that had arbitrarily assumed the role of state builders in contravention of the people's sovereignty, the Sindh High Court declared the "cabinet of talents" illegal.

If this early instance of judicial activism had prevailed, a firm basis might have been laid for the supremacy of the rule of law over political expediency in Pakistan's history. But with Punjabi chief justice Muhammad Munir in tow, the civil and military combine managed to get a judicial verdict in its favor. Instead of determining the validity of the governor-general's action, the judges of the federal court ruled by four to one that the Sindh High Court had no jurisdiction to decide on the matter. By grounding themselves in technicalities, the judges evaded the real issue of the balance of powers between the executive and Parliament to the detriment of the future of democracy in Pakistan. In later years, Justice Munir defended his controversial decision by arguing that principles of public law were found not in books but in the force of political events. Confusing his role as judge with that of an administrator, Munir maintained that the court did not rule against the federal government because it had no means of enforcing its writ. Such a lame excuse cut no ice with Justice A. R. Cornelius, who in his dissenting note stated that the constituent assembly was a sovereign body. The governor-general had to act within the framework of the constitution prepared by the constituent assembly. It followed that the governor-general's assent was not needed for the validation of constitutional laws. To insist on such a requirement on laws of a constitutional nature was "a direct affront to the position and authority of that body."[39]

Within a week of the federal court's landmark decision, the governor-general declared a state of emergency. This prevented additional references to the court against the dissolution of the constituent assembly. Ghulam Mohammad had a more insidious aim. He wanted to use his emergency powers to frame a constitution without reference to the representatives of the people. The federal court struck this down on the grounds that constitution making could not proceed through ordinance. But in the absence of a national legislature that could validate laws nullified by the federal court, the entire political, legal, and administrative edifice of the state was rendered invalid by the court's ruling. The constitutional impasse brought the pliant chief justice back into line. In a politically contorted reading of Hans Kelsen's theory of revolutionary legality, the federal court invoked the law of state necessity to sanction the governor-general's emergency powers.[40] But it insisted that only an elected constituent assembly could frame the constitution. The existing provincial assemblies duly elected a new constituent assembly. With no party enjoying an absolute majority, the second constituent assembly had a divisive tenure. This made it more open to manipulation. Instead of sound constitutional principles, the politics of pragmatism and compromise shaped the constitution that was formally implemented on March 23, 1956, after sustained conflict along regional and ideological lines.

Parity between the two wings was the foundational principle of the constitution that was adopted by the second constituent assembly. Pakistan was to be an Islamic republic and the Objectives Resolution of 1949 inserted as the preamble to the constitution. The repugnancy clause was incorporated, but Islam was not declared as the state religion. Rights of equal citizenship were guaranteed to all, irrespective of religion or sect. The liberal democratic concept of a government limited by the rule of law was enshrined in the constitution. There was an elaborate list of inalienable fundamental rights, and the judiciary was empowered to enforce them against encroachments by the executive and the legislature. With the potentially disruptive issue of the role of Islam in the state temporarily out of the way, the praetorian guard and its mandarin friends sanguinely accepted the constituent assembly's stance on fundamental rights. As they knew only too well, the proof of the pudding lay in the eating.

The constitution provided for a form of parliamentary democracy that was as close to a military-bureaucratic conception of a presidential system of government as was possible. Pakistan was to have a federal system of government but a unitary central command. The powers of the president, an office the notorious intriguer Iskander Mirza reserved for himself, far exceeded those normally conferred on a ceremonial head of state in a unicameral parliamentary system. As head of state, the president could select and dismiss the prime minister and the cabinet regardless of the Parliament's wishes. The prime minister held office at the pleasure of the president and along with the cabinet was expected to aid and advise the head of state on matters pertaining to the federation. Nothing bound the president to accept the advice of the cabinet, whose only recourse was to comply or resign. The head of the state had wide-ranging discretionary powers and made all the key appointments. As the supreme commander of the armed forces, the president selected all three service chiefs. The central and provincial civil services were directly answerable to the president, who also appointed the provincial governors. It was practically impossible to remove the president. A successful impeachment motion required a three-fourths majority, a virtual impossibility in a country where politicians were known to sell their loyalties at a drop of the hat.

The 1956 constitution reflected rather than remedied the institutional imbalances that had crept into the evolving structure of the state. But even the flawed product of nine difficult years of constitution making was a positive step in Pakistan's uncertain quest for a system of government based on the rule of law rather than the arbitrary whims of whoever happened to be at the top. During the two and a half years that the constitution was in operation, general elections were repeatedly postponed due to concerns about the nature of the political configuration they might throw up. While politicians wearing an array of party badges were shunted in and out of office, a military and civil bureaucratic combine exercised real power. Without absolving the politicians in any way, such cultivated instability could only further impair the political process. Mirza arrogated to himself the authority to make and break governments. There was a rapid succession of prime ministers. H. S. Suhrawardy, the dynamic populist leader of the Awami League in East Bengal, which was renamed East Pakistan, replaced the staid and reliable Chaudhri Mohammad Ali in September 1956. Suhrawardy's efforts to secure a better deal for the eastern wing incurred the wrath of the center's big business supporters, forcing him to resign in October 1957. Shaky coalition governments led by I. I. Chundrigar of the Muslim League and the Republican Party leader Feroz Khan Noon ensued.

On October 7, 1958, Mirza declared martial law. The decision was taken in close consultation with Ayub Khan and other top-ranking military officers. Ironically enough, Mirza told the American ambassador that he was taking the action to prevent the army from seizing power in Pakistan. A civilian martial law to foil a military takeover was a bizarre move in a country that was to witness many more. Unwilling to countenance a Bengali-led political configuration at the center upsetting the flow of much needed American military assistance, senior army officers were firmly against holding elections. Amid mounting turmoil, routine promotional matters in the army were tampered with for political reasons. This heightened professional jealousies, often along regional and sectarian lines. Between 1955 and 1958, Ayub succeeded in getting three extensions as commander-in-chief. In the words of a future commander-in-chief, this frustrated the ambitions of "megalomaniacal senior officers" who,

having made their way to the top with almost indecent haste, were looking for higher horizons. Appointments made by Ayub to consolidate his
position ushered in a culture of mediocrity and "blind obedience bordering on obsequiousness." The system of organizational discipline demanded "total compliance by subordinates" and suspension of debate. Senior officers evaded responsibility by blaming their juniors, with the result
that "a profound sense of despondency permeated the lower ranks."[41]

Mirza was mindful of the pressures building up in the army. Senior
army officers were perturbed by intelligence reports about the creeping
Indian influence in East Bengal. They blamed politicians for maladministration and corruption. What this perspective overlooked was the role of
the president in generating political instability by using the intelligence
agencies to achieve the desired political results. Mirza exercised powers
well beyond the provenance of a head of state in a parliamentary system
of government. Irrepressible at the best of times, he ensnared the ruler of
Kalat into seceding from Pakistan and promptly used that as an excuse to
tighten the center's noose around that state. The swift military action
against Kalat on October 6, 1958, came in the face of a series of political
and economic crises. A dramatic drop in industrial production during the
summer of 1958 was accompanied by soaring inflation and the shortage of
essential commodities because of hoarding and smuggling. Together with
the unresolved problem of refugee resettlement and property allotment,
there was enough combustible material to light a million fires. In September 1958, the death of the deputy speaker on the floor of the house after an
angry member of the assembly flung a paperweight at him during a parliamentary brawl served to pour oil on troubled waters. Mirza and Ayub
used this shameful breakdown of parliamentary decorum and the political situation in Balochistan as a pretext for the military takeover and dismissal of the assemblies. The political system did not simply break down.
Senior civil and military officials with British and American blessings
broke it down. Far from stepping into a "power vacuum," senior civil and
military officials exploited the internal political fissures to their own advantage and manipulated their international connections in a concerted
effort to depoliticize Pakistani society before it slipped into the era of mass
mobilization.

FOUR

PITFALLS OF MARTIAL RULE

ON THE NIGHT OF OCTOBER 7, 1958, with the populace in the depths of slumber, President Iskander Mirza put an unceremonious end to parliamentary democracy in Pakistan. The American ambassador and the British high commissioner were among the first to find out. They were summoned to the presidency just before midnight and, in General Ayub Khan's presence, informed that martial law had been imposed in the country. The new government was to be more pro-Western than before. Under military dictatorship, local political headaches would no longer distract Pakistan from honoring its international commitments in the Cold War against communism. Mirza suspended the constitution, dismissed the central and provincial governments, dissolved assemblies, banned political parties, postponed elections indefinitely, and placed the prime minister and his cabinet under house arrest. Justifying these drastic measures, the president noted that for the past two years he had been "watching with deepest anxiety the ruthless struggle for power, corruption, the shameful exploitation of our simple, honest, patriotic and industrious masses, the lack of decorum and the prostitution of Islam for political ends." Such "despicable activities" had "created a dictatorship of the lowest order." The "mentality of the politicians had sunk so low" that he was "unable to any longer believe that elections will improve the present chaotic situation." What Pakistanis needed most was not elections but freedom from "political adventurers, smugglers, black marketers and hoarders." The coup was "in the interests of the country."[1]

Addressing the nation on radio in his capacity as chief martial law administrator and the new prime minister designate, General Ayub Khan endorsed Mirza's reasoning. The army had "always kept severely aloof from politics" since the inception of Pakistan. Left to the politicians, "a perfectly sound country" had become the laughingstock of the world. Though taking the drastic measure, the army had no intention of running the day-to-day affairs of the state. Martial law was to be administered through the existing civilian organs of government. The "ultimate aim" of the military regime was to "restore democracy" but a democracy "people can understand and work." First, the country had to be put on an even keel by eradicating disruptionists, opportunists, and hoarders, the "social vermin" of whom soldiers and people alike were sick and tired. "History would never have forgiven us if the present chaotic conditions were allowed to go on any further," Ayub contended.[2] Knowledge of the exact timing of the coup was confined to a small circle of three to four generals. It took a fortnight to fine-tune the troop movements, giving their commanding officers an inkling of what was afoot.

Executing the military coup was a momentous decision. The new regime was committed to centralizing state power in disregard of regional sentiments and the pro-federation consensus. This augured poorly for the future of center–province relations. An imposed unity of the sort Mirza and Ayub had in mind carried an even greater likelihood of fragmentation than the provincialism they derided. The institutional shift from elected to nonelected institutions in the first decade, which the military intervention of 1958 sought to confirm, was to endure for decades to come. Pakistan's first military intervention coincided with anti-Western takeovers in Iraq and Burma and a pro-US one in Thailand, underlining the effects of Cold War politics on the domestic calculations of national armed forces. An anatomy of the coup with its far-reaching impact on civil–military and center–region relations offers key insights into the nature of Pakistan's military-dominated state.

A "Silent Revolution"

The efficiency with which the army assumed control of Pakistan under "Operation Fair Play" made for an impressive contrast with the political disarray of the recent past. Except for troops guarding some key installations, there was no evidence of anything unusual. Public reactions to the coup were mixed. Some were profoundly relieved to see an end to the political shenanigans of the past several years. Among the middle classes there was genuine and rational regret that parliamentary democracy, though disappointing in its operation, had been replaced by a dictatorial regime. Unable to mount opposition to the new regime, even conscientious objectors sullenly fell into line. Newspapers, which had been writing paeans to democracy, came out with editorials praising the regime's achievements.[3] Civil servants started working harder, claiming it was their last chance to get the country on its feet. Yet there was no spontaneous burst of enthusiasm or rush to adorn city streets with portraits of the new regime's leaders.

Ordinary citizens were gratified to see martial law authorities wielding the stick against shopkeepers who, fearing punishment for overpricing, adopted a code of fair practice. Prices dropped; smuggled goods vanished from the market and medicines in short supply became readily available. Those with money went on shopping sprees, stashing goods the regime was helping release from hoarders. The streets were cleaner, with fewer beggars in sight. Pedestrians seemed more disciplined, and cinema audiences stood up to hear the national anthem with military obedience.[4] This apparent transformation of the national character, as a *New York Times* correspondent reported, was attributed to "the new regime's apparent determination to make a record as the champion of the harassed man in the street." In Karachi, bus drivers were more polite. There was quiet satisfaction with the crackdown on former parliamentarians, who had been peddling influence, accepting bribes, hoarding, and trafficking in import licenses—the get-rich-instantly formula that had become the favorite pursuit of the go-getters in the land of opportunity. The politically more sophisticated, however, worried about the implications of the army action, pointing out that Pakistan's problems were far more complicated and that the generals might find it difficult to relinquish power to the civilians.[5]

They were right. Cosmetic changes were no answer to Pakistan's deep-seated political and economic problems. Politicians may have disgraced themselves with their intrigues and corruption, but the new masters—senior army officers and civil servants—were hardly exempt from these traits. The more far-sighted citizens worried about the prospects of the army becoming entangled with corruption. Instead of stabilizing politics, they feared that the suspension of democratic processes and the replacement of the 1956 federal constitution with a Punjabi-military-dominated unitary state would heighten center–province tensions and do irreparable damage to the fragile unity of the country. Under the martial law administration, concerted steps were taken to enhance border security. An anti-smuggling campaign called "Operation Close Door" was launched in the eastern wing that led to a reduced flow of goods between the two Bengals. The drying up of the commodity trade was reflected in diminished food stocks in Calcutta markets, leading one senior Pakistani Army officer to confidently assert, "Partition has now taken place for the first time." West Pakistani officers at the brigadier level in the eastern wing favored turning to the Turkish model and establishing semiautocratic rule for a quarter of a century. Indicative of the contempt in which they held their Bengali compatriots, they advocated adopting an uncompromising attitude toward East Pakistan and eradicating the cancer of provincialism. The regime could easily take the "wind out of the sails of potential opponents among the politically conscious minority" by replicating the supposed British example of providing the poor with access to cheap food and clothing, a reasonable administration, and a fair chance at getting justice. But these military officers also realized that they could not wait for years to show the results.[6]

Stability eluded the new dispensation at the very outset. The joint authority of president and commander-in-chief was untenable and did not last more than a few weeks. Even before the coup, Mirza had been conspiring to replace Ayub as commander-in-chief. By appearing to go along with the president, Ayub bought precious time. Once the Supreme Court headed by Chief Justice Munir dignified the coup as a revolutionary necessity, Ayub sprang into action to establish himself as the undisputed leader of Pakistan. With the backing of his top military commanders, he packed off Mirza to permanent exile. Ayub justified his action by accusing the former president of trying to intrigue with discredited politicians and creating factions within the armed forces through unwarranted interference. Styling himself as an enlightened strong man who believed in effective action, Ayub made the consolidation of state power and an externally stimulated economic development strategy the main pillars of his military regime. Upon assuming the office of president, he made known his preference for a system of government that was closer to the American rather than the British model. He vowed to give people access to speedier justice, curb the crippling birth rate, and take appropriate steps, including land reforms and technological innovation, to develop agriculture so that the country could feed itself. The sweeping reforms envisaged by the military regime demanded greater centralization of state authority and better coordination between the different arms of government.

Upon becoming lord of the land, Ayub Khan withdrew the army from martial law duties, declaring the successful restoration of the civil administration. Barring those specifically on martial law duties, the bulk of the army was kept out of civilian matters. Ayub relied heavily on the two military spy agencies, the Inter-Services Intelligence (ISI) and Military Intelligence (MI), as well as the civilian Intelligence Bureau (IB), which now worked directly under the chief martial law administrator. This helped secure his base within the army and cement his alliance with the civil bureaucracy. Needing to stretch his network of support more widely, Ayub used a predominantly Punjabi army and civil bureaucracy—the establishment in Pakistani political parlance—to dispense patronage to social and economic groups with political bases that were neither extensive nor independent of the state apparatus so as to pose a serious threat to the regime.

Some of the best senior officers of the Civil Service of Pakistan (CSP) and the brightest legal minds were pressed into the service of the regime. Aziz Ahmad was appointed deputy martial law administrator. Qudratullah Shahab became Ayub's personal secretary and top media point man before being replaced by Altaf Gauhar as information secretary. They were among the most prominent members of the senior civil bureaucracy in this period. Brandishing the rousing doctrine of a strong leadership that could weld Pakistan's disparate constituent units into a single nation and fend off India's hegemonic designs, Ayub's bandwagon attracted politicians who were willing to cut their losses and serve as junior partners to a military usurper. These included the flamboyant thirty-year-old Sindhi landlord and lawyer Zulfikar Ali Bhutto, who was retained from Mirza's inner cabinet. Muhammad Shoaib, the pro-American former executive director of the World Bank, was made finance minister. The stage was set for the enactment of a one-sided drama in which the main character was the prosecutor, defender, and juror all rolled into one.

Needing to secure support from his main constituency in the armed forces, Ayub appointed a staunch loyalist, General Muhammad Musa, as the new commander-in-chief before turning to neutralize other potential threats. However, his breaking of the law to establish a new order did not go unnoticed. In a telling poetic repartee, Faiz asked:

> Lifeless are the sick, why don't you administer the medicine?
> What kind of messiah are you, why don't you provide the cure?
> . . .
> Will you do justice after the people have been annihilated?
> Arbiter that you are, can't you see the rising tumult?[7]

Such impertinence was duly punished. The press was suppressed and newspaper editors told to toe the line or face grave consequences. A state-controlled media advertised the regime's success in punishing black marketers and venal politicians and putting the engine of government back on track. But it did not report how intellectuals were silenced and marginalized, particularly those suspected of communist sympathies. In keeping with the regime's buzzword—targeting corruption—an estimated 1,662 members of the federal bureaucracy were disciplined and 813 dismissed on charges of inefficiency, corruption, and misuse of office. Although most belonged to the lower tiers of the state administration, a few hundred middle and higher-ranking officials had to face disciplinary action, and a dozen members of the hitherto invincible CSP were sacked.[8] Politicians were given the unenviable choice of quitting politics or facing prosecution for corruption and misuse of office under the Electoral Body Disqualification Ordinance (EBDO) of 1959. This deprived Pakistan of the services of several experienced politicians and administrators. Ayub had concluded that the people of Pakistan were temperamentally unsuited for parliamentary democracy and needed a presidential form of government in order to be tutored in the art of democracy. With all the pieces of his jigsaw puzzle of Pakistan seemingly in place, Ayub turned his attention to the mechanics of establishing a modicum of legitimacy.

Although fundamental rights remained suspended, the regime tried earning popular support by tackling two of the most contentious issues of the period in West Pakistan: the mismanagement of evacuee property and the inequitable land tenure system. There had been unbridled corruption in the allotment of evacuee property throughout the first decade; the property distribution system was streamlined and made relatively more efficient, though not necessarily more equitable. Reforming the land tenure system in West Pakistan posed a thornier problem. Some 6,000 landlords owned huge tracts of land and controlled access to canals vital to the agricultural prosperity of Punjab and Sindh. According to one estimate, 80 percent of the landowners in the western wing had less than one-third of the cultivable land whereas about six-tenths of one percent owned a fifth of this area. Most of the agricultural units were less than five acres each, while the big landlords had holdings ranging from 500 to several thousand acres.

The concentration of political and economic power in the hands of eighty or so large landlord families in West Pakistan posed a formidable barrier to land reforms. By contrast, the Estate Acquisition Act had breezed through the East Bengal assembly in 1950. The land reforms announced by Ayub in January 1959 were little more than a calculated sham in the redistribution of wealth. In keeping with the regime's intention to effect social and political change without any significant economic transformation, the Land Reforms Commission was asked to recommend ways of ensuring increased production while also providing social justice and security of tenure to the cultivators. The commission in its report noted that social justice and economics were not easily reconcilable. Under the circumstances, the best that could be done was to strike a delicate balance by fixing the ceiling at a level that would "eradicate the feudalistic elements" with "minimum necessary disturbance of the social edifice" while providing incentives to allow for higher levels of production. Consequently, the reforms neither addressed the problem of landless labor nor pretended to offer security of tenure. The ceiling of 500 acres for irrigated and 1000 acres for non-irrigated land was on individual rather than family holdings. This effectively exempted middle-sized landlords, raising objections from one member of the commission, Ghulam Ishaq Khan, who thought the ceiling should be much lower. He pointed out that most landlord politicians with access to state power had already parceled out land in excess of the ceiling to their family members in anticipation of the impending reform.[9]

Other loopholes in the form of exemptions for teaching, religious, and charitable institutions as well as orchards allowed West Pakistan's influential landlords to emerge unscathed from this ostensible attack on their power. Most of the acreage resumed by the state was wasteland, while huge sums were paid to the landlords as compensation. The principal beneficiaries of the reforms were the army's recruiting grounds in the sparsely watered Potwar plateau, while traditional landed families in the rest of Punjab and Sindh lost out. Baloch tribesmen were the hardest hit, claiming that 2.3 million of the 2.6 million acres recouped by the government belonged to them. Resentful at not being forewarned like the bigger Punjabi, Pathan, and Sindhi landlords had been, the Baloch offered the most significant opposition to the regime over the land reforms.[10] There was, however, no other major resistance to the land reform scheme. Some 20,000 peasants were given land, but without the requisite capital to develop it, most of them could not take advantage of the change in their fortunes.[11] Much of the appropriated land in the irrigated plains and pastoral deserts of West Pakistan was sold cheaply to the regime's supporters among army and civil officials. This was an important first step in a strategy of internal colonization designed to secure a loyal political constituency for the army outside its traditional stronghold in northern Punjab. The almost simultaneous shift in the capital from Karachi to Rawalpindi in the north left no scope for doubt that the army and not the landlords were the new power brokers in Pakistan. Ayub had struck a Faustian bargain according to which, in return for continued economic privileges, landlord politicians would accept a subservient role in the power-sharing equation. Instead of carping and complaining, the more enterprising of the landed families responded by moving capital from land to industry while others clung to their money until the regime showed more of its hand.

Controlled Democracy and Its Discontents

Ayub did not keep the country guessing very long about his vision of the future political system. While staying at the Dorchester Hotel in London, he had drawn up a plan for a controlled form of democracy that he believed was better suited to the "genius" of the Pakistani people. Presented as a fait accompli, the Basic Democracies Order of 1959 was authored by the eminent constitutional lawyer Manzur Qadir, who was foreign minister at the time. A blatant attempt at institutionalizing bureaucratic control over the political process, the basic democracies system virtually disenfranchised the more volatile sections of urban society—industrial labor and the intelligentsia in particular. The scales were loaded in favor of the rural notables who would dominate the new political system. They would elect most of the 80,000 representatives, later increased to 120,000, equally divided between the wings. Known as Basic Democrats, or BDs, the representatives were to be elected on the basis of universal adult franchise to union councils and union committees in the rural and urban areas, respectively. These union-level representatives would then indirectly elect the next tier of local bodies as well as the district and divisional councils. They would also serve as the electoral college for the election of the president as well as the national and provincial assemblies. All four tiers of the system were closely monitored by the civil bureaucracy, which nominated nearly half the members of the district and the divisional councils.

In consolidating the state's hold over society by extending the scope of bureaucratic patronage—both political and economic—to the rural localities, Ayub was trying to bolster central authority by neutralizing parties with provincial bases of support. Such a controlled political system in which the representatives of the people could gain entry only by abject loyalty to Ayub was open to graft and corruption and fraught with problems for Pakistan's federal state. Designed to insulate the center from the campaigners of provincial rights, the basic democracies system simulated the British colonial policy of preventing the aggregation of nationalist demands. The first round of elections for basic democrats was held in January 1960. The following month, a record 95.6 percent of the BDs voted to endorse Ayub Khan as president and authorize him to frame the new constitution. Three days after being elected president, the chief martial law administrator appointed a constitutional commission to examine the reasons for the "failure of the parliamentary system" in Pakistan.

For a man whose retainers told him he could be king, Ayub was now completely beholden to his favorites in the civil bureaucracy. The confluence of sycophancy and unchecked powers of patronage produced impractical ideas, including the notion of indirectly elected party-less assemblies. This proposal was rejected by the constitution commission's report. Ayub skirted around the difficulty by appointing a cabinet subcommittee to study the report. After getting his way, the general on March 1, 1962, gave the nation a constitution based on a one-chamber legislature with equal representation for both wings and a presidential form of government. The Bengali minister of law Muhammad Ibrahim, who had advocated the need for a federal constitution in the preceding months, relinquished his office on April 11, 1962. Ayub Khan acknowledged that on essentials like the constitution, the two men were "poles apart," adding that accepting Ibrahim's views would have entailed "laying the foundation of a bloody revolution in the country."[12] By railroading the 1962 constitution of his choice, Ayub may have done just that.

The state's designation was changed from the "Islamic Republic of Pakistan" to the "Republic of Pakistan," and all references to the Quran and the sunnah in the 1956 constitution were deleted. Amendments to the constitution required a two-thirds majority in Parliament and presidential concurrence. The judiciary was stripped of powers to question any law passed by the legislature. Ayub justified the concentration of powers in presidential hands by pronouncing Pakistan incapable of working the Westminster system. The secret of the British parliamentary government's success, he maintained, was a higher level of education, prosperity, public spirit, integrity, and, above all, "a really cool and phlegmatic temperament" that "only people living in cold climates seem to have."[13]

Vain, arrogant, and quick-tempered, Ayub Khan was wary of letting "rabble-rousers" provoke people's emotions. Cast in the mold of British colonial thinking, he planned on running Pakistan as a unitary state with a no-nonsense attitude toward proponents of regional rights. Ayub found a perfect instrument for his authoritarian rule in Malik Amir Mohammad Khan, the Nawab of Kalabagh in Mianwali district of northern Punjab, who was appointed governor of West Pakistan in April 1960. A ruthless administrator and a wily political manipulator, the thick-mustached Kalabagh kept firm controls on the press and used the police to silence the regime's opponents. Stories of his tyrannical methods have passed into Pakistani folklore, making him Ayub's most feared and hated lieutenant. Yet he functioned primarily as Ayub's point man and did everything with the president's sanction, hounding those opposed to the president and taking blame for his unjust acts.[14] Frustrated by the regime's autocracy, the politically sidelined former Unionist premier of undivided Punjab, Khizar Hayat Khan Tiwana, suggested that the best assurance for stability might be for Pakistan to become a monarchy so that succession could remain in Ayub's family.[15] The projection of the president's imperial affectations by the official media invoked ideas of Ayub as the perpetual ruler of Pakistan. As he himself mused, the "real trouble" was that the people of Pakistan had "never been the masters of their own destiny" and, as a result, were "instinctively suspicious of their rulers."[16]

Whatever the justification for Ayub's dictatorship, the regime needed to cloak itself in some semblance of democracy. Within weeks of the promulgation of the new constitution and the lifting of martial law, the Political Parties Act legalized the formation of parties. This brought the Muslim League out of the woodwork, a pale shade of its illustrious forebear, split between the Council Muslim League, representing the stalwarts of the old party, and the progovernment Convention Muslim League. In a typically Pakistani all-in-the-family twist to politics, the president's estranged younger brother, Sardar Bahadur Khan, who headed the Muslim League's parliamentary party in the West Pakistan assembly before the coup, became leader of the opposition in the assembly. The rift between the two brothers was personal, not political. They had fallen out when Ayub Khan married his daughter Nasim to the Wali of Swat's heir instead of Sardar Bahadur's son, to whom she had been promised. Tall, round-faced, and sporting a brushed-up moustache, Sardar Bahadur was the spitting image of his elder brother. Objecting to Ayub's rejection of a more open political system but using his relationship with the president for political advantage, he provided loyal opposition rather than a real threat to the regime.

Even a foolproof political system that made the will of the people irrelevant did not guarantee the general's hold on office. No sooner had martial law been lifted than the opposition denounced the 1962 constitution as undemocratic. The ban on hundreds of politicians disqualified by the regime was retained, limiting the value of the initiative in the eyes of the opposition. Yet elections to the national assembly brought in several politicians who demanded the restoration of fundamental rights in the constitution. In October 1962, a National Democratic Front was formed consisting of more than half a dozen parties, including the Council Muslim League, the Awami League, the National Awami Party, and the Jamaat-i-Islami. They demanded adult franchise and objected to the arbitrary displacement of parliamentary democracy by a highly centralized presidential system and indirect elections. With Kalabagh showing excellent results in obstructing, if not breaking up, the opposition in West Pakistan, Ayub now needed someone comparable in East Pakistan. Abdul Monem Khan, a Bengali lawyer who had been elected unopposed to the national assembly and served as health minister in the first central cabinet formed after the 1962 constitution, was chosen as governor of the eastern wing. An Ayub loyalist by necessity, Monem Khan's corruption and strong-arm tactics against the political opposition in the eastern wing made him one of the regime's die-hard supporters.

Amid growing acrimony with the opposition that was greatly embittered by gubernatorial arrogance in both wings, Ayub could not amend the constitution in the absence of the necessary parliamentary majority. In a clear defeat for the government, the first amendment to the constitution made fundamental rights defensible in the law courts. The appointment of Justice Cornelius as the chief justice of the Supreme Court gave a fillip to the fundamental rights lobby to the detriment of the military-controlled legislative and executive organs of the state. But here was the rub. While giving the 1962 constitution a democratic touch, the first amendment conceded the ulema's demand to change the nomenclature of the state by adding "Islamic" before the "Republic of Pakistan." This and subsequent amendments to the constitution demonstrated to the soldier-statesman that, try as he may, there was nothing to prevent politicians from coalescing with the ulema to undermine his vision of stability and progress. Despite his aversion to party politics, Ayub took the decisive plunge and added the presidency of the Convention Muslim League to his already colorful assortment of offices.

Ayub's formal entry into politics in 1963 made it doubly important to strengthen his support among the elected representatives. Providing differential economic patronage to a freshly cultivated leadership in the rural areas and the regime's supporters among business and state officials in the urban areas was essential for the success of the basic democracies system. In a cash-starved state, this was possible only by soliciting handsome doses of foreign assistance. Aiming to industrialize and militarize Pakistan in the shortest possible time, Ayub wanted to wash his hands of all political constraints by getting Parliament to rubber-stamp his policies. This included an unabashedly pro-American foreign policy that ran the risk of jeopardizing Pakistan's national security by antagonizing the Soviet Union irreparably. These were, however, concerns for a later day. For now, Ayub had no hesitation in joining hands with the United States in the hope of raising a credible military defense against India.

Foreign Policy and Domestic Dissonance

As early as December 1958, Zulfikar Ali Bhutto, the youthful commerce minister, said at a meeting of the federal cabinet that Pakistan was depending far too much on America and needed an independent foreign policy consistent with its sovereignty. Ayub countered this by saying that Pakistan's foreign policy was driven by security concerns. One had to approach foreign policy in a "realistic manner without being sentimental about it." The hard truth was that "our country would have ceased to exist if the U.S. economic and military aid had not been forthcoming." The only other option available was for Pakistan to look toward the Soviet Union for money, and that would almost certainly "reduce us to the level of a satellite country."[17]

If securing the territorial integrity of Pakistan was the primary motivation of Ayub's foreign policy, Kashmir and water disputes with India topped his agenda. Advocates of an independent foreign policy like Bhutto maintained that the tilt toward America was inconsistent with Pakistan's need to resolve Kashmir and the Indus water issue since Washington would stop short of doing anything that might upset New Delhi. In a startling admission of the limitations of his carefully cultivated pro-American policy, Ayub conceded that security pacts with America had "rendered the solution of Kashmir more difficult" as India pointed to the changed military balance in the region to justify its stance on the issue. However, the military assistance these deals had fetched for the armed forces had "underwritten the integrity and security of Pakistan." "We might not be able to go to war with India with the strength that we had," Ayub declared, but now Pakistan was "strong enough to deter India from attacking us."[18]

Washington's generosity included assistance under the Atoms for Peace program to help Pakistan develop expertise in nuclear science and technology as well as a multimillion dollar agreement to finance a rural development program needed to sustain the basic democracies system. In return, Ayub permitted the Americans to carry out surveillance flights from Pakistan Air Force facilities. These were monitored from Badaber base near Peshawar. It was from here that Francis Gary Powers flew the U-2 spy plane that was shot down on May 7, 1960, by the Soviets. Apart from the sheer embarrassment of being caught red-handed facilitating a US covert operation, the U-2 affair exposed Pakistan to the Soviet threat without any commensurate improvement in the quality or quantity of American military assistance. The continued American presence in Badaber spotlighted Pakistan's compromised sovereignty. A request by the acting foreign minister Bhutto to visit the base was turned down by the Americans, who incurred his abiding wrath by keeping him confined to the cafeteria.

The U-2 incident might have created a national uproar, if not brought down the government. With a military dictator and a toothless Parliament, however, the blow to Pakistan's strategic security was allowed to wear off quietly. If Ayub had cushioned his pro-American policy against attack, his regime's modernist and secular vision was acutely vulnerable to a popular whiplash by would-be religious divines looking for an opportunity to make a dramatic impression in politics. Ayub held the self-appointed guardians of Islam in utter contempt. He believed they distorted the spirit of Islam, "flourish[ed] on the ignorance of the people," and were the "deadliest enemy of the educated Muslim."[19] Though he never wavered in his low opinion of those who peddled religion for popular consumption, his determination to resist the ulema visibly weakened after an initial spurt of modernist reforms. Using the cover of martial law, Ayub in March 1961 had introduced changes in Muslim family laws. These strengthened women's rights by imposing restrictions on polygamy and the verbal pronouncements of divorce. The ulema raised a storm against this unwarranted interference in Muslim law that, following colonial practice, they believed was their jurisdiction. Ayub remained steadfast in the face of agitation against the family law ordinance, although he later not only agreed to change Pakistan's name to an Islamic republic but also constituted the advisory Council of Islamic Ideology in August 1962. An Institute of Islamic Research was also set up the same year.

These gestures to Islam did not alter the essentially secular thrust of state policies until the mid-1970s. But there was a contradiction between the emphasis placed on Islam in the discourse on national unity and the desire to keep right-wing parties using religion as a cover for their political ambitions at bay. In the opinion of the former chief justice and first law minister under the 1962 constitution, Muhammad Munir, "one of the most serious threats to the future political stability and well-being of Pakistan was the multiplication of Islamic parties." He thought it "characteristic of a society like Pakistan's that when political life began on a mass scale it should express itself first in terms of religious fanaticism, since the people were so much more religiously than politically minded."[20] Even Daultana, who had pushed for land reforms giving peasants security of tenure, thought no "secular political party" could unite Bengalis, Punjabis, Pathans,

Balochis, and Sindhis into a single unit. He deplored the reluctance of certain East Pakistani politicians to revive the Muslim League in preference for a party that non-Muslims could join. Islam, he claimed, was "the only common value binding the people of East and West Pakistan together."[21]

The tactic of keeping Islam in play, in order to keep the so-called religious parties out, produced a bittersweet harvest. On the positive side, the decision gave the modernist viewpoint on Islam an upper hand. Ayub projected his own notion of Islam for nation-building purposes. There was no contradiction between his insistence on a strong center and Islam, which was the "prime mover in attaining . . . progress, prosperity and social justice."[22] This exposed him to acerbic criticism from Mawdudi's Jamaat-i-Islami, which accused the government of undermining Pakistan's Islamic ideology both in form and substance. In November 1963, the student wing of the Jamaat-i-Islami, the Jamiat-i-Tulaba, led student protests against the regime in key cities of West Pakistan. Proving its martial colors despite the civilian guise, the regime banned the Jamaat-i-Islami in January 1964. The Supreme Court declared the government action to be in violation of the fundamental right of association. This hinted at the judiciary's role as the sleeping giant that could, if it so wished, keep more effective watch and ward on the powers of an overweening executive than an ineffectual legislature. Though bolstering the confidence of political parties, the decision made Ayub more suspicious of politicians, whether of the liberal or of the socially conservative ilk.

The withering effect of ideological differences over the role of Islam in the affairs of the state was the lesser of the challenges confronting Ayub's regime. Far more dangerous for the sustainability of the regime was its willful disregard of regional sentiments in the name of national unity based on Islam. Bengalis continued to be poorly represented in the military and the upper echelons of the civil bureaucracy. Anxious to step up the industrialization of the country, the regime opted to give a variety of tax incentives to big business at the cost of agriculturalists and small bazaar merchants. The bonus voucher scheme, introduced in 1959 as an export control measure to protect domestic industry, enabled well-connected businessmen to multiply their profits in no time and contributed to the concentration of wealth in the hands of a few industrial houses.[23] Economic policies emphasizing growth rather than redistribution heightened disparities between the two wings and made the lines dividing the rich from the poor starker than ever. Political denial matched by the dubious mantra of functional inequality—enhancing production rather than re-distribution—as necessary for rapid economic growth bred hostility toward Ayub's regime, especially in East Pakistan, where demands for provincial autonomy were backed by charges of West Pakistani coloniza-tion. Containing 55 percent of the country's population, the eastern wing's export earnings from raw jute had been financing industrialization in the western wing. The Ayub regime's policy of state support for the private sector paid rich dividends in West Pakistan, where urbanization gathered pace, while the eastern wing, a river delta barely above sea level, was left out in the cold.

At the time of independence, West Pakistan's per capita income was 10 percent higher than in the eastern wing. The Indo-Pakistan agreement on the Indus waters negotiated under the auspices of the World Bank in 1962 was not matched by a similar settlement on the sharing of the eastern riv-ers. Nor were steps taken to cope with the perennial problem of flooding in East Pakistan. By the late 1960s, the western wing had stolen the march with a per capita income that was nearly 40 percent more than East Paki-stan's.[24] Inequalities in growth rates of income between the two wings ought not to distract from variations in the incidence of poverty within West Pakistan. A few dozen industrial families, wealthier and innovative farmers, civil servants, and members of the armed forces reaped the fruits of foreign-aided development policies. With the exception of a few dis-tricts, there were pockets of acute poverty in many parts of Punjab. The problem of intraprovincial inequalities, however, took a back seat amid a charged debate on provincial autonomy fueled by feelings of discrimina-tion in East Pakistan. Bengalis were galled to see non-Bengali families controlling the few large-scale industries in their province. They com-plained of central neglect in the granting of import licenses and receipt of development funds. Feeling isolated and alienated, Bengali economists in the national Planning Commission advocated the "two economy" thesis, according to which the economies of the two wings had to be considered separately. Apart from obvious differences between them due to geo-graphical and cultural factors, the main justification was the discrimina-tory effects of the center's investment policies. Drawing on the logic of investing in areas that offered the highest economic return, the policy was not appropriate in a country where the limited mobility of people and goods between two far-flung wings prevented the spread of the gains evenly.

Intended to underscore the economic deprivations of East Pakistan, where per capita income lagged behind that of West Pakistan, the thesis was flayed by officialdom as proof of an Indian conspiracy to break up the country. The situation was only marginally better in the western wing, where the non-Punjabi provinces loathed the one-unit system, which they saw as a ruse to deny them their due share of political and economic power. The concentration of political power and wealth in the hands of a few notable landed and industrial families in the country meant that even in Punjab there were few genuine supporters of the military regime. After donning the civvies, Ayub relied on the loyal support of a charmed circle made up of landed politicians-turned-basic democrats, around 15,000 senior civil servants, 500 senior military officers, and the scions of under two dozen wealthy urban families who controlled the industrial, banking, and insurance assets of the country. One fierce bend in the wind could bring down Ayub's regime like a house of cards.

With the intelligence agencies preparing reports based on rumor, gossip, and surmise more than an assessment of the political situation on the ground, the president was oblivious of the discontent brewing at home. The regime's takeover of Progressive Papers owned by the leftist Mian Iftikharuddin in 1959, the imposition of a system of "press advice" under which government laid down rules for what journalists could report, and the setting up of a National Press Trust in 1964 served to put an end to any serious intellectual debate in the country. Offensive antigovernment comment in the press ran the risk of newspaper establishments being shut down in a flash. The government's use of advertisements, both as reward and punishment, forced even the most obstreperous journalists to observe an intellectually deadening self-censorship. Plans to start a state-controlled television service promised to intensify the policy of indoctrinating the public in the cause of "national progress." This augured poorly for the regime's ability to keep abreast of the shifting moods of the populace and remain flexible in its approach to the challenge of governance. In the astute evaluation of the *Times* of London correspondent, "only a freeing of the political and intellectual climate" could "bring the government into a fruitful relationship with the intellectual and popular trends in the country." The supreme irony was that Ayub, with an impregnable hold on power, faced no danger in taking this oppressive course of action while "continued enforced conformity" was more than likely to result in "alienation as well as sterility."[25]

Surrounded by lackeys in the CSP, the Central Sultans of Pakistan as the civil servants were sarcastically called, Ayub was unaware of the mounting dissatisfaction with his policies, particularly in the eastern wing. If he had been unsure before, the soldier-turned-dictator was by now impervious to such intimations of trouble. As far as he was concerned, the people of East Pakistan were "incapable of seeing beyond their nose." They had squandered an empire in 1905 by siding with the Hindus against the partition of Bengal and with "one false step" could "go back to serfdom under the Hindus for another couple of centuries."[26] If his historical understanding was flawed, Ayub had amazing reserves of hubris. Not content with the authority he had already mustered, the soldier-president elevated himself to the rank of field marshal without having fought a single battle. This made him the supreme commander of the military. Facing a reelection campaign, the president needed an uplift of this kind. Any presidential election held within the confines of the basic democracies system was bound to be a cakewalk for Ayub. The electoral arithmetic gave him an overwhelming advantage. As many as 3,282 of the BDs constituting the electoral college were government nominees from the semiautonomous tribal areas of Pakistan's northwestern frontier. Elsewhere, too, the BDs could hardly be expected to perform collective suicide by subscribing to the opposition's call for the restoration of parliamentary system of democracy based on direct elections.

Hoping to make the most of the opening provided by a presidential election, the opposition parties formed the Combined Opposition Parties, representing a wide spectrum of public opinion in the two wings ranging from the far left to the extreme right. Their only common objective was to get rid of Ayub. What rattled the regime was not this ragtag alliance but its choice of presidential candidate—Fatima Jinnah, the sister of the founder of the nation. In an overreaction that was to later cost him dear, the entire administrative machinery was mobilized in Ayub's favor. What followed was a thoroughly rigged electoral process. There were blatant financial irregularities, misuse of government resources, and extensive electoral malpractice. Ms. Jinnah nevertheless gave Ayub a few palpitations

Ayub Khan with Fatima Jinnah at a reception on January 16, 1959. *The White Star Photo Pvt. Ltd. Archive.*

with her good showing in East Pakistan and Karachi, the commercial hub of Pakistan. When the results of the January 2, 1965, elections were counted, Ayub had won a comfortable majority, bagging 49,951 votes against his opponent's 28,691. Dismissing the election as a farce, Fatima Jinnah portentously stated that "the so-called victory of Mr. Ayub Khan" would turn out to be "his greatest defeat."[27]

She was right. Even if the regime's media gurus could conjure up ways to claim successes on the domestic front, there were tangible difficulties in pronouncing any victories vis-à-vis India. In a setback to Ayub's American-centered foreign policy, relations with Washington soured during John F. Kennedy's tenure as president in 1960. The fanfare surrounding Ayub's visit to Washington in 1961 soon died down. The new Democratic administration considered India a better bet for both strategic and economic reasons. The Sino-Indian War of 1962 only confirmed the US White House of this view. In the aftermath of the war, India became the recipient of generous flows of military and economic assistance from the

West. Ayub was deeply worried about Pakistan's sagging relationship with the United States and feared that a potentially debilitating strategic imbalance was being created by the Western rearmament of India. The feisty Zulfikar Ali Bhutto, who was now foreign minister, persuaded Ayub that the best retort to the shift in US priorities was to forge stronger ties with China. Though a member of SEATO, Pakistan needed to take a more independent line on American policies toward Vietnam in order to establish its credentials in Asia and Africa. British policies east of Suez, most notably in Malaysia, also came in for hard questioning.

The Pakistani government's newfound anti-imperialist stance aimed at correcting the negative public impression of the directions taken in the past on the foreign policy front. Far more substantive were the series of trade and military agreements negotiated with China that helped establish a number of industrial projects in Pakistan. To propel the new relationship into greener pastures, Bhutto advocated settling Pakistan's boundary with China. On March 2, 1963, he signed the Sino-Pakistan boundary agreement delimiting some 300 miles of their common boundary separating Hunza and Baltistan from Sinkiang. In return for acknowledging Chinese sovereignty in large swathes of northern Kashmir and Ladakh, Pakistan got 1,350 of the 3,400 square miles in dispute, including 750 square miles previously under Chinese control. It was a typically Bhutto move. Lacking the requisite firepower to take on India, Pakistan underlined its rejection of the status quo by voluntarily giving away a part of the disputed territory to China. The stroke of genius qualified Pakistan for Chinese economic and military largesse at a time when American assistance was beginning to dry up.

The 1965 War with India

The success of his China initiative encouraged Bhutto to try and assert himself more on the foreign policy front. He began hobnobbing with Aziz Ahmed, the foreign secretary, and Major General Akhtar Hussain Malik, the commander of the Twelfth Division stationed near Indian-occupied Kashmir. They agreed that Pakistan had to try and take Kashmir before India edged ahead decisively on the military front with the help of Western armaments. The situation on the ground looked propitious. There was growing disaffection in Kashmir with New Delhi's meddling designed to erode the autonomy of the former princely state. On December 27, 1963, the underlying ferment in the state erupted into popular protests after the theft of the Prophet Muhammad's hair from the Hazrat Bal shrine. The relic was recovered, but to the dismay of Kashmiri Muslims, the culprits were never punished. In April 1964, the preeminent Kashmiri leader, Sheikh Abdullah, jailed in 1953 because of differences with Nehru, was released from prison. After he returned from a visit to Pakistan, where he received a warm welcome and held talks with Ayub and Bhutto, Abdullah was rearrested, infuriating his Kashmiri supporters. Anger toward India did not necessarily translate into pro-Pakistan sentiments but was nevertheless an opening worth exploiting further.

Relations with Afghanistan, too, were less overtly hostile than ever, releasing critical pressure on the Pakistani Army in the north as well as along much of the western front. This would enable the Pakistani Army to use its full force against India. These musings received a boost when in the spring of 1965 Pakistan appeared to have got the better of India militarily in a clash over the Rann of Kutch, an arid desert abutting Sindh and Indian Rajasthan. Bhutto wrote a ten-page memorandum calling for a military push into Kashmir and, more implicitly, for a Pakistani-backed Kashmiri uprising against India. Taking comfort in India's defeat at Chinese hands and its misadventure in the sand dunes of the Rann of Kutch, Bhutto argued that the Pakistani Army could outclass its rival despite being outnumbered by four to one. "The situation precipitated by India" in the Rann of Kutch gave Pakistan "an opportunity to hit back hard in self-defence, maim and cripple her forces in such a way as to make it virtually impossible for India to embark on a total war against Pakistan for the next decade or so." Timing was of the essence. With the "advent of massive U.S. military assistance," India's "desire to administer a crushing defeat to Pakistan is bound to increase with the passage of time." Although any conflict could potentially spiral out of control, India was "at present in no position to risk a general war of unlimited duration for the annihilation of Pakistan." Apart from economic difficulties, India had to contend with the "relative superiority of the military forces of Pakistan" in terms of equipment and morale. India in all probability would want to take some military action to restore the self-esteem of its armed forces after being discomfited in the Rann of Kutch. However, Bhutto thought it unlikely that India would take retaliatory action across Punjab's frontier, where

Pakistan's forces were well poised or, for that matter, disturb the status quo along the cease-fire line in Kashmir. It might be tempted to take military action in East Pakistan, where Pakistani defenses were vulnerable, but it could do so only at the risk of provoking the Chinese.[28]

As commander-in-chief of the Pakistani Army General Musa realized, it was a tactically ingenious but strategically flawed plan. The success of a forward thrust in Kashmir depended on India not attacking West Pakistan along the international border. In a firm but politely worded note to Bhutto, Musa disputed the notion that India would at most strike in the southwestern sector of East Pakistan and that a general war of even a short duration was improbable. On the contrary, Musa thought Pakistan had to be fully prepared to take immediate and effective counterretaliatory measures on several fronts. Nothing could be more "futile" than to take territory in Kashmir that "we might lose due to our failure to protect it."[29] What seems to have ultimately clinched the argument for Ayub was his foreign minister's confident assertion that as far as Kashmir was concerned, it was a matter of acting now or never. By early 1965, the prospects of an Indo-Pakistan rapprochement on Kashmir looked remote. India openly dismissed the UN resolutions on the issue as "obsolete" because of Pakistani and Chinese aggression in Kashmir. Even General Musa agreed with Bhutto that regardless of whether Pakistan managed to maintain a military balance with India, it would be too late two to four years down the line to take Kashmir. Playing on the president's fears of the new direction in American policy toward the subcontinent, Bhutto wrote impishly: "just as today we have to be thankful to the United States for placing us in a position in which we can wage a war of self-defence, two years from now, our people will curse the United States for giving India the capacity to launch a war of annihilation on Pakistan."[30]

In the first week of July 1965, Bhutto found his opportunity to go for the kill once Washington abruptly announced a two-month postponement in the meeting of the consortium of countries set up to sanction foreign aid to Pakistan. In a flurry of memos directed at persuading Ayub to approve military action in Kashmir, the foreign minister interpreted the delay as a political move by President Lyndon Baines Johnson. Facing escalating domestic and international pressure over his government's policy in Vietnam, Johnson was seen to be angling for Pakistan's acquiescence in America's global policy of pitting India against China. This would be "disastrous" because the United States wanted to align Pakistan behind India in "a de facto Akhund Bharat arrangement" that would "mean the complete surrender of Jammu and Kashmir and the relegation of the Pakistani people to the position of second class citizens suffering the same fate as that of Muslims in India." No regime could survive such a disastrous course of action, as Pakistanis "will never accept a position of subservience to India."[31]

In an assessment fluctuating between passages of acute perceptiveness and extreme emotion, Bhutto told Ayub to take a tough stand with Washington. During the three years since the Sino-Indian War, Pakistan had demonstrated "utmost restraint" toward US policies that had "gone to the extent of endangering our national security." Despite all the "valuable contributions" they had made to the American cause internationally as a member of CENTO and SEATO, Pakistanis were being threatened and browbeaten. A modest concession to the US hope of aligning Pakistan behind India in order to contain China would result in losing all the advantages of the carefully cultivated pro-Chinese policy. Pakistan would lose respect domestically and internationally. Gamal Abdul Nasser had shown the way with his gallant stand when threatened by the Americans over the Aswan Dam. Nasser told them to "go drink from the Red Sea." Washington's immediate reaction was to retract its position, illustrating the Anglo-Saxon tendency "to exploit decency and moderation" but "speedily come to terms with obduracy and firmness." It was time Pakistan showed stiff resolve against American dictation. Even if Washington withdrew all its aid, which was doubtful, "the Pakistan nation will not crash like a stock exchange." The national economy was sturdy enough to tide over the crisis with some adjustment in its development goals and help from other sources.[32]

With the American stock sinking sharply in the Asian political market because of the Vietnam quagmire, Bhutto did not think the United States could afford to lose Pakistan. If Pakistan could seize the advantage by making as many territorial and tactical gains as possible in Kashmir within a week or two, the UN would be forced to intervene and enforce a settlement. In his considered opinion, the people of Pakistan were more united than at any other time in the country's history and would support any attempt to resist American interference. Bhutto accused the American Peace Corps stationed in Pakistan of engaging in unacceptable activities against the regime during the 1965 elections. "They are in our hair, under our nails—they are to be found every where," he bellowed. Bhutto concluded by warning that the United States was now seeking to get rid of him and "even the President himself."[33]

Linking the military action in Kashmir to Ayub's own political future was a masterstroke. Bhutto is thought to have laid the snare along with hard-liners in the civil service, such as the foreign and information secretaries Aziz Ahmed and Altaf Gauhar, to advance his own political future. The 1965 elections had underlined the difficulty of ejecting Ayub from within the confines of his bureaucratically monitored political system. So an exit strategy had to be imposed on him instead. Officials at the Indian Ministry of External Affairs attributed the incursions to "a struggle for power going on in Pakistan," with the faction led by the foreign minister "working to remove President Ayub and substitute Bhutto as the head of the Government."[34] Whatever Bhutto's ultimate reasons for advocating a limited war in Kashmir, the president fell for it and gave the green signal for the operation. Expectation that India would not attack Pakistan if it meddled in Kashmir proved to be a chimera, sustained by faulty intelligence provided by the military's main spy agencies. The ISI and MI assumed that there would be a spontaneous popular revolt in Kashmir soon after the incursions, which were timed to coincide with a general strike. They were wrong. Support for the 5,000 or more infiltrators, styled as "liberators" by the local populace, was passive in light of the heavy concentration of police and armed forces in Srinagar.[35]

What followed was a bungled operation called Gibraltar, which was supplemented by Operation Grand Slam to take Akhnoor and threaten India's hold over Kashmir. Significantly, the military high command remained lukewarm in its support for both operations, convinced that the conflict could not remain confined to Kashmir. But once Ayub had bitten on the bait, there was no scope for dissent among the officer corps. If GHQ was a less than willing participant, most Kashmiris were too absorbed with everyday struggles to earn a living to risk taking on the Indian security forces. There was no spontaneous popular revolt. Trained guerillas from camps in Azad Kashmir, some of whom were originally from Srinagar, had been organized into groups named after famous Muslim military heroes under the command of the Pakistani Army. They were supposed to pave the way for a decisive military thrust into Kashmir. Instead of performing heroics, the infiltrators were caught the instant they entered Indian-occupied Kashmir in August of 1965. Four of them divulged the secret operational plans on All-India Radio.

India used this as the pretext to launch a three-pronged attack on Pakistan along the international border at Wagah near Lahore in the early morning hours of September 6, 1965. The attack was repelled. There were extraordinary displays of gallantry, adding to the pantheon of national heroes. Washington's decision to cut off arm supplies and stay neutral in the war came as a rude shock for Pakistan, America's most loyal ally in Asia. Unable to replenish its rapidly depleting ammunition, the Pakistani war machinery could neither best its rival nor make a decisive move to take Kashmir. As Bhutto had anticipated, the outbreak of hostilities between the subcontinental neighbors came at a most inconvenient time for the Americans, who were thoroughly engrossed with Vietnam and, closer to home, with a controversial intervention in the civil war in the Dominican Republic. The Soviets, too, were perturbed by conflict on their southern flank. It might lead to interference by outside powers, forcing them to back India against the Chinese with consequent damage to Soviet interests in North Vietnam. A cease-fire between India and Pakistan was, therefore, a top priority for Moscow, which had strategic differences but a common tactical interest with the Western powers in bringing a quick end to the war under the auspices of the UN Security Council. Recognizing that the Soviets had a stake in the resolution of the dispute, the British in unison with the Americans backed efforts by the UN Secretary General to negotiate a cease-fire while at the same secretly encouraging Moscow to take the lead in getting India and Pakistan to agree to a long-term settlement in Kashmir. This saved Pakistan from humiliation. The suspension of military supplies from the United States had grounded most of its air force and left the army capable of fighting for only a few more days.

These hard realities were a stretch removed from popular expectations in West Pakistan. Programmed by official propaganda into believing that one Pakistani solider was equal to ten Indians, people in the western wing responded to the war with an unprecedented show of patriotism. Poets and singers volunteered their services to Radio Pakistan, which aired a series of patriotic songs that remained part of the national repertoire long after the 1965 war had slipped from public memory. The courage of the citizens of Lahore in withstanding the Indian attack and repeated aerial bombardment was celebrated with special gusto. Pakistan's leading female singer, Noor Jahan, won hearts and minds with her inspirational and melodious songs in praise of the men in arms. Miraculous stories were circulated during the short-lived war, encapsulating the spirituality embedded in regional cultures on the one hand and, on the other, the impact of the officially encouraged belief in the superiority of the Pakistani forces over their Indian foes. Journalists returning from battlefields reported that Indians surrendered because they thought they were completely outnumbered when the Pakistani forces were actually small in number. The idea melded well with the yarn that men in white had descended from the heavens to assist the Pakistani Army. A letter appeared in the Urdu daily *Jang,* claiming that the Holy Prophet had been sighted in Medina riding a horse "Going on Jihad in Pakistan."[36]

Notwithstanding the fantastical elements, the 1965 war elicited a rare sense of national solidarity in the west. Citizens assisted by students organized demonstrations in Karachi and Lahore in support of Pakistan's demand for a plebiscite in Kashmir. Substantial Pathan representation in the armed forces also ensured support in the NWFP. However, backing for the war was noticeably absent in the eastern wing, where Kashmir and the related Indus water dispute were nonissues. From the East Pakistani perspective, the center's preoccupation with Kashmir was a barrier to improved relations with India without which there was no real prospect of settling the dispute over the sharing of the Ganges river waters between the two Bengals. Bengalis had always resented the Pakistani military credo that the defense of East Pakistan lay in the west. They saw concrete proof of their place in the priorities of the national security state when they were left defenseless during the war. The Chinese "ultimatum" to India on September 17, 1965, demanding the removal of Indian fortifications along their disputed border in Sikkim, fell miserably short of giving East Pakistanis a sense of security. There was no chance of China intervening militarily from the north to defend Pakistan's eastern wing, but Beijing used the opportunity to condemn India's designs in Sikkim and Kashmir. This raised alarm bells in several capitals across the globe and, most important, in New Delhi. Once India promptly complied with the demand, the Chinese were at pains to deny that they had ever issued the "ultimatum."[37] Ayub himself was wary of encouraging a Chinese intervention, recognizing that it would mean international condemnation and likely expulsion from the Western bloc. After the 1965 war, Pakistan accused New Delhi of pushing Muslims from Assam into East Pakistan and abruptly sealing its borders with India. This incensed Bengalis, who made a living from a thriving two-way trade in smuggled goods, and intensified feelings of alienation toward West Pakistan.

These were ominous signs in view of the economic fallout of the seventeen-day war. Heavily dependent on foreign aid, Pakistanis were astounded by Washington's suspension of military and economic assistance to protest the violation of the understanding that American arms would not be used against India. Drastic cutbacks in foreign aid followed, adversely affecting all sectors of an economy that just the previous year had grown at a rate of 6.5 percent. The official government report on the state of the economy in 1963–64 had presented a rosy picture of the future, no doubt with a view to the forthcoming presidential elections. Despite structural problems in the agricultural sector and a spiraling population growth rate, crop yields had been higher, export earnings were better than expected, and the Second Five Year Plan's ambitious target of a 24 percent national growth rate had seemed within reach. But the robustness of an aid-dependent economy could always be exaggerated. As soon as international aid was reduced to a trickle, development funds had to be scaled down in order to divert resources to defense expenditure. With debt servicing already accounting for 10 percent of the export earnings, the impact of the 1965 war on Pakistan's economic prospects were grimmer than anyone had anticipated.

Fighting a hugely expensive war against India to a stalemate was not an achievement Ayub could gloat about. The war revealed the weaknesses and incoherence in the Pakistani Army's command and execution skills. Rapid promotions through the ranks had bred a culture of sycophancy and a consequent decline in standards. The war itself exposed the army's abject dependence on the continued supply of American weapons. A US embargo on arms and ammunition to the two combatants hurt Pakistan more than India. Many in Pakistan saw this as a betrayal in their moment of dire need and led to America being dubbed a "fair-weather friend." Bhutto is generally seen to have plotted the war to sideline the pro-American party in the government and, in due course, to turn the popular rage against Ayub himself. Regardless of the veracity of the charge, the foreign minister managed to overcome his pride to plead with the Americans not

to bring the Pakistani military machine to a grinding halt. If the necessary military supplies could not be given on the usual grant basis, then
Pakistanis were ready to pay cash. They would "sell all their possessions,"
Bhutto asserted emotionally, "even their family heirlooms in order to get
the means to continue the struggle until the Indian invasion [was] re-
pulsed and Kashmiri rights established."[38]

The sentiment was widely shared in the urban centers of Punjab. Government propaganda had led people to think they were winning the war. A
corollary to this misinformation was the officially planted view that Pakistan had been in a position to take Kashmir but had been forced by the international community under UN auspices to accept a cease-fire. Bhutto
was among the most eloquent advocates of this view. Perturbed by Ayub's
expressions of anger at US betrayal, the Americans turned to their point
man in the Pakistani capital—the finance minister Muhammad Shoaib—to
assess whether the disappointing progress of the military campaign in
Kashmir had changed the field marshal's attitude. On the thirteenth day of
the war, Shoaib met with Ayub and reported that he was "disenchanted
with Bhutto's reckless adventurism," "grieved" by the losses Pakistan had
suffered, reluctant to forge any alliance with the Chinese, and willing to
compromise with India. But Ayub knew that an admission of failure after
the sacrifices made would cause the fall of his government.[39]

By that time Pakistan was fast running out of firepower. So it accepted
the UN-sponsored cease-fire on September 22, 1965. Official media hacks
created the illusion that Pakistan had "won" the war, a difficult proposition to sustain considering that India's grip on Kashmir remained un-
shaken. Pakistan's attempt to link the withdrawal of troops from the border to a settlement of the Kashmir dispute made little headway. India for
its part insisted on the prior removal of all the infiltrators before it pulled
back its troops. This made for an uneasy peace along the cease-fire line
and gave the Americans and the British incentive to back the Soviet initiative to invite the leaders of India and Pakistan to Tashkent to discuss
the formal cessation of hostilities. President Johnson summed up the
American attitude when he said that both sides had to agree to the cease-
fire unconditionally. The United States had to remain "strictly neutral"
and issue "no threats," but India and Pakistan "just can't afford to have
this World War III. . . . They can't have that kind of crime around their
necks."[40]

The 1965 war was a turning point in the US–Pakistan Cold War alliance. Built on mutually contradictory interests from the outset, the relationship had been on a downward incline since the Sino-Indian War in 1962, but the myth of the "special relationship" persisted. Untutored in the subtleties of international relations, ordinary Pakistanis felt betrayed and accused America of stabbing them in the back. The closure of smaller American facilities by the government was matched by public displays of outrage against the United States in the streets of West Pakistan. Mobs in Karachi were seen with handbills of a newspaper article that had appeared in the *Daily Telegraph* about how the CIA started the 1965 war in an effort to get rid of Ayub. The Americans suspected Bhutto's hand in this and condemned his political gamesmanship. But they were more irked by the discovery that some of their Pakistani friends had sent photographs of mobs damaging the United States Information Service (USIS) installations in Karachi to the Turks, presumably to instruct them on how to deal with American facilities.[41]

In an effort to salvage something out of their damaged relationship and, in the process, douse the anti-American fires in Pakistan, President Johnson invited Ayub Khan to Washington in December of 1965 for a tête-à-tête. The discussions were to be based on certain ground rules that were interpreted in Pakistan as an "ultimatum," creating a public outcry against the president going to Washington. The visit only served to underscore the State Department's misgivings about Bhutto and strengthen American resolve not to be drawn into the Kashmir dispute beyond what was acceptable to India. In an uncompromising mood, Johnson candidly told Ayub that he should "get it out of his system" that the United States could pressure India on Kashmir. American differences with India were economic while those with Pakistan were political. Johnson then proceeded to muddy the waters by calling the 1965 war between India and Pakistan a "civil war." As if this were not enough, the American president, sensitive to criticisms of his Vietnam policies, went out of his way to snub Bhutto by giving greater importance to the foreign secretary, Aziz Ahmed. The final straw was Johnson's assertion that he was prepared to resume economic aid to Pakistan if the interests of the two countries converged. If this was the inducement, Ayub Khan was subtly reminded that the price for noncompliance with Washington's purposes could mean his being ousted like other dictators who had fallen out of favor.[42] Knowing on which side his bread was buttered, the Pakistani president told his American hosts that he wanted "nothing to do with the Chinese" but was "trying to prevent [Pakistan] from being eaten up."[43]

After their meeting in the Oval Office on December 15, 1965, President Johnson talked about "how close he felt to Ayub" and how well he understood the Pakistani president's fears and problems. He had assured Ayub that the United States would not let India "gobble up Pakistan." In return, Pakistan had to keep China at an arm's length.[44] Ayub's "ecstatic" account of his final round of talks with Johnson led to much conjecture in Pakistan. On Bhutto's instructions, the report prepared by the Foreign Office on the president's visit to the United States stated that a "secret understanding" appeared to have been reached that entailed sacrificing the Pakistani foreign minister.[45] Tensions between Ayub and his erstwhile protégé were registered in Washington and London before they made themselves felt on the Pakistani domestic political scene. The real opening for the mercurial foreign minister came after Ayub Khan signed the Tashkent Declaration in January 1966 with Prime Minister Lal Bahadur Shastri of India. American approval of the declaration gave weight to Bhutto's contention that Ayub had bartered away Pakistan's interests in Kashmir at Tashkent. Misled by the state's propaganda machinery into overestimating Pakistan's defense capabilities, people widely held that the war had been won militarily but lost politically. Bhutto exploited the trend in popular opinion by insinuating a possible deal between Ayub and Shastri at Tashkent. The impact of the foreign minister's "revelation" on a volatile political situation was explosive. In June 1966, Bhutto "resigned," ostensibly under American pressure, after being issued a notice to quit in January. According to informed sources, it was "the British who had more influence in removing Mr. Bhutto than the Americans." In a private conversation with the Pakistani president, Prime Minister Harold Wilson had commented that he was "puzzled by the fact that Ayub and his foreign minister spoke with different voices." Ayub was thought to have leaked the story to order to counter criticism in Pakistan that he had "given way to the Americans in sacking Bhutto."[46]

Aftershocks of War

If the 1965 presidential elections had underscored the impossibility of dislodging Ayub through the basic democracies system, an inconclusive war with India opened the floodgates for his downfall. The costs of the war burned a gaping hole in the central exchequer's pocket. Depletion of military stores and the continued suspension of American military assistance saw defense expenditure being hiked by 17 percent during 1965–66, imposing strains on a stumbling economy. Business confidence had been badly shaken, leading to a fall in private investment and a corresponding slowing down of Pakistan's previously impressive growth rate. As industrial production dropped sharply, inflation skyrocketed. The introduction of "Green Revolution" technologies led to hikes in production for larger landlords, who acquired land previously cultivated by tenants and squeezed out middling farmers, aggravating social polarization in the agrarian sector. Increased landlessness led to a sharp rise in rural–urban migration, heightening pressures on already congested cities. Two consecutive monsoon failures in 1965 and 1966 resulted in a food shortage, particularly acute in East Pakistan, forcing the government to import food at a time when foreign aid had declined by as much as 25 percent.

Political resentments in the different regions, inflamed by the economic duress of social classes marginalized by capitalist-orientated growth strategies, were a potent brew for a regime facing international disdain for its abortive military adventurism. The 1965 war was an eye-opener for the Bengalis. They always objected to the West Pakistan–centered military doctrine, but now discovered to their dismay that their security against any Indian misadventure had been outsourced to China. For the proponents of the two-economy thesis, this was concrete evidence of the inherent injustice of East Pakistan being made to contribute to the center's defense budget while its own population lived a marginal existence.

Paradoxically, the real opportunity for the advocates of autonomy for East Pakistan came just as the economic trends were registering a slight decrease in regional disparities. West Pakistan's export earnings had started outpacing those of East Pakistan. Some Bengali entrepreneurs had begun emerging. The Ayub regime was plowing more development funds into the eastern wing and taking steps to improve Bengali representation in senior ranks of the civil service. But after the 1965 war and the adverse economic effects of restrictions on cross-border trade with India, these palliatives were an instance of too little, too late.[47] The combined impact of the center's differential economic policies and postwar inflation had reduced the already low standard of living in the East Pakistani countryside, home to a large proportion of the industrial labor force and university students. Against the backdrop of labor militancy and radical student activism, the main political parties demanded an immediate return to democracy, the end of "one unit" in West Pakistan, and the devolution of political and economic power to the constituent units. The leader of the East Pakistan–based Awami League, Sheikh Mujibur Rahman, unfurled a six-point program for provincial autonomy in February 1966, pointing to growing economic disparities between the two wings and the inadequate representation of Bengalis in the military and the civil bureaucracy.

The Awami League's six-point program was the firecracker that lit the tinderbox of disillusionments in Ayub's Pakistan. Instead of permitting an open discussion to flush out the merits and demerits of the Awami League's program for provincial autonomy in public, a paranoid West Pakistani establishment accustomed to functioning like a semipolice state, dubbed the demands secessionist. It was a colossal mistake. The opposition to Ayub in West Pakistan was at sixes and sevens and in no position to seriously challenge the regime. Bhutto was a potential menace, but the state's coercive arms were deployed to the fullest extent to restrict his political activities. Ironically, it was Ayub's own inability to read the direction in which the wind was blowing that hastened his political demise. In September 1966, he broke off with the Nawab of Kalabagh, accusing him of deviousness and betrayal, and appointed the loyalist and former commander-in-chief General Musa as governor of West Pakistan. The removal of the regime's most dreaded official opened up space for long-suffering opposition politicians in the west. In December 1966, the end of the ban on 5,000 disqualified politicians led to some of them joining Ayub's Convention Muslim League, which he intended to turn into a mass-based party in both parts of the country. For a regime that was fast becoming a police state and completely out of touch with the people, this was little more than a pipe dream.

East Pakistan posed the single biggest threat to the regime. Bengalis were united in opposition to the central government and Ayub's chosen governor, Monem Khan, had become an object of public disdain. The elected representatives were self-servingly corrupt and incapable of countering the rising popularity of the discourse on autonomy, some of which bordered on secession. In May 1967, the Council Muslim League, the Jamaat-i-Islami, and the Nizam-i-Islam parties coalesced with the Awami

League in the Pakistan Democratic Movement Although not going as far as the six-points policy, they demanded the restoration of parliamentary government based on direct elections and universal suffrage; a federal center restricted to defense, foreign affairs, currency, communications, and trade; separate foreign exchange accounts for the two wings based on their export earnings; relocation of the naval headquarters from Karachi to East Pakistan; and the achievement of parity in the state services within ten years.

By the summer of 1967, Ayub appeared to be vacillating before the force of demands for autonomy in East Pakistan. He had been struck by the strength of the provincial sentiments voiced by Bengali politicians attending the national assembly session in Rawalpindi. Some of the younger West Pakistani officers around Ayub also impressed on him the need to establish a looser relationship between the two wings as this was the only hope left for a united Pakistan. A firm believer in keeping secessionists on a tight leash, the general had gone to the other extreme and was leaning toward a confederation. The Bengali opposition leader Nurul Amin "opposed the idea and said he and his friends do not want a confederation." The president was extremely concerned about foreign policy matters. He wanted peace with India but was "disheartened" by New Delhi's attitude. Ayub is reported to have sounded "very anti-American" and was "very worried" because he feared "the CIA was plotting against him all the time."[48]

Ayub's posthumously published private dairies provide a different take on his state of mind at a time of intensifying pressure. "I am giving them all the resources possible for development," he bitterly complained, but "both the provincialists and the secessionists" have "combined to blackmail the centre and sow discord between East and West Pakistan." To spite their coreligionists in West Pakistan, Bengalis were "consciously Hinduizing the[ir] language and culture" and "Tagore has become their god." All the signs in East Pakistan, even number plates on vehicles, were in Bengali, with the result that "a West Pakistani feels like a foreigner in Dacca."[49] Ayub's line of thinking was unmistakable. Further concessions to the Bengali majority demanded their adherence to the dominant narratives of nationhood authored in the west. The more East Pakistanis wanted closer ties with India, the stronger would be the authoritarian center's disciplinary response. In an ill-conceived step, the regime decided to extend the state of emergency that had been declared at the onset of the 1965 war.

All opposition politics were now equated in the language of officialdom as subversive antistate activity—a very wide and flexible category. In early 1968, the Awami League leader Mujibur Rahman and thirty-four others were accused of plotting with India to dismember the country. Known as the Agartala Conspiracy Case, the court proceedings provoked an outburst of Bengali anger. The regime was forced to withdraw the case. Mujib now was the icon of a surging Bengali nationalism.

Developments in the west also spelled disaster for a regime that dealt with provincial autonomy demands from a rigid national security perspective. Just as the Indian bugbear was used to delegitimize Bengali demands for a better share out of resources with the center, Balochi calls for an end to "one-unit" governance and a higher percentage of the royalties from natural gas resources at Sui were treated as part of a treacherous plot to make common cause with Afghanistan. Trapped by the limiting vision of its national narratives, the Ayub regime was unable to pacify the Baloch sardars or cultivate support among the provincial middle classes with its development projects, many of which were put into place from a security perspective. The building of military installations in conflict areas during the early 1960s provided the catalyst for armed insurgency in the Marri, Mengal, and Bugti tribal areas. By 1964 a point had been reached when Kalabagh's stick had broken off all contacts between the tribes and the government. Upon becoming governor of West Pakistan, General Musa, a Hazara of Afghan origin who was born in Balochistan, made special gestures to placate the tribal chiefs and reconcile them to Pakistan. Except for this short-lived interlude, Balochistan remained up in arms for most of the Ayub period, forcing the central government to seek recourse in army action and aerial bombing.

No less ominous was the unrest in Sindh, where opposition to Ayub was gaining momentum. Bhutto had stormed into the limelight with his belligerent stance on the Tashkent Declaration. Bhutto had attributed Washington's decision in April 1967 not to resume military assistance to Pakistan and India after the 1965 war to the imperatives of an escalating war in Vietnam. He characterized American policy toward Pakistan as a "please–punch" approach. To achieve its national objectives, the United States pushed Pakistan closer into its global orbit with a gesture to "please" in the form of economic assistance. This was followed by a "punch" and then another round of economic palliatives. The United States would continue imposing its strategic objectives until Pakistan drew the line and said "no further."[50] On December 1, 1967, Bhutto launched the Pakistan People's Party (PPP), comprising leftists and liberals of varied hues. Vowing Islam as its faith, democracy as its politics, and socialism as its economy, the PPP promised all power to the people and adopted the populist slogan: "Food, clothing and housing is everyone's demand." Before the PPP could sink its roots among a disaffected populace, there was a mass uprising against Ayub that knocked the bottom out of his exclusionary and repressive political system. In 1967 he had launched his autobiography, *Friends Not Masters,* with considerable fanfare as part of a public relations exercise to promote the regime both at home and abroad. While Pakistanis were agitating to protest its failures, the regime's deep inner circle trumpeted Ayub's accomplishments through an expensive and intrusive media blitz. The people's rage against this blatant propaganda was palpable.

Bhutto inflamed students and lawyers with detailed descriptions of the regime's crimes and misdemeanors, drawing attention to the corruption of Ayub's sons and extended family; administrative inefficiency; graft and venality; heightening social and economic disparities; and, most egregiously, the stifling of any free expression of public opinion. The regime had become irremediably unpopular. Anyone with the courage to take on its coercive arms could acquire an instant following among a disenchanted and directionless populace. Bhutto was quick to snap up the opportunity and cash in on student discontents. His moment came on November 7, 1968, when 3,000 students in Rawalpindi defied a ban on meetings to welcome him. Two people were killed when police opened fire, inciting student protests in all major cities of West Pakistan. Lawyers and civil society groups joined unprecedented street demonstrations to protest the regime's imperious treatment of the students. The USIS library in Peshawar was ransacked. On November 10, Ayub survived an amateur assassination attempt by a disgruntled pro-Bhutto student while addressing an open-air meeting in Peshawar, leading many to suspect that it was an official plot to discredit the opposition.[51]

On November 13, 1968, Bhutto was arrested along with Wali Khan, the leader of the NWFP-based National Awami Party, under the Defense of Pakistan Rules (DPR). The former air marshal Asghar Khan also joined the fray, condemning Ayub for maladministration, nepotism, and corruption. But it was Bhutto who captured the popular imagination. Students inspired by contemporary movements spearheaded by their counterparts in other parts of the globe, such as Paris and Mexico City, rallied to his side. In the affidavit challenging his detention, Bhutto ranted against a regime of which he until recently had been a key defender. He was not planning a violent overthrow of the government, but its "misrule and oppression" had alienated the people. "The popular agitation in the country," Bhutto declaimed, was "a spontaneous verdict of the people against the excess of the regime, its corruption, its selfish purposes, its contempt for the rights of man, its corroding of institutions, its dependence on an oppressive bureaucracy, its failure to serve the common weal, its pedantic approach to culture, its insulation from the people and its insatiable appetite for family fortunes." He used the "weapon of language" only to rouse the people while the government, which had "slandered" the word "revolution" in describing its own illegal takeover, was capriciously using the "language of weapons" to suppress a democratic movement: "Everywhere the blood of innocents has watered the land, sometimes in Baluchistan and sometimes in East Pakistan. On occasion it is in the Punjab and Sind; on others, in the ramparts of our northern regions." Every bit the populist, Bhutto waxed eloquent on the virtues of democracy. More than a feeling, democracy was about "fundamental rights, adult franchise, the secrecy of ballot, freedom of the press and association, independence of the judiciary, supremacy of the legislature, controls on the executive—in short, everything that was sorely missing under the current regime."[52]

Between November 1968 and March 1969, students, industrial labor, lower-grade government servants, and even the ulema took to the streets in key urban centers to protest the regime's sins of omission and commission. Their demand was categorical: "Ayub must go." An unrepentant Ayub called Bhutto and Asghar Khan "charlatans and self-seekers" and bemoaned the "gangsterism" and "madness" parading the streets. In the president's opinion, the opposition was "paving the way for the disintegration of the country." "My fight," he stated self-righteously, "is to save us from this disaster." He could not have been more wide of the mark. The restrictions on political activities, controls on the media, and suppression of free speech were coming back to haunt the dictator. After a serious heart attack in January 1968, Ayub was relieved of effective power by his trusted commander-in-chief, General Yahya Khan. A virtual palace coup had taken place. Once the turmoil took a turn for the worse in early 1969,

Yahya began preparing for the kill. In a desperate attempt to save himself, Ayub announced that he would not contest elections again, leading his information secretary and propaganda maestro Altaf Gauhar to utter: "Pakistan has committed suicide."[53]

Coming from Ayub's top spin doctor, the comment reflects just how much the military–bureaucratic clique surrounding the president was isolated from the actual realities. Even the long suppressed media was breaking loose and criticizing the regime. More ominously, the army was getting politicized and split four ways among supporters of Ayub, Bhutto, Asghar Khan, and Yahya Khan. Lacking an effective political party to counter the growing opposition, the president banked on the continued support of the civil service, the police, the army, and sections of the rural population. Although no longer enjoying a false sense of security, he had not changed his approach to Pakistani politics. He remained opposed to opening up the political system so long as politicians were airing demands like the six-point program. Ayub's contempt for politicians and distrust of intellectuals were so embedded in the regime's thinking that adjusting to the tumult rising from below proved impossible. Other than a few minor concessions to students, the government made no effort to take the public into confidence or try and redress their more ingrained grievances.

At the end of a long and lonely road, Ayub's parting shot was to convene a round table conference to thrash out differences with a political opposition whose internal rifts offered him an outside chance to save face. Held in Rawalpindi on March 10, 1969, all the main opposition politicians attended the conference except Bhutto and Maulana Abdul Hamid Bhashani, the pro-Chinese leader of the East Pakistani left. Days before the meeting, the government tried to assuage the political mood by lifting the emergency in place since the 1965 war. Though united in opposition to the regime, each of the politicians had their own definition of parliamentary democracy. With Mujibur Rahman pressing the six points, and most West Pakistani politicians unwilling to go so far as to concede them on the plea of not wanting to undermine the unity of the country, the conference made no headway before breaking for the Muslim festival of Eid to mark the culmination of the annual pilgrimage to Mecca. Apart from agreeing to dissolve "one unit" in West Pakistan, restore parliamentary government, and hold elections based on universal adult franchise, there was no agreement on key constitutional issues for center–province relations.

On February 21, 1969, Ayub had announced his decision not to contest the next presidential elections and soon after withdrew charges against Mujib in the Agartala Conspiracy Case. Mujib's participation in the round table conference raised doubts about his ability to carry the Awami League's rank and file with him. By then, radicalized students in East Pakistan were dictating the terms of the political debate. Their conditions for dialogue with the government were presented at a rally on February 9, 1969, attended by 100,000 students and urban workers: (1) winding up the Agartala trial, (2) lifting the state of emergency, (3) releasing all those arrested under DPR, and (4) ending all political cases. A student leader conveyed the mood when he asserted that the government's failure to meet these demands would "set the whole of East Pakistan aflame."[54] With such clear warnings from the eastern wing, there was a gnawing sense that groups other than those participating in the round table conference would eventually decide Pakistan's future. Mujib sent a draft amendment bill to Ayub providing for a highly decentralized Pakistan with representation at the center on a population basis. He not only made concessions to West Pakistani regional sentiments by calling for the end of "one unit" and the restoration of the provinces but also indicated that the powers to be retained by the central government were open to negotiation. In private conversations, Mujib repeatedly said that he favored a united and prosperous Pakistan and did not want the eastern wing to secede.[55]

This made for a sharp contrast in attitude with the West Pakistani–dominated establishment and its industrial and landlord supporters. Unwilling to accept a decentralization of power to make way for an open political process, they advocated military intervention to put down labor militancy and regional unrest in the east. There was evidence of growing cynicism among West Pakistani bureaucrats and businessmen, some of whom had come to accept a parting of ways between the two wings as unavoidable and desirable. Senior West Pakistani civil servants opposed fresh allocations of funds to East Pakistan, an ill-conceived policy that further riled the Bengalis. Hard statistics underlined the case for regional disparity in no uncertain terms. In 1966–67, per capita income in the east was Rs.348 compared with Rs.467 in the west, where electricity costs were 40 percent less than in East Pakistan. In an early sign of disengagement by West Pakistanis, big industrial houses like the Adamjees, Dawoods, and Ispahanis were cutting their losses and moving their investments out of the eastern wing. The flight of capital from East Pakistan led to the depreciation of an artificially overvalued rupee by more than half. Economic and political uncertainties compounded fears among the military top brass about their ability to hold the country together in the event of a renewed burst of antigovernment demonstrations in East Pakistan. The men in khaki manning GHQ had other more pressing concerns on their mind. Removing disparities between the two wings invariably meant apportioning larger outlays of investment for the east and a corresponding slowing down of the growth rate in the west. More awkwardly, it meant inducting a larger number of Bengalis into the ranks and a corresponding reduction of recruitment from West Pakistan. The prospect of senior Bengali army officers influencing the future course of Pakistan's national security was a chilling prospect for a Punjabi-dominated military high command.

By the time the governor of East Pakistan, Monem Khan, submitted his resignation on March 2, 1969, the decision to impose martial law had been taken. General Musa, the governor of the western wing, had resigned earlier. Indication that the top generals were planning to intervene for some time was the steady dispatch of additional troops and military equipment from West Pakistan to the eastern wing. Ready to take on the malcontents, they were no longer prepared to serve Ayub. Tainted by the corruption of his sons, the president carried no moral authority. Most Punjabi officers had not forgiven Ayub for his "surrender" at Tashkent. The junior cadres were drawn mainly from the lower classes and, being more politically minded than their predecessors, shared the grievances of the protestors. So on March 3, 1969, when the question of imposing martial law was formally raised, Yahya Khan cited the unreliability of the army, leaving the beleaguered president no option except to step down. In his final address to the nation on March 25, Ayub Khan reaffirmed his conviction in the need for a strong Pakistani center. He had accepted the opposition's demand for a parliamentary government in keeping with that objective, but now the politicians wanted to split the country up into different parts, leaving state institutions ineffective and powerless. The defense services would be crippled and the political entity of West Pakistan abolished—all this at a time when the national economy was in shambles, civil servants were intimidated by mob rule, and serious matters were decided in the streets rather than in parliament house. "I cannot preside over the destruction of my country," Ayub declared disingenuously, before calling on the commander-in-chief to perform his "legal and constitutional responsibility" to not only defend Pakistan from external threats "but also to save it from internal disorder and chaos."[56]

Elections under Martial Law

By the time Ayub Khan abdicated, a sizeable contingent of troops and equipment had been sent to East Pakistan, with more in the pipeline if the need arose. The strength of the army in East Pakistan had risen to a corps of three divisions, making for approximately 40,000 men, including 12,000 of the mainly Bengali paramilitary East Pakistan Rifles.[57] Reasonably satisfied with the security arrangements, GHQ was in no mood to apply the soothing balm to the festering sore in the east. This was overly optimistic as the loyalty of the Bengali component of the security forces remained deeply suspect. But Mujib's demand for an immediate decentralization of power accompanied by the threat of renewed trouble in the east had persuaded the generals to intervene. Ayub's letter asking Yahya Khan to do his "constitutional" duty was supposed to provide a fig leaf of legality to the new dispensation. There was no constitutional provision for martial law. Under the constitution, the speaker of the national assembly Abdul Jabbar Khan from East Pakistan was the legal successor. The imposition of martial law was seen in the eastern wing as a ploy to prevent a Bengali from becoming head of state. This underlined the severe strains in the federal equation due to the chronic imbalance between military and civilian institutions. While most of the western wing quietly accepted the reimposition of martial law, Bengalis were despondent about the turn of events, which they considered an unwarranted occupation by West Pakistan. With food shortages in the countryside from where many university students came, there was far more resentment against than support for the martial law administration in East Pakistan.

Upon becoming the new chief martial law administrator (CMLA), Yahya abrogated the constitution, dissolved the national and the provincial assemblies, and issued a flurry of regulations detailing offenses and punishments as well as trial procedures. The state of martial rule was parading in its full colors. But 1969 was not 1958, when martial law was received with far less consternation. In his opening speech to the nation, Yahya called for sanity as a precondition for constitutional government. Justifying martial law to protect the life and property of citizens and revive the administrative machinery of the state, he promised elections on the basis of adult franchise and a constitution framed according to the will of the people. Keen observers of the political scene could see that the return to martial law in Pakistan was yet another puerile attempt to freeze the problem of democracy. Whatever the merit of Yahya's stated intention to restore democracy, there was now a very real "danger that in East Pakistan martial law w[ould] in effect be only a prelude to the total collapse of the country."[58] Soon after the coup, Yahya slotted himself into the presidential office and declared that the country would be governed as closely as possible to the 1962 constitution. For someone who described himself as a caretaker and a simple soldier who preferred the barracks to the presidential palace, he was in no rush to relinquish power.

Agha Yahya Khan was a Shia from the Qizilbash family of Persian descent. He rose to rule a Sunni-majority country by besting rival generals who contested his credentials to replace Ayub. A boisterous fellow and determined drunkard, Yahya Khan had a penchant for cavorting with abandon. His nocturnal activities were the talk of the nation, with stories about the overweening influence of his procuress Akleem Akhtar aka "General Rani" occupying center stage on the elite gossip circuit. These excesses exposed Yahya to criticism, sparking a struggle for power within the military high command. Although he eventually prevailed, it took him eight months to announce on November 28, 1969, that general elections based on universal adult franchise would be held the following year, on October 5, 1970. The amalgamation of the provinces in the west under "one unit" was to be abolished and the princely states of Chitral, Dir, and Swat merged into West Pakistan. A reversion to a federal parliamentary system of government was conceded in principle. The long-standing Bengali demand for representation according to population was grudgingly conceded. To guard against endless delays in constitution making, the elected national assembly was given 120 days to complete the document, failing which it was to be dissolved and a new assembly elected in its place. A conspicuous omission was the absence of any reference to Bengali demands for provincial autonomy enshrined in Mujib's six points. This was a subtle signal that, notwithstanding the change of guard, there would be more continuity than discontinuity in the regime's policies toward the eastern wing. In keeping with the army's conception of national interests, Yahya considered Bengali demands for autonomy as a subterfuge for secession. Although offering the opposition a few carrots, he was ready to wield the big stick to perpetuate Ayub's policies of centralization.

The new year saw the resumption of political activity and the start of an inexplicably long election campaign. In a clear indication of the regime's wariness of what the elections might throw up, Yahya on March 30, 1970, announced a Legal Framework Order (LFO) that gave him the power to veto any constitutional document prepared by an elected assembly. The LFO was a nonnegotiable template for the future constitution. The only matter left for the people's representatives to decide was the distribution of powers between the center and the provinces. There was to be maximum autonomy for the provinces, but only to an extent consistent with the federal center possessing the requisite powers to preserve the independence and territorial integrity of the country. In a conspicuous omission, the LFO made no mention of the voting method to be employed by the elected assembly in framing a constitution within 120 days. It was apparent that Yahya had given in to the army hawks and diluted popular sovereignty beyond recognition.

All this was designed as an insurance against any political move after the elections to alter the balance of state power to the disadvantage of the military and the civil bureaucracy. For the military mind-set, in particular, any electoral reference to the populace was an inherently destabilizing activity. "The curse of the parliamentary system," Ayub had written in his diary in November 1969, "is that the politicians compete with each other in making fabulous promises to catch votes and find it difficult to retreat from the positions taken."[59] The army high command distrusted Mujib, who they believed was working with India to dismember Pakistan. Bhutto, too, was not above suspicion, especially once he began flirting with socialist ideas. Amid widespread economic distress caused by a shortfall in food production in East Pakistan as well as continuing labor and student unrest, the intelligence agencies feared that the left-leaning parties might have a field day at the polls. A special fund was created for the intelligence agencies to enhance the electoral chances of the so-called pro-Islam parties. The minister of information General Sher Ali Khan played a key role in the regime's efforts to deploy Islamist parties, notably the Jamaat-i-Islami and the Jamiat-i-Ulema-i-Pakistan (JUP), against the PPP and the

Awami League's left-leaning tendencies. Whether out of a misplaced sense of superiority or plain incompetence, the military's intelligence agencies overestimated their success in taking the wind out of the Awami League's and the PPP's sails. The Awami League was expected to get between forty and seventy of the 162 elected national assembly seats from East Pakistan and the PPP no more than twenty to thirty of the 138 elected seats for the western wing.[60]

If wishes were horses, Yahya Khan might have ridden the political twister with exemplary nonchalance. No amount of raw intelligence could exactly predict the outcome of Pakistan's first national election based on universal franchise. Prone to misreading the popular mood, particularly in the east, the intelligence agencies erred in assuming that the electorate would return a hung Parliament, with half a dozen or so parties splitting up the electoral booty. This would give Yahya a controlling hand in the postelectoral scene and, barring the unavoidable concessions to provincial autonomy, shepherd the straying flock of Pakistani politicians into accepting a constitution that upheld all the sacred idioms of the military–bureaucratic state. These assumptions were rocked by events beyond the control of the military intelligence agencies. Monsoon rains in East Pakistan caused heavy flooding, exacerbating the food situation and leading to a postponement of the elections until December. On the night of November 12, a massive cyclone accompanied by high tidal waves devastated the coastline of East Pakistan. One of the deadliest natural disasters in modern history, the cyclone left 200,000 people dead and millions of starving people homeless.

The West Pakistani–based central government's tardy response to the human catastrophe was pilloried in East Pakistan, gifting the Awami League an unexpectedly easy victory that was beyond anything Mujib had anticipated. Bengali middle-class professionals, students, businessmen, and industrial labor, left out of the distribution of economic rewards in Pakistan, would have voted for the Awami League's six-point program for maximum provincial autonomy without an act of God. The main victims of government negligence in the face of a human calamity—the poverty-stricken peasantry in East Pakistan—voted en masse for the Awami League. More than 50 percent of the total electorate in the eastern wing voted in the 1970 elections. Coming at the end of more than a decade of virtual political disenfranchisement, the first general elections on the ba-

sis of universal adult franchise in Pakistan were a remarkable demonstration of the voters' maturity in using the secret ballot to decide their own
future without the traditional influences of mullahs, landlords, or local
leaders. Three-quarters of the votes were cast for the Awami League, giving it all but two of the 162 seats from East Pakistan in a national assembly
consisting of 300 elected and thirteen nonelected members. In the western wing, the PPP surprisingly won more than two-thirds of the seats in
Punjab and Sindh, or eighty-one of the 138 elected seats in the national
assembly from West Pakistan, plus an additional seven reserved for the
Federally Administered Tribal Areas (FATA). The margin of victory of
both the Awami League and the PPP in individual constituencies was
very large. But neither party won a single seat in the other wing, a poor
omen for the postelectoral negotiations to determine how power was to be
shared.

By emphasizing the links between the center and the localities, the basic democracies system had sought to undermine provincial politics. No
amount of gerrymandering or ideological manipulation could alter the
regional basis of politics in Pakistan. Far from diluting the strength of
provincial feelings, a decade of basic democracies under tight administrative control had heightened demands for provincial autonomy from an
unrepresentative and overweening center. Once he did not get the fragmented Parliament of his dreams, Yahya Khan and his top generals took
comfort in the LFO. Although agreeing to hold the first ever national election on the basis of adult franchise, they were strongly averse to transferring power to any political group, from the eastern or the western half of
the country, that aimed at circumscribing the interests or reducing the
dominance of the military and the bureaucracy. In the late 1940s and early
1950s—when the state was still in the process of formation—the sharing of
power between the two wings may have been a matter for the main political party or parties to settle. By 1970–71, the institutional stakes of the
military and the bureaucracy within the existing state structure were
much greater than those of the diverse social groups represented by Mujib's Awami League and Zulfikar Ali Bhutto's PPP. This, rather than the
supposedly irreconcilable differences between east and west Pakistani
electorates and the intransigence of certain politicians, was the more important reason why no political formula for power sharing could be found
to prevent the tragic disintegration of the country.

FIVE

TOWARD THE WATERSHED OF 1971

DURING A VISIT TO DHAKA in the late summer of 1968, Zulfikar Ali Bhutto declared Bengali demands for provincial autonomy to be in the best interests of the country. He assailed civil bureaucrats, the CSP in particular, for treating the people of the eastern wing as "Kala Admees," literally black men. This derogatory attitude had misled the government into implicating Sheikh Mujibur Rahman in the Agartala Conspiracy Case when they might have tried negotiating with him. Self-interested quarters in West Pakistan had started attacking the Awami League's demands the moment they were announced by Mujib without examining their merits and demerits. Bhutto regretted that Mujib had refused his invitation to debate the six points set forth in public. Only two of the six points were "totally unacceptable" to the PPP leader, who was prepared to discuss the others in order to "remove doubts and misgivings." He urged the government to "find some political solution of the problem" as "such issues cannot be solved with force."[1]

Three years later, when the golden hues of eastern Bengal's lush green landscape had been turned red with the steely might of oppression, the sharp-witted Bhutto stood knee deep in the bloodshed in East Pakistan alongside the leadership of a hated military junta. Upon returning to Karachi from Dhaka after the military crackdown on the night of March 25, 1971, the former foreign minister thanked the Almighty for saving Pakistan. He defended the military action publicly and accused Mujibur Rahman of conspiring with India to dismember the country. In private, he conveyed to Yahya Khan that even if limited military action had been found necessary to counter the threat of secession, a resolution of the crisis demanded a political solution that gave the people of the eastern wing their due share of both political and economic power. "If the correct course is not followed," Bhutto wrote in a memo to Yahya Khan, "why should East Pakistanis want to stay as part of Pakistan—what stake would they have left in Pakistan with their due rights denied to them?" Bhutto warned Yahya against projecting discredited Bengali politicians and strongly recommended providing economic relief to the rural populace of East Pakistan who had not yet been swept away by the Awami League's propaganda. It was dangerous to create a situation in which the government was left facing "a hostile public in both Wings during this national crisis, particularly when India is waiting to take advantage of the situation."[2]

The military regime was disinclined to countenance civilian rule until the successful conclusion of the counterinsurgency operations in East Pakistan. Mindful of the risks involved in attacking the junta, Bhutto confined himself to calling for a transfer of power in the west, which he defined as democratization to deflect criticisms of his thirst for power. Similar steps were to be taken in the eastern wing whenever circumstances became conducive. Despite clear differences in their stances, Bhutto has come to be regarded as Yahya Khan's accomplice in the making of the colossal human tragedy that culminated in the breakup of Pakistan in December 1971. Bhutto vehemently denied the charge. His differences with Mujibur Rahman were "not in the nature of a power struggle" but "a struggle of conflicting equities." For the Awami League leader, "equity lay in an independent Bengal, . . . for me in the retention of Pakistan." Mujib claimed that the six points were the property of the people of the eastern wing. For Bhutto, "Pakistan was the property of the people" and the Awami League's demands a "concealed formula for secession." It was in this that "our points of view clashed."[3]

The question of who ultimately was responsible for the 1971 debacle has spawned a rich harvest of commentary. At the political level, the debate on the causes of Pakistan's disintegration has three sides to it in much the same way as the one about India's partition. The Pakistani Army might be seen as replacing the British at the base of the triangle, with Bhutto and Mujib substituting the Muslim League and the Congress as its two sides. As in 1947, the primary hurdle in the way of a mutually acceptable arrangement was how power was to be shared between the main political contenders within a federal state. The similarities between 1947 and 1971 should not be allowed to obfuscate the key difference between them. Unlike the British, who were transferring power before leaving the subcontinent, the Pakistani Army wanted to secure its own interests before passing the mantle to the victorious political parties. Despite the army's self-interest in the outcome of the negotiations with the Awami League, a powerful current of popular opinion in Pakistan and Bangladesh has held that Bhutto in his greed for power bamboozled a mentally and physically unfit Yahya Khan into dismembering the country. On this view, a conniving and unprincipled politician tricked the army into committing national suicide. Although there may be some merit in this view, the events of 1971 also had a fourth dimension in the form of India's role, which had a direct bearing on the Pakistani Army's calculations. To make sense of the single most important watershed in the subcontinent's postindependence history, therefore, requires tracing the evolution of the Awami League's demands for provincial autonomy within the context of the formation and consolidation of Pakistan's military–bureaucratic state structure.

The crisis in East Pakistan had a much longer history than the twelve weeks of post-1970 electoral machinations orchestrated by Bhutto and the military top brass. Even before the creation of Pakistan, there were doubts about the viability of a country separated by a thousand miles with two wings that had nothing in common except adherence to the same religion. Eastern Bengal had formed no part of Muhammad Iqbal's conception of a Muslim homeland. The Lahore resolution of 1940 had spoken of more than one Muslim state in the northwestern and northeastern parts of the subcontinent. On the eve of partition, Jinnah himself had given his blessing to the idea of a united and independent Bengal, commenting that he was certain that it would be on very good terms with Pakistan. Soon after partition, however, Jinnah spoke glowingly of East Bengal as "the most important component of Pakistan, inhabited as it is by the largest single bloc of Muslims in the world." He left no scope for anyone to doubt that the new state was determined to keep its two wings together: "those people who still dream of getting back East Bengal into the Indian Union are living in a dream-land."[4]

The Politics of Denial

Starting its independent career without the semblance of a center, Pakistan showed its determination to parry external and internal threats to its survival by developing an elaborate hydra-like state structure during the first two and a half decades of its existence. Steeped in the classical tradition of colonial bureaucratic authoritarianism, the state sought to penetrate society, extract resources from the economy and manipulate the polity rather than devolve responsibilities or serve as a two-way channel of communication between the rulers and the ruled. The early demise of representative political processes shored up the centralizing logic of bureaucratic authoritarianism, replacing the democratic requirements of consensus with the dictatorial methods of coercion. The primacy of the central state in all spheres of a society characterized by regional heterogeneities and economic disparities generated rancor among the constituent units, breeding a web of political intrigue and instability that affected the functioning of state authority at the local and the provincial levels.

Unable to reconcile the imperatives of state building with those of nation building, successive ruling combinations tried to gain legitimacy by playing up the Indian threat and paying lip service to a vaguely defined Islamic ideology. With a narrowly construed security paradigm defining the center's conception of national interest, the perspective of the provinces was sidelined, if not altogether ignored. Rumblings of protest in the provinces were put down with an iron fist or given short shrift by invoking the common bond of religion. Islam in the service of a military authoritarian state proved to be divisive. Far from unifying a people fractured along regional and class lines, the state's use of religion encouraged self-styled ideologues of Islam to nurture hopes of one day storming the citadels of the Muslim state. The great populist poet Habib Jalib poured scorn on the state's appropriation of Islam to promote national unity. "Islam Is Not In Danger," he cried out in a memorable poem. It was the idle rich, the exploiters of the peasantry and labor, the thieves, tricksters, and traitors in league with Western capitalists who were endangered.[5]

Proponents of such populist ideas were hounded and winnowed out. With the press in chains and civil society the target of novel forms of social and political engineering, the odds were stacked against the advocates of democracy. After derailing the political process in 1958, the military–bureaucratic establishment tried securing its bases of support. This meant bypassing political parties and using state power to bring segments of dominant socioeconomic groups under the regime's sway through differential patronage and selective mobilization. During the heyday of modernization theory in the late 1950s and early 1960s, Pakistan under military rule was hailed in some quarters in the West as a model of social harmony and political stability in the developing world. These expectations were sorely belied by the realities on the ground. The methods employed to construct and consolidate the state exacerbated provincial grievances, with dire consequences for Pakistan's political stability and tenuous federal equation. State-sponsored processes of political inclusion and exclusion, the economics of functional inequality, and neglect of regional disparities made it increasingly difficult to administer two geographically separate parts, triggering the ignominious downfall of two military regimes and sowing the seeds of the disintegration of the country.

The breakup of Pakistan was the result of the autocratic policies of its state managers rather than the inherent difficulties involved in welding together linguistically and culturally diverse constituent units. Islam proved to be dubious cement not because it was unimportant to people in the different regions. Pakistan's regional cultures have absorbed Islam without losing affinity to local languages and customs. With some justification, non-Punjabi provinces came to perceive the use of Islam as a wily attempt by the Punjabi-led military–bureaucratic combine to deprive them of a fair share of political and economic power. Non-Punjabi antipathy toward a Punjabi-dominated center often found expression in assertions of regional distinctiveness. But politics more than cultural difference stoked regional resentments. Clarion calls for provincial autonomy were effectively demands for better job opportunities, basic social services, and a larger cut of state finances.

Here the fault lines in the Pakistani state structure played a decisive role. The demands of the military establishment on the state's meager resources left little for development in the provinces. Seeing India as a near and present danger, the military–bureaucratic establishment used Pakistan's geostrategic location to attract American military and economic assistance in return for supporting Washington's Cold War agenda. Once a partnership had been struck with the United States, a security-conscious state fostered a political economy characterized by high defense and low development expenditure. The primary goal of the state's development initiatives was to enhance revenue rather than social welfare—a process that saw the nonelected institutions edging out the elected institutions in the struggle for dominance in the new state. These nonelected institutions carried a legacy of uneven recruitment patterns from the colonial era, compounding the difficulties in integrating diverse linguistic and socio-economic groups.

An overarching reason for the Pakistani state's faltering steps in the quest for social support and legitimacy was that the federal center came to represent the interests of the dominant nonelected institutions more effectively than those of the regional socioeconomic groups to which at different stages it was loosely tied. Apart from extending patronage to its functionaries and locating them in key sectors of the economy, the state defined the field of political privilege. In the absence of democratic politics, the dominance of a predominantly Punjabi civil bureaucracy and army heightened the grievances of non-Punjabi provinces and the linguistic groups within them. The entrenched institutional supremacy of a Punjabi army and federal bureaucracy, not Punjab's dominance over other provinces per se, had emerged as the principal impediment to restoring democratic processes in Pakistan. In the face of chronic tensions between the center and the regions, the religious glue of Islam alone could not bind a diverse and disparate people into a nation.

The proposed homeland for India's Muslims was envisaged in the Lahore resolution of 1940 as a federation of "sovereign" and "autonomous" units. This hint of confederalism quickly fell by the wayside in the heady aftermath of 1947. The first requirement of the new government in Karachi was to establish its writ over two geographically distinct constituent units. In the absence of a preexisting central apparatus and effective political party machinery in the provinces, pragmatism was the better option. The Government of India Act of 1935 was adapted as the provisional constitution and later made the bedrock of the 1956 and the 1962 constitutions. Aimed at perpetuating, not terminating, colonial rule, the Act of 1935 retained certain unitary features of the British Indian state to counterbalance the concessions to federalism. Unlike most federal systems of government, the constituent units were made subject to a single constitution. The federal center arrogated superior powers in legislative, financial, and political matters. Soon after independence, the provinces were deprived of the financial autonomy granted to them under the act and made dependent on central handouts which, given the severe shortage of funds, were wholly inadequate for their development needs.

The future course of democracy was imperiled in a country whose federal configuration to begin with consisted of fifteen different entities—five provinces and ten princely states—of vastly uneven size and political importance. Troubled by the political implications of an overall Bengali majority in the federation, officialdom in West Pakistan gave enthusiastic support to the merger of the western wing under the one-unit scheme. Unlike the western wing, with its heterogeneities, East Bengal was in relative terms linguistically and culturally homogeneous. It was also politically more volatile than parts of West Pakistan. Bengalis felt passionately about their autonomy and were prone to leftist ideologies and sporadic bouts of violence. They resented the use of their hard-earned foreign exchange to beef up a military establishment wedded to the curious strategic doctrine of defending the eastern wing from West Pakistan. Seeing an Indian hand in Bengali demands for provincial autonomy, the federal government declared them seditious and, in turn, used this to justify its centralizing and homogenizing designs. But neither the threat of India nor the allure of Islam could save the center from the wrath of constituent units reduced to being hapless appendages in a state that was federal in form and unitary in substance.

If East Bengal was a thorn in the side of the federal establishment, the fourteen units composing the western wing presented a political and constitutional conundrum. Most of the princely states claimed some semblance of sovereignty and had to be cajoled and coerced into acceding to Pakistan before being summarily bundled into the one-unit scheme of October 1955. Those that resisted—Kalat, for instance—were clobbered with an iron hand. As the largest of the tribal states in Balochistan, Kalat enjoyed the allegiance of tribal chiefs who, though monitored by the British resident in Quetta, had retained autonomy over their local affairs during the colonial period. The Pakistani center's encroachments on Balochistan threatened to alter a jealously guarded status quo. Sporadic eruptions of armed insurgency became a recurrent feature of politics in Balochistan. This was not too difficult given the impoverishment of the people and the absence of the most rudimentary forms of infrastructure for the economic development of the province. During the 1960s, Sher Mohammad Marri spearheaded the resistance under the umbrella of the Baloch Liberation Front. The battles fought by the Pakistani Army in the rugged terrain of Balochistan shaped its institutional psyche in decisive

ways. Baloch nationalists were labeled "miscreants" working hand in
glove with either Afghanistan or the country's premier enemy. This perception did not remain confined to the military. Tarring regional demands with the Indian brush became such an entrenched part of the official discourse of nationalism in Pakistan that the managers of the centralized
state regarded legitimate demands for provincial autonomy with deep
suspicion.

Consequently, even in the relatively quiescent parts of West Pakistan,
there was no love lost for an unresponsive center that continued swallowing
up larger and larger chunks of provincial revenues without contributing
much for the development of local infrastructure and social welfare. The
massive demographic changes accompanying partition strained the
limited administrative capacities of Punjab and Sindh to breaking point.
While the exodus of non-Muslims disrupted the economic and educational networks in these provinces, accommodating the bulk of the 7.2
million Muslim refugees from India within a short span of time was impossible without the sustained help of the central government. Preoccupied with matters of defense and its own political survival, Karachi's assistance to the provinces fell well short of expectations. In the absence of
funds and efficient administrative solutions, the rehabilitation of refugees
was quickly transformed into an explosive political issue. Several provincial politicians used it to chip away at the center's uncertain authority.

Accounting for 10 percent of Pakistan's population by 1951, the refugees
permanently altered the political landscape of Punjab and Sindh. Despite
taking in a much larger percentage of Muslims fleeing parts of East Punjab ravaged by violence, Punjab had a relatively easier time absorbing the
mainly Punjabi-speaking migrants into its social fabric.[6] By contrast, the
influx of mainly Urdu-speaking migrants into Sindh created a clutch of
political and cultural problems for the provincial administration. More
than half a million refugees came to Sindh during the initial years of independence. Almost two-thirds of them opted for urban centers like Karachi and Hyderabad while the remainder settled in the rural areas of this
overwhelmingly agricultural province. In principle, the incoming migrants were expected to replace the non-Muslims in both the urban and
the rural areas. However, the problem of resettlement was far more complicated and the ensuing tensions between local Sindhis and the newcom-
ers much fiercer than in Punjab. For one thing, the outflow of Hindus to

India was slower in Sindh than in Punjab.[7] For another, some of the more powerful Sindhi Muslim landlords are said to have grabbed nearly two-thirds of the agricultural land vacated by Hindus before migrants from UP, Hyderabad Deccan, or East Punjab could make their presence felt. The situation was particularly fraught in Karachi, a thriving cosmopolitan city of 400,000 in 1947, but one in which construction activity had not kept pace with the growth in population due to World War II. The preferred destination for a majority of uprooted Urdu-speakers from north India's urban areas, Karachi had thinly spread municipal facilities, whether for health, communications, water supply, electric power, or housing, that were incapable of bearing the burden of its new population.

The sheer pace of the sociocultural and political transformation of Sindh can be seen by the jump in the number of Urdu speakers from a mere 1 percent of the population in 1947 to 12 percent by the time of the 1951 census. With just a sprinkle of Urdu speakers at the time of partition, Karachi by the late 1950s had become a migrant city with more than half of its population claiming Urdu as their mother tongue. This would not have been possible if the provincial government had succeeded in getting its way. Within a year or so of partition, relations between the center and the Sindh government had nose-dived over the forcible separation of Karachi from the province. Justified on the grounds of national interest, the loss of Karachi rankled the Sindhis all the more because they were not compensated for the loss of the province's primary revenue earner. Under the circumstances, the center's advocacy of the Urdu-speaking migrants' right to space, gainful employment, and adequate political representation was perceived as a deep-seated conspiracy to displace Sindhis from a position of dominance in their own province. The center's preference for authoritarian methods over democratic ones even during the first decade after independence only confirmed the worst fears of the Sindhis. Calling themselves *muhajirs,* or refugees after the early community of Islam that migrated from Mecca to Medina, the Urdu speakers believed that their sacrifices of life and property for Pakistan entitled them to a privileged position in the new state. Lacking a provincial base of their own, the class, occupational, and emotional profile of many Urdu speakers made them particularly susceptible to the appeal to religion by self-styled "Islamist" parties like the Jamaat-i-Islami and the JUP, which had made Karachi the focus of their oppositional politics. Paradoxically enough, their religious pretensions and claims of cultural superiority over other linguistic groups suited a West Pakistani establishment, harping on the Islamic identity of Pakistan and Urdu as the cultural motif of its national unity, much more than political parties with provincial bases of support.

The concordat between the center and the better-educated Urdu-speaking *muhajirs,* many of whom held top positions in the federal bureaucracy, had large implications for Pakistani politics. Even before the first military takeover of 1958, the migrants' success in creating a social and political niche for themselves, especially in Karachi, was intensely resented not only by Sindhis but also by Punjabis, Pathans, Gujaratis, and Balochis who had come to the city looking for employment and a better quality of life. Antipathy toward the Urdu-speaking migrants was not a facet of the Sindhi sociopolitical scene alone. It extended to other provinces where the educated classes felt slighted by the cultural pretensions of the Urdu speakers. This was true even of those members of the urban Punjabi middle and upper classes who accepted Urdu as their lingua franca in the interest of national cohesion. Urdu was much less prevalent in the NWFP and Balochistan. The Pathan provincial elite gradually took to it for pragmatic reasons without abandoning their own mother tongue, Pashto. In Balochistan, Urdu was resisted as an alien imposition by a rapacious and indifferent center.

The suspension of democratic government in October 1958 gave a fillip to these sentiments and, in turn, provoked the center into taking draconian measures in the name of national unity. Disgruntled politicians with regional bases of support were either locked out of Ayub's bureaucratically controlled political system or locked up in jail on various grounds. Pakistan under military rule flouted the elementary norms of federalism, accentuating strains in center–province relations. As the nonelected institutions were the main beneficiaries of administrative centralization and democratic denial, their overwhelmingly Punjabi character caused bitterness among non-Punjabis. Unable to allocate financial resources equitably to the provinces and unwilling to grant them their share of power, the federal union of Pakistan was built on a fragile branch that was liable to break under the weight of its own contradictions.

To prevent this eventuality, steps had been taken as early as 1949 to placate the non-Punjabi provinces by instituting a quota system for recruitment to the federal government services. This failed to provide adequate, far less equitable, representation to the provinces or the linguistic minorities within them. Instead of correcting centrifugal trends, a centralization drive by an administrative bureaucracy dominated by Punjabis and Urdu speakers fanned provincialism. Bengalis led the non-Punjabi charge in demanding better representation in the civil, diplomatic, and armed services. The federal center was accused of pursuing policies of internal colonization by posting Punjabi and Urdu-speaking civil servants to the non-Punjabi provinces to pilfer their meager share of resources. Instead of consulting with the provinces or making a prior reference to the legislature, the federal center soon after independence had temporarily withheld the share out of income tax. In an audacious move, the center arbitrarily took away the right of the provinces to collect the sales tax, the single most elastic source of their revenue. Justified in the name of national interest, the center's monopolization of the entire gamut of fiscal and financial arrangements to pay for a debilitating defense burden extinguished such hopes as existed of generating a measure of federal bonhomie.

The nub of Bengali hostility toward the West Pakistani establishment was the pernicious logic of functional inequality. Once militarization and industrialization became the twin pillars of Pakistani officialdom's developmental rhetoric, an astonishing range of special concessions were offered to West Pakistani–based business families at the expense of the agricultural sector in East Pakistan. Raw jute grown in the eastern wing was the leading foreign exchange earner during Pakistan's first decade of independence. In the fall of 1949, Pakistan exercised its financial sovereignty by refusing to follow the example of Britain and India and devaluing its currency. As the center's economic wizards had correctly calculated, this boosted export earnings by nearly 40 percent. The nondevaluation decision brought down jute and wheat prices while those of other essential commodities increased. By imposing heavy export duties to the detriment of agriculture, the central government augmented its foreign exchange reserves. The additional foreign exchange was used to finance the defense procurement effort and the industrialization of West Pakistan. Bengali grumbles about being used as a milk cow for the security and development of the western wing were dismissed or conveniently misread as evidence of secessionist and pro-Indian tendencies.

So long as even the most compromised form of a federal parliamentary system was in place, it was impossible to leave the provinces completely in the financial lurch. Soon after the controversial erosion of provincial fiscal rights, the central government entered into negotiations with the provinces to arrive at a more mutually acceptable allocation of financial resources. An official of the Australian treasury, Jeremy Raisman, had been asked by the Pakistani government to examine the existing financial arrangements between the center and the provinces. In January 1952, the Raisman Report increased the provincial proportion of federal finances. It gave East Bengal just under two-thirds of the export duty on raw jute but turned down Punjabi and Sindhi requests for a cut in the export duties in view of the federal government's precarious financial position. Raisman also rejected provincial demands that the sales tax should be distributed among them and not shared between them and the center. Although a positive development in an otherwise grim federal landscape, the Raisman Award did not go far enough in alleviating center–region frictions over the all-important issue of financial autonomy.

If the center's tight-fistedness could be justified in the light of the strategic and economic consequences of partition, its overbearing attitude toward the cultural sensitivities of the provinces was inexcusable. There were powerful undercurrents of cultural alienation in provincial demands for autonomy. Bengali outrage at the center's Urdu-only language policy was just the tip of the iceberg, concealing a deep-seated resentment at the marginalization of their culture in the emerging narratives of the Pakistani nation. The wounded pride of the Bengalis had met with a rude shock on February 21, 1952, when the center's crackdown on the student-led language movement in Dhaka led to the killing of four students and injured several more. Commemorated as Martyrs' Day by Bengalis ever since, the incident is thought to have marked the beginning of the politics of dissent that culminated in Bangladeshi nationalism and independence. Bengali linguistic nationalism, however, was one among several factors that led eventually to the breakup of Pakistan.

Bengalis were not alone in feeling aggrieved by the center's imposition of Urdu as the official language. A section of Punjabis, belonging mostly to the lower and less well-off middle classes, bemoaned the loss of their linguistic tradition in the rush to embrace Urdu. They felt alienated by the state's artificial attempts to imitate the mores of the Mughal court. Their opposition was not to Urdu but to its patronage by the federal center at the expense of Punjabi, a language with a rich and vibrant oral and written literary history spanning a thousand years.[8] Confusing cultural assertion with parochialism, the central government harassed Punjabi intellectuals working to promote their regional language, declaring the more recalcitrant among them as "antistate." The suspension of parliamentary government in 1958 dealt a hammer blow to regional linguistic aspirations not only in Punjab but also in the non-Punjabi provinces. Fancying himself as the great unifier, General Ayub suppressed regional literary associations, dubbing some of them as extensions of the banned Communist Party.[9]

State coercion could at best curb the growth of mass-based language movements, not dilute the enthusiasm of the more ardent protagonists of linguistic regionalism. Bengalis defied the government's crude attempts to prevent them from celebrating the birthday of the revered Bengali poet Rabindranath Tagore. The ban on his works in the state-controlled media heightened Tagore's appeal as a symbol of Bengali resistance against an intrusive and dictatorial center. Bengali writers and poets used Tagore, along with socialist and communist themes, to highlight the exploitation of East Pakistan and attack the state's Islamic ideology. In West Pakistan, too, regional languages like Punjabi, Pashto, and Sindhi continued to expand their readership by increasing their literary production independently of the state. Advertising the risks of forcibly regimenting cultural traditions, Urdu came to be seen as an alien implant at the service of a neoimperialist agenda.

The center's myopic handling of provincial sensibilities on language was matched by ham-handed attempts at marshaling Islam in the cause of nation building. With the religious ideologues agitating for the introduction of the sharia, senior bureaucrats set about feverishly establishing the religious credentials of the state. The result was a strange convergence of interest between an authoritarian center, besieged by a crescendo of demands for provincial autonomy, and a spectrum of Islamic ideologues looking for ways to squeeze through the woodwork to the apex of state power. Although it is possible to exaggerate the extent of the symbiosis between these two distinct forces, the state's emphasis on its religious identity lent greater legitimacy to the would-be ideologues of Islam than the ground realities merited.[10] But there was a world of difference between using religious preachers to advance the state's homogenizing logic and a commitment to turning Pakistan into a conservative, hidebound Islamic state modeled on a narrowly construed reading of Islam.

Ever since the Objectives Resolution of 1949—ostensibly a victory for modernist interpretations of Islam—the so-called religious parties had chastised the state overlords for not living up to the ideals of Islam. Mawdudi, the leader of the Jamaat-i-Islami, lent ideological starch to this argument. In his opinion, it was the duty of a state created in the name of Islam to mold the hearts and minds of its citizens according to the tenets of their religion.[11] There was no scope for citizens to influence or contest the state's understanding of Islam. Mawdudi defended this on the grounds that because sovereignty in an Islamic state was vested in Allah, such perfect justice and equity will prevail that dissent would amount to apostasy. The Jamaat ideologue had pretensions about pressing his credentials as an Islamic scholar with infallible authority to interpret the divine will. Consistent with his view of the state in Islam as a spiritual democracy, Iqbal had proposed reposing that authority in an elected Parliament. In Mawdudi's authoritarian conception of the Islamic state, there was no possibility of Parliament debating, far less defining, God's will. Muslims not conforming to his idea of Islam were implicitly excluded from Mawdudi's definition of a believer. In another significant departure from the poetic visionary of Pakistan, who had held that the idea of the state was not dominant in Islam, Mawdudi considered the acquisition of state power vital to attain the ideal Islamic way of life. He proposed a jihad to seize state power and declared the lesser jihad (against the enemies of Islam) to be more important than the greater jihad (with one's inner self). Jihad was justified against internal Muslim "others" quite as much as against non-Muslims, sharpening the edges of the fault lines in the battle for the soul of Pakistan. There was no place in this scheme of things for any mutually negotiated coexistence between Muslims and non-Muslims. The Islamic state was the ideological embodiment of Muslim belief in one God and the Prophet Muhammad. Consequently, non-Muslims had to be debarred from holding key positions of responsibility. The same logic led Mawdudi to propose that Indian Muslims, a rump of a once significant community, had no choice but to live according to the dictates of the Hindu-majority community.

Mawdudi's idea of indoctrination and his strident anti-Indian rhetoric coupled with an insistence on Islam held out attractions for a military-dominated state. However, there was no question of the decision makers in the military and the civil bureaucracy letting the clerics rule the

Islamic roost. During Ayub Khan's era of enlightened Islam, *Mawdudism* became a word of execration and also fear. The religious lobby's potential to kick up a popular storm to the detriment of an authoritarian regime fully dawned on the general within years of his usurpation of state power. Moon sighting for the Muslim festival of Eid was a source of contention among the believers, with the clerics using it as an opportunity to enhance their public reach. When the Ayub regime tried rationalizing the process in 1967 by setting up a committee that proceeded to announce a day for Eid, the ulema led by Mawdudi protested this unwarranted intervention by the state in a sphere they regarded as their exclusive preserve. Five of them were quickly put behind bars, including Mawdudi, and the press prohibited from reporting on the matter. Throughout the Ayub era, Mawdudi bore the brunt of the state's coercive apparatus and was dragged through the courts in lengthy and financially withering legal battles. Ayub vented his fury against the Jamaat leader, calling him a "traitor and true enemy of Islam." "In any other country," the dictator opined, "[Mawdudi] would have been lynched like a dog, but in Pakistan we have rule of law of which the traitors take full advantage and protection."[12]

A gaggle of senior civil bureaucrats close to Ayub's way of thinking set about conjuring up the idioms of an Islamic ideology designed to expedite national integration rather than any visible kind of religiosity. What ensued was a scrappy tug-of-war between self-styled ideologues at the helm of state power and the bearded legions with their prayer rosaries, whether in the mosques, seminaries, or the streets, over the authority to interpret the message of Islam. Among the main casualties of the struggle was the center–province equation, with dire consequences for the federation. The state's recourse to religion was designed to counter claims based on cultural diversity and difference. Intended to facilitate unity among Pakistan's diverse regions, cynical uses of Islam served to undermine any sort of consensus on national identity. For a largely destitute populace seeking to eke out a decent living, matters to do with Islam's ritualistic, doctrinal, and spiritual aspects were not the primary issue. Singling out Islam as the only thread in the intricate regional weave of Pakistan's national identity was a crudely conceived policy of homogenization through which the military–bureaucratic state succeeded in making an issue out of a nonissue. A citizenry more in tune with the eclectic and varied social makeup of the country was quite comfortable wearing multiple affinities of region, religion, and nation. Policies of national indoctrination in the name of Islam generated derision, dismay, and dissension, most noticeably in the eastern wing.

The votaries of the Pakistani state's centralizing and homogenizing project arrogantly dismissed dissenting reactions as products of ignorance, insularity, and, worse still, secessionist inclinations. General Ayub had a visceral dislike for the advocates of provincial rights, who he thought were disrupting the economic progress of the country. The Pakistan Council for National Integration was established with the explicit objective of promoting better understanding among the people of the two wings in order to fashion a common national outlook. Reading rooms were opened in key cities, and lectures, seminars, and symposia were held on the theme of national unity and integration. Some of these did help lift the veil of ignorance between the two halves of the country. But without qualitative changes on the political and economic front, integrative rhetoric without concrete action was wholly ineffective in bridging the gulf separating the Bengalis from the people of West Pakistan.

Ayub had banked on the leavening effects of his economic development policies to justify keeping tight curbs on political activity. This was excessively optimistic, as he soon found out. Under his regime's externally stimulated development policies, East Pakistan received a bigger share of state resources than in the 1950s. But with 55 percent of the population, a share of 35 percent of the total development expenditure was neither fair nor equitable. The centralized nature of the state-directed development effort, in any case, ensured that the economy of the eastern wing continued to lag well behind that of the western wing. The regime's growth-oriented strategies increased regional income disparities without any improvement in Bengali representation among army officers, which remained at a lowly 5 percent. The higher income levels in West Pakistan were ascribed by officialdom to the effects of the "Green Revolution" and the leap in agricultural production that had ensued after the introduction of new technologies. In fact, interregional discrepancies in growth and development were a direct result of the policy to use East Pakistan's export surplus to finance West Pakistan deficits. The federal government's hollow propaganda incensed Bengali popular opinion further, galvanizing support for the Awami League but, at the same time, threatening to subsume its campaign for provincial autonomy with cries for full independence.

Losing East Pakistan

East Pakistan's possible secession had always troubled Pakistan's first military ruler. Ayub Khan's worst fears came true when the radical Bengali leader Maulana Bhashani, after sitting out the 1970 elections, upped the ante by calling for an independent and sovereign state of East Bengal as envisaged in the Muslim League's Lahore resolution of March 1940. The general pondered whether he was "witnessing the beginning of the end." This was what "most Bengali nationalists always meant when they talked of complete provincial autonomy." The fiery left-leaning maulana may have been venting his fury against West Pakistani callousness toward the recent cyclone victims and, by the same token, cashing in on an opportunity to take some of the shine off the Awami League. Even before the results of the 1970 elections were out, Ayub suspected that Bhashani's firecracker would spur Mujib into lighting the bonfire of Pakistani unity. The sheikh seemed to have been "waiting for such an opportunity"—"making independence a common cry of Bengal and turning it into an irresistible movement." Several of Ayub's visitors, including former as well as serving members of the federal cabinet, agreed with him that it was now only a matter of time before the eastern wing separated from the rest of Pakistan. With the Awami League's landslide victory, Mujib was "no longer a free agent" but "a prisoner of his vast support." Bhutto, too, would be loath to make any compromise that could allow his opponents to accuse him of "selling West Pakistan down the drain."[13]

As the architect of a political system that was threatening to fall apart, Ayub's forebodings offer a poignant insight into his reading of history. On January 4, 1971, he recorded the "strange irony of fate" that had seen Pakistan "escap[ing] the tyranny of an inflexible and hostile Hindu majority," only to end up facing an untenable situation where one wing was about to establish its permanent majority "without bearing a proportionately higher burden or higher liability." The alternative to this "artificial alliance" was independence or a loose confederation. Ayub thought that Bhashani's call for independence, if premature, was more representative of the "inner feelings of his people." The president was unimpressed by the fact that Mujib was not asking for independence but wanted complete autonomy for the eastern wing within a federal arrangement. From Ayub's angle of vision, Mujib was stalling for time in a calculated attempt to "milk

Punjab and Sindh" of their surpluses before opting out. Although in the 1970 elections, Punjab and Sindh "sold themselves to Bhutto and have no voice of their own left," Ayub wondered whether "they would not rebel against such an idea." He surmised that "the demand for separation may well start in these provinces once the reality dawns, as it is bound to in course of time, that they are being robbed."[14]

Ayub had put his finger on the crux of the 1971 crisis. Who was liable to secede from whom, the majority in the eastern wing or sections of the minority in the west? If Pakistan was to remain united, by what democratic or federal principle could anyone prevent the majority population in the eastern wing from redressing past injustices by diverting resources from the western wing to develop its own economy? Mujib interpreted the Awami League's absolute majority as a validation of his six-point program for provincial autonomy. But the program had not formed part of the electoral debate in West Pakistan, where the Awami League did not win a single seat. Bhutto had taken the PPP into the 1970 elections on a socialist platform. The PPP leader told the commission investigating the causes of Pakistan's military defeat in 1971 that he had refrained from attacking the Awami League's program at public meetings because they were venues for emotional outbursts, not reasoned arguments about the political and constitutional niceties of the six points. Bhutto had criticized the Awami League's provincial autonomy demands at smaller gatherings of lawyers and intellectuals in West Pakistan, arguing that they were not in the best interests of the country and could lead to secession.

In the run-up to the 1970 elections, right-wing parties opposed to the PPP in the western wing were more vocal in criticizing the Awami League's six points, which they often equated with the breakup of the country. After the elections, the PPP reaffirmed its commitment to a constitutional settlement within the framework of Pakistan. Because Pakistan was a federal and not a unitary state, Bhutto argued, it was vital to secure the consensus of the federating units. He never explained how a consensus was to be obtained after the elections. Though it emerged as the majority party in West Pakistan, the PPP's support base was confined to Punjab and Sindh. In the NWFP and Balochistan, the Deobandi-oriented Jamiat-i-Ulema-i-Islam (JUI) fared better at the polls. Along with the defeated parties and politicians of West Pakistan, the JUI led by Maulana

Mufti Mahmud could not be shut out of discussions on the future constitutional arrangements.

This made Bhutto's claim to speak on behalf of West Pakistan indefensible and hints at the essence of his dilemma. On the threshold of a historic opportunity, the PPP chairman found himself between a rock and a hard place. The PPP had done well but not well enough. Although the party's radical program accounted for its electoral success in central Punjab, where the "Green Revolution" coupled with the Ayub regime's irrigation projects had made the most impact, Bhutto's controversial decision to enlist the support of conservative landlords in south Punjab and Sindh had played an equally important part in the PPP's victory. Tensions within the left and the right wings of the PPP threatened to split the party even before Bhutto had succeeded in registering his claim to power. To make matters worse, in cutting a deal with Mujib, Bhutto ran the risk of being denounced as a traitor in West Pakistan. Wary of becoming the butt of West Pakistani criticism if he compromised with Mujib, Bhutto miscalculated his ability to withstand the ill effects of becoming a willing pawn in the regime's game plan to thwart the Awami League's bid for power. If he wanted to avoid being called a traitor to West Pakistan at all costs, Bhutto was equally determined not be cast in the role of arch-conspirator in the breakup of Pakistan. Bhutto's role in the post-1970 election crisis has to be assessed in the light of the positions taken by Mujib and Yahya Khan, not to mention the structural obstacles in the way of a smooth transfer of power from military to civilian rule in Pakistan.

The basic democracies system had been designed to safeguard the center from challenges mounted by political parties with broad-based support at the provincial level. Instead, opposition to Ayub's exclusionary political system crystallized in East Pakistan in the form of the six points, which, for all practical purposes, made the center redundant. Most political parties in the western wing wanted an effective, if not a strong, center that could lend credence to the existence of Pakistan as a sovereign independent state. There was scope for discussions between the representatives of the two wings, leading to a narrowing of differences on the question of center–province relations. But the localization of political horizons under the basic democracies system had prevented the forging of meaningful alliances between political parties both within and between the two wings.

This in large part explains why the six points elicited such different responses in East and West Pakistan.

The main bone of contention between the two wings was the powers of the federal center. The Awami League's vision of a limited center was a red flag for the gendarmes of the Pakistani state. The first of the six points called for the creation of a federation of Pakistan in the true spirit of the Lahore resolution with a parliamentary form of government based on the supremacy of a legislature directly elected on the basis of universal adult franchise. The second point confined the powers of the federal government to defense and foreign affairs and vested all the residual subjects in the constituent units. According to the third point, there were to be two separate but freely convertible currencies for the two wings and, if that proved unworkable, a single currency for the whole country with constitutional safeguards to prevent the flight of capital from East to West Pakistan. Moreover, the eastern wing was to have its own reserve bank and a separate fiscal and monetary policy. The fourth point stripped the federal center of its powers of taxation and revenue collection and handed them to the federating units. Turning the twenty-four-year logic of military fiscalism in Pakistan on its head, the fourth point made the federal center dependent on handouts from state taxes to meet its expenditures. If this did not raise the hackles of the military brass, the fifth point certainly did. It envisaged separate accounts for the foreign exchange earnings of the two wings, with the federal center getting an agreed percentage of their financial resources. Indigenous products were to move free of duty between the two wings. But this gesture to federalism was offset by the provision empowering the constituent units to establish trade links with foreign countries. The sixth point's demand for a separate militia or paramilitary force in East Pakistan was anodyne by comparison to the drastic readjustment that was being proposed in the apportioning of finances between the federal center and the federating units.

Yet for all the clouds darkening the political horizon, there was also an element of creative ambiguity in the postelectoral context. It was evident that Mujib's six points were negotiable, and he was not thinking of secession. His conception of a free Bengali nation was not incompatible with something less than a fully separate and sovereign state. If the military junta had seized this opening to negotiate the terms for a transfer of power with the newly elected representatives of the people, the course of

Pakistani history might have been different. Stung by election results that were completely contrary to the intelligence reports, Yahya delayed announcing a date for the meeting of the national assembly, which was to function as both the legislature and the constitution-making body. This aroused Bengali suspicions, prompting Mujib to take a more rigid stance on the six points. On January 3, 1971, at a mass meeting of a million people at the Dhaka Race Course ground, all the Awami League members of the national and provincial assemblies took an oath of allegiance to the six points. Most telling was Mujib's assertion that the six points were "the property of the people of Bangladesh" and there could be no question of a compromise on them.

Yet when he met Yahya Khan in the second week of January 1971, Mujib was a paragon of moderation. As the general had not bothered studying the six points, Mujib explained them to him and asked whether he had any objections. Yahya said he had none but noted that the Awami League would have to carry the West Pakistani political parties, the PPP in particular. Mujib urged him to convene the national assembly by February 15 and predicted that he would "obtain not only a simple majority but almost 2/3 majority." Admiral Ahsan, who was then still governor of East Pakistan, noted that with its absolute majority, the Awami League could "bulldoze their constitution through without bothering about West Pakistan's interests." Mujib was quick to the defense: "No, I am a democrat and the majority leader of all Pakistan. I cannot ignore the interests of West Pakistan. I am not only responsible to the people of East and West Pakistan but also to world opinion. I shall do everything on democratic principles." Mujib wanted to invite Yahya to Dhaka three or four days before the assembly session to see the draft constitution. "If you find objections," Mujib told Yahya, "I will try to accommodate your wishes." Toward that end he promised to seek the cooperation of the PPP as well as other parties in West Pakistan. The Awami League realized that the western wing did not need the same measure of autonomy as East Pakistan. In a telling statement of the inner thinking of the Awami League leadership, Mujib said that although he was prepared to be of help, he did not wish to interfere in any arrangements that the West Pakistani leadership may wish to make. Looking forward, Mujib talked about drafting Yahya's address to the national assembly, which he wanted convened no later than February 15, and went so far as to say that the Awami League intended to elect the general as its presidential candidate. Mujib spoke of "a democratic parliament" and discussions on issues to "find acceptable formulas inside and outside the Assembly." The meeting ended with Yahya flattering Mujib by calling him the next prime minister of Pakistan.[15]

An uncompromising public posture contrasted with private reassurances exchanged by the main actors and complicates the story of the tripartite negotiations that preceded the military action in East Pakistan. As far as Mujib was concerned, a formula could be worked out to save the unity of Pakistan even while pursuing legitimate Bengali demands. Soon after the elections, Mujib is said to have conveyed to Bhutto through a personal emissary that he could have the "big job" in return for accepting the six points and joining hands with the Awami League to force the military back into the barracks. Taken aback but excited by the idea, Bhutto declared that he was personally not opposed to the six points but had to carry the party with him.[16] Secure in the knowledge of his powers under the LFO, Yahya Khan exploited Bhutto's uncertainty about the PPP's reactions to striking a deal with the Awami League. On his return to West Pakistan, Yahya stopped off in Larkana to visit Bhutto at his ancestral home. There is no record of what transpired at the meeting, but the president would almost certainly have mentioned his conversation with Mujib, though he did not tell Bhutto about the Awami League leader's readiness to discuss the outstanding constitutional issues both inside and outside the national assembly.[17] Yahya might also have hinted at the limits to which the regime was prepared to go to accommodate the Awami League's demands. Any reference to the LFO and Pakistan's national interest would have alerted Bhutto to the military establishment's distaste for the six points.

The junta downplayed the meeting between Yahya and Bhutto, describing it as coincidental. There were several subsequent consultations between the two men that were far from incidental. The existence of a secret channel of communication between the PPP chairman and the martial law administrator pointed to collusion, generating a rash of negative speculation in the eastern wing. Bhutto was already held in high suspicion when he arrived in Dhaka on January 27 for the first round of talks with the Awami League leader. Bengali doubts about Bhutto's intentions were strengthened when, after eight hours of being holed up alone in a room with Mujib, the PPP leader did not go beyond seeking clarifications on the six points. There was no mention of joining hands to oust the military regime. Mujib was understandably "disappointed" and "puzzled" by these tactics.[18]

Upon returning from East Pakistan, Bhutto denied any differences with Mujib and said that their talks had been "exploratory" in nature. Before these statements could have a salutary effect, two Kashmiris hijacked an Air India Fokker on January 25, 1971, and forced it to land in Lahore. While Mujib condemned the hijacking on principle, Bhutto rushed to Lahore airport to greet the "freedom fighters" who were granted asylum by Pakistan. That the regime and the PPP chairman had been ensnared soon became apparent when the hijackers blew up the plane two days later and New Delhi reacted by banning all Pakistani interwing flights from using Indian airspace. This increased the distance between East and West Pakistan from 1,000 to 3,000 miles around the coast via Sri Lanka. The hijacking widened the gulf between Bhutto and Mujib and brought Indo-Pakistan relations to an all-time low, especially once the tribunal set up to investigate the incident concluded that the hijackers were not heroes but Indian agents. Mujib's stance on the hijacking intensified Punjabi hostility toward him, making it more difficult for Bhutto to compromise. On February 21 a PPP convention vowed to abide by the chairman's decision not to attend the session of the national assembly scheduled for March 3.

Yahya Khan used the excuse of a deteriorating political situation and the Indian threat looming on the borders to dismiss his civilian cabinet and invest the governors with martial law powers, a first step to clearing any hurdles in the way of a military action. The decision indicated the president's semi-isolation and made him more dependent on the military hawks in the National Security Council (NSC). On the evening of February 22, he presided over a conference in Rawalpindi attended by the governors, martial law administrators, and intelligence officials, where a decision was taken in principle to deploy force in East Pakistan. An operational plan was discussed that envisaged the deployment of troops and the mass arrest of Awami League leaders on charges of sedition.[19] The governor of East Pakistan, Admiral Ahsan, was the only one to raise his voice in objection. Along with General Sahibzada Yaqub Ali Khan, the commander of the eastern forces, the governor insisted on the imperative of finding a political solution and openly expressed dismay at the unthinking jingoism of West Pakistani officials who "regarded the people of East Pakistan as a vast colonial population waiting to be proselytized."[20] Until the third week of February, Yahya had appeared to endorse his views, but now the tide had turned. On arriving in the capital from Dhaka, Ahsan was "alarmed to notice a high tide of militarism flowing turbulently." There was "open talk" at the conference of a "military solution according to plan."[21] Ahsan's refusal to endorse such a course of action made him unpopular with his colleagues, who thought he had sold out to the Bengalis.

There is no indication that Bhutto was privy to the regime's plans to clamp down on the Awami League leaders. Publicly, he persisted in calling for a political solution acceptable to both wings. Signs of the military leaning on Bhutto, albeit for its own institutional reasons, created the impression of complicity. The election results had blown Yahya's cover under the LFO. A counterfoil was needed to stop Mujib's thunderous march to power. In his narrative of the events, Brigadier A. R. Siddiqi, the head of the military's Inter-Services Public Relations (ISPR) wing, maintains that after the elections, General Gul Hassan, the chief of the general staff, told him, "Let's back Bhutto."[22] In his memoir, Gul Hassan holds both Bhutto and Mujib in contempt and refers to them as "creative liars" whose ambition and vindictiveness made them prone to fabrications if that served their political purpose.[23] What is undeniable is that the army had a clear self-interest in the outcome of the postelectoral negotiations. According to Siddiqi, the "right of a provincial-cum-regional party to frame the national Constitution and run the national government for the next five years, was not acceptable" to the military high command. Bhutto was preferred not because he was more worthy of trust than Mujib. The generals knew that the Awami League leader was no friend of theirs and feared he might try to seek a drastic cut in the army's size and power. Circumstantially, Bhutto had better credentials. The PPP's biggest majority was in Punjab, home to 75 percent of the army's rank and file. This would force Bhutto to be "more reasonable and not touch the army."[24]

Encouraged by the regular exchange of missives with Yahya Khan and his contact with other top generals in the regime, Bhutto became more insistent on not attending the national assembly. While denying any fundamental opposition to the six points, he charged the Awami League with wanting to impose its preferred constitution on West Pakistan. Letting the majority frame a constitution of its choosing would make sense if Pakistan was a unitary state. In a country split into two parts that lacked any semblance of political cohesion, the federal constitution had to be based on the consensus of all the federating units. In the interest of national unity, Bhutto agreed to the six points barring the second and the fifth relating to currency, taxation, international trade, and foreign assistance. When push came to shove, he was prepared to accept all the points except the one pertaining to foreign trade and aid. If these were adjusted in favor of the center, the PPP was prepared to cooperate with the Awami League in formulating the constitution.

The more ruthless of Bhutto's critics have persisted in accusing him of stalling for time at Yahya's behest. There is no question that Bhutto overestimated his ability to get the better of the general. Spurning Mujib's offer to help eject the military from the political arena was an error for which history cannot absolve Bhutto. Like any politician, Bhutto needed the support of his party leadership. Notwithstanding the PPP's studied public silence on the Awami League's demands, Bhutto remained remarkably consistent in his stance on the six points. Raising the PPP's objections to the conception of the federation in the six points, he noted that there was no federation in the world without a second house of parliament, a proposition Mujib had rejected. Equally objectionable was the fact that although some of the points upheld the principles of federalism, others implied a confederal arrangement between the two wings. The Awami League wanted West Pakistan to assume responsibility for the bulk of the external debt of the federal government. East Pakistan was to contribute only 24 percent of the center's running costs, and even this sum was to be set against "reparations" due from West Pakistan for its past exploitation of the eastern wing. On this basis, the entire central levy would have to be borne by the western wing for several years to come.[25]

For a West Pakistani politician, let alone a Sindhi, to agree to such an arrangement was political suicide. Right-wing parties considered the six points blasphemous and would invariably denounce Bhutto for being opportunistic and, worse still, a traitor. His own ideologically divided party cadres were liable to revolt, certainly in Punjab, where the PPP had received strong electoral support in military cantonments. Leery of the Awami League's absolute majority, Bhutto stuck to his guns about discussing the main points of difference before the meeting of the national assembly. If Mujib had wanted Yahya to call the national assembly by mid-February, Bhutto wanted the meeting postponed until the end of March so that the two parties could thrash out all the contentious issues. Ignoring Bhutto's arguments but also falling short of accepting Mujib's, Yahya had announced on February 13 that the national assembly would meet on March 3, 1971. Bhutto said his party would not attend unless assurances were given that it would be heard. The PPP was not boycotting the assembly but asking the Awami League to reciprocate its gesture of accepting four out of the six points. Likening the constitution to an essay, Bhutto said "we accept the essay written in East Pakistan—but we want to write some concluding paragraphs which are of vital national importance." "We have gone a mile to accommodate the Six Points," he continued, and "request our East Pakistani friends to move at least an inch to accommodate our views."[26] In a deliberate act of omission, Yahya Khan did not tell Bhutto about Mujib's readiness to engage in discussions outside the assembly. This implies that far from colluding with Bhutto, or for that matter with Mujib, as the PPP claimed, Yahya was looking to extend his regime's continuation in office by pitting the two main parties against each other.

The tactic worked. Sensing the army's reluctance to transfer power, Bhutto went on a verbal rampage through the populist alleyways of the historic city of Lahore. In a stormy speech to a mammoth crowd at Lahore's Mochi Gate on February 28, he reiterated his line that Mujib had decided on the constitution and wanted the PPP to rubber-stamp the document. Bhutto demanded a postponement of the national assembly or an extension of the 120-day period for the formulation of the constitution. Getting carried away by the force of his own words, he threatened to break the legs of anyone, whether from the PPP or any other West Pakistani party, who attended the national assembly session in Dhaka. This was provocative in the extreme. The die had been cast; the Awami League leadership's distrust of Bhutto was complete. Egged on by the intelligence agencies, most political parties in West Pakistan refused to attend the assembly session. On March 1 Yahya used the excuse to postpone the national assembly and aggravated matters by not announcing an alternative date for its meeting. While this sparked disappointment in West Pakistani political circles, the eastern wing exploded in violent frenzy. In clear evidence of serious differences in higher military circles, both Admiral Ahsan and General Yaqub resigned from their positions. With the removal of the two senior most West Pakistani officials who still believed in the need for a political solution, the military gunned down several demonstrators in East Pakistan on March 2 and 3 before returning to the barracks.

From March 1 until the fateful moment on March 25, 1971, when a crackle of gunfire disrupted the silence of the night in Dhaka, Bengali antipathy for the Pakistani military presence in East Pakistan soared. Food sellers refused to supply meat and fresh produce to the army while West Pakistanis and pro-government Urdu-speaking Biharis were targeted by the Awami League muscle men. Despite clear and present provocation, the army desisted from taking any action, purportedly to allow the political negotiations to succeed. Yet since a decision to resort to military action had been taken in principle, the lack of any remedial measure on the part of the military can equally well be seen as marking time to fly in troop reinforcements from West Pakistan. The state's inaction after a vicious display of its coercive power emboldened Awami League workers to begin taking over state institutions. After March 2, Mujib, popularly known as Bangabandhu (friend of Bengal) was running the civilian administration in East Pakistan from his unassuming two-storied home at 32 Dhanmandi. The three-member Hamoodur Rahman Commission set up to investigate the causes of the military defeat in East Pakistan chastised the military regime for letting the situation get out of hand, with the result that much greater use of force was needed later to regain control. There was no reason why keeping the door open for negotiations with Mujib was inconsistent with maintaining law and order. As far as the commission could discern, the majority of the people of East Pakistan were not in favor of secession. But with the government doing nothing to stop the violence, it was difficult to prevent people from thinking that it was "making ready to pack up and go." Even those who may have wished to oppose the Awami League were deflected from doing so.[27]

By the time Yahya came around to announcing that the national assembly would meet on March 25, Mujib's stance had stiffened. Mindful of the extreme views in the Awami League cadres, who considered the six-points nonnegotiable, he now demanded the immediate withdrawal of martial law and a return of all military personnel to the barracks, an inquiry into the loss of life, and an immediate transfer of power to the representatives of the people. Reluctant to transfer power, Yahya could not agree to these demands prior to the completion of the constitution-making process. But he was prepared to ask the army to hold their fire until he had gone through the motions of trying to make Mujib see sense. Banking on the inability of the two main political parties to agree, Yahya Khan had eased into a life of excess in wine, women, and song. Yet the Hamoodur Rahman Commission did not attribute the general's "dereliction of duty" to his heavy drinking. The supreme commander of the armed forces held his drink, though his mental reflexes had evidently slowed down. The information garnered by the commission indicated that Yahya Khan, flanked by a close circle of military officials, "played out a game in which no clear cut decision could be reached."[28]

Such a game was played out in the vitiated atmosphere of the negotiations. Yahya had set the tone on March 6 while announcing a new date for the national assembly. Slamming the Awami League for misunderstanding his reasons for postponing the meeting of the national assembly, he had said: "I will not allow a handful of people to destroy the homeland of millions of innocent Pakistanis." It was "the duty of the Pakistan Armed Forces to ensure the integrity, solidarity and security of Pakistan," and it was "a duty in which they have never failed."[29] With Bhutto demanding time out at the decisive moment in the match, and the junta cloaking the threat of force in the flighty language of national unity, the Bangabandhu had few options. Mujib was now even more of a captive of his Awami League supporters who, realizing that the regime had no real intention of either sharing or transferring power, wanted Bengalis to fight and take what was theirs by right.

On March 7, 1971, Mujib addressed a massive political rally at the Ramna Race Course in Dhaka. A skilled public orator in Bengali, the Bangabandhu delivered a stirring speech that reflected the mood of his people. He called for every Bengali home to be turned into a fortress. As blood had already been shed, he was prepared to offer more blood to free the people of his country. "The struggle this time is a struggle for freedom. The struggle this time is a struggle for independence," he proclaimed passionately, before concluding with the slogan "Jai Bangla" (Victory to Bengal). A virtual declaration of independence, Mujib's March 7 speech did not, however, completely shut the door on further talks.

The negotiations that got under way in Dhaka in mid-March 1971 were peculiar in many respects. The presidential team closely choreographed the meetings. No minutes were kept, making it impossible to cross-check and verify either Yahya's or Bhutto's testimony to the Hamoodur Rahman

Commission. Mujib did not appear before the commission. He was assassinated in 1975, and the report was not declassified until 2001. Whatever the limitations of the inquiry commission's findings, they do make it possible to piece together a proximate account of what transpired at the negotiations. At his first meeting with Yahya, Mujib demanded the immediate lifting of martial law and convening of the national assembly. There was to be a simultaneous transfer of power at the center and the provinces. Yahya accepted all the demands except the lifting of martial law on the rather lame excuse that this would create a legal lacuna. By the time the two men met again on March 20, their aides had worked out the modalities for ending martial law. Power was to be transferred to all five provinces but not for the time being at the center, where Yahya was to remain in office. The national assembly was to be divided into two committees, one for each wing. These committees were to meet together to frame a constitution on the basis of their respective reports.

This was a circuitous way to keep a divided country united. But, then, Pakistan was no ordinary country. Considering the Lahore resolution of 1940, the idea of a confederation was not nearly so far-fetched. On arriving in Dhaka on March 21, 1971, Bhutto rejected the proposal to divide the assembly into two parts on the grounds that it pointed to a confederation and paved the way for secession. This was in line with Yahya's own thinking. That night Bhutto consulted other PPP leaders, who concurred with the assessment. The next morning when the three protagonists met together for the first and only time, Yahya said that the PPP's agreement was required for the Awami League's proposals. Mujib bluntly told Yahya that it was up to him to persuade Bhutto. The discussions ended with the two politicians saying nothing to each other in the president's presence. Outside the presidential salon, Mujib took Bhutto aside and asked for his help to overcome an increasingly grave situation. Afraid that the conversation might be tapped, the two walked out into the verandah and sat in the portico, where Yahya saw them, "honeymooning with each other," as he snidely commented later.[30] Mujib told Bhutto to become the prime minister of West Pakistan and leave the eastern wing to the Awami League, warning him not to trust the military, as it would destroy both of them. Bhutto replied that he would "rather be destroyed by the military than by history." While agreeing to consider the Awami League's proposals, the PPP leader urged Mujib to place them before the national assembly, as he was not prepared to give a personal pledge on such a serious matter. According to Bhutto, Mujib rejected the idea of the national assembly being convened even briefly.[31]

The only direct exchange between Mujib and Bhutto in the tripartite talks ended in a stalemate, though the two had planned on meeting again in secret. For a second time within a matter of months, Mujibur Rahman had solicited Bhutto's help in dislodging the military regime. That the effort failed is not surprising once the haze is lifted from the moves and countermoves in the final days of a united Pakistan. Recourse to thick narrative detail reveals that the principal hurdle in the way of a united Pakistan was not disagreement on constitutional matters but the transfer of power from military to civilian hands. More concerned with perpetuating himself in office, Yahya Khan was strikingly nonchalant about the six points. He left that to the West Pakistani politicians, in particular Bhutto, who, contrary to the impression in some quarters, was more of a fall guy for the military junta than a partner in crime. In his testimony to the Hamoodur Rahman Commission, Yahya blamed Bhutto for the failure of the negotiations to make headway. What he did not reveal was that the policy of divide and rule had survived colonialism and become the preferred policy instrument of the postcolonial state in handling an intractable and increasingly violent polity. It was a recipe for disaster at the service of a drunken and dissolute ruler, more capable of dividing than ruling according to any known norms of governance.

Given the historical evidence, the verdict on apportioning responsibility for the 1971 debacle in East Pakistan must go decisively against Yahya Khan and his senior military associates in the NSC.[32] What clinched the issue for the military high command was the law-and-order situation in East Pakistan, where the Awami League was running a parallel government with bruising effect on the morale of the armed forces. Irritated by the daily abuse levied at the military presence by the Bengali press, they were incensed to find that India was actively supporting the dissidents. What the military's eastern command did not gauge, thanks to a linguistically impaired intelligence network, was that its own Bengali troops strongly supported the Awami League "miscreants." Although the decision to use military force in East Pakistan was taken only on February 22, plans had been put in place much earlier. As early as December 1970, East Pakistan's martial law administrator, General Yaqub Khan, had worked out the operational aspects of imposing law and order in what was code-named "Operation Blitz." Yaqub subsequently resigned, warning against taking military action in a situation that required a political resolution. The alarm bells went off on March 23 when the Awami League marked Pakistan Day by hoisting Bangladeshi flags but fell short of declaring independence. There were reports of Jinnah's portraits being defaced. More seriously from a military point of view, fighting broke out in Chittagong that day, with the East Pakistan Rifles and East Bengal Regiment joining hands with the dissidents against the West Pakistani forces, completely paralyzing the port city. Faced with supply difficulties, the eastern command under General Tikka Khan was implementing the first stages of its "Operation Searchlight" plan, while Yahya Khan and his aides continued their talks with Mujib and Bhutto.

It is commonly held that military action followed the breakdown of negotiations. But the talks never actually broke down; they were unilaterally abandoned on the orders of the president acting in unison with his inner military circle in Rawalpindi. A transfer of power acceptable to Mujib and Bhutto was still not outside the realm of possibility. The PPP leaders saw the Awami League's revised proposals on March 25. These called for a "confederation of Pakistan" and two constitutional conventions, instead of the separate committees in the earlier version, which were to frame the constitutions for each wing. The conventions would then meet to frame a constitution for the confederation. In shifting from a vaguely federal to a clearly confederal arrangement, the Awami League addressed the PPP's main objection that the six points said contradictory things about the future constitutional structure. Separate constitutions for the two wings, followed by one for the confederation of Pakistan, accommodated the PPP leader's fears of being diddled out of power by the Awami League. On March 14, he had made a similar demand at a public rally in Karachi's Nishtar Park. Remembered in Pakistan as his *udhar tum, idhar hum* (you there, us here) speech, Bhutto had maintained that power ought to be transferred to the Awami League in the east and the PPP in the west. He was widely condemned in West Pakistan for sanctioning the division of the country. Dismissing accusations of colluding with Yahya Khan and being responsible for the political gridlock, Bhutto spoke of "one Pakistan." The "rule of the majority" for the whole country could become applicable only if the six-point demand with its secessionist overtones was dropped. As that was not being done, the rationale and logic of the six-point demand necessitated agreement of the majority parties of both the wings.[33]

Bhutto's two-majority thesis was conceded in the final version of the Awami League's constitutional proposals. However, the notion of a confederation was wholly alien to the thinking of the military command in Pakistan. Having run Pakistan as a quasi-unitary state despite its federal configuration, the guardians of military privilege were not about to concede ground to those they saw as traitors. Instead of trying to bring the situation under control by disarming the East Pakistan Rifles and the East Bengal Regiment, the army gave vent to its rage by unleashing a reign of terror. Dhaka University was stormed and many students, faculty, and staff killed. There was indiscriminate killing of civilians, with Hindus and intellectuals serving as the main targets. The sheer ferocity of the military action ensured that Dhaka was quickly subdued, but fighting continued to rage in Chittagong and other key cities while the countryside remained in ferment. In a glaring instance of strategic oversight, Yahya and his aides moved to pummel the Awami League without fully considering India's or, for that matter the world's, likely reaction. The Pakistani Foreign Office should have had no difficulty anticipating India's likely response. But the merrymaking general and his inner coterie of military generals in their ineptitude cut themselves off from the thinking of the Foreign Office. They also had made no clear plans on how to deal with East Pakistan after the objectives of the crackdown were achieved. Yahya Khan left for West Pakistan a few hours before the start of the military operation. From his room in the Intercontinental Hotel, Bhutto watched the army setting ablaze the horizon with breathtaking ruthlessness. Punitive action without any thought to reopening the political dialogue made no sense. Yet at no time after the first shots were fired in the barricaded streets of Dhaka on March 25, 1971, did Yahya Khan restart negotiations with the Awami League. While most of the top Bengali leadership fled across the border to West Bengal, Mujib was promptly arrested and transported to a West Pakistani jail. Apart from a facetious trial in which he was given a death sentence, the regime made no effort to initiate dialogue with the Awami League leader.

With the international media flush with harrowing tales of the army's atrocities and the plight of millions of refugees who had fled to India,

Pakistan's stocks slumped internationally. Archer Blood, the American consul general in Dhaka, thought it unconscionable for the United States to turn a blind eye to the reality of the oppression Bengalis were facing and to which the "overworked term genocide is applicable." The only likely outcome of the conflict was "a Bengali victory and the consequent establishment of an independent Bangladesh." It was "foolish" to give "one-sided support to the likely loser."[34] In contrast to 1965, China politely distanced itself from a regime charged with genocide. Washington was a bit more forthcoming because the Pakistani government had recently helped the secretary of state, Henry Kissinger, to make contact with Beijing.[35] But American support was more symbolic than real—a morale-boosting assurance that India would not be permitted to rip through West Pakistan. It did not extend to absolving the Pakistani regime of its crimes and misdemeanors. The story of the junta's botched international diplomacy is a trifle less appalling than its abysmal failure on the military front. A brutal military crackdown in late March and April may have resulted in a semblance of order in key urban centers and around the cantonments. Once the monsoon set in, however, the army was constantly harried by the Bangladesh Mukti Bahini (Liberation Army) resorting to guerrilla tactics in the watery terrain of the Bengal delta. In August 1971, India, which was actively training the Bangladesh liberation forces, buttressed its international position by entering into a treaty of friendship and cooperation with the Soviet Union. The Pakistani Army's strategic doctrine of defending East Pakistan from the western wing exploded in its face when India launched a full-scale attack on the eastern front. There were no effective lines of communication between key players in the regime and an internally divided GHQ,[36] far less between them and the eastern command. Pakistani troops did fight the advancing Indian troops effectively in key sectors. The United States sent its nuclear carrier USS *Enterprise* from the Seventh Fleet into the Bay of Bengal to hover on the edges of Indian territorial waters. But the surrender of 93,000 soldiers without a whimper on December 16, 1971, highlighted the magnitude of the defeat suffered by the Pakistani Army at the hands of its primary rival. General Amir Abdullah Khan Niazi, then in command of the eastern front, alleged that the "ignominy of surrender," which is "a death warrant for a soldier," was "imposed" on him and his men by "our selfish rulers and selfish officers sitting in GHQ" in order to save West Pakistan. "We accepted humiliation to save our homeland," the disgraced general claimed in his memoir.[37]

Strategic blundering and political ineptitude combined to create a horrific nightmare for a military high command that was ill equipped to handle the situation. Once orders had been given to put boots on the ground and enforce law and order, pent-up frustrations shredded the last remnants of humanity still adorning the hearts of the West Pakistani troops. The ethical dilemma of killing fellow Muslims was quickly overcome. Bengalis were not just black men; they were Muslims in name only and had to be purged of their infidelity. Whatever the reasoning of the perpetrators, nothing can justify the horrendous crimes committed in the name of a false sense of nationalism. As in any war, there was violence on both sides against unarmed men, women, and children. But there was a world of difference between organized state coercion against a largely unarmed populace and the targeted violence of armed dissidents against known collaborators of the military regime.

A blackout on national and international news from East Pakistan kept the majority of the people of West Pakistan in a state of blissful ignorance. Some accounts of the massacre of civilians and rape of women in East Pakistan by the national army and its hastily raised Islamist militias known as *razakars* did filter through. Some West Pakistanis registered their protest. But few in the western wing were listening, convinced that the armed forces were performing their duty to protect the national integrity of the country against Indian machinations. This makes the words and actions of those brave souls from the western wing who did speak out that much more significant. Habib Jalib bewailed the savagery that had ravished East Pakistan. "For whom should I sing my songs of love," he asked, when "the garden is a bloody mess," when there were battered flower buds and blood drenched leaves everywhere despite an unstoppable rain of tears.[38] Jalib had sensed that nothing could wash away the sins of the cabal of generals who had presided over the most inglorious moment in the history of Pakistan. The noted Urdu poet Faiz Ahmad Faiz also wrote poems in 1971 lamenting that events in East Pakistan had shaken his faith in humanity. Three years later when he visited Dhaka, Faiz felt a strange kind of estrangement upon meeting with intimate Bengali friends. "After how many more meetings," he wondered, "will we be that close once again?" How many monsoons would it take to usher in a spring of unstained green in east Bengal? The end of love had been so cruel and pitiless that the crushed heart longed in vain just to quarrel once again with old friends. Faiz had gone to Bangladesh, ready to offer everything, even the gift of his own life. Such was the distance between him and his closest friends that these healing words remained unspoken after all else had been said.[39]

More than four decades after the bloody separation, the gulf between the erstwhile wings of Pakistan has grown wider in the absence of any remedial measure. Unable to forget, the people of Bangladesh might at least try and forgive if presented with a formal apology by their former tormentors. Unwilling to learn the lessons of their own history, successive rulers of what remained of Pakistan in the west avoided owning up to the crimes committed by their defeated and disgraced predecessors. The tragedy of East Pakistan had been partially foretold by the willful manipulation of center–province relations in the 1950s and 1960s by a military-dominated state. Yet a fully separate and sovereign state was an option of the last resort in the spring of 1971 once the military junta shut down all prospects of realizing Bengali national aspirations within a federal or confederal framework. What came in the wake of 1971 promised to be an endless trial by fire for the constituent units of a Pakistani federation that the military in league with the central bureaucracy insisted on governing as a quasi-unitary state.

SIX

THE RISE AND FALL OF POPULISM

PICKING UP THE PIECES of a dismembered and demoralized country was a monumental task that fell on the eager shoulders of Zulfikar Ali Bhutto. A self-styled populist who was proud of his sense of history, Bhutto had anticipated criticism of his role in the breakup of Pakistan. Soon after the military action, he wrote that the historical verdict would depend on whether the weight of the evidence showed the Awami League and Sheikh Mujibur Rahman wanting secession or provincial autonomy. "Whether we are right or wrong," he asserted, "whether our actions have been correct or incorrect, whether our initiatives have been influenced by supreme national interest or by personal ambition, will be judged in that light." What mattered was the "intention" as there was "a very thin line between maximum autonomy and secession" and, depending on one's interpretation of the six points, "little to distinguish between a loose federation, confederation and near-independence."[1]

Bhutto expected to be vindicated and the six points exposed as a subterfuge for secession. He was dead wrong. The Awami League's proposals were vague on the federal or confederal features of the future constitutional arrangement because, like any negotiable political demand, they aimed at securing the maximum possible share of power for the eastern wing within Pakistan. Even though the idea of the Bengali nation was imbued with new cultural and linguistic meaning since 1952, the scope and form of the state that could embody the idea remained open to negotiation until March 25, 1971. The divergence between intention and consequence flowed from clashing interests of the military establishment and the two main political parties. The critical factor influencing political postures was the military junta's unwillingness to relinquish power without adequate safeguards for its institutional and other interests. Faced with the prospect of sitting in the opposition at the federal center and aware of the structural constraints of Pakistan's military-dominated state, Bhutto chose to work within the existing status quo. Politics is the art of the possible, as the PPP leader knew better than anyone else. What can be queried is not Bhutto's ambition but his sense of history, his skewed definition of "national interest," and consequently his decision to back the keepers of an inherently inequitable and antidemocratic state system.

In the aftermath of a devastating military defeat, Bhutto received his calling when disaffection among a group of junior officers forced Yahya Khan to step down. This was achieved once the chief of general staff, Lieutenant General Gul Hassan, won the backing of the air chief, Air Marshal Rahim Khan. A defeated and disgraced army needed time to regroup, retool, and restore morale. More urgently, a way had to be found to secure the return of the 93,000 prisoners of war being held in Indian camps. This was a more volatile issue than military defeat and the loss of the eastern wing. As the leader of the largest party in West Pakistan, Bhutto was the logical front-runner, with the Muslim League leader Khan Abdul Qayum Khan a distant second. Bhutto was already the deputy prime minister, a capacity in which he had represented Pakistan at the UN Security Council while the terms of the cease-fire resolution were being debated. His gutsy speech, refusing to surrender to Indian aggression, accompanied by a dramatic walkout, had been roundly applauded in West Pakistan. In one of the typical legal innovations for which Pakistan was becoming renowned, Bhutto assumed charge both as president and as the first civilian chief martial law administrator. For a man who knew the complex modalities of exercising power in the Pakistani context, he would not have had it any other way.

In his first speech to a stunned nation, an emotional Bhutto stated that he had been "summoned by the nation" at a "critical hour" when "we are at the edge of the precipice." He denied any hunger for power. "I stood by the people," Bhutto avowed, "isolated from the ruling junta, from the bureaucracy, from those who matter in the land." In return, he faced five assassination attempts and a sustained media onslaught. He was "the authentic voice of the people of Pakistan," not by virtue of his dual offices, but because of the electoral verdict the people had given him. "Every institution of Pakistan has either been destroyed or threatened," and it was imperative "to rebuild democratic institutions . . . to rebuild confidence . . . to rebuild hope in the future." Donning the populist garb, Bhutto swore to bring about the biggest turnaround the ill-fated country had ever seen. He would restore democracy, frame a constitution, and establish the rule of law so that the people would never again be "under the capricious will of any individual."[2]

These noble words were fraught with irony. While inveighing against the previous regime for feeding lies to the people, Bhutto was unwilling to concede the bitter reality of military defeat or the obvious fact that East Pakistan was now the independent state of Bangladesh. Long after the signatures on the surrender document had dried, he insisted that the eastern wing remained "an inseparable and indissoluble part of Pakistan." "We have not lost a war," Bhutto stated disingenuously, "we have not failed." The "gallant armed forces" and the people of Pakistan had nothing to be ashamed of. Bhutto pledged to stick by the people through thick and thin and to never deceive or betray them. All he asked in return was their cooperation. With the people's cooperation, he could "look over the Himalayas"; without them he was "simply nobody." Ending on an uplifting note, Bhutto proclaimed Pakistan as the crystallization of a great ideal that was imperishable. Pakistanis would see to it that the stigma of defeat at India's hands was wiped out and national honor fully vindicated, "even if it has to be done by our children's children."[3]

Zulfikar Ali Bhutto: The populist. *Author's archive.*

Toward that end, Bhutto decided to fulfill his long-held dream of using Pakistan's existing nuclear energy infrastructure to embark on a rapid nuclear weapon's program. As minister for fuel, power, and national resources in Ayub Khan's cabinet, he played an active part in the formation of the Pakistan Atomic Energy Commission (PAEC). A strong proponent of acquiring nuclear capability, Bhutto faced stern opposition from Ayub who was worried about the repercussions this could have on Pakistan's pro-Western foreign policy.[4] Pakistan's need to regain prestige in the international arena after the loss of East Pakistan made the acquisition of nuclear capability urgently important. On January 20, 1972, Bhutto called a historic meeting of the country's senior nuclear scientists in Multan to solicit their views on the possibility of building a bomb within a short period of time. Dr. Ishrat Hussain Usmani, the chairman of Pakistan's Atomic Energy Commission, was the only one who opposed Bhutto's idea of redirecting the nuclear program to develop a nuclear deterrence against India. The remaining scientists, including Pakistan's sole Nobel laureate, the physicist Dr. Abdus Salam Khan, endorsed the plan. An elated Bhutto promised to spare nothing to achieve the objective and gave the scientists three years to make the vital breakthrough. Usmani was replaced and the bomb lobby empowered to work under Bhutto's watchful eye. The nuclear weapons program was a gambit that could make or break his hold on state power.

Opportunity and Failure

If not yet the tragic hero of whom epics are told, then certainly the "chosen leader" he had aspired to become, Bhutto readily accepted the crown of thorns offered to him by the new power brokers of the military establishment. Restoring national morale after a shattering defeat posed a stern test for a party powered into high office by a tsunami of rising expectations. Matters were made worse by a set of interlocking economic problems. The loss of East Pakistan had administered a rude shock to the West Pakistani economy. A way had to be found to restructure trade and find alternative markets for West Pakistani goods, 50 percent of which had been absorbed by the eastern wing. In dire need of foreign exchange, the government agreed to the International Monetary Fund (IMF) and World Bank conditions for debt rescheduling and devalued the rupee from

Rs.4.75 to Rs.11 to one US dollar. Although this helped reorient exports, it also created inflationary pressures which, together with a series of natural and man-made disasters, complicated the PPP government's efforts to pull the country out of the economic doldrums. It was an unenviable task and one Bhutto's government performed with admirable zeal, albeit with mixed results and the usual chorus of praise and opprobrium.

The populist buzzword of social justice was enshrined in the PPP's motto: "Islam is our faith, democracy is our polity, socialism is our economy, all power to the people." Employed with electrifying effect, Bhutto vowed to remake Pakistan according to the lofty principles of the father of the nation. Calling on Jinnah's legacy to legitimize their sins of omission and commission has been a standard tactic of Pakistan's mainly landlord politicians. What made Bhutto different was his rhetorical evocation of the will of the *awam* (people), which he identified as the moving force in Pakistan's past, present, and future. The momentum of the national struggle had emanated from the people, but they were shamelessly let down by a succession of rulers. Now when Jinnah's Pakistan cut such a sorry figure in the comity of nations, it was reassuring that the people of Pakistan were the "rulers of their nation" and "the arbiters and architects of their destiny."[5] Giving the common man a sense of ownership in a country whose very basis was under question was an artful device that served Bhutto well as he moved quickly to neutralize potential challenges and consolidate his grip on state power. He used the state-controlled media and the government machinery to project himself as the Quaid-i-Awam, the leader of the people, a counterpoint to Jinnah's designation as the Quaid-i-Azam, or the great leader. Bhutto manipulated the vehicle of populism consummately to create the impression that his decision to release Sheikh Mujibur Rahman and let him return to Bangladesh was willed on him by the people.

An actor who came alive under the full glare of the limelight, Zulfikar Ali Bhutto planned on scaling the heights to ultimate power in Pakistan's military-dominated state on the heady wings of populism. A Sindhi landlord with a Western education and a liberal lifestyle, Bhutto was not a man to be pinned down by contradictions. Deploying his powers as chief martial law administrator with a flourish, he announced a spate of political, economic, and administrative reforms. One of his first actions was the nationalization of a swathe of heavy industries and public utilities. This earned him the abiding wrath of big business houses, accustomed to reaping the boon of their lucrative partnership with the military–bureaucratic state. But there was little business groups could do except look on with chagrin as Bhutto announced the Economic Reforms Order sanctioning the state's takeover of ten categories of industries for the "benefit of the people of Pakistan."[6] The decision could not be challenged in any court of law. This gave the central government and its handpicked managing directors complete immunity in the day-to-day running of the industries, resulting in disastrous consequences for the economy.

The PPP's election manifesto drew on the global populist wave against capitalism led by the socialist critique of the growth-oriented development of the 1950s and 1960s. It was the handiwork of urban, educated, middle-class professionals like Mubashir Hasan and J. A. Rahim, socialist ideologues who had assembled around Bhutto because of his national stature. It was an improbable, if not inexplicable, choice on their part. To expect a scion of one of the largest Sindhi landowning families, who had earned his stripes in the service of the first military regime, to bring about a socialist and democratic transformation was a calculated gamble. In the absence of organized political parties at the grassroots level that could offer a credible middle-class leadership, a landlord politician with a populist bent seemed the best bet. A shrewd politician, Bhutto sensed that Pakistan was ripe for reform and democratic change to assuage the seething political and socio-economic discontentment sweeping the rural and the urban areas.

A distinctive feature of the PPP's nationalization of industries was the takeover of the management rather than the shareholdings. Foreign investment was left untouched in the hope of attracting the continued flow of badly needed capital from overseas. However, the speed at which the regime moved to assume control of the management of the industries proved to be the undoing of the PPP's nationalization policy. No attempt had been made to survey the actual situation on the ground. Some of the nationalized industries were in the red, while others were barely worth the name. Without stopping to gauge the effects of the first round of nationalization, Bhutto hurtled ahead with a fresh attack against monopoly capitalism by abolishing the managing agency system under which industrialists stashed away profits with impunity. This was followed by the nationalization of insurance companies, including those linked to foreign firms. The speed of the reforms shattered business confidence and undermined the fledgling industrialization process. Apart from diversifying into trade, construction, and the service sector, the bigger industrial houses diverted capital and entrepreneurial skills overseas.

Anxious to gild the lily, Bhutto issued martial law orders to seize the passports of leading industrialist families and even to jail some. Matters did not stop there, as the PPP chairman muzzled the press, used intelligence agencies to suppress opposition parties, and locked up his most vocal opponents. A martial law regulation was issued to carry out a major shake-up of the administrative bureaucracy that affected 1,300 government servants. The actions were widely seen as vindictive. Bhutto's detractors accused him of fascistic tendencies wrapped in the fig leaf of the people's will. He responded by unleashing a campaign of intimidation against political opponents and those with whom he had an axe to grind. A culture of fear and distrust meshed uneasily with the new populist order that the PPP was trying to build. Bhutto had seen enough of the workings of politics in Pakistan during his apprenticeship in Ayub's cabinet. He knew that power not only flowed from the barrel of the gun, it was the best antidote to the emergence of any significant opposition.

The use of coercion to bludgeon opponents into silence required the close cooperation of the security forces, especially the army. Taking advantage of the general disrepute into which the army had fallen after its humiliating defeat, Bhutto tried to extend his control over the institution. He ordered Pakistani television to telecast a film on the army's surrender in Dhaka on December 16, 1971, to the shock of a population still in denial. Among one of his earliest decisions was to constitute the Hamoodur Rahman Commission to investigate the causes of the military defeat in 1971. These moves brought him into conflict with General Gul Hassan, his chosen commander-in-chief. Relations between the two became strained the instant the new commander-in-chief took charge. Hassan demurred when Bhutto requested the army's help in putting down labor unrest. When a police mutiny erupted in Lahore and also Peshawar, the army chief overruled an order for intervention by Bhutto's newly appointed national security adviser, retired Major General Akbar Khan of the 1951 Rawalpindi Conspiracy fame. The mutiny was put down through a dramatic display of people's power in Lahore, deftly orchestrated by the Punjab governor, Ghulam Mustafa Khar. GHQ's noncompliance with a civilian request for assistance was used by Bhutto as the rationale for setting up the Federal Security Force (FSF), a virtual private army that the soon-to-be-ousted commander-in-chief likened to Hitler's storm troopers. Gul Hassan became convinced that Bhutto was "hell-bent on wrecking the army" when he learned that the PPP chairman had plans to put the men in uniform under the scanner of civil intelligence agencies. Hassan stood his ground and so was summarily removed. The retired general in his memoirs portrays Bhutto as "an out and out autocrat" who "thrived on subterfuge, threats, vindictiveness, and was a master in the art of overawing people" but who was cheered by the masses. A carefully cultivated cult of personality inflated Bhutto's vanity, "adding more tonnage to the apprehensions of those Pakistanis who wished to live in a decent environment."[7]

Not long after his assumption of office, Bhutto's style of governance came to be condemned as "feudal," a term loosely used in Pakistan to refer to personalized rule. The impression was reinforced by the government's recourse to the Defense of Pakistan Rules under which civil liberties and fundamental rights remained in abeyance. Bhutto's penchant to harass critics and lock them up drew the wrath of sections of the print media and the intelligentsia who, along with senior military officers, labor, and student groups, were among the first to begin withdrawing support. Air Marshal Rahim Khan, who with Gul Hassan had facilitated Bhutto's takeover, was given marching orders for demanding the release of a former military-officer-turned-business-tycoon, General Habibullah. If Gul Hassan was guilty of insubordination, the air marshal was seen as overstepping his authority. In a carefully staged drama, Bhutto secured their resignations and arranged for his top aides to drive them to Lahore, where they were kept overnight in the safety of governor's house. It was overkill as Hassan and Rahim, though initially shaken, made no effort to resist. The incident underlined Bhutto's intense wariness of the army. After axing Hassan, he selected a servile army chief, Lieutenant General Tikka Khan, the notorious "butcher" of Balochistan and Bangladesh.

If appointing compromised individuals to key positions gave Bhutto a sense of security, the constant invocation of people's power was his political lifeline. Whatever the misgivings of the urban intelligentsia, big business, or the military establishment, his populist oratory won him the hearts and minds of a sizeable segment of the populace in Punjab and Sindh. Aware of the source of his strength, Bhutto deliberately timed the removal of the two top guns in the military establishment on March 3 with a holiday to celebrate the land reform program he had announced the previous day. The land reforms of 1972 did not go far enough in redressing the problem of rural inequities. But they were an advance on Ayub Khan's land reforms and established Bhutto's credit with the masses. As in the past, the new reforms were based on individual and not family holdings. The individual ceiling was reduced from 1,000 to 300 acres of nonirrigated land and from 500 to 150 acres of irrigated land. As with the 1959 reforms, several loopholes blunted the efficacy of the 1972 land reforms. Land transfers made to family members prior to the benchmark of December 20, 1971, were declared valid.

Influential landlords, including Bhutto himself, divided their holdings among family members before the provisions of the land reform became operative. The actual ceilings on individual holdings, in any case, were appreciably higher as they were based on evaluations of land productivity made in revenue settlements dating back to the 1940s. The actual area resumed was 0.6 million acres compared with 1.9 million acres resumed under the previous reforms. Most of the resumed area consisted of uncultivated land, making for a mere 0.01 percent of the total cultivated area. The political gains for the PPP far outweighed the limited impact of the 1972 land reforms on the highly skewed structure of agrarian relations in Pakistan. Steps were taken to curb the privileges of the big landlords. The costs of production were spread out more equitably and tenants given the right of preemption of the land under their tenancy. The excess acreage acquired by the government was given free of charge to the tenants tilling the land. Nearly 13,000 tenants are estimated to have received property rights through this method. In addition, 40,000 families were given land in Swat, Chitral, Dir, and the NWFP.[8]

The nationalization of private colleges and schools was also pushed through as a martial law regulation. Intended to provide teachers with better working conditions and prevent private owners from defrauding the state through tax evasion, the nationalization turned out to be an ill-conceived step that expedited the decline in educational standards registered since 1947. Several of the schools and colleges taken over by the federal and the provincial governments were better run privately. As with the earlier reforms, there was no possibility of challenging the state's takeover of the management of privately run institutions in the courts. This incensed the urban middle classes, who were unable to funnel their resources into new institutions of learning. What ultimately destroyed the functioning of many of the nationalized educational institutions was the misconception of their employees that the ownership had also been transferred to the government, thereby relieving them of their normal obligations. The result was a precipitous drop in the teachers' work ethic.

A similar problem dented the PPP's otherwise potentially progressive labor reforms. Soon after coming into power, the government had to put down striking industrial workers, to the dismay of the PPP's left-wing cadres. But in the summer of 1972, a comprehensive reform package sought to seal the party's substantial support base among industrial labor. Masterminded by pro-labor finance minister Mubashir Hasan, the reforms raised the minimum wage and gave workers employment benefits, including pension, medical, and welfare funds. Workers were given the right of free association, collective bargaining, greater security of service, and representation in the running of industrial enterprises. Small-scale industries were hard-hit by the sudden decision to extend the purview of the reforms to cover firms employing five or more persons. Yet the reforms did extend to workers benefits they had never enjoyed before.

The PPP's labor reforms stunted the profit-making capacities of the nationalized units and triggered a series of unanticipated labor problems. There were serious labor troubles in Karachi's Landhi and Korangi industrial estates. During the month of Ramadan in early October 1972, a purportedly pro-labor central government sent in paramilitary forces and the police to clear the Dawood Cotton and Gul Ahmed Textile mills, where left-leaning workers linked to a pro-China group had taken over. The government forces fired indiscriminately on the workers. Officially, there were four deaths and fifty injuries, but eyewitnesses put the mortality figures appreciably higher. The labor leaders escaped into the neighboring hills and, after the killing of three more people, had to be brought under control by the army. If the PPP had hoped to win back labor with the reforms, its objective remained unfulfilled in Karachi, where linguistic divisions between Urdu-speaking and non-Urdu-speaking workers played an even more important role than class solidarity.[9] Karachi was not a PPP city, while concessions made to labor led to the party losing substantial support among the proprietors of small-size units in Punjab. All roads to the center ran through Punjab, something that would come to plague the PPP in its later incarnations as it trawled for electoral support in the 1980s.

In the short term, the government crackdown on industrial workers and trade unions improved business confidence, which had been shaken by the labor reforms. The mood in business circles remained upbeat despite statements by Bhutto and other central ministers that the PPP government would always side with labor in industrial disputes. There was a general feeling among businessmen that given stable conditions, they could generate the wealth necessary for Pakistan's development. But they were suspicious of the PPP's socialist rhetoric and doubted whether Bhutto's government had the political will to sustain such conditions. A member of one of the country's leading business families summed up the attitude well when he told the British consul general in Karachi at a social gathering that Pakistan was "incapable, in her present stage of development, of operating a democratic form of government and . . . the army would have to take over again in the near future."[10] With the army under the command of Tikka Khan, a loyalist, there was no immediate danger of a coup, an abiding fear that influenced Bhutto's tactics at each step of his rise up the slippery pole of power in a military-dominated state. He knew all too well that an army intervention could never be ruled out. Wedded to their security paradigm, the generals would consider any threat to the national integrity of Pakistan—whether in the form of widespread internal disorder, a regional secessionist movement, or perception of surrender to India—as cause for intervention.

No single policy measure can explain Bhutto's breathtaking rise to power and equally swift decline in fortune. A casualty of his own success, he distrusted any institution that could threaten his authority. His primary target was the military and, to a lesser extent, the civil bureaucracy, which invariably contained willing collaborators of any government, whether elected or nonelected. The logical step to take was to strengthen civilian institutions, Parliament in particular, and correct the long-standing institutional imbalances that had brought Pakistan to such a shameful pass. Fearful of the army and distrustful of the bureaucracy and the judiciary, Bhutto found cold comfort in Parliament. A PPP majority notwithstanding, several smaller parties and independents represented the fissures in the electorate to the detriment of the party agenda to bring about a state-sponsored socialist transformation of Pakistan. The PPP formed a coalition with the Muslim League led by Qayum Khan, who was made interior minister, largely because of his rivalry with the National

Awami Party (NAP). More awkward for a party needing strong centralized authority to implement its reforms, there were coalition governments of the NAP led by Wali Khan and Mufti Mahmud's JUI in NWFP
and Balochistan.

Yahya Khan had banned the NAP and imprisoned Wali Khan. The PPP
government lifted the ban and opened negotiations with Wali Khan. Tall
and silvery haired, the impressive looking Pathan politician thought the
Pakistani president was completely untrustworthy. "Bhutto was like the
unholy trinity," Wali Khan railed, "he stood for I, Me and Myself" and
"put himself above his Party and his Party above Pakistan, in that order."
Denying that the NAP and JUI ever agreed to extend martial law until
August 14, 1972, Wali Khan contended that they had said only that the
national assembly should decide the matter. No opposition party could
ever support martial law.[11] After marshaling a range of arguments for its
continuation, including the misleading claim that half the country was in
Indian hands, Bhutto on April 21, 1972, lifted martial law in return for the
opposition's endorsement of an interim constitution. He was forced to do
so in the wake of a landmark judicial decision in the *Asma Jilani* case.
Overturning the *Dosso* ruling that had upheld the legitimacy of Ayub's
martial law, the Supreme Court pronounced Yahya Khan a usurper and
declared his martial law illegal. Bhutto was ruling under the 1969 martial
law proclamation. So the need for constitutional legitimacy became criti-
cally urgent. The long-delayed meeting of the national assembly was called
on April 14, and on April 17 a clear majority passed an interim constitution, providing for a presidential form of government at a strong center
and parliamentary government in the four provinces. On October 20,
1972, the leaders of the parliamentary parties met under Bhutto's chair-
manship and unanimously adopted the outlines of a constitution prepared by a parliamentary subcommittee.

Wali Khan chose not to attend the meeting and asked Mir Ghous Baksh
Bizenjo, the governor of Balochistan, to negotiate on behalf of the NAP.
To Wali Khan's horror, his representative was lured into conceding extensive powers to Bhutto as prime minister for the next fifteen years. At a
meeting on November 18 to discuss the draft constitution, the NAP's general council expressed disquiet, noting that the document fell short of the
party manifesto, people's aspirations for undiluted democracy, and maximum provincial autonomy. Apart from being opposed to Bhutto's powers,

the NAP was against the uneven distribution of power between the two houses of Parliament and the three-quarters majority required to dismiss an elected government. But instead of rejecting the accord, and endangering the future of Pakistan, the NAP decided to focus its energies on pushing the national assembly to make amendments to the final version of the constitution. For all his misgivings about the PPP chairman's political gyrations, Wali Khan did not favor overthrowing him as he could "not think of anyone else to replace Bhutto." He was confident that Bhutto would concede the NAP's amendments. Bhutto was "stubborn" and "tried to bully others" but "gave in where he could not exert pressure."[12]

There was still scope here for a negotiated compromise on the constitution. While formally soliciting the support of the NAP and JUI in constitution making, Bhutto in his eagerness to slot the PPP into office in the NWFP and Balochistan began plotting for the removal of their coalition governments. This poisoned relations between the two political adversaries. Bhutto set the bureaucracy into motion to garner evidence against Wali Khan's anti-Pakistan lineage dating back to his father, Khan Abdul Ghaffar Khan (known as the "Frontier Gandhi"), who had supported the Congress instead of the Muslim League in the final decades of colonial rule in India. It took the engineering of a diplomatic incident to give the central government an excuse to move against the non-PPP governments in the NWFP and Balochistan. On February 10, 1973, a cache of Soviet-made weapons was seized in a raid on the Iraqi embassy in Islamabad. The government alleged that they were meant for separatist elements in Balochistan. American intelligence thought the arms might have been intended for southeastern Iran, where the Iraqis wanted to stir up trouble.[13] Bhutto saw things differently. He suspected the Soviets of wanting to establish a grip on Afghanistan and of furtively fanning a separatist movement in Balochistan. Presidential rule was imposed in Balochistan and Bizenjo replaced as governor with Sardar Akbar Bugti. The governor of the NWFP was also dismissed, resulting in the NAP–JUI government resigning in protest.

On March 4, 1973, at a well-attended public meeting in Karachi, Wali Khan retaliated by starting a movement to restore democracy and the rule of law. Press censorship had to be lifted and the tyranny of one-man rule ended. He reiterated his controversial demand for an open trial of Yahya Khan to establish responsibility for the breakup of the country. Wali

Khan's backsliding on the constitutional accord and hobnobbing with minor opposition parties had done nothing for his credibility. An article in the government-controlled *Pakistan Times* attributed the arrest of Sher Mohammad Marri, the Baloch nationalist leader known as General Sheru, to his role in raising a guerilla force to liberate parts of Balochistan with the help of the former NAP government. Bhutto openly accused the NAP of colluding with Afghanistan. There was a coordinated media blitz about a "London Plan" chalked out by the NAP leadership to bring about the disintegration of Pakistan. Later, in February 1975, the assassination of Hayat Mohammad Sherpao, the popular leader of the PPP in the NWFP, provided the pretext for banning the NAP and implicating Wali Khan in a conspiracy against the state.

These measures exploded Bhutto's democratic façade and, in exposing his lukewarm commitment to federalism, seriously damaged the prospects for political stability in Pakistan. The PPP chairman needed the legitimacy of the 1973 constitution to tighten his hold on state power. Faced with inner party discord in his strongholds in Sindh and Punjab, Bhutto was not inclined to rely on the PPP organization. The result was his increasing use of the newly created paramilitary FSF as well as the police and civil bureaucracy to achieve his political purposes. In an inconvenient piece of timing, the PPP governor of Sindh, Rasul Baksh Talpur, resigned over differences with Bhutto on the federal provisions of the constitution and a bruising power struggle with Bhutto's cousin, the provincial chief minister Mumtaz Bhutto. There was a wave of political arrests in all four provinces, including that of the Jamaat-i-Islami leader, Mian Tufail, who publicly called for army intervention in the light of the delicate political situation in Balochistan created by Bhutto's dictatorial methods.

With the opposition parties threatening to take their campaign for democracy to the streets unless their constitutional demands were met, Bhutto upped the ante. Warning of the "deadly crisis" facing Pakistan, he convened the national assembly to discuss the draft constitution. The opposition decided to attend the parliamentary debate in the hope of demonstrating that the constitution had only minority support in three provinces. In the event, Bhutto won an overwhelming endorsement for his preferred constitution. On April 10, 1973, 125 out of the 135 members of the national assembly voted in favor of the draft document. For a defeated and divided nation, a consensual constitution was a remarkable feat that had required special exertions on the part of the PPP negotiators. Compromises were struck with the opposition parties and unwritten promises made. In an interesting move for a politician committed to eliminating US involvement in Pakistan's domestic affairs, Bhutto solicited the help of the American chargé d'affaires to win over Bizenjo, whom he had just dismissed as governor of Balochistan. The NAP voted for the constitution because it wanted to join the PPP's urban dissidents to put some sort of a leash on Bhutto's unrestrained exercise of power. Bhutto later took credit for this metamorphosis, asserting that Wali Khan had "vehemently opposed" the constitutional draft. "I led him by his pretty nose to agree to the 1973 constitution," he boasted and, through skillful maneuvering, "smashed him into becoming a Pakistani."[14] Bhutto had wanted a presidential system of government but deferred to the opposition's demand for a parliamentary democracy and took over as prime minister. By giving the impression of conceding more than any of the other parties, the PPP was able to pilot the 1973 constitution through Parliament. Pakistan's third permanent constitution came into operation on the twenty-sixth anniversary of independence. Two days later, key leaders of the opposition in Balochistan were arrested on charges of corruption and sedition, undermining Bhutto's claim that the new constitution marked the end of palace intrigues and violence in politics. If it had been implemented both in letter and spirit, the new constitutional framework may well have provided the political impetus for recasting Pakistan's federal configuration.

The future of Pakistan depended on striking a more equitable balance between the federal center and the four provinces. With the loss of the eastern wing, Punjabi dominance of the state structure became unassailable. Constituting 60 percent of the total population of Pakistan, Punjabis made up 70 percent of the military personnel. They also dominated the federal bureaucracy and had a significant presence in the provincial civil services and the police force in Sindh and Balochistan. Antipathy toward the dominance of the administrative and security services by Punjabis and Urdu speakers in Sindh announced itself in the form of a serious language crisis not long after the formation of a PPP government in the province. Encouraged to see one of their own as prime minister at the center, Sindhis demanded national status for their regional vernacular. They wanted 90 percent of the regional radio and television broadcasting to be in Sindhi. Bhutto called for calm reflection and the spirit of give and take, reminding the Urdu speakers that they owed it to their Sindhi hosts to accommodate, if not embrace, the provincial cultural traditions. While promising the Urdu speakers a fair deal, he regretted that Sindhis had been reduced to a position of a minority in some parts of the province.

There had been violent clashes in Sindh during the summer of 1972 whose reverberations were felt in the political arenas of Punjab, where there was strong support for Urdu. Headed by Bhutto's "talented cousin," Mumtaz Bhutto, the Sindh provincial government had to somehow square the circle of the conflicting demands of the two main linguistic communities. The compromise formula had the prime minister's stamp of approval. Sindhi was made the official language of the province, but Urdu was retained as the national language. For twelve years non-Sindhi speakers were not to be placed at a disadvantage in either the public services or their transactions with the government. The Sindh government was instructed to deal lightly with those arrested during the language disturbances and give monetary compensation to the victims of violence. Although the trouble was scotched through political negotiations, the language crisis of 1972 sowed the seeds of an acrimonious linguistic divide between Sindhi and Urdu speakers, transforming key urban centers like Karachi and Hyderabad into war zones during the 1980s and 1990s.

With the experience of the language disturbances in Sindh fresh in his mind, Bhutto knew that the only way to alleviate the sense of marginality on the part of the non-Punjabi provinces was to provide them with more effective representation at the center. Suspicious of Punjabis, he tried controlling the politics of the province by pitting the earthy populist Ghulam Mustafa Khar against the clement intellectual-politician Hanif Ramay. Bhutto was accused of staging Punjabi dogfights. To be fair to the great PPP leader, he used much the same sort of tactic to manipulate politics in his own home province of Sindh as well as the more distant NWFP and Balochistan. Experience had taught him that the only way to rule Pakistan was to divide. This helped him in hammering compromises with the opposition to arrive at an agreed constitutional document. Bhutto's biggest contribution to Pakistan had been preceded by head-on confrontations with the NAP and other opposition parties. The situation in Balochistan was coming to a boil. Akbar Bugti's appointment as governor led to heightened rivalries among Bugti, Marri, and Mengal tribesmen. Baloch hostility toward the center threatened a repeat of the situation in

East Pakistan. In the discerning analysis of the US State Department's intelligence report on Pakistan, Bhutto and the opposition leaders succeeded in striking compromises after learning to accept their limitations. If this process of political bargaining, so intrinsic to a democracy, was allowed to continue, there was a possibility of Pakistanis "developing procedures to deal with one another so as to reduce the risk of violent confrontations." However, resorting to repressive measures against non-PPP politicians and the press, Bhutto "forced the opposition to accept compromises on his own terms" with "an adroit use of carrot-and-stick tactics." Although this had strengthened his position, it had also provoked regional antagonisms. A political process based on Bhutto's continuing ability to outmaneuver the opposition was "not likely to provide for the integration of conflicting groups required for stability over the longer term."[15]

On the face of it, the 1973 constitution was sensitive to the needs of the smaller provinces. They were given equal representation with Punjab in the Senate, the upper house of a two-chamber federal legislature. But the upper house did not have the requisite legislative and financial powers to redress the numerical disadvantages of the non-Punjabi provinces in the lower house. Some financial concessions were made to the provinces. They were entitled to the proceeds of excise duty, royalties on gas, and profits of hydroelectric power, partially reducing their financial dependence on the center. A Council of Common Interests was established to ensure the smooth functioning of the federation and safeguard the rights of the smaller provinces. Despite these concessions to federalism, the authority of the central government was left essentially unchanged. A three-quarter majority was required to dislodge the government. As prime minister, Bhutto could exercise vast powers as the chief executive while the president, Fazal Ilahi Chaudhry, was reduced to being a figurehead. The chances of a healthier federal union, however, were dashed not so much by the structural constraints of the system but by the honoring of the constitution in the breach rather than in the observance. There were seven amendments to the constitution between 1973 and 1977, all of them at the expense of the judiciary and individual rights.

Instead of directing reforms to strengthen the role of Parliament and the judiciary vis-à-vis the military and the civil bureaucracy, Bhutto focused on stamping his own authority on the two main nonelected institutions of the state. Daunted by the power wielded by the army, Bhutto encouraged criticism of the military's role in politics through the state-controlled media. He flayed the "Bonapartic" tendencies in the armed forces, where "some professional Generals turned to politics not as a profession but as a plunder."[16] Taking the indictment a step further, Bhutto asserted that the Pakistani Army played no role in the struggle for independence and had been "more concerned with the distribution of the regimental silver than the partition of the subcontinent."[17]

Such contempt was not incompatible with wanting to keep the army on his side. While curtailing the growth of the military's commercial ventures,[18] Bhutto not only espoused the military's hawkish views on India but also lent them a populist touch that resonated well with his constituents in Punjab. This ensured his continuity in office, giving him time to rein in a military institution that exerted such a powerful influence on the country's politics. Bhutto's meeting with Prime Minister Indira Gandhi at Simla in July 1972, the first since the Indo-Pakistan War the previous year, was a potential opening for placing relations between the two countries on a new footing. Wary of popular opinion in Punjab, Bhutto used the opportunity primarily to negotiate the return of the prisoners of war and Pakistani territory occupied by India. Both sides agreed to honor the cease-fire line in Kashmir, which was renamed the Line of Control (LOC). There was no softening of the official rhetoric against India, far less a major rethinking of the state's security imperatives after the dramatic shift in the subcontinental balance of power stemming from the loss of Pakistan's eastern wing. This took away the sting from Bhutto's restructuring of the military's command and control system in the spring of 1972. The office of commander-in-chief was abolished as a remnant of colonialism and members of the three services placed on an equal footing. The tenure of the army chief of staff was reduced and a decision taken not to give extensions to any of the service chiefs. A special clause was inserted into the 1973 constitution, making it illegal for the military to intervene in politics.

With the new army chief, General Tikka Khan, at his beck and call, Bhutto looked to impose his imprimatur on the country's premier institution. Soon after the Iraqi arms incident, Bhutto presided over a meeting of the federal cabinet that was briefed by representatives of the civilian Intelligence Bureau (IB) and the army's ISI. There was a paucity of funds and little coordination between the intelligence agencies, which were unduly focused on protective security rather than offensive counterintelligence.

Indira Gandhi and Zulfikar Ali Bhutto on the lawns of Raj Bhawan, Simla, June 30, 1972.
Author's archive.

Bhutto complained about the lack of information he was getting from the ISI Directorate on the political situation in the country. The army intelligence reports were also not made available to him. He had learned only from party sources that mullahs in their sermons to the soldiers were attacking the government. It seemed as if the army was still unreconciled to constitutional democracy. Almost 90 percent of Pakistan's federal budget was spent on defense, leaving little for economic development or the social needs of the people. Despite their privileged position, army officers were criticizing government actions and questioning valid orders. It was imperative that the ISI chief keep him fully posted on undercurrents in the defense forces.[19]

In his directive to the ministry of interior, Bhutto called for the establishment of a reserve force that would be the final repository in dealing with serious agitations and breaches of law and order. Looking to reduce his dependence on the army in putting down civil unrest, Bhutto used the FSF as a private militia. The newly set up Federal Investigation Agency served as his personal intelligence network. He began spending an inordinate amount of time reading false and half-baked reports from secret informants. Most of the intelligence related to the private lives of others, friends and foes, which Bhutto deployed both to his political advantage and personal amusement.[20] Eager to carve out a support base in the army, Bhutto retained the services of several senior officers whose role in the 1971 debacle was derided by the junior ranks. Angered by Bhutto's use of the army for his own political purposes, a group of young army officers began planning a putsch. They were infiltrated by military intelligence, arrested in March 1973, and tried in the Attock Conspiracy Case.

Politicizing the army was a far cry from placing it under civilian control and correcting the institutional imbalances between elected and nonelected institutions of the state. Ever conscious of the potential for a military intervention, Bhutto was disinclined to strengthen Parliament or the judiciary. He firmly believed that only a strong civilian political authority in control of the executive, legislative, and judicial branches of government could keep ambitions within the army in check. Nor did he see the wisdom in building up the PPP's organizational machinery. Pakistan in his opinion could be governed only through coercion and dashes of populism emanating from his charismatic personality. A virtuoso in dispensing with one hand and withholding with the other, Bhutto jacked up the salaries, allowances, and other perks for the senior and junior officers of all three services. No stone was left unturned to procure weaponry for the defense forces. The PPP government successfully negotiated the lifting of a ten-year American embargo on arms to Pakistan. When in 1974 India tested a nuclear device, reiterating his famous claim with renewed vigor, Bhutto promised to push ahead with Pakistan's nuclear program even if the country had to "eat grass." This dismayed Washington, the one capital he could not afford to alienate if he was to keep the army and the national economy on an even keel.

Making light of the law of unintended consequences, Bhutto followed his drastic nationalizations with a revamping of state institutions through radical administrative reforms. Speaking at the PPP's fifth annual convention on November 30, 1972, in Rawalpindi, Bhutto accused civil servants of creating discord between PPP workers and members of the national and provincial assemblies. He would "break the back of bureaucracy" and "convert these Brahmins and Pundits into Moslems."[21] At a stroke, the 1973 constitution eliminated constitutional guarantees giving civil servants protection of service—a measure that would be blamed in later years for the decline in the bureaucracy's institutional ethos and inclination of civil servants to seek the patronage of political parties. The top level of the superior bureaucracy, the CSP, was abolished and merged into a linear all-Pakistan-based unified grade structure. Bhutto introduced a lateral entry system to induct skilled talent into the civil service and the police. These were popular measures and could have gone a long way in bolstering the PPP's support base if they had been used to pare down the vast powers exercised by the administrative services. Instead, the need for civil servants to run the nationalized industries saw a distinctive increase in bureaucratic power. The expansion of the public sector with the nationalization of thirty-two private-sector industries created vast opportunities for political graft and corruption. In the much-vaunted age of populist reforms, members of the former CSP were better placed than the new technocratic and professional recruits to influence the cut and thrust of greater state interventions in the economy.

Reinforcing dependence on the administrative services was the unintended result of Bhutto's reforms. Fortunately, the PPP government did a reasonable job managing the economy given the enormity of the challenges. By looking westward to the oil-rich Muslim countries and beyond, Pakistan was able to replace the markets lost in Bangladesh. Bhutto broke the power of the twenty-two business families that controlled the vast majority of the country's industrial assets and tempered his regime's pro-labor rhetoric by helping widen the circle of entrepreneurs. There was a string of unlucky setbacks. In 1973, considerable havoc was wreaked by flash floods; there was a costly mishap at the Tarbela Dam, which was under construction; oil prices quadrupled in September 1973; and the crushing impact of global inflation was felt in a country in the grips of drought. The PPP government was aware of its economic vulnerabilities. Policies were adopted to expedite Pakistan's quest for self-sufficiency in food production. The goal was to achieve a growth rate that could help distribute wealth more evenly than had been the case under military rule. Efforts were made to persuade the World Bank and the IMF, aid donors, and, above all, the oil-producing countries that Pakistan's economy was worth supporting. By the spring of 1974, Pakistan seemed to be in a healthier economic position than India and Bangladesh.[22]

Yet at the end of three years in office, Bhutto had lost the support of the urban middle and lower middle classes in Punjab and Sindh without a commensurate consolidation of his base among industrial labor and the urban poor. But what Bhutto lost in popularity, he gained in power. The adoption of the 1973 constitution offered him a wide berth to handle all the provinces except Balochistan, where recourse to military action gave the army an upper hand. In Sindh, he got rid of the chief minister, Mumtaz Bhutto. Soon after soaring in popularity for convening his version of the Mughal durbar (i.e., a court) in the form of a conference of Islamic heads of state, Bhutto sacked the governor of Punjab, Mustapha Khar. His disdainful treatment of a loyalist party boss like Khar, the self-proclaimed "lion of Punjab," made it plain that the PPP was becoming less and less important to Bhutto in ruling Pakistan. He relied increasingly on the bureaucracy, police, the intelligence agencies, and his own FSF, ensuring that while the provinces had the accoutrements of democratic government, real authority remained exclusively in the hands of the center. The arrangement was workable only so long as Bhutto kept the defense forces in good cheer. He tried doing so by refusing to heed calls to bring Yahya Khan to trial, thereby avoiding opening up a can of worms related to the army's sordid actions in East Pakistan. The Hamoodur Rahman Commission's report would be allowed to gather dust with only a select few privy to its contents. Moving forward with one eye fixed on the all-powerful army was not easy for a politician whose policies had riled influential segments of the dominant social classes into outright opposition to his regime.

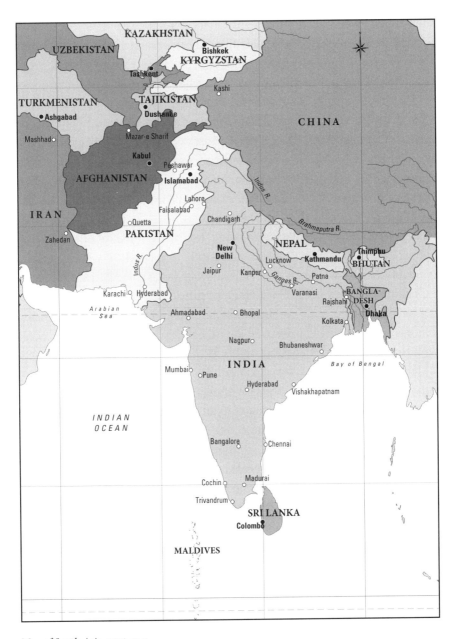

Map of South Asia, post-1971.

Foreign Policy Initiatives

Bhutto had always been a vocal proponent of an independent foreign policy. The PPP's manifesto was committed to suspending all "entanglements with imperialist neocolonialist powers" that were using Pakistan as "a pawn" for their international games and hampering its "freedom of action" in securing the liberation of Kashmir.[23] In line with this policy, Bhutto took Pakistan out of the Commonwealth and SEATO but upgraded relations with CENTO. The bedrock of his foreign policy was close friendship with China and the Muslim world, friendly relations with America, and a guarded attitude toward the Soviet Union, which was accused of assisting the Indians in the dismantling of Pakistan. After the Arab-Israeli War and the quadrupling of oil prices in 1973, Bhutto redoubled his efforts to reaffirm Pakistan's ties with Muslim oil-producing countries, especially Iran, Libya, and Saudi Arabia, all of which contributed monetarily to Pakistan's nuclear program. The acclaimed father of Pakistan's nuclear bomb, Bhutto fancied himself as a leader of the Muslim world. His crowning achievement on the foreign policy front was hosting the Islamic Summit Conference in late February 1974, a glittering occasion that he used to extend Pakistan's formal recognition to Bangladesh.

Held in Lahore, the Islamic Summit Conference was cohosted by Bhutto and King Faisal of Saudi Arabia. In a traditional display of Pakistani hospitality, the city elite moved out of their luxurious homes to accommodate the delegates. The Shah of Iran was conspicuous by his absence, preferring to receive a visiting Indian minister rather than attend an extravaganza hosted by his archrival, the Saudi monarch. King Hussain of Jordan also stayed away because of the Palestine Liberation Organization (PLO) representation at the conference. Taking full advantage of the high-profile occasion, Bhutto hogged the limelight, defiantly appealing to transnational Muslim solidarity. Muammar Gaddafi, Yasser Arafat, and Mujibur Rahman were among other favorites of the press. Outperformed at his own party, the Saudi monarch showed his displeasure by leaving a measly tip rather than paying his expected share of the costs.[24] The cooling of relations between Riyadh and Islamabad could not last long. Bhutto's new policy directions, especially the nuclear weapons program, were heavily dependent on Saudi largesse. Asked how he would fund his reforms, he responded, "God will give." Pakistan's economy

Chinese premier Chou-en-Lai receiving Zulfikar Ali Bhutto at Beijing Airport, late January 1972. *Author's archive.*

needed a gift from God, but Bhutto was willing to settle for some part of the soaring oil profits in Saudi Arabia, the Gulf States, and Iran. The Arabs and the Iranians had better places to invest than Pakistan. Promoting the export of manpower was the next best choice for the PPP government.

Bhutto's foreign policy departures had a direct bearing on the domestic political scene. Making a bigger play of Pakistan's Islamic credentials encouraged the electorally routed religious parties to organize their political comeback. Instead of using his populist reforms to stretch the PPP's bases of support as widely as possible, Bhutto opened up several fronts against himself without creating a safety net in the form of a party organization. The blue serge uniforms worn by Bhutto and his ministers gave the illusion of party solidarity, which was belied by the organizational realities. Soon after taking office, Bhutto began purging the radical left elements from the PPP and recruiting bigger landlords, whom he lambasted at

Zulfikar Ali Bhutto with Mujibur Rahman at Lahore Airport, February 23, 1974. *Author's archive.*

public rallies for their greed and exploitation. The reversal of commitments put off the PPP's left-wing constituency, dampening the spirit of party workers just when the land and labor reforms were generating enthusiasm for the PPP. It was the classic quandary of a populist politician who had successfully made his way to the apex of state power by playing to all factions within his party.

Like Indira Gandhi in India, Zulfikar Ali Bhutto feared the consequences of leading a truly democratic political party. Relying on their personal appeal to the masses, both leaders opted not to organize their respective parties at the grassroots level. Inner party democracy was dispensed with as a threat to their preeminent power at the national level. Both relied on the powers of the centralized state to project themselves as the main repository of political patronage. Bhutto's task was doubly difficult because the army, notwithstanding its humbling by India, remained the most powerful state institution in Pakistan. The FSF could quell urban dissent but not an insurgency. After creating the conditions for Balochistan to erupt in a tribal uprising, Bhutto made the fatal mistake of calling in the army to crush the revolt. The army was soon at odds with the Balochistan governor, Akbar Bugti, who resigned, making the problem more intractable. Even with a loyalist as chief of staff, it was now only a matter of time before the army returned to the political arena. The insurgency took on the proportions of a civil war, drawing the active interest of the Shah of Iran, who feared Pakistan's local troubles might spill over into Iranian Balochistan and draw Soviet backing. Wali Khan countered by objecting to the Shah's interference in Pakistan's affairs and accused Bhutto of letting Iran take over Balochistan. In a related development, a group of Pakistani students in London, most of them with urban Punjabi upper middle-class backgrounds and leftist leanings, joined the tribal militants in their mountain redoubts to fight against Bhutto's tyranny.[25]

It was against the backdrop of an armed revolt in Balochistan and widespread opposition to the PPP government that the religious right found its moment of glory. Emboldened by the regime's cultivation of an Islamic image for Pakistan, the Jamaat-i-Islami capitalized on Mawdudi's close ties with Saudi Arabia, in return for which the party became the recipient of benevolence, in both cash and kind. The Saudi ruler Shah Faisal wanted to use the petro-dollar windfall to seal a dominant place in the international arena and, in the process, counteract the Shah of Iran's rising regional influence. Projecting their Wahabi ideology with a newfound confidence, the Saudis called for the excommunication of the Ahmadis and began denying them Haj visas. Delighted with the turn of events, the Jamaat-i-Islami and like-minded Islamist parties joined a group calling itself the Khatam-i-Nubuwwat (Finality of Prophethood) to reopen the controversy to declare the Ahmadis non-Muslims. The basis had been laid in the 1973 constitution, which provided the legal and political machinery for the implementation of the sharia as defined by the orthodox religious clergy. Anxious to win a strong endorsement for the constitution, Bhutto made the first of his many cynical concessions to the so-called religious lobby—effectively a gaggle of parties with a political agenda to assume state power by harping on all things Islamic. Under the new constitutional provisions, a special oath had to be taken by the president and prime minister, stating that they were Muslims who believed in the finality of Muhammad's prophecy and firmly denied the possibility of any prophet after him. The need for a statement of the obvious was dictated by the single-minded agenda of the religio-political parties to purge the Muslim community of any strains of Ahmadiyat. This was the capstone of the Islamist demand to establish the golden age of the Prophet Muhammad.

The anti-Ahmadi agitation drew on a historically constructed narrative that billed Ahmadis as British agents, who were deliberately put up by the colonial masters to undermine the finality of Muhammad's prophethood. More recently, Ahmadis were accused of being Israeli agents. These "fifth columnists" wanted "the creation of another Israel for themselves in this part of the world," claimed Agha Shorish Kashmiri, the pro-Jamaat-i-Islami and anti-Bhutto editor of the right-wing Urdu weekly *Chatan* from Lahore. The danger was political, not sectarian, as was mistakenly believed. Ahmadis had "dug into different important positions in the Defence, Finance, and Broadcasting departments of Pakistan government and are busy in paving the way for their political domination."[26] Kashmiri's opinion reflects the hard-line attitude against Ahmadis, particularly in Punjab. During the Islamic Summit, King Faisal indicated to Bhutto that

King Faisal greeting Zulfikar Ali Bhutto at Hamar Palace, Jeddah. *Author's archive.*

Saudi aid would be contingent on Pakistan declaring Ahmadis a non-Muslim minority. In April 1974, the Rabita al-Alam-al-Islami (Islamic World Congress) meeting at Mecca called on all Muslim governments to declare Ahmadis a non-Muslim minority and debar them from holding sensitive positions in the state. While calling for an immediate social and economic boycott of Ahmadis, the Rabita left it to each country's legislature to deal with the political aspects of the issue. In May 1974, the Jamaat-i-Islami colluded with parties operating under the umbrella of the movement to uphold the finality of Muhammad's prophethood to instigate a fresh wave of anti-Ahmadi disturbances. The catalyst for the violence was a clash on May 29, 1974, between some students of Nishtar Medical College and Ahmadis at the railway station in Rabwah, the sect's spiritual and organizational home. Members of the community were knifed, their properties burned down, and their mosques and graves desecrated throughout Punjab and also parts of the NWFP.

In the 1970 elections, Ahmadis had solidly supported Bhutto after the leader of the community instructed them to vote and donate generously to the PPP. The Ahmadi vote in the upper middle-class neighborhoods of Lahore was critical in Bhutto winning with a margin of 40,000 votes against Javed Iqbal, the son of the city's esteemed poet and philosopher Muhammad Iqbal. Ahmadis were rewarded with key positions in the Bhutto administration. Aziz Ahmad, the minister of state for defense and foreign affairs, was an Ahmadi. By mid-1972, Ahmadis were commanding both the air force and the navy while about a dozen or so held senior and sensitive positions in the army, including that of corps commander. This is what most irked the would-be defenders of the Prophet. Bhutto had contempt for the anti-Ahmadi agitators, deeming them to be "too narrow minded and out-moded." It was a "fallacy to think that a simple and expedient tilt towards such forces serves the country's interest or even that of a regime."[27] Once in high office, he found it advantageous to go against his own better judgment. Aware of the potency of anti-Ahmadi sentiments in certain pockets of Punjab, Bhutto feared becoming a casualty of the campaign against the sect. He convinced himself that only an orthodox Sunni prime minister could survive the implications of a liberal resolution of the Ahmadi controversy. This mistaken assumption led him into making the grievous error of thinking the Islamists could be kept at bay by conceding their main demand for the Islamization of the state.

In a defining moment for Pakistan, the national assembly unanimously passed an amendment to the constitution on September 7, 1974,
pronouncing the Ahmadis a minority. Any definition of a Muslim by the
state was bound to throw open the floodgates of bigotry against smaller
and more vulnerable sects. Declaring Ahmadis non-Muslims laid the basis for an exclusionary idea of citizenship, undermining the Pakistani
nation-state's commitment to equal rights of citizenship. The PPP government presented the second constitutional amendment act as a preemptive measure for the protection of Ahmadis. It was Bhutto's lowest
moment as a politician and a statesman and one he was willing later to
acknowledge. But even in compromise, he was more pragmatic than ideological. Aziz Ahmad retained his position in Bhutto's cabinet. However,
the Nobel prize–winning physicist Mohammad Abdus Salam, another
key Ahmadi serving as science adviser to the government and overseeing
the development of the nuclear weapons program since 1972, resigned his
position to protest the amendment. Bhutto accepted the resignation but
asked Salam to continue giving informal advice. "This is all politics,"
Bhutto declared, "give me time, I will change it." When Salam asked if
Bhutto would write this down in a private note, the crafty politician politely declined.[28]

Bhutto had let political expediency triumph over principle. The ramifications of his decision soon became apparent as the prime minister came
under increasing pressure from the religio-political parties. Looking to
convert their victory on the Ahmadi issue into definite electoral advantage, they demanded the immediate institution of an Islamic system of
government. The charge of the religio-political combine that it was the
state's lack of religiosity, and not the inadequacies of Islam as a force of
cohesion, that had broken up the country appealed to broad sections of
society still unable to come to terms with the blow to their national pride.
The religiously minded lower middle classes, consisting of small shopkeepers and petty merchants, teachers, as well as the semiprofessional and
educated unemployed, were particularly susceptible to this kind of propaganda. Once the ground had been prepared, the Jamaat-i-Islami and like-
minded Islamist parties turned the PPP government's lack of religiosity
into a potent political weapon. The aspersion stung all the more given the
Jamaat-i-Islami's public denunciations of the PPP chairman for his hand
in the disintegration of Pakistan.

Bhutto realized that the call for an Islamic revival was a ruse by the Islamist parties to orchestrate a movement to oust him from office. Once he had nationalized the vegetable oil industry on the advice of his socialist finance minister, Mubashir Hasan, small- and medium-scale entrepreneurs, who owned a considerable portion of the cooking oil industry, rose up against him. There was a public outcry against Bhutto's deception—he had assured business that there would be no further nationalizations. Business groups hit by the PPP's nationalization and labor reforms vented their fury by filling the opposition's coffers. The coup de grâce for large businesses came with the nationalization of banks, petroleum products, and maritime shipping. Prominent businessmen now were not just financing the opposition; they were actively working to bring down the government. Bhutto responded to the uproar in business circles by getting rid of most of his original team of socialist ministers. A cabinet reshuffle in the fall of 1974 saw Bhutto bringing in the "feudal lords," hated by the PPP's ousted left-wing intellectuals, and relying increasingly on a select group of bureaucrats. Even while benefiting from the regime's pro-agrarian policies, the landed gentry as a whole was unhappy at the prospect of more land reforms. The urban middle classes, for their part, were incensed by the government's failure to control galloping inflation and the denial of the most rudimentary kind of civil liberties.

These negative perceptions were offset by Bhutto's popularity among the urban and rural poor. The PPP's reforms created a sense of optimism among the toiling masses, especially in the rural areas. By turning the terms of trade in favor of the agrarian sector, the Finance Ministry under Mubashir Hasan reversed over a decade of policies promoting industrial interests. Pro-poor measures adopted during the phase of left-wing dominance of the PPP ensured its popularity among the downtrodden and disempowered. In keeping with its promise to provide food, clothing, and housing, the government intervened in the market to control and subsidize prices for essential commodities like sugar, cooking oil, and cloth. The PPP's educational policy, calling for free universal education for everyone up to the age of fifteen, appealed to the poor. So did the objective of a comprehensive public health-care program. In the absence of increased financial allocations to these sectors, neither policy made any difference in eradicating illiteracy and providing basic health care. But they associated the PPP with the poor, assuring it mass support well after the thrust of populism had been blunted. The decision to facilitate the export of migrant labor in order to take advantage of the employment boom in oil-producing Muslim countries had a more enduring impact. It not only helped the families of these workers skirt around the problems of unemployment and high inflation but also brought huge amounts of remittances that bolstered the country's foreign exchange reserves.

The PPP has been charged with economic mismanagement and the adoption of policies to serve the left's main constituencies in the urban areas.[29] Yet on the whole the PPP regime did a reasonable enough job of reviving Pakistan's economy in a challenging international environment. Despite a succession of devastating floods, drought, and an earthquake in the north, to say nothing of the shock transmitted by the fourfold hike in oil prices, the economy showed resilience and performed well in certain sectors. The gross domestic product, led by the agricultural sector and the expansion of public investment, grew at an average of 5.5 percent per annum between 1972 and 1977. An effort was made to divert resources more equitably to all four provinces as well as the northern areas. This included a more acceptable allocation of the Indus River water between Punjab and the non-Punjabi provinces. As the largest province and the PPP's stronghold, Punjab was the main beneficiary of public investments in the heavy engineering, fertilizer, and cement industries. But there were road works and electrification programs in Balochistan and the NWFP, while Sindh witnessed the setting up of industries in its rural areas and the start of major projects like the Steel Mills and Port Qasim near Karachi.

The PPP's blitz against monopoly capitalism may have lost it the support of big business. But it more than made up for this with the political capital gained from the economic populism of its first three years in office. Certain of winning the numbers game, Bhutto decided to seek a renewal of the PPP's mandate by announcing general elections in early 1977. A stronger electoral performance could give the PPP control of the Parliament and the provincial assemblies, providing Bhutto with an impregnable hold on power. His miscalculation lay in believing he could neutralize the extreme right and the left by stealing their thunder. Pleased about warding off the Islamist threat by declaring the Ahmadis a minority, he made sure that the PPP's election manifesto highlighted it as one of the main achievements of his government. Bhutto now decided to try beating the left at its own game by championing the interests of the smaller farmers. Using nationalization as an instrument for rewarding supporters and punishing opponents, Bhutto announced the state takeover of flour and rice husking mills as well as cotton ginning factories on July 17, 1976. It was an imprudent decision taken in consultation with an inner circle of bureaucrats rather than the PPP leadership. Most of the nationalized units were medium or small businesses, making for a management nightmare.

The political fallout of the decision was to prove catastrophic. Nationalizing agro-industries hit the electoral support base of the Islamist parties the hardest. More than any threat these parties could pose in the name of religion, the PPP was electorally vulnerable to the wrath of the religio-political parties' main constituents among the urban middle to lower middle classes, including small- and medium-scale traders, merchants, shopkeepers, and middlemen. Once Bhutto had thrown down the gauntlet by announcing general elections, a cross-section of commercial and trading groups coalesced to secure not just the victory of the self-styled Islamists but also a change of regime. Realizing their limited support base, the Jamaat-i-Islami, the JUP, and the JUI formed a rainbow coalition with six other parties.[30] Known as the Pakistan National Alliance (PNA), the nine-party combination had nothing in common except hatred for Bhutto and Bhuttoism. Their intention, quite simply, was to dismantle the PPP regime.

The 1977 Elections and Their Aftermath

A much-maligned monster in the opposition's lexicon, and less popular than he had been in 1970, Bhutto would have won the elections even if his lieutenants had not fudged the results. On January 4, 1977, on the eve of his forty-ninth birthday, Bhutto announced a new round of labor reforms. He kicked off the celebrations the next day by giving a "personal gift" to the people in the form of new land reforms. Land ceilings were reduced from 150 to 100 acres of irrigated land and from 300 to 200 for nonirrigated land. Some elements in the PPP's left wing had wanted the ceiling reduced to twenty-five acres. The more daring step was the decision to tax agriculture and broaden the tax base.[31] In the torrent of pre-electoral good news was a surprise for the business community—an unexpected cut in the top personal income tax rate and company supertax rate. Bhutto was covering all bases. A peasant's charter had already been announced earlier.

There was a hike in pensions for the state's civil and military employees, who were eagerly awaiting the announcement of new salary scales by the Federal Pay Commission. The PPP government's other successes were the rehabilitation of Pakistan's international profile, the restoration of diplomatic relations with India in 1976, and stronger ties with the Islamic world. Domestically the economy was doing reasonably well despite a growing debt burden. With a roll of incentives to the voters, no one doubted Bhutto's ability to defeat a fragmented opposition. The only unknown factor was how large a majority he would seek.

The credibility of the elections was dented with the unopposed election of the prime minister and several PPP candidates before the campaign had got under way. Bhutto scoffed when exhorted to hold free and fair elections, commenting that elections had never been free or fair in Pakistan. He was equally eager to avoid giving the impression that the polls were rigged, especially since this was one of the nine-party opposition alliance's main lines of attack. On the eve of the elections, he instructed the commissioners of Punjab to ensure that the balloting was fair and impartial. But PPP stakeholders in the electoral contest thought otherwise. The results exceeded all expectations: the PPP won 136 seats against the PNA's thirty-six and, most questionably, 112 out of the 116 seats in Punjab. Bhutto was troubled that such a landslide was a sure recipe for opposition protests.[32] The addition of representatives from FATA gave the PPP a throttle-hold over the national assembly, with 81.5 percent of the seats. Yet of the 17 million votes cast in the 1977 elections, the PPP got 10 million and the PNA bagged 6 million. The margin between the votes cast and seats won was not unusual in a system of parliamentary government. But 93 percent of the seats in Punjab stretched the limits of credulity and hinted at the culpability of the civil administration. There were cries of foul play by the opposition parties, who announced a boycott of the provincial elections. In a conspicuous display of the party mood, PPP workers did not resist the PNA protestors who thronged the streets calling for Bhutto's resignation and the holding of impartial and fair elections.

If saner counsels had prevailed, the "undisputed leader" might have postponed provincial elections on March 10 until the allegations of rigging in the parliamentary elections had been investigated. Not only were the provincial assembly elections held on schedule, but they were so massively rigged as to suggest a bureaucratic conspiracy of killing the party with the kindness of an overwhelming victory. In the final analysis, how-ever, the provincial assembly results were more significant in confirming public doubts about the authenticity of the national assembly results. The Election Commission admitted that some half a dozen seats were rigged in Punjab. Like a cornered tiger, Bhutto called for dialogue with the PNA while arresting some of its main leaders. There was violence in Lahore and other parts of Punjab on the day the provincial assembly was convened. The government underplayed the number of casualties, but the damage had been done. Between March and July 1977, the cities and market towns of Pakistan were the venues for remarkably organized and well-funded political protest. A broad cross-section of Pakistanis took to the streets calling for a return to the Prophet of Islam's system of government, a counterpoint to the perceived "Westernized" decadence of an immoral PPP regime, signaling an Islamist takeover of the opposition movement. The strongest presence was of commercial and trading groups aligned with the religio-political parties. A flurry of desertions from the PPP, in-cluding Mubashir Hasan, made Bhutto visibly weaker and more desperate.

Unable to comply with the PNA's insistence that he had lost the moral right to govern and should resign, the prime minister cynically agreed to "Islamize" his government. On April 17 he announced the introduction of the sharia within six months and imposed an immediate ban on alcohol, gambling, and nightclubs. The prime minister's closest aides were as flum-moxed as his supporters. A week earlier, Bhutto in a reflective mood had said in private that the "rightists can never be appeased"; "their demands will keep escalating and I know I could not accept them in the ultimate analysis."[33] This did not prevent him from visiting Maulana Mawdudi and asking for his support in resolving the crisis. Placating the Islamists may have been Bhutto's way of keeping a line open to Allah. He needed a di-vine miracle. His hold over the *awam*, in which he took such great pride, was shakier than it had ever been. The army he so dreaded was sullenly acting on his orders in Balochistan and in three key urban centers of Pak-istan. Hundreds of protestors had been killed and over a thousand injured amid widespread damage to both public and private property.

Bhutto's domestic troubles coincided with a change of administrations in Washington. A strong proponent of nuclear nonproliferation, the new Democratic administration under Jimmy Carter was publicly opposing Pakistan's impending purchase of a nuclear processing plant from France.

The American stance was related to the issue of nonproliferation, not on any deep understanding of the geopolitical situation in South Asia. This was in contrast to the sympathetic attitude shown by the Republican administration toward Pakistan's strategic vulnerability vis-à-vis India. Henry Kissinger, the secretary of state of the outgoing Ford administration, had also urged the Pakistani prime minister to drop the idea or, at the very least, delay matters. However, on a lighter note, Kissinger revealed that after their last visit to India, in October 1974, the head of his policy planning staff concluded: "we should give nuclear weapons to both Pakistan and Bangladesh."[34] On a more sober note, Kissinger queried the logic of Pakistan acquiring a processing plant before possessing a large enough reactor capacity. An American reactor was offered as a nostrum. Upon failing to get the Pakistanis to cancel the French contract, the US secretary of state warned that the new administration was bound to "make a massive attempt" to stop the sale and "would like nothing better than to have somebody to make an example of." To underscore that he was saying this with the best of intentions, Kissinger told the Pakistani ambassador to the United States, Sahibzada Yaqub Khan, that "there was no leader to whom I am personally more attached than your Prime Minister."[35] The outgoing American ambassador, who had become his personal friend, frankly told Bhutto to back down on his nuclear ambitions if he wanted to remain in power. With such friends, Bhutto needed no enemies. After US pressure had led the French to cancel the deal, his relations with Washington soured. In retaliation, Bhutto is alleged to have made overtures to Moscow, including an offer to allow the Soviets use of Pakistan's Makran coast.[36]

April was a cruel month for the icon of populism in Pakistan. The speed with which the anti-Bhutto campaign gained momentum surprised everyone, including the PNA leadership. The ready flow of funds for the PNA movement aroused Bhutto's suspicions. On April 27 he received a fillip when the military establishment affirmed support for the "present legally constituted government." In Parliament the next day, Bhutto spoke of an international conspiracy to dislodge his government and pointed the finger at the "superpower" that had lost the Vietnam War.[37] The "bloodhounds are after my blood," he claimed, because he was daring to defy their pressures and proceeding with the purchase of the French nuclear reprocessing plant. Without actually naming them, he charged US intelligence agencies and the American embassy in Islamabad for instigating and financing the opposition. There had been an inexplicable increase in the value of the rupee vis-à-vis the US dollar. Condemning the efforts to destabilize Pakistan, he asked in a highly emotional tone, what would be the security of Oman, the United Arab Emirates, the Gulf States, and even Saudi Arabia "if, God forbid, Pakistan crumbles, and becomes an international cockpit of intrigue and they receive a stab in the back?"[38]

Later Bhutto was to name the leader of the Jamaat-i-Islami, Mian Tufail Muhammad, as co-conspirator with America and the chief of army staff, General Zia-ul-Haq, in the conspiracy to bring down his government. Bhutto had appointed Zia-ul-Haq as the army chief, superseding six generals. He claims to have done so on the recommendation of Lieutenant General Ghulam Jilani, the director general of the ISI. The decision was finalized only after Bhutto was satisfied that the Pakistani Army under Zia-ul-Haq, a lower-middle-class migrant from East Punjab with no independent base of support in the army, would be amenable to dancing to his tunes.[39] Taken in by his fawning demeanor and display of excessive self-effacement, Bhutto had selected Major General Zia-ul-Haq to head the tribunal set up to try those accused in the 1973 Attock Conspiracy Case. Zia had served in the Pakistan military advisory group in Jordan. He defied the orders of his superiors and joined the Jordanian Army in cracking down on Palestinians in battles that gave rise to the Black September movement. General Gul Hassan saved Zia from being court-martialed.[40] Educated at St. Stephen's College in Delhi, Zia had joined the British Indian Army in 1944. He served as a commissioned officer in the cavalry and did service in South East Asia at the end of World War II. A devout Muslim with a quirky resemblance to the British comic Terry Thomas, the unassuming general had affinities with the Jamaat-i-Islami, whose leader, Mian Tufail Muhammad, was his kinsman. Cutting a figure in humility compared with Bhutto's flamboyance, Zia adroitly played a duplicitous game. After the imposition of martial law in Lahore, Karachi, and Hyderabad, the army chief started attending meetings of the federal cabinet, never missing an opportunity to reassure the prime minister of his loyalty. A circular issued by Zia in May urging the military to remain firmly behind the government deluded Bhutto into thinking that he had the army under control, a mistake he was to rue until the end of his life.

If the PPP's "supreme leader" had learned his lessons from Pakistani history, he might have averted the military coup of July 5, 1977. Unduly sanguine about his army chief, he dragged out the negotiations in the expectation of outflanking the PNA. For someone accustomed to getting his way without bending, Bhutto was a revelation when it came to making concessions for short-term political gains. He agreed in principle to hold new elections and conceded to all of the PNA's demands, except for the one calling for his resignation. The basis of an accord between the PPP and the PNA was eventually worked out on July 3. Elections were to be held at the center and the provinces; all political prisoners were to be released; there was to be a new and impartial Election Commission with greater powers and an implementation council consisting of an equal number of PPP and PNA members. But the PPP government had been late on the uptake. The delay gave the PNA time to establish contact with the army high command. It also fanned the inherent distrust in which Bhutto was held by most of the PNA leadership. After the PNA's negotiating team had taken account of the views of Sherbaz Mazari, leader of the National Democratic Party, and those of the NAP, nine additional demands were added to the original list. The opposition now wanted not only new elections but a repeal of constitutional amendments restricting individual liberties and judicial authority, the withdrawal of the army from Balochistan, and the termination of the special Hyderabad tribunal deliberating on the NAP's alleged conspiracy against the state.

General Zia-ul-Haq rejected the last two demands, only to agree to them after assuming power. This has led to considerable speculation that he all along intended to grab power and had an interest in seeing the negotiations fail. By early July 1977, planning for a military coup had been finalized. Significantly, General Jilani, the ISI chief who became one of Zia's close aides after the takeover, advised the prime minister to sign the agreement with the PNA on July 3. Bhutto asked for time to consider, by now fully aware that the military was gearing up to strike. The whole of the next day went by without any statement. Around the midnight hour on July 5, a tired and prickly Bhutto, wagging a fat cigar in the air, told the press that though he too could come up with new conditions, he was not helpless like the PNA negotiating team and would sign the accord in the morning. It was an uncharacteristic climbdown for a politician who had faced more formidable challenges with greater fortitude and determination. For all his shortcomings, Bhutto had not only revived Pakistan's standing in the international comity of nations following the defeat by

India in 1971 but also had given new direction to his dispirited country-men with a spate of some long-delayed populist reforms. Where he mis-calculated was in choosing a servile army chief in the vain hope of using his loyalty to ward off the one institution that had repeatedly undone elected governments in Pakistan with impunity. Bhutto had made an ir-reparable error of judgment. Later that night General Zia-ul-Haq gave the green signal for the military coup. Even if he did not act on American in-structions, as Bhutto alleged from his prison cell, the general's subsequent moves demonstrated that he had a definite agenda, which had the en-dorsement of the military top brass. With Bhutto negotiating from a posi-tion of weakness and the opposition kicking up a storm about his un-Islamic style of life and governance, a far less ambitious and more self-effacing gen-eral than Zia-ul-Haq might not have been able to resist the temptation of plucking the prize cherry.

SEVEN

MARTIAL RULE IN ISLAMIC GARB

AS THE HOT AND SULTRY NIGHT OF JULY 4 made way for the dew-soaked dawn of July 5, 1977, early morning risers in Pakistan heard on the 6:00 a.m. radio bulletin that the armed forces had taken over the country's administration and placed the top political leadership under "temporary protective custody." There was no mention of who had carried out the coup or why. An eerie silence hovered over the prime minister's house nestled in Rawalpindi's sprawling national park named after Ayub Khan. Outside the walls of the colonial style compound that served as Bhutto's official residence, it seemed like business as usual except for the presence of armed troops. The more fertile minds among the urban chattering classes initially thought the coup aimed at bolstering the PPP regime. A towering populist with a substantial following, Bhutto had appeared invincible. Carefully choreographing his public utterances, he remained defiant until the bitter end. In an interview to the *Times* of London correspondent in April 1977, he slammed the "myopic men" of the opposition who wanted to grab power. "Being a politician is like a spring flower, he blossoms, he blooms and a time comes for him to fade," Bhutto noted wistfully, "but that time was not in the present critical context."[1]

Sadly for Bhutto, the generals led by Zia-ul-Haq had concluded otherwise. Disbelief at the turn of events soon gave way to despair in pro-PPP circles. Jubilant PNA supporters thronged the streets distributing sweets and shouting victory slogans. These mixed reactions signaled the new reality—Bhutto out of office was a more divisive factor than in power. While bracing for another bout of the khaki jackboot, no one quite realized at the time that the third military intervention in as many decades was about to herald unparalleled changes in the political and ideological profile of the Islamic Republic of Pakistan. At the same time, no one anticipated the longevity of this new spell of military dictatorship. That Zia's rule came to rival Ayub Khan's eleven-year reign owed much to international factors that came into play two years after the military takeover.

The army action, code-named "Operation Fairplay," was carried out with clinical precision without a single shot being fired. Bhutto, who dubbed the coup "Operation Foulplay," was put under house arrest and whisked off to the hill station at Murree in the morning to cool his heels. The national and the provincial assemblies were dissolved; politicians were detained and martial law imposed. In his inaugural address to the nation, General Muhammad Zia-ul-Haq, acting as CMLA, blamed politicians for pushing the country to the brink of anarchy by refusing to compromise. Describing himself as "a true soldier of Islam" with no political ambitions whatsoever, he promised free and fair elections within ninety days. In a clear sign that ideology was paramount for him, Zia applauded the Islamic spirit of the PNA movement. Created in the name of Islam, Pakistan could survive only by establishing an Islamic system of government. Until that could materialize, the existing political structure, notably the presidency and the judiciary, was to be retained. The 1973 constitution was held in abeyance. No judicial authority could challenge the proclamation of martial law or question the orders of the CMLA. Pakistan had seen military authoritarianism before. What was to be distinctively different about its reimposition after 1977 was the fusing of martial rule with a state-sponsored Islamic ideology.

"You Can Forget Elections"

Islamic ideology and military might were the twin pillars on which General Zia-ul-Haq began building his new order.[2] Senior civil bureaucrats who encountered him could see that the political ethos of the government had changed dramatically. Unlike the two "modernist" coup makers of the past, Zia was wedded to the idea of taking the country back to the times of the Prophet Muhammad. At his first meeting with government secretaries, the CMLA singled out the Ministry of Religious Affairs and Haj arrangements for criticism.[3] He reshuffled the Council of Islamic Ideology for which provision had been made in the 1973 constitution. In a move that had detrimental effects on the expanding waistlines of civil bureaucrats, the regime promoted the national dress *shalwar kameez,* a long, loose shirt with baggy trousers, over the customary Western-style suits. To make good Muslims out of civil officials, prayers were introduced in government offices and religious piety upheld as a virtue to be considered in promotion decisions. The colonial culture of army messes underwent similar change. Drinking officers were frowned upon and the visibly pious identified for promotion. Often attributed to Zia's personal whims, these changes were a sign of the times. The global Islamic reassertion spearheaded by Saudi Arabia and Arab petro-dollars was making itself felt in Pakistan. There were unmistakable signs of the Saudi imprint on Zia's locally honed ideological agenda. The proud champion of Islam liked giving Mawdudi's writings as official gifts and awards. For the first time in the history of Pakistan, the Jamaat-i-Islami had found a soul mate at the helm of government. The ensuing transformation of Pakistan's liberal and moderate social landscape was swift and brazen.

Needing to consolidate power and win a semblance of legitimacy to implement his "Islamization" policies and neoliberal economic agenda, Zia emulated the tactics of the proverbial camel who slowly inched his master out of the tent. Promising the people free and fair elections within three months, he soon switched gears upon realizing the extent of the PPP's continuing popularity. This became painfully evident to the military high command on August 8, 1977, when a sea of people gave the deposed prime minister a rapturous welcome in Lahore. Bhutto did not help matters by abusing Zia and threatening to try him for high treason under article 6 of the constitution. Upon being released from custody, the PPP populist harangued the junta in no uncertain terms. He maintained that the military had started planning the coup before the elections and that there was a foreign conspiracy to prevent Pakistan from acquiring the French nuclear reactor. Fearing stern retribution, the army high command began looking for ways to silence and, better still, disqualify Bhutto and the PPP from participating in the elections. Bhutto was accused of ordering the FSF to murder Ahmad Raza Kasuri, a supporter-turned-political-opponent, whose father, Nawab Mohammad Ahmad Khan, ended up getting killed in the firing on their motorcade. The incident that resulted in Ahmad Raza Kasuri's father's death had occurred three years earlier, and the evidence was circumstantial. Bhutto was arrested but soon released on bail by the Lahore High Court. Seeing an opportunity to rid himself of his principal foe, Zia had Bhutto arrested under a martial law order.

The CMLA, soon to be known as "Cancel My Last Announcement" for constantly going back on his word, now claimed that he had taken over power to enforce Islam and not simply to hold elections. The date of the elections was "not in the Quran," and there was nothing sacrosanct about the constitutionally stipulated ninety days. In his opinion, the armed forces and not the politicians could keep Pakistan together.[4] The armed forces were the guardians of not only the territorial but also the ideological frontiers of Pakistan. Parties with manifestos opposing the ideology of Pakistan were to be debarred from participating in the elections, which Zia was prepared to hold only if he could get "positive results." Unruffled by the legal implications of his arbitrary position, he dismissed the constitution as a mere booklet with a dozen or so pages that he could tear up at will and he rested assured that the political bigwigs would follow him with "their tails wagging."[5] This is not the sort of banter expected of a humble, gracious, and God-fearing man. Such bravado, however, had become a vital part of the performative repertoire for governing a wayward country like Pakistan.

By the early fall of 1977, Zia and his top military associates were actively working to block Bhutto's political comeback. Coining the slogan "First accountability, then elections," the military regime wagered its future on the outcome of the murder charge against the former prime minister. Jittery at the prospect of being charged for violating the constitution, it kept up the public pretense of leaving the matter to the better judgment of the honorable judges of the Supreme Court. At the same time, steps were taken to ensure that the judiciary remained as obliging as always. Zia replaced the chief justice whom he found to be soft on Bhutto. On September 20, the Supreme Court headed by Justice Mohammad Yaqub Ali flustered the junta by accepting Mrs. Nusrat Bhutto's petition against Bhutto's detention. Relying on the *Asma Jilani* case, Mrs. Bhutto's counsel argued that military intervention was banned under article 6 of the constitution. Consequently, the laws under which Bhutto and his colleagues had been detained were illegal. On November 10, the Supreme Court headed by the new chief justice, Anwar-ul-Haq, rejected the petition by invoking the fabled doctrine of necessity. Citing the existence of civil war conditions and a constitutional breakdown after March 1977, the ruling legitimized the coup as a necessary step taken in the interest of the state and the welfare of the people.

The judicial ruling gave Zia the power to amend the 1973 constitution unencumbered by legal niceties. Conferring authority on a military dictator to alter the constitution at will was to set a dangerous precedent with dire consequences for Pakistan. Still unsure of the judiciary, Zia contemplated trying Bhutto in a military court. The idea was dropped once he was satisfied that the judiciary would endorse the official plot. Zia wanted nothing less than Bhutto's removal from the political arena. He found a willing accomplice in Justice Maulvi Mushtaq Hussain, who after being superseded twice for promotion as chief justice of the Lahore High Court under the PPP regime harbored a personal grudge against Bhutto. A cantankerous and vindictive man, Mushtaq was acting chief justice and governor of Punjab when entrusted with the task of presiding over the high-profile case. He later became chief justice of the Lahore High Court. With a hostile judge and a turncoat in the form of the former FSF chief, Masood Mahmood, as approver, the scales were loaded against Bhutto. On March 18, 1978, a five-member bench under Justice Mushtaq found Bhutto and four others guilty of a criminal conspiracy to murder and sentenced them to death. In a blatant display of subjective considerations rather than hard evidence, the judgment was based on determining the commitment of the accused to Islam and Pakistan's ideology. Bhutto was declared unfit to rule—he had violated the constitution and lacked real belief in Islam, presumably because his mother was a convert from Hinduism.

The hearings were marred by procedural irregularities. Improper record keeping and well-documented charges of bias against Justice Mushtaq topped the list. Bhutto boycotted the proceedings. His defense was confined to questioning the fairness of the trial and arguing that the case was fabricated. Bhutto's counsel, Yahya Bakhtiar, filed an appeal in the Supreme Court, where a nine-member bench headed by Chief Justice Anwar-ul-Haq was constituted to hear the case on May 20, 1978. Bhutto wrote to the chief justice from his death cell in Lahore's high-security Kot Lakhpat jail, charging him with prejudice and asking him not to serve on the bench. By "zealously collaborating" with the martial law regime, Justice Anwar-ul-Haq and his cohort Justice Mushtaq had placed the highest judicial office at the service of a dictatorial executive. Haq's only hope for redemption was to recuse himself from the case.[6]

Anwar-ul-Haq not only presided over the appeal proceedings, two judges thought to be leaning toward acquitting Bhutto did not serve until the end of the hearing. One retired and was not asked to stay on until the case concluded, while the indisposition of the second judge did not occasion a postponement of the hearing. After initially being open to the public, the trial was held behind closed doors and continued despite Bhutto's illness and absence from court. It was an embarrassment of justice unprecedented in Pakistan's history. Worse was to come. On February 6, 1979, the seven-member bench of the Supreme Court gave a four-to-three verdict divided along provincial lines. All four judges in favor of sentencing Bhutto were Punjabis, while the opposing trio came from non-Punjabi provinces. If the original nine judges had decided the case, the verdict would have gone in Bhutto's favor. Normal judicial procedures were flouted with startling ease. Otherwise, it would have been impossible to pronounce a death sentence given the circumstantial nature of the evidence, to say nothing of the split verdict. The dissenting judges had questioned the reliability of the principal approver's evidence and the admissibility of statements made by dead men. This was overruled by a majority opinion of the bench, which demonstrated its partiality by producing the verdict desired by the military regime. Zia had said that he would uphold the judicial decision. Though the Supreme Court gave him the option of turning Bhutto's sentence to life imprisonment, the general was in no mood for mercy. The former prime minister was made to rot in a narrow and dark death cell while the regime tried making the most of its well-orchestrated campaign to malign him in public. A five-volume white paper detailing Bhutto's misdeeds in office and his electoral malpractices was published, excerpts of which were carried widely by the print media.[7] State-run radio and television networks broadcast programs about his crimes and personal failings. Bhutto was a doomed man even before the dubious judicial ruling shook the country and distressed the international community. Ignoring appeals from Western capitals, the Soviets, China, and even friendly Muslim countries to spare Bhutto's life, Zia ordered the execution. He had taken to heart the witty aphorism making the rounds that there was only one grave and two bodies to fill it, Bhutto's or Zia's.[8]

Against the backdrop of the Iranian revolution and the unceremonious fall of the Shah, Zia was unwilling to take risks with Bhutto. Little did he realize that Bhutto in death was a more potent symbol of resistance than all the people's power he might have tried mustering in his lifetime. Focused on personal survival, the general turned down Mrs. Bhutto's appeal to save her husband's life. At 2:00 a.m. on April 4, 1979, an emaciated but unbowed Zulfikar Ali Bhutto was "hanged" in Rawalpindi jail and his body flown to Larkana shortly afterward for burial. His grieving wife, Nusrat, and elder daughter, Benazir Bhutto, were flown in for the funeral. Many of Bhutto's supporters maintain that he was never sent to the gallows and that his death occurred in the prison cell after he was tortured for refusing to sign a document taking responsibility for the loss of East Pakistan. Reduced to living in subhuman conditions, Bhutto in his final hours showed character by refusing to buckle under mental and physical pressure. Proud and unbending in the face of acute adversity, he refused to ask Zia for clemency. In his final hours, he demanded hot water to shave as he did not wish to die looking like a mullah. Bhutto's state of mind is summed up in a few lines written to his defense lawyer. He had passed through many fires and was "big enough" to admit guilt if had committed the crime. That would have been "less of an ordeal and humiliation than this barbarous trial which no self respecting man can endure." As a Muslim, he was at peace with his conscience and left his fate in God's hands.[9]

An unbearable heaviness hung over the Rawalpindi district jail on April 4, 1979, a tragic day for Pakistanis, whatever their political stripes. Even those happy to see the fall of Bhutto regretted the sham of a judicial hearing given to a former prime minister and president of Pakistan. They were now appalled by the hasty execution. Many had expected a last-minute executive pardon. Emotions ran high among pockets of PPP support, and there were instances of self-immolation by passionate young men. But the sea of people Bhutto thought would drown his tormentor was never permitted to rise. The security juggernaut was tightened to scotch the first signs of trouble by the PPP, most of whose top ranking leaders and workers were populating jails across the length and breadth of the country. But the apparent calm disguised a more uncertain reality. The military establishment's decision to get rid of Bhutto through trial and execution rather than hold free and fair elections had crippled hopes for a politically stable and democratic Pakistan. Long after the third general to command their destiny had disappeared from the scene, Pakistanis have not recovered from the psychological trauma of seeing an elected prime minister sent to the gallows in disregard of domestic and international calls for mercy. The sense of national shame was more profound for those who realized that the trial of Zulfikar Ali Bhutto and his "judicial murder" were the last stop in the Pakistani judiciary's abject subservience to military juntas.

A sprightlier and more confident Zia had been hard at work to secure a prolonged and productive spell of military rule in Pakistan. In pursuit of his stated aim to create a morally upright nation of Muslims, General Zia-ul-Haq on February 7, 1979, introduced a constitutional amendment through a presidential order giving the high courts jurisdiction to establish Shariat Benches to determine whether a law was repugnant to Islam. Taking a first step toward "Islamization," Zia presented this as the fulfillment of the people's demand. He was misinterpreting the popular will. What people wanted was a system based on social justice and equity, regardless of whether it was called socialist or Islamic. Exposing the politically motivated nature of his "Islamization" policies, Zia avoided taking the perilous course of trying to recast the economy in the light of Islamic principles of egalitarianism. While undertaking to introduce interest-free banking, the focus was on imposing prohibitive or punitive laws that gave differential weight to the testimony of Muslims, non-Muslims, and Muslim women. Discrimination on the basis of religion and gender made a mockery of justice.

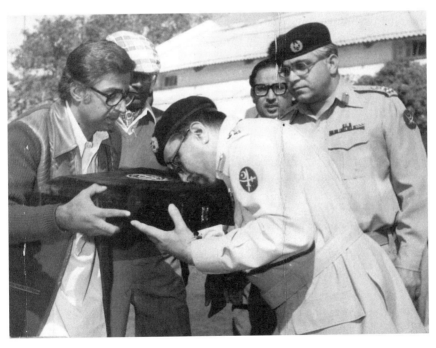

General Zia-ul-Haq receiving a rare copy of the Quran, Hyderabad, 1979. *The White Star Photo Pvt. Ltd. Archive.*

The self-styled vice-regent of Allah was undeterred by these awkward truths. Zia projected his regime as the moral antidote to Bhuttoism. The production, distribution, and consumption of alcohol and narcotics were banned and made punishable by lashing and imprisonment. The requirement of two credible male witnesses made enforcement of the full punishment difficult, and so lighter sentences were permitted. Those charged with theft or robbery risked amputation of the right hand up to the wrist for the first offense and the left foot up to the ankle in case of a second offense. Here again the strict standards of evidence necessitated the lighter punishment of a jail sentence. By far the most egregious of Zia's initial volley of Islamic laws were the Hudood (literally limit or restriction) ordinances introduced in February 10, 1979 specifically targeting women. The *zina* ordinance obscured the distinction between adultery and rape. Anyone accused of adultery *(zina),* even in the case of rape, was liable to be stoned to death. An act of fornication was punishable by one hundred whips in a public place. These acts had to be attested to by four male witnesses, an absurd requirement that provided plenty of scope for the privileged to avoid punishment. Downtrodden women bore the brunt of this injudicious and inhumane law.[10]

Minorities were the other victims of the state of martial rule's turn to piety. Islamist parties had long demanded separate electorates for religious minorities to gain some electoral advantage against parties like the PPP. Zia leaped at the opportunity. The Representation of the People's Act of 1976 was amended, stripping minorities of the right to vote in general constituencies. Paradoxically, none of the minorities had ever demanded separate electorates. Using retrograde and implausible methods to keep the lid from boiling over was to become the leitmotif of Zia's imperiled regime. "Islamization" aimed at perpetuating the junta by manipulating Islamic sentiments. It was also a convenient way to appease the religio-political parties, eager to make the most of the regime's ideological predilections. Although personally inclined toward Mawdudi's idea of the Islamic state, Zia had to strike a delicate balance between the imperatives of office and his own institutional support base on the one hand and the conflicting demands of the Islamist parties on the other. While applauding Zia's "Islamization" policies, the Islamist parties were insistent on elections. An early reference to the electorate, the removal of all constraints on political activity, and the introduction of an Islamic system were the conditions on which the PNA had agreed to join the national government in August 1978. The following month Zia elevated himself to the presidency. His alliance with the PNA played a crucial role in helping the regime weather popular reactions to Bhutto's judicial murder. The understanding collapsed within days of the execution, forcing Zia to reconstitute the federal cabinet without the PNA. Even the Jamaat-i-Islami, whose cadres had tried setting the popular tempo by cheering Bhutto's death, was loathe to brazenly associate with authoritarianism.

The election mantra was a thorn in the general's flesh. Unable to establish legitimacy without broadening his regime's social bases of support, he called nonparty local body elections in an attempt to mobilize support among the landed groups. This stirred up a hornet's nest. Politicians across the political spectrum lashed out at the regime, suspecting that, like earlier army dictators, Zia was seeking a long stint in office. With rampant inflation fueled by the abolition of the wheat subsidy in the hugely unpopular new federal budget, the call for local elections attracted ordinary voters. The electoral results showed the martial law administration standing alone against the entire political spectrum. In a resounding reproof of the regime, candidates affiliated with the PPP calling themselves "friends of the people" won handsomely. Shaken by the results, Zia banned all political activity and postponed elections.

For the general in his labyrinth, the only comfort came from loyalists in the army, who were equally averse to a PPP victory at the national polls. Some senior generals disapproved of the effects of martial law duties on army morale and preferred returning the affairs of government to civilians. But they posed no threat to Zia, who had taken care to reshuffle or retire most of the corps commanders of 1977. Nearly all of Zia's corps commanders held civilian positions, four were provincial governors, and two were federal ministers. Federal Labor Minister General Faiz Ali Chishti was from Zia's hometown of Jullundur while the corps commander of Quetta and governor of Balochistan, General Rahimuddin, was related to Zia by marriage. The grafting of military officers in top civilian and diplomatic posts was another way to strengthen his main base of support in the army. Despite a solid loyalist inner chain protecting his hold on power, Zia was vulnerable at home and isolated internationally after sending Bhutto to an untimely death. The general needed an act of divine mercy. Relations with the country's main international patron were in the doldrums after Washington imposed sanctions on Pakistan for its nuclear ambitions—ironically the one issue on which Zia was at one with popular opinion. US–Pakistan ties remained extremely tenuous after Bhutto's execution until the Soviet invasion of Afghanistan in December 1979 dramatically altered the tide in favor of the beleaguered military regime.

Zia's precarious hold on power was underlined in a report by the American embassy in Islamabad. His limited support was likely to evaporate if he postponed elections again. "A wide-ranging popular wave against him on that issue if accompanied by violence," the report surmised, "could be the catalyst to force the army leadership to choose a successor to Zia from among themselves." A mere reshuffle at the top, however, was unlikely to moderate the "heavily Punjabi and Sunni" thrust of the military regime, the cause célèbre of resentments in the non-Punjabi provinces. Darkening the horizon was a major economic crisis whose systemic basis was obscured by impatient international donor communities and angry consumers dreading the implications of the new federal budget. With one of the highest birth rates and one of the lowest living standards in the world, Pakistan's chronic problem of living beyond its means was coming home to roost. Beyond elections, the political leadership agreed on nothing. Without forging a consensus on the future shape of representative institutions in a federal system capable of mediating regional interests and creating a sense of national identity, elections, even if free, American diplomats feared, "could be a very empty and destabilizing exercise."[11]

The British concurred for the most part with their American counterparts but had a better understanding of the military regime's dilemma: "how to hand over to a civilian Government not committed to Bhutto." Even if he was coming to enjoy the trappings of power, as his many detractors feared, Zia lacked the political skills to elicit popular support. Desperately in need of legitimacy, he opted to ride on the wings of a global reassertion of Islam. But in advocating the notion of a representative democracy without elections, the general ran the risk of becoming a victim of his Islamization fixation. In the opinion of the British ambassador in Islamabad, although Zia's "absence of political feel may be excusable," the time and energy he seemed to be devoting to the "Islamization of Pakistani life are not." The promised economic revitalization had not taken place, and a major crisis was looming large. The consumer price index was rising. A negative balance of trade had been made worse by mishandling the wheat growers' problems, forcing the government to import one and a half million tons of wheat. There were few new investments because of an overriding sense of political uncertainty. If not for over $1.2 billion in annual remittances from Pakistani workers abroad, the country would be in dire straits.[12]

Knowing his limitations, Zia not only canceled elections indefinitely, he turned his lack of popularity into a justification for his authoritarian rule and went on to become Pakistan's longest surviving ruler. Elections were not held until 1985, making it impossible to assess the full extent of the rigging in the 1977 elections. To avoid deepening his regime's crisis of legitimacy, Zia encouraged the spread of a pseudo-Wahabi strain of Islam while instituting measures to bring about a systematic fragmentation of politics. But popular legitimacy still eluded him. Bhutto in death was proving to be an indestructible foe. The Iranian Revolution and the April 1979 communist coup led by Nur Muhammad Taraki in Afghanistan introduced a critical new dimension into the military high command's calculations. Wary of the fallout from the Shah's removal and apprehensive of the prospect of Kabul reviving its "Pakhtunistan" propaganda and fomenting secessionist tendencies in Balochistan with Indian and Soviet help, Zia and his generals were taking no chances with any kind of elections. Pakistanis had to forget about elections, become pious Muslims, and defend their homeland against ungodly communists.

Playing the Afghan Card

Zia's grand reprieve came in the form of a chain of events stretching from Saudi Arabia and Iran to Pakistan. The year 1979 is best remembered for the Iranian Revolution and the Soviet occupation of Afghanistan. What made it a pivotal year were three spatially disconnected incidents in Tehran, Mecca, and Islamabad that underscored the rising potency of anti-American sentiments in the Muslim world. The epicenter for the first lay in Tehran, where on November 4, 1979, pro-Khomeini students stormed the American embassy, taking nearly a hundred hostages. Mecca was the site of the second incident when during the annual pilgrimage of Haj, on November 20, 1979, the Kaaba, the holiest of Muslim places of worship, was attacked by 500 armed men led by Juhayman al-Otaibi, a former Saudi national guard. The attackers included Egyptian, Pakistani, and

American converts to Islam. Modeling themselves on the Ikhwan, the religious militia that helped establish the Saudi state, Otaibi and his men claimed to be disciples of Muhammad al-Qahtani, a poet with mystical leanings whom they considered a Mahdi, the rightly guided spiritual and temporal ruler expected to rule the world before the Day of Judgment. Tens of thousands of Muslim pilgrims were taken hostage by the gun-toting zealots and told to pray behind Qahtani. A news blackout in the kingdom fueled a virulent conspiracy mill. Washington hinted at Iranian involvement, while others spread rumors, later backed by Khomeini, that the attack might have been an American and Israeli plot. Tempers were already at a boil when the Voice of America reported that President Carter, who hinted at the use of force to rescue Americans still being held hostage in Tehran, had ordered US naval ships into the Indian Ocean.

Amid unverified rumors of a US and Zionist hand in the desacralization of the Kaaba, a Radio Pakistan broadcast reporting the incident exploded into a torrent of well-coordinated expressions of anti-Americanism in all the main urban centers, including Azad Kashmir. In Lahore, the American Cultural Center was set ablaze and the consulate general sacked while angry crowds in Rawalpindi burnt down the US Information Center and the British Council Library. There was considerable damage to properties, several diplomatic vehicles were torched, but there were no fatalities. The attack on the American embassy in Islamabad symbolized the Muslim rage underlying the partnership between a shaky military ruler and Islamist politics in Pakistan. Around 1:00 p.m. on November 21, 1979, Quaid-i-Azam University students belonging to the Jamiat-i-Tulaba, the youth wing of the Jamaat-i-Islami, surrounded the US embassy in Islamabad. In what was evidence of preplanning, the students came equipped with inflammable materials and implements to break down the embassy walls. More than 600 strong, the students broke the police cordon. Shouting anti-American slogans, they proceeded to set fire to the embassy and gutted a block of flats housing diplomats. Nearly 5,000 people from the twin cities of Islamabad and Rawalpindi joined the students. The conspicuous participation of Iranian and Palestinian students, the former with the active encouragement of the Iranian embassy, signified the serious global ramifications of the incident. A small detachment of troops arrived on the scene but watched from the sidelines while army helicopters hovered over the embassy compound.[13]

Evidence of state complicity, if not actual sanction, was the inactivity of both the police and the army as the students ransacked the embassy, killing two Americans, including a marine. The embassy staff was forced to take refuge in a vault located on the second floor of the building. It took nearly five and a half hours before Zia, who had gone bicycling through crowded Rawalpindi to promote Islamic values, ordered the Pakistani Army to take action against the violent mob. Zia's performance on his bicycle was comical except that his romp around town tied up a large number of security forces in the midst of a potentially explosive international crisis. The president's biking expeditions elicited ridicule at the time. Isolated like his predecessors by a ring of mediocre and sycophantic advisors, the only remedy Zia could come up with was to do things the Islamic way. Instead of responding to the emergency, he avoided doing anything that might stir Shia–Sunni troubles. Letting the populace vent its anger at America was a safer bet. If he had ordered the army to fire on the belligerent students, there was every possibility of their deaths becoming the catalyst for a political backlash against his shaky regime. At 3:05 p.m. Pakistan standard time, with the siege of the American embassy under way, Zia blithely got off his bicycle at a crowded marketplace in Rawalpindi to bemoan the attack on the Grand Mosque in Mecca. Muslims were undergoing "an extremely difficult time" but had to stay calm and pray for deliverance as Allah would protect the Kaaba.[14] A pontificating dictator can do more damage than an incompetent or roguish one. Zia's prestige in the army plummeted. A tough martial law administration had been unable to keep order in its own capital. His generals were "extremely angry."[15] There was talk of the "generals being dissatisfied with Zia" but "being unable to agree which of them shall replace him."[16]

In a different time, Washington would have read the riot act to the Pakistanis for their tardy response to a major diplomatic crisis that led to six deaths, including two of US nationals. Up to its neck with the hostage crisis in Iran, the Carter administration's reaction to the attack on the American embassy in Pakistan was surprisingly muted. Zia's apology for the incident was accepted without recrimination. Some 300 American personnel were evacuated from Pakistan with a verbal assurance from the secretary of state that no change was intended in the formal diplomatic relationship between the two countries. An uncharacteristically feeble response, it was seen as signposting the erosion of US power in the Muslim world, which had been in ample evidence ever since the Iranian hostage crisis. The Kremlin's decision to commit the Red Army to Afghanistan gave the Americans an opportunity to rebuild ties with the believers. Often attributed to the Soviet Union's fabled quest for warm water ports, the invasion had more to do with the Kremlin's fears of the impact that an Islamic revival in Afghanistan could have on its Muslim republics. Seeing the Soviet occupation of Afghanistan through the prism of Cold War politics, US policy makers responded by striking a Faustian bargain with strands of Muslim anticolonial nationalism espousing Islamist aspirations that directly contradicted American notions of democracy and freedom.

A clear recognition of the risks notwithstanding, the United States had by the end of 1979 decided to increase assistance to the Afghan mujahidin, a throng of tribal warlords with a narrow worldview and no coherent ideology other than the cry of jihad as the armed struggle of the faithful. The strategic attractions of using the weighty Islamic concept of jihad to justify the war against ungodly communism led American policy makers into developing their own nemesis. The rise of Khomeinism had knocked out the Nixon doctrine of using Iran and Saudi Arabia as the two main props of American policy in the Middle East and the Persian Gulf. Finding their options restricted in the Middle East, the Americans turned a blind eye as the House of Saud implemented its understanding with the conservative religious establishment after the attack on the Kaaba by pouring large sums of money into Saudi-backed global networks promoting radical Islam in the Muslim world.[17] Well aware of the potential dangers of radical Sunni Islamic thinking, the Americans took the dictum of "my enemy's enemies are my friends" to heart in a final lunge to defeat the Soviets at their own game. Basking in the glory of Allah's grace, or so he believed, Zia used this opportunity to wriggle out of his domestic political corner and bid for the prize most coveted by his predecessors—leadership of the Muslim world. This was the elusive crutch he used to confirm his reputation in Pakistan as the *amir-ul-momineen*, the leader of the faithful.

Coming in the wake of the Iranian Revolution, Moscow's military misadventure altered the balance of power in the region with profound consequences for Pakistan's security. Strategic calculations and not Islamic ideology dominated thinking in the dramatically changed geopolitical situation. From the Pakistani Army command's angle of vision, the Soviet occupation was a matter of global and not just regional concern. Recognizing that the West had no choice but to back the Zia regime, they saw a rare opportunity to end Afghan opposition to the Durand Line and exert influence in the former buffer state on its western border to gain "strategic depth" against India.[18] By creating an expansive state-supported transnational network of Muslim militants, the anti-Soviet campaign violated the sanctity of borders with audacious ease. In later years it would be said that if Afghanistan sneezed, Pakistan catches a cold while Iran and India suffer from severe symptoms. The causes of this contagion can be located in policies pursued during the 1980s even if its broad parameters had a prior history. In a little discussed irony, Zia was the unintended beneficiary of Bhutto's policies in the NWFP and their spillover into Afghanistan. To counter Kabul's "Pakhtunistan" propaganda claiming the Pakhtun parts of NWFP and Balochistan, the PPP government had pumped development funds into the federally administered northwestern tribal areas and encouraged their participation in the Gulf bonanza of the early 1970s. Huge inflows of development funds were disbursed to win the loyalty of local tribal leaders to the federal center. Like his forerunners, Bhutto was concerned about the Soviet Union's hegemonic ambitions in the region. He told Washington that Pakistan could talk to the Americans and the Chinese, but the Soviets were prone to "bullying and browbeating and no self-respecting nation could accept this."[19]

An Afghan cell had been set up in the Foreign Office in 1973. The following year Bhutto asked the ISI to forge contacts with antigovernment Islamists in Afghanistan. The main beneficiary of this policy was the pro-Jamaat-i-Islami leader of the Hizb-i-Islami, Gulbadin Hekmatyar. The American CIA had its own reasons for keeping close tabs on Afghanistan. In July 1973, a successful coup led by Mohammed Daud Khan with Soviet-supported Marxist help had ended more than 200 years of monarchy controlled by the Durrani-led tribal confederacy. Although Daud soon purged the Marxists and distanced himself from the Soviets, Pakistan reacted to his promotion of "Pakhtunistan" by increasing support for its Islamist clients. In the political struggle that ensued, it was the Marxists who prevailed in what came to be known as the Saur Revolution of April 1978. The Marxist takeover of Afghanistan alarmed the Pakistani defense establishment and set the stage for covert American intelligence activity in the country, supplementing that of the ISI. On July 3, 1979, President Carter approved covert aid—a modest half a million dollars—to insurgents ranged against the pro-Soviet regime in Kabul.[20] Much less than what the Pakistanis were angling for, this was open provocation for the Soviets, who were acutely concerned about US and Pakistani interference in Afghanistan. Fearful of the brittleness of the pro-Moscow regime in Kabul, the Soviet Union fell into the deadly trap of invading Afghanistan.

Pakistan's relations with Afghanistan were never cordial. Afghanistan was the only country to oppose Pakistan's membership in the United Nations. The reason was Kabul's rejection of the 1893 British-drawn Durand Line, which divided the Pakhtun tribes and served as the de facto border between the two countries. Bhutto's response to this irritation on the northwestern border was to splurge development funds in FATA, well aware that the tribal elders were misappropriating them for their personal benefit. By continuing the colonial policy of bribing the tribes, the postcolonial Pakistani state deliberately postponed integrating the tribal areas into the federation. The Pakistani Army had used Pathan tribesmen to invade Kashmir immediately after independence with less than satisfactory results. Faced with a powerful enemy on the east, the military high command backed by the government saw an accommodation with the badlands of northwestern Pakistan as the best way of avoiding the onerous responsibility of defending a second frontier in the west.

The strategic paradigm served the short-term political objectives of earlier regimes. The Soviet invasion of Afghanistan and American-backed international support for jihad wrought a qualitative shift in this policy. A veritable cash cow, the anti-Soviet Afghan jihad gave a new lease of life to the sagging political fortunes of the military regime. Zia won national kudos when in keeping with Pakistan's recently acquired nonaligned status and close ties with Saudi Arabia and the Gulf states, he dismissed the initial American offer of $400 million in aid as "peanuts," a snide reference to the peanut-growing occupant of the White House. Getting the backing of the Islamic bloc was preferable to relying on America and lent credibility to Pakistan's claim to nonalignment. However, once most Muslim and nonaligned countries openly opposed the Soviet invasion, Zia saw sense in striking a lucrative deal with the Americans. Apart from demanding several times more millions in aid, he insisted that the United States earmark all assistance to the Afghan mujahidin through the Pakistani Army.

In agreeing to the demand, the Americans knowingly walked into a web of corruption and financial irregularities. By keeping his nerve, Zia succeeded in extracting a far better package from the United States. Despite intelligence and media reports about Pakistan's rapidly developing nuclear program, Washington not only reaffirmed its 1959 commitment to come to Pakistan's aid in the event of a Soviet attack but under the Reagan administration provided billions of dollars in assistance for the Afghan mujahidin through the Pakistani Army and the ISI. Saudi Arabia pitched in with generous doses of money. Overall $7.2 billion was channeled to the Afghan militants through the Pakistani defense establishment, offering ample scope for senior officers to make family fortunes. The ready flow of external funds enabled the regime to use state power and patronage to help all three services further entrench themselves in the political economy.

That was not all. Threatened by the surge in Shia sentiments in Iran and afraid of the Soviets embarking on their perceived objective of gaining access to warm waters through Balochistan, General Zia-ul-Haq used the greenbacks to recruit civilian militias. These units could act as surrogates for a Pakistani Army that was simultaneously expanding its hold on state power and the political economy. Radical clerics in the tribal areas belonging to the Deobandi school of Sunni Islam were encouraged to give the call of jihad to their madrasa students in return for large sums of money. In the NWFP, the JUI led by Maulana Fazlur Rahman and the breakaway faction of the party led by Maulana Samiul Haq extracted maximum advantages from the policy. Many future leaders of the Afghan Taliban, notably Mullah Omar, were educated at the madrasa managed by Samiul Haq. While the JUI leadership went from rags to riches, the flow of easy money into FATA shifted the balance of power from the tribal elders to the suddenly enriched and well-armed radical clerics who had typically depended on the *maliks* (tribal elders) for their wherewithal and personal security. Informal state support was extended to Sunni militias, loosely labeled mujahidin, with a view to waging jihad in Afghanistan and snuffing out any signs of a Shia resurgence or any remote possibility of a Marxist implosion in Pakistan. Zia's fears of Shia assertion of power proved to be correct. In July 1980, members of the sect, outraged by the blanket imposition of the Sunni law of *zakat*, the Islamic wealth and welfare tax, thronged Islamabad under the umbrella of the newly formed

Tehrik-i-Nifaz-i-Fiqah-i-Jafria (Movement for the Enforcement of Jafari Law). Forced to retract, the government waived the collection of *zakat* from Shias. It was a tactical retreat that enraged hard-line Sunni opinion. To retrieve lost ground and ensure a steady supply of recruits for the Afghan war, the regime started arming Sunni surrogate militias, destabilizing not only the tribal areas but also the rest of the country.

The emergence of Pakistan as a frontline state gave rise to a parallel arms and drugs economy, the uncontrolled influx of over 3 million Afghan refugees, and a lethal culture of violence in the name of Islam. In a shocking oversight, no attempt was made by the martial law regime to register the refugees or keep them apart from the rest of the population. Those with money were allowed to settle in key urban centers while the vast majority were accommodated in refugee camps. Radicalized Pakhtun clerics recruited new blood for the Afghan jihad from these camps. The regime's active encouragement of jihad and sponsorship of chauvinistic publications proclaiming jihad as a duty for believing Muslims had wide-reaching effects. Poorly educated Punjabi youth from the lower strata with few lucrative means of employment were recruited to fight the Soviets. Turning jihad into an instrument of state policy, the Zia regime ensured its own longevity by deploying the state-controlled media to wage a vigorous campaign to purify Pakistani society. An ultraorthodox brand of Islam, owing more to Saudi Wahabi thinking than to local cultural traditions, was foisted on the people. A pro-regime former Jamaat-i-Islami propagandist, Maulvi Israr Ahmad, appeared every night on prime time state television for half an hour. His forte lay in warning people of a terrible life in the hereafter if they did not strictly adhere to Islamic tenets. As a direct result of such admonishments, an Urdu book, *Maut ke Baad Kiya Hoga* (What Will Happen after Death) became one of the best-selling texts.

The premium on piety and a state-promoted ideology of armed struggle in the name of Allah was consistent with Zia's motto for the army, "Islam, Piety, and Jihad." Adopting it as the bedrock of the foreign policy of a strategically vulnerable and politically unstable country had devastating consequences. Fortunately for the self-styled soldier of Islam, the Americans had their own reasons for smiling on his regime's jihadi rhetoric. Buoyed by the influx of dollars, the general oversaw the transformation of the ISI into a vital pillar of the state to the chagrin of some of his closest associates. Established as a small organization under the command of GHQ as early as 1948, the ISI's involvement in the Afghan war proved hugely profitable for its operatives and created a vested interest in perpetuating the business of jihad. With help from the CIA and its Saudi counterpart, the General Intelligence Directorate (GID) led by Prince Turki Al-Faisal, the ISI under General Akhtar Abdur Rahman built a robust infrastructure to become a state within a state. Using an external threat to the country's security as a weapon, Zia publicly dropped the idea of elections exactly two years after the Soviet invasion. Elections had "given birth only to goons and chaos and confusion."[21] Basing his paternalistic view of governance in the Islamic concept of promoting good and forbidding wrong, Zia lectured, "somebody else has to tell them this is good for you and this is bad for you."[22] The results of the 1979 local body elections had shown him that a majority of Pakistanis wanted what was bad for them. They had to be corrected. A 350-member consultative body, the Majlis-i-Shura, was created to give the martial law regime a civilian face and, more important, to bring sections of the dominant socioeconomic classes within the state's ambit of patronage and privilege. By cultivating a political constituency, Zia calculated, elections to the provincial and national assemblies could be manipulated to produce the desired results.

It took another four years before nonparty elections were held in 1985. During this period of "defunct" parties and politics, the political pulse dropped appreciably. Bhutto's legacy still posed the biggest threat. Rifts within the PPP and tactical mistakes by the leadership played into the regime's hands. In her first statement on Afghanistan, Mrs. Nusrat Bhutto accused Zia of "blowing up" the Soviet invasion and exaggerating the number of Afghan refugees in the country. A PPP government, she said, would never permit the Afghan rebels to use Pakistani territory to interfere in Afghanistan.[23] This was anathema for a military high command committed to the Afghan resistance movement. Both Nusrat and Benazir were kept under house arrest in Bhutto's mansion in Karachi's wealthy Clifton neighborhood. "How can they be so afraid of two women?" Benazir asked, likening the security blanket around her home to "some silly James Bond thriller."[24] Keeping the Bhutto women out of the public eye was vital to prevent crowds from gathering in city streets and open spaces in rural hamlets. It was part of Zia's command-and-control strategy. With the main opposition leadership out of commission, his regime managed to weather the political storms unleashed by the Movement for the Restoration of Democracy (MRD). Formed in February 1981 to collectively oppose military rule, the MRD consisted of the PPP, former PNA parties like the JUI, Asghar Khan's Tehrik-i-Istiqlal, and several smaller parties. Citing irreconcilable differences with the PPP, the Jamaat-i-Islami stayed away and continued tacitly supporting Zia.

The threat from an opposition coalition formed with the sole objective of toppling Zia and holding elections would have been greater if events had not taken an unexpected turn. On March 2, 1981, a Pakistan International Airlines (PIA) plane en route from Karachi to Peshawar with 148 passengers on board was hijacked by PPP supporters armed with pistols and hand grenades, queering the pitch for the MRD movement. The hijackers forced the plane to land in Soviet-occupied Kabul. An organization called Al-Zulfikar led by the executed prime minister's two sons, Murtaza and Shahnawaz, took responsibility and demanded the release of political prisoners in exchange for the passengers. Murtaza later denied ordering the operation but accepted that the hijackers were his men.[25] Looking to avenge their father's judicial murder, the brothers opted for armed struggle without the approval or knowledge of their mother and sister. After the hijacking, pro-regime elements held the Bhutto women culpable. The regime's supporters pointed to simultaneous protests by lawyers, students, and thousands of railway workers in Lahore against the arrest of thirty-seven members of the MRD, the high cost of living, the denial of civil liberties, and government repression of trade unions. The protests had drawn a positive response from lawyers in Karachi and Peshawar. Teachers and doctors were staging their own strikes for higher salaries, forcing the closure of schools and hospitals throughout the country. It was the most widespread demonstration against military dictatorship since Bhutto's execution. Set under popular siege, the regime used graphic details of the ordeal of the passengers, especially the brutal killing of a young army officer-turned-diplomat and intensified the government campaign of maligning the PPP and portraying its women leaders as a national security risk. Murtaza Bhutto was seen on television accessing the plane in Kabul, and the Afghan government was shown providing the hijackers with weapons and moral support.

Pakistani authorities alleged that the plot had been hatched by the Soviet-backed Kabul regime to win international recognition. The hijack-

General Zia-ul-Haq addressing the nation. *The White Star Photo Pvt. Ltd. Archive.*

ers were said to have met Carlos the Jackal, the notorious Venezuelan considered to be the kingpin of international terrorism at the time. The
thirteen-day drama ended with the regime releasing fifty-four political prisoners, paying $50,000 to the hijackers, and letting them seek asylum in
Libya. Less than twenty-fours hours after the hostages were set free in Da-
mascus, Zia went on radio and television to denounce the hijacking as an
anti-Pakistan conspiracy by "unpatriotic politicians and a foreign government." It was designed to punish Pakistan for standing in the way of another
nation's "foreign designs," a reference to the fifteen-month Soviet occupation
of Afghanistan. Charging the PPP leadership of collusion with the Soviets
and the Afghan government, Zia intended to wreak maximum political
damage. The "snakes in the sleeve" inside the country belonged to a group
that believed in the "politics of violence" and opposed Pakistan's ideology.[26]

Worried about the opposition's street power, Zia exploited anti-PPP sentiments with his characteristic mix of cajoling and coaxing. He expanded

the federal cabinet to induct twelve civilians, all political nonentities. The policy of co-option was a case of too little too late and did nothing to restore the credibility of the government. Facing the wrath of a combined opposition of banned political parties, Zia relied on the advice of the attorney general, Syed Sharifuddin Pirzada, a constitutional lawyer whose legal contortions legitimizing military dictators have earned him the nickname "magician of Jeddah." In late March 1981, a Provisional Constitutional Order (PCO) was issued that further undermined an already toothless judiciary and did away with the fundamental rights granted under the 1973 constitution. The Supreme Court, which had earlier granted Zia the power to change the constitution, was now deprived of the right of judicial review against any law or action of the military administration. Zia could appoint and remove judges without consulting senior judges. Not every serving judge was invited to take the mandatory oath on the PCO, an artful device used to eliminate those suspected of pro-PPP sympathies and weed out those, like Justices Mushtaq and Anwar-ul-Haq, who had become political liabilities for the regime. The oath was humiliating even for a judiciary known for its supine adherence to executive will and led to the resignation of a few judges who put principles first. For the majority of the judges, the lure of office was irresistible. In the anguished words of a prodemocracy lawyer, the "generals could not be entirely blamed for this unfortunate episode" as "everyone was busy saving his own office and did not care what he had to pay in terms of self-respect to retain it."[27]

In a country where the functioning of civil courts had been replaced by either Islamic or military tribunals, neutralizing the superior judiciary was a final blow to any semblance of judicial independence. The crippling of the judiciary took the sting out of the opposition's challenge, establishing Zia as a seasoned politician. Deploying the specter of Soviet power, Islamic ideology, and the martial rod of order with consummate skill, he belied his critics by steering the course for a long stay at the helm. His eleven years in office wreaked havoc with the fragile threads holding the Pakistani federation together. Lighting fires to protect his berth at the top, Zia not only gagged and fractured politics. He promoted Punjabi chauvinism and a virulent kind of Sunnism, accentuating the alienation of non-Punjabi provinces and destroying the internal sectarian balance. Sindh was the most restive of the provinces and the principal site of the

MRD movement. Rejecting another round of local body polls before controlled elections in March 1985 as a subterfuge to perpetuate the regime,
the alliance of eight banned political parties launched a civil disobedience
campaign on the thirty-sixth anniversary of Pakistan's independence.
Large crowds burned government vehicles and properties in rural Sindh,
sabotaging railway lines, breaching canals, and setting inmates free from
a local jail. Rallies in major urban centers were lackluster by comparison.
With the main leadership in jail, house arrest, or exile, the demonstrations
never showed signs of shaking Zia's grip on power. Opposition leaders still
on the loose berated him for denying the people an elected Parliament, a
constitutional government, civil rights, and political liberties for six long
years. Realizing that his intention was to change the constitution to amass
powers in an indirectly elected presidency at the expense of the prime
minister and Parliament, they condemned the proposed elections as a futile exercise. Claiming he wanted an Islamic and not necessarily a presidential form of government, Zia gave a renewed pledge to eliminate corruption and announced plans to create a new system of Islamic courts to
guarantee swift and inexpensive justice for the average citizen.[28]

A Fractured Backlash

While keeping the idea of democracy alive, the MRD movement did not
derail Zia so much as expose the woeful absence of political unity among
the constituents of the federation. Confined to Sindh in the main and
drawing no significant response from the other three provinces, the protest against martial law wilted in the face of the regime's heavy-handed
methods. The failure of the MRD leadership to mobilize support in Punjab, a bastion of middle- and upper-class support for the regime, proved to
be decisive. Overall more than sixty perished, hundreds were injured, and
several thousand were arrested in the early 1980s protests. Intimidation
and the threat of imprisonment crushed political debate as the national
press took to the demeaning task of exercising self-censorship. The ruthless
mowing down of the political opposition makes one vignette of resistance
cry out for attention. Looking to reclaim the one province that had risen
in such violent resistance to his regime, Zia toured Sindh. As the presidential motorcade drove past the shuttered shop windows of the empty streets
of Dadu, protestors threw stones and waved their fists at him.[29] This was

mild compared with the 400 stray dogs that were unleashed on the streets bearing the slogan "Zia is a dog." The offending dogs were shot or clubbed to death by the local martial law authorities. Taking out insurance for Zia's future public appearances, orders were issued to kill all stray dogs in Pakistan. In a related incident, dozens of donkeys carrying banners marked "Death to Zia" were let loose in another town the general visited. No donkeys were killed, one observer mused, because "perhaps the country had a more urgent need of the animals."[30]

A veiled allusion to the mulish attitude of the populace, notably in Punjab, it summed up the MRD's movement. Back to playing his election game, Zia hinted at holding the polls earlier than 1985 and sent the army to restore control over Sindh. Seeing the options closing, Nusrat Bhutto, in Europe for medical treatment, called on the army to oust Zia, release political prisoners, and set a date for free elections. Zia lacked legitimacy; his removal would end the political stalemate between the government and opposition and prepare the way for consultations leading to a peaceful transfer of power.[31] It was an impolitic statement, which added to the general's rising good luck tally. He needed it once the bar associations became energized against the regime. In early October 1983, 4,000 lawyers marched from the Lahore High Court to the Punjab Provincial Assembly shaking their fists and shouting "Down with Martial Law" and "Pakistan Forever."[32] They forcibly entered the assembly grounds and placed the national flag and a copy of the 1973 constitution in front of the building's main entrance, noting that martial law was just brute force and had no legal authority.

Political protests during the Zia era were acts of extreme daring in the face of excessive use of force. Falling well short of triggering an outburst of popular fervor, they failed to ruffle a dictator whose ruthlessness was tempered only by his extraordinary good fortune emanating from global political developments. The steady flow of international funds for the Afghan war created options for the regime that had eluded Bhutto. A significant proportion of the dollar windfall was surreptitiously diverted to the nuclear program centered at the Research Laboratories, set up in 1976 by Bhutto in the picturesque setting of Kahuta, about twenty miles from Islamabad. Once Washington relaxed its insistence on denying Pakistan the nuclear option, the program, based on the little-known centrifugal technology for the enrichment of uranium, developed by leaps and bounds.

Though officially code-named Project 207, Pakistani agents running the procurement operations called it "Operation Butter Factory." Headed by Abdul Qadeer Khan, the nuclear program at Kahuta thrived on Western ignorance of the implications of the spread of centrifugal technology and the consequent laxness of export controls on sensitive materials. Whether out of naïveté or active complicity, European countries displayed a surprising eagerness to sell vital parts and equipment to Pakistan. "They literally begged us to buy their equipment," Qadeer Khan later boasted.[33] By April 1978, Pakistan had broken the Western monopoly by enriching uranium while also continuing the plutonium-based program at the PAEC. It took another five years before Zia publicly admitted that Pakistan could enrich uranium. His canard denying any intention of building nuclear weapons convinced no one. But Zia did not care. The nuclear program was his regime's most treasured asset. Immensely popular at home, the quest for nuclear parity was considered Pakistan's best hope of resisting India's claims to regional hegemony.[34] A vigorous pursuit of the nuclear option pleased the army, the one institution Zia had to keep on an even keel. His sedulous control over the upper echelons of the army helped him survive coup attempts. A plot in 1980 by Major General Tajammul Hussain to assassinate Zia on Pakistan Day had been thwarted, as were subsequent coup attempts, one of which was linked to Bhutto's sons.

Capping the general's remarkable run of good fortune was a robust economy—the combined result of American assistance, six good harvest seasons, and $3 billion in annual remittances from 6 million Pakistanis working in the Persian Gulf. Zia was capitalizing on Bhutto's dream of turning the Middle East boom into Pakistan's opportunity to the grave detriment of the PPP's constituency in Punjab. The remittance money whetted the middle-class appetite for consumer goods and took the pressure off the government. It was raining money through other means as well. Heroin was by now Pakistan's largest export, earning billions of dollars in illicit money. The army's National Logistics Cell was known to be involved in the transport of narcotics from the northwest to the port city of Karachi. In 1980, the country acquired its first heroin-producing laboratory. Not all the heroin was exported, with as much as one-third serving the needs of a growing population of heroin addicts. By 1983, a conservative official estimate projected 150,000 addicts. In 1987, the Narcotics Control Board placed the number of heroin addicts in Pakistan at 650,000 out of 1.9 million drug users.[35] Unofficial figures were appreciably higher. Estimates in 1988 put the number of heroin addicts at 1.5 million, and this in a country where a decade earlier there had been none.

An alarming rise in drug addiction was among the poisoned gifts of Zia's Islamic era. Displaying his value system in no uncertain terms, he is known to have wistfully asked whether it was not possible to produce heroin exclusively for export. Drug money laundered through the Bank of Commerce and Credit International (BCCI) gave added buoyancy to the national economy. Punjab was the main beneficiary of the state's enhanced ability to dispense patronage. Small-scale Punjabi entrepreneurs prospered as a result of the rise in consumer demand while the provision of development funds for the rural areas of the province gave the regime the rudiments of a political constituency. To neutralize the sting of the Islamist parties, Zia declared it a crime for Ahmadis to preach or propagate their religion. As the date for the 1985 elections approached, restrictions on dissent were tightened. Student unions were banned in March 1984 and the press treated to additional curbs on threat of imprisonment and closure. Newspapers were prohibited from publishing any information related to political parties, most of which were arrayed against the government. In this martial wonderland, elections were to be held on a nonparty basis. Candidates and voters were to be screened in accordance with newly incorporated Islamic provisions to the constitution. To add insult to this injury, a directly elected president was to have the power to dismiss both the Parliament and the prime minister.[36]

The MRD, now a mismatch of eleven parties, accused Zia of wanting to hold on to power. They were right. But he was even more unwilling to risk facing any kind of electorate. In any fair election, the political parties would mobilize people against dictatorship. This would require Zia to manipulate the vote, a dangerous gamble that could easily backfire. There was already a great deal simmering below the apparent surface calm to worry the government. Students were fighting gun battles with the police to protest the ban on student unions. Lawyers, journalists, intellectuals, and other civil society groups were incensed by the clampdown on dissent and efforts to control people's behavior through monstrous intrusions into their personal autonomy. The ban on alcohol was nearly a decade old. State-promoted religiosity under Zia carried a hollow ring given the growing ranks of heroin addicts and the sudden increase in cases of depression and mental illness. Like the bonfire of national education lit by the regime in its efforts to rout the PPP from the country's educational campuses, the false claims of Islamic morality had a pernicious impact on the Pakistani mind. The full extent of the damage would be reaped by future genera-tions, much like the economically crippling and mounting debt burden while the ruling coterie enriched itself.

To ensure his continuity in an elected civilian setup, Zia came up with the ingenious, if odious, device of holding a referendum. A brainchild of his advisers, the referendum would ask people whether they approved of the regime's Islamization program. An answer of yes would give Zia an-other five years in presidential office. The unapologetic blend of deceit and hypocrisy enraged people well beyond the official opposition. Bhutto's final words anticipated the new twist in Zia's theater of the absurd. The country wants a constitution, the nation wants democracy, the people want Parliament, the provinces want autonomy, the proletariat and the peasantry want the PPP: "This is what the people want. Stop trying to be a Mehdi."[37] With the legitimacy of absolute power lurking just around the corner, Zia dismissed criticisms and marshaled his gag brigade to pre-vent politicians from voicing them publicly. During a whirlwind cam-paign tour through Punjab, he promised elections and the lifting of mar-tial law in return for a mandate to continue dabbling with his version of Islam. Proof of the electorate's sophistication and the national consensus on democracy, the referendum on December 19, 1984, was boycotted in unison from Khyber to Karachi. Optimistic estimates put the turnout at 10 percent of the registered vote. There was massive fraud; nonregistered voters were permitted to cast their votes, including some opponents of the general who gleefully voted more than once. Unfazed by the snub, the chief election commissioner declared a 97.7 percent "yes" vote by 62 per-cent of the electorate, sealing Zia's claim to another half a decade in presi-dential office.

Pleased with the outcome of his referendum charade, the general pro-ceeded to tighten the screws on the opposition. The MRD led by Benazir Bhutto, who was by then based in London, made the tactical error of boy-cotting the nonparty elections scheduled for February 1985. Zia responded by putting the entire opposition under lock and key for the duration of the polls. This emptied the field for his henchmen to manipulate the vote to ensure the election of parliamentarians the regime could work with.

Given the first opportunity to express their opinion in eight years, people came out in droves for both national and provincial assembly elections. Several close associates of Zia lost the election, and the Jamaat-i-Islami, the only party permitted to contest, was vanquished in all except a couple of urban constituencies in Lahore. The turnout for elections to the national assembly was 53.69 percent nationwide, while 57.7 percent of the electorate voted in the provincial assembly elections.[38]

Such a thumping response for an electoral exercise, flawed though it may have been, deprived the MRD leadership of any political leverage during Zia's remaining three years in power. Benazir in the splendor of her isolation and exile had not realized just how successfully the regime had used the pennies dropping from heaven to transform the face of Pakistani politics. Ideology took the back burner as Zia the Islamic ideologue presided over the commercialization of social values and the crass monetization of politics. Focused on development issues in the immediacy of their constituencies rather than on distant national objectives, PPP members flouted the party decision and participated in the elections. In the opportunistic rush to join the ranks of those enjoying the benefits of state patronage and privilege, politics were bent out of shape. Those who entered the political fray did so more as a business, fully aware that the more one spent in electioneering, the greater the future rewards. While benefiting the commercial art industry and ancillary businesses, the monetization of elections in Pakistan did precious little to educate the electorate about the main issues. Personalities, not issues, dominated voters' choices, proving Zia's dictum that a thwack of the whip was all that was needed to get politicians to fall into line.

An assorted flock of representatives, many of them political greenhorns worthy of local and provincial arenas, made it to Zia's Parliament. A mild-mannered Sindhi landlord, Mohammad Khan Junejo, was picked as prime minister. Ironically enough, the regime's anointed formed a parliamentary party and called it the Pakistan Muslim League to deflect comment on its strange pedigree. The controversial Eighth Amendment to the constitution was piloted through the assembly with help from this political grouping. It had a transformative effect on Pakistani politics whose significance has to be understood in the light of constitutional amendments enforced through a presidential order before the first meeting of the national assembly on March 23, 1985. Zia preempted the newly elected

Parliament by passing a Revival of the Constitution of 1973 Order, which altered the spirit of the constitution. The Objectives Resolution of 1949, which had served as the preamble of all Pakistani constitutions since 1956, was made a substantive part of the constitution in order to expedite the Islamization of state and society. Apart from indemnifying the entire gamut of the regime's actions, the RCO gave the president overarching powers over the prime minister and invested centrally appointed governors with authority to sack elected provincial chief ministers. Zia had wanted to create a National Security Council, which was widely seen as a move to give the military a permanent say in politics. Zia dropped the idea of giving the military a constitutional role in Pakistani politics. In return, the members of the national assembly agreed to give the president powers to dismiss an elected cabinet and dissolve the assembly. It was the price they believed had to be paid to get Zia to lift martial law on December 31, 1985.

By then the shortcomings of a civilian government under the military's thumb had become painfully evident. Zia frankly stated that power was being shared with, not transferred to, civilians. The Eighth Amendment was the jewel in the president's crown. It implanted the spurious notion of presidential "discretion" without providing safeguards against the exercise of arbitrary power. Exploiting Pakistan's geostrategic importance for American Cold War purposes in the 1980s, Zia smothered internal political dissent. What money could not buy, the arms of the state obtained by coercion. Without denying the important role played by the MRD opposition, oppressive controls on freedom of expression and political activities helped Zia consolidate his grip on power by silencing the populace.

Only the people could not be wished away. Seeking social and economic opportunities, not ideological lessons from a self-serving ruler, the democratic aspirations of Pakistan's disempowered found voice in Habib Jalib's populist resistance poetry:

> Why should we fight America's war
> And color our land with blood?
> We are awaiting light ourselves
> Why should we throw stones on light?
> O tyrant, have you ever thought
> Why all of God's creation is fed up with you?

We are the forerunners of peace and freedom
Why should we become the accomplices of a usurper?[39]

Pakistanis from various walks of life and ideological persuasions vocal-
ized their opposition to Zia both at home and abroad. One London-based
group calling itself "Pakistanis for Democracy" wrote a hard-hitting letter
to the US senator Frank Church, then the chairman of the Foreign Relations Committee, warning him of the hazards of granting military assistance to their country:

> Mr. Senator, you will pardon the people of Pakistan if they do not
> readily perceive the threat to freedom by whatever the Russian
> troops may or may not be doing in Afghanistan. They know that
> their own freedom has been despoiled not by the Russian Army but
> by the gallant Pakistan Army on whose upkeep they have been
> squandering over 70% of their budget every year since the country
> attained independence.

It was the "Army which would not let democracy take root in Pakistan."
Under the present regime, the army as an institution was becoming an
object of disdain. However, Zia was the primary target of popular hatred
because of his "sanctimonious pose . . . palpable dishonesty and untruth-
fulness." Any "unconditional aid to General Zia and his junta would be
planting a time bomb of instability in the region which would be quite the
opposite of what America wants and what the interests of America demand."[40] These ominous words would come back to haunt US policy
makers two decades later.

Resistance to Zia's dictatorial regime were more likely to be found in
artistic and intellectual expression than in outbreaks of political protest.
Determined to keep the streets clean of angry demonstrators, the martial
law regime actually contemplated banning the use of the word "politics"
from public discourse. Just below the surface—capped by strict curbs on
the media, martial law ordinances, and punitive Islamic laws—flowed a
flourishing subculture of resistance whose strength lay in its resolute opposition to dictatorship rather than in numbers. Ahmad Faraz wrote the
uplifting "Mahasara" (Besieged), one of the most celebrated poems of resistance against military dictatorship, in which he renewed his intellectual

vow to wield the pen against deceit and oppression, whatever the cost.[41] Punished with public floggings for exercising their fundamental right of expression and deprived of their livelihoods, depressed and hounded journalists, civil rights activists, labor leaders, and intellectuals met in underground coffee houses and the privacy of homes to vent their anger at Zia, his Punjabi-Sunni prejudices, and hypocritical "Islamization" policies. A few courageous journal editors tried issuing warnings against upstart publicists whose "misguided interpretation of the principle of Islamization rests on their love of authoritarianism."[42] Creative writers began experimenting with political allegories to capture life under military rule and also to register their utter disdain for the farce of "Islamization." Visual and dramatic artists also used symbolism to remonstrate their loss of freedom and denial of dignity. Zia may have ruled Pakistan with an iron fist, but he failed to capture the hearts and minds of Pakistan's resilient intelligentsia and dynamic artistic community.

Popular cinema of the period reveled in heroic violence against tyranny, most notably in the Punjabi blockbuster *Maula Jat,* whose release coincided with Bhutto's death sentence and hanging. The lionized Punjabi actor Sultan Rahi was cast in the title role as the people's savior against an egomaniacal control freak, played by Mustafa Qureshi (Nuri Nath), whose ruthless grab for absolute power symbolized the martial law regime. Presented as a story of good and evil, the plot foregrounds women's oppression to expose the hollowness of rural Punjab's patriarchal morality. Eventually the people join hands with Maula Jat, literally a wandering king, to defeat the villain and his clansmen. Martial law authorities banned the film for excessive violence, but it ran consecutively for two and half years, pending a review of the filmmaker's appeal in the high court. Brash in its depiction of the divine battle between God's justice and Satan's injustice, the film broke box office records and became an icon of success for Pakistani cinema. Significantly, the film was most successful in the PPP's strongholds in Punjab and rural Sindh. Where Bhutto's support was limited, such as Karachi and Balochistan, the audience response to the film was at best lukewarm.[43]

When an overzealous member of the national censor board arranged for Zia to see censored clips of films produced before and during the Bhutto era, he was so outraged by the eruption of immorality on celluloid that he instantly banned all films produced in the preceding three decades.

A stringent code of morality was enforced that was so all encompassing as to scare most filmmakers. The state's attempts at cultural policing sounded the death knell of Pakistan's struggling film industry, which had been badly hit by the loss of the East Pakistan market, but did nothing to improve moral standards. Starved for entertainment, audiences turned to watching Indian television. Pirated Indian and Western film videos did roaring business, defeating the purpose of the controls imposed on the film industry. The craze for Indian films and stars reached new heights as many among the faithful combined visitations to local mosques for daily prayers with viewings of Bollywood's improbable and formulaic yarns intermeshed with romantic sequences of song and dance and blood-curdling violence. The general's own family was not immune from the popular craze for Hindi cinema in Islamic Pakistan. The guest list at Zia's daughter's wedding included the Indian actor Shatrughan Sinha, who went on to join the Bharatiya Janata Party (BJP).[44]

Shameless about wearing hypocrisy as a badge of Islamic morality, Zia cultivated a new political culture where displays of piety came to signify social status and power. For all those who were swayed by the state-controlled media's daily diet of an Arabized and punitive Islam, there were many more who resisted with wit and grit. Debarred from directly flaying the military regime, critics attacked the government by writing reviews trashing programs aired by the state-run Pakistan Television (PTV). Newspaper readers knew that the mostly anonymous critiques were aimed at the government and not PTV, then the country's only television channel and the primary source of information and entertainment for a nation of 90 million, mostly poor and illiterate Pakistanis. Television critics pilloried the news coverage for being biased and highly selective. When PTV decided to shut down its broadcast for two hours as a sign of piety during the month of Ramadan to allow viewers to start and break the dawn-to-dusk fast, critics hailed the move as the best thing PTV had ever done. They regretted that the suspension of service was short-lived and thought PTV's redemption lay in going off the air permanently.[45]

Some of the most egregious measures to enforce public morality were targeted at women. Female announcers on state television were told to wear the *chadar,* a large wrap, and keep their heads covered. The sanctity of the *char diwari,* or the four walls of the home, was drummed into a populace susceptible to religious conservatism by Wahabi ideologues like

Maulvi Israr Ahmad. Popular television serials portrayed working women as immoral breakers of family values, the object of disdain and outright rebuke. Rebel writers like Saadat Hasan Manto and revolutionary poets like Faiz Ahmad Faiz, along with Jalib and Faraz, were blacklisted. Bhutto's regime had tried opening up public spaces for women, who not only found employment in state services but also flourished in other fields where they competed with men on more than equal terms. Zia sanctioned the conservative backlash by making the social control of women a central plank of his "Islamization" policies. Advised by a seventeen-member Council of Islamic Ideology, he made a series of objectionable laws that effectively reduced women to the status of second-class citizens. Several of the Islamic laws approved by the advisory council bore an unmistakable Saudi imprint.

The rigid view of transgressions and punishments was in contrast with the more flexible attitude of Hanafis, the main school of jurisprudence among Muslims in the subcontinent. Fearing challenges to his laws in civil courts, Zia withdrew his earlier decision to vest the high courts with power to decide whether a law was repugnant to Islam. Completing the process of setting up a parallel judicial system consisting of sharia benches, Zia established a Federal Shariat Court with appellate powers to hear any case pertaining to convictions and sentences under the Hudood laws he had promulgated in 1979 as part of his "Islamization" policy. Paradoxically, the general's self-appointed court overthrew the law of death by stoning (*rajm*) for adultery, creating an uproar among the self-appointed guardians of the faith. The ulema now demanded a place in the august court to make sure that the judges did not dilute the Islamic character of the laws with their limited Westernized education. Zia complied by passing an amendment to the constitution, sanctioning the appointment of three representatives of the ulema to the five-member Federal Shariat Court. The inclusion of the ulema ensured a reversal of the court's earlier judgment on stoning to death for adultery.[46] The concession raised expectations among madrasa-educated clerics, for whom the slogan of "Islamization" was a means to empowerment by getting key positions within the state bureaucracy or, at the very least, some other sinecure. Zia was well on his way to cultivating the political constituency that had eluded him before the Afghan war. He had also made himself indispensable to Western capitals in the final round of the Cold War with the Soviet Union.

Women protesting against the Zia regime in Lahore. *The White Star Photo Pvt. Ltd. Archive.*

With sections of the ulema willing to approve Zia's equation of his regime with the introduction of an Islamic system of government, the liberal intelligentsia was left fighting a losing battle. While resistance assumed multiple forms, urban and middle-class women led the street protests against Zia's so-called Islamization policies. The stimulus came from a law that reduced a woman's evidence in certain commercial cases to half that of a man's. Zia's law of evidence stirred an elementary uprising among educated, urban, upper-class women that found strong support among many men. As enraged women organized the Women's Action Forum (WAF) and took on the baton-wielding arms of the state, they were beaten and hurled into jail. Saeeda Gazdar's inspirational poem "Twelfth February, 1983" immortalized the moment:

> The flags of mourning were flapping
> the hand-maidens had rebelled
> Those two hundred women who came out on the streets
> were surrounded on all sides

besieged by armed police.
Tear gas, rifles and guns
wireless vans and jeeps
every path was blockaded
there was no protection
they had to fight themselves . . .
You ask for two
We [twenty million] . . . women
shall testify
against this tyranny and cruelty
hurled at our heads
in the name of the law of evidence
Not us, but you
deserve to be murdered
for being the enemies of light and truth
for being the murderers of love.[47]

The long night of the Zia years mutilated much more than just the spirit of truth and love. It uprooted the Pakistani national consciousness from its moorings in the vision of its founding father:

> No nation can rise to the height of glory unless your women are side by side with you. . . . It is a crime against humanity that our women are shut up within the four walls of the houses as prisoners. . . . There is no sanction anywhere for the deplorable conditions in which our women have to live.[48]

Women bore a major brunt of the sea change in the cultural complexion of Pakistan during the heyday of "Islamization." But they emerged from the Zia era as a more assertive force than at any other time in Pakistani history. Though confined to urban middle- and upper-class women in the main, the battle for women's rights was now an intrinsic part of the struggle for democracy. The symbolism of women leading the opposition to the general's rule is a telling comment on the significance of the Zia era in bringing the women's rights movement into prominence. But there were still a multitude of promises to be kept and miles to go before the women's movement could truly come into its own.

Zia's high-handed amendments to the 1973 constitution were to make the task doubly difficult. Using the fig leaf of a representative Parliament, he inserted his name into the constitution. Declaring himself president for life, Zia assumed powers to dismiss elected governments and legislatures. The Eighth Amendment made him the supreme commander of the armed forces with authority to make key senior appointments without needing to consult the prime minister, whom he could dismiss along with the elected assembly on a whim. Able to intervene in the political process under constitutional cover, the armed forces now had no need to directly intervene in politics. The generals could just prevail on the president to dismiss unpalatable governments. While making martial law unlikely, the measures were inimical to the growth of democratic institutions in the country.

Once all the pieces for perpetuating himself in power were in place, Zia lifted martial law on December 31, 1985. What was being anticipated as an occasion for celebration became a dirge for democracy and, by implication, the future of a moderate and stable Pakistan. The first street demonstrations to rock the urban areas were organized by the PPP on the occasion of Bhutto's birthday on January 5, 1986. Denouncing the civilian face of martial law, protestors chanted slogans, "Death to Zia" and "Zia is an American stooge," as they huddled around 130-pound garishly decorated cakes honoring the memory of their fallen leader.[49] The sea of more than 4 million people that came out in Lahore to welcome Benazir Bhutto with rose petals on her return from exile in early April 1986 gave fresh impetus to the movement to oust Zia. It took several more street protests, a spate of untimely deaths, and thousands of arrests before Pakistan's longest surviving general-politician could be ejected from office.

More than constitutional doctoring, Zia's continued grip on power flowed from his retention of the office of army chief. This blocked promotions within the army and was a potential source of disaffection. With the war against the Soviets in Afghanistan entering its final stages, Zia could not risk losing control over the country's premier institution. He distrusted New Delhi, which only recently had backed away from attacking Pakistan's nuclear facilities with Israeli collusion. Instead India opted to display its military prowess by launching a massive war game called "Brasstacks" in January 1987 along its border with Pakistan. The general deftly defused tensions by engaging in some cricket diplomacy. He flew to

India to watch a match between the Indian and Pakistani teams. Playing games with big brother India was child's play compared with achieving the army's desired objectives in Afghanistan. Zia and his inner circle of generals wanted nothing less than a pro-Pakistan government in post-Soviet Kabul. This was deemed crucial to preventing Pakistan from facing hostile neighbors on both the eastern and the western fronts, a lesson initially learned during the 1965 war and one that was painfully confirmed in 1971. Once the introduction of the portable surface-to-air Stinger missile tilted the balance in favor of the mujahidin, Moscow began looking for ways to pull out of Afghanistan without losing face. The search had begun soon after the invasion with the Soviets hoping to use the withdrawal of the Red Army as leverage for getting Pakistan and Iran to stop assisting the rebels fighting against the communist government in Kabul. By its insistence on installing pro-Pakistan resistance leaders in power, the Zia regime contributed to prolonging the war in no uncertain terms. The army high command's singular determination to reap maximum rewards for their tenacious support of the mujahidin saw the Afghan war spilling into Pakistan. During 1987, there were a spate of terrorist bombings in nine cities, killing 150 people. Blamed on communist agents, the blasts ushered in a new era where the state's inability to govern a burgeoning population was overshadowed by its abject failure to protect life and property.

The ready availability of weapons of all manner of lethal intensity seriously compromised the state's monopoly over the instruments of coercion, making Pakistan a scary place in which to live and work even during Zia's own time. Instead of the much-fabled Muslim unity that was supposed to be the bedrock of Islamic Pakistan, a noxious outpouring of sectarian hatred manifested itself in print culture and, most menacingly, in increasing violence by armed militias. The simultaneous mushrooming of mosques and madrasas, each with its own narrowly construed point of view, compounded the problem. Pakistan's drift toward sectarian conflict was matched by growing antagonism between linguistic groups in urban centers like Karachi and Hyderabad. Living in congested cinderblock slums, the different linguistic groups could erupt in an orgy of violence at the hint of a provocative rumor. Even as agents of the Afghan secret service KHAD and the Soviet KGB set off bombs in crowded shopping centers in Karachi, Lahore, and Rawalpindi, linguistic tensions stirred by the regime's use of colonial divide-and-rule tactics ripped apart the brittle social peace in

Pakistan's financial hub and sole seaport in the south. The meteoric rise of the Muhajir Qaumi Movement (MQM) led by a student-leader-turned-demagogue, Altaf Hussain, was engineered by army intelligence to weaken the PPP's support base at university campuses. Exploiting local frustrations to its political advantage, the MQM's emergence in Karachi pitted Urdu speakers against Pathan and Punjabi settlers. Disaffected youth armed with Kalashnikovs waged war on rival linguistic communities in pitched battles for control over urban spaces. Religious divines for their part staked their political claims by promoting sectarian tensions. Far from gaining strategic depth in Afghanistan, the military top brass had recklessly wagered away the keys to Pakistan's own internal security.

It was not until April 1988 that an agreement was inked in Geneva by representatives of Pakistan and Afghanistan, with the United States and the Soviet Union acting as guarantors. Under the terms of the Geneva Accords, Islamabad and Kabul undertook to respect each other's sovereignty and stick to the principles of noninterference and nonintervention. Both sides also agreed on ensuring the voluntary return of Afghan refugees living in Pakistan. Zia had opposed signing the Geneva Accords. They fell well short of his goal to replace the pro-Soviet government in Kabul with one pieced together by the ISI from among the mujahidin groups and, for good measure, headed by the deposed Afghan king, Zahir Shah. The international tide that had shored up his regime since 1979 was, however, now decisively turning against his interests. His efforts to delay the signing of the agreement were rebuffed by Washington, befuddled at the apparent insanity of postponing the Soviet withdrawal after expending so much effort to achieve precisely that end. Based on the principle of negative symmetry, the Geneva Accords required the Soviets and Pakistan to suspend arms supplies to their respective proxies in Afghanistan. By rushing in military supplies to bolster the chances of their Afghan clients, Zia and the ISI wanted to tip the scales against the communist government before the agreement came into effect.[50]

To their utter dismay, those responsible for the carefully vetted new civilian dispensation had other ideas. Egged on by Foreign Office stalwarts and backed by Parliament, Prime Minister Junejo wanted to honor the accords in letter and spirit. But there was no getting around the military's strategic planners, now seeing the whole cake within Pakistan's grasp in Afghanistan. It was a serious case of optical illusion for which both Afghanistan and Pakistan ended up paying an unacceptably hefty price. The

Zia regime's strategic brinkmanship plunged Afghanistan into a withering civil war whose destabilizing effects would in time seriously threaten
global security. Pakistan was the first to suffer the blowback. The Zia regime's social and political engineering had produced a jumble of civil
wars at home along linguistic, sectarian, and ideological lines. Coupled
with administrative paralysis and unconscionable levels of corruption in
high places, the foundations of the federation had been shaken to the core.
As a disillusioned politician put it, "corruption had by now seeped through
every level of society; from electricity meter readers to high court judges."
Businessmen left briefcases stashed with money at government ministries,
having discovered an easier way to make money than market competition. "There were no checks whatsoever."[51]

The last thing Pakistan needed was an overadventurous army high
command and intelligence services waging a proxy war in a neighboring
country. Sensing the growing impatience among politically conscious
Pakistanis with the army's meddling in Afghan affairs, Prime Minister
Junejo decided to flex his political muscle. Angry about being kept out of
the loop by Zia on matters pertaining to Afghanistan, Junejo allegedly told
the Foreign Office to clear all cipher telegrams with him before sending
them on to the president.[52] If true, the defiance could not escape its comeuppance in military-authoritarian Pakistan. More grist for the anti-Junejo
army mill was provided by the prime minister's decision to call an all-
parties conference on the Geneva Accords. If this was intolerable civilian
interference in military matters, Junejo's attempts to cut the bulging costs
of preserving the pomp and circumstance of the generals sealed his fate.

Even a military dictator enjoying unlimited constitutional powers
needed a justification to dismiss a civilian prime minister. The opportunity for Zia came in the form of massive blasts in Ojhri Camp, an ammunition dump housed in vintage World War II brick- and tin-roofed barracks in Faizabad—a heavily populated area lying athwart the twin cities
of Islamabad and Rawalpindi. It was an ordinary spring day on April 10,
1988, with the sun beaming its soft golden rays on the busy roads as the
morning rush hour wound to a close. At 9:35 a.m., a series of explosions
transformed the relative calm of Islamabad–Rawalpindi into an inferno
that many likened to *qiamat,* or the Day of Judgment. An estimated 7,000
tons of arms and ammunition went up in flames as hundreds of missiles
and shells rained on an unsuspecting citizenry, killing over a hundred

and injuring more than a thousand. An unaccounted number of small children were among the casualties. Eyewitnesses related harrowing tales of police running away from the scene of destruction but finding time to rob the local residents. Hell had broken loose.

A major transit facility for arms and ammunition for the Afghan mujahidin, Ojhri Camp was run by the ISI. A request by the Americans to visit the camp had sent panic waves in the senior echelons of the ISI. Zia's close consort General Akhtar Abdur Rahman, who headed the ISI during the first eight years of the Afghan war, is known to have amassed a handsome fortune as director-general. Nicknamed the silent general, Rahman was replaced in March 1987 by the excitable and voluble General Hamid Gul. Well before the Ojhri Camp disaster, Washington was needling Islamabad to recover the Stinger missiles from the Afghan rebels, furious upon discovering that they had been sold to clandestine buyers and had ended up in Iran and other Middle Eastern countries.[53] Determined to arm their favorite Afghan mujahidin, the ISI had been shipping huge quantities of weapons from Ojhri to the western border. The discovery of any sign of pilfering would have disgraced Zia and his two top generals, embarrassing the army. If avoiding an American inspection gave the ISI handlers a motive for blowing up the ammunition dump, the possibility of sabotage by communist agents or a fatal accident moving inflammable materials was also plausible.

The report of the military commission set up to investigate the causes of the blasts was never made public. Those privy to the commission's findings have intimated that it was inconclusive and attributed the blasts to an accident. Junejo appointed a second parliamentary commission. On May 29, 1988, an infuriated Zia summarily sacked the man he had honored with his trust amid much fanfare about the restoration of democracy. Befuddled Pakistanis heard that the government's dismissal and the simultaneous dissolution of the national assembly had been prompted by the steep decline in public morality owing to Junejo's reluctance to speed up "Islamization" in deference to the Parliament. More incredulous was the charge that the elected government had failed to control a deteriorating law-and-order situation. The story behind the strange progression of events after Ojhri was not confined to Pakistani drawing rooms. Newspapers were rife with speculation about Zia wanting to win the war in Afghanistan within three months and his perception of Junejo as a tiresome obstacle in the army's efforts to capitalize on its "investment." The more Zia

tried justifying his decision, the more he implicated himself in the controversial move. His unconstitutional decision to appoint a caretaker cabinet
minus a prime minister and retain favored chief ministers in the provinces did not go down well. The general's incredible run of luck, it seemed,
was finally coming to an end.

Feeling acutely vulnerable, Zia prolonged his ministrations and went
out in public less and less. Angered with the Pakistani president's devious
tactics on Afghanistan and fed up with his dissimulations on the nuclear
issue, Washington was reviewing the implications of its continued identification with an increasingly isolated and unpopular president. This
presaged the end for Zia who, fearing an assassination attempt, went into
virtual seclusion behind the high-security walls of Army House in Rawalpindi. A prisoner of his own policies, the general was eager to keep up
pretenses. Against his better judgment, he flew to the southeastern city of
Bahawalpur to inspect a display of the latest US Abram battle tanks that
the Pakistani Army was considering purchasing. It was a fatal error. On
August 17, 1988, a preoccupied Zia glumly watched the tank exercises
flanked by the US ambassador Arnold Raphel, the American defense attaché Brigadier General Herbert M. Wassom, and a bevy of top Pakistani
generals. The trials were a sham; the tanks performed disastrously in
the desert conditions of southeastern Pakistan. After a hurried lunch, Zia
boarded Pak One, the redesigned luxury Hercules C-130 plane, taking Raphel with him at the last minute as a safety measure. General Akhtar Abdur Rahman followed them onto the plane, as did Wassom and twenty-
seven others. Also on board was said to be a case of mangoes.[54] Minutes
after the plane took off, it began losing height before making a steep dive
straight into the ground and going up in a ball of fire.

What the political opposition could not achieve had happened in a
flash. There were no survivors. In just a few moments of high-decibel
history making, Zia and almost the entire senior Pakistani military
leadership had been reduced to ash. Many a committed democrat would
rue the loss of an opportunity to hold Zia accountable in the people's
court. A plethora of conspiracy theories heaped confusion on the charred
rubble of the plane. For the few who believed it was an act of divine intervention, many more thought it was a straightforward case of sabotage,
with some subscribing to the American view that there was a mechanical
fault in the C-130 plane. No one would ever know the real reasons for the

crash. With time few would doubt that it was anything but a successful assassination plot. The deed done, it was time to pick up the fragments of a pulverized and terrorized nation that, more than ever before, needed leaders with the political will to turn a fresh page in its history. There was no dearth of inspiration for those with their hand on the people's pulse. In the spirited words of the great resistance poet Faiz Ahmad Faiz, who had passed away four years earlier:

> We shall see
> No doubt we too will see
> the day that has been promised
> When these high mountains
> Of tyranny and oppression
> will fly away like pieces of cotton
> And we oppressed
> Beneath our feet will have
> this earth shiver, shake and beat
> And heads of rulers will be struck
> With crackling lightning
> and thunder roars.
> When from this God's earth [Kaaba]
> All false icons will be removed
> Then the pure of heart, condemned by zealous keepers of faith,
> Will be invited to sit on the altar and rule.[55]

EIGHT

DEMOCRACY RESTORED?

GENERAL ZIA-UL-HAQ PASSED AWAY INTO HISTORY without fulfilling his oft-repeated and rescinded pledge to restore democracy in Pakistan. A pair of dentures was all that survived the C-130's incineration to confirm his identity. Like other assassinations of public figures in Pakistan's troubled history, Zia's death remains shrouded in mystery and idle speculation. None of the conspiracy theories matched the gripping simplicity of Benazir Bhutto's comment that it was an act of God. Denied the satisfaction of dislodging Zia through the ballot box, the opposition found comfort in the prospect of free and fair elections on November 16, 1988. Pakistan at long last stood poised to join the ranks of formally democratic countries in the developing world. The heroic display of people's power in the Philippines led by the unassuming Corazon Aquino against the twenty-year rule of Ferdinand Marcos had invigorated prodemocracy movements as far afield as Latin America, Eastern Europe, and Africa. With democracy bursting forth on the global stage, supporters of the thirty-five-year-old Benazir—hailed as the symbol of democracy—were itching for an opportunity to emulate the trend. They could now hardly believe their luck.

A hushed silence hung over Rawalpindi and Islamabad as a shocked but composed nation awaited word of the next move at the top. The elimination of the country's top command came at a time when the Soviets were halfway through withdrawing from Afghanistan. Troops quickly took control of strategic locations in the capital. Zia's provincial chief ministers recommended postponing elections and imposing martial law. They were overruled by the military high command, purportedly on

American instruction. The Senate chairman Ghulam Ishaq Khan, an experienced bureaucrat, became acting president with the backing of the new army chief, Major General Mirza Aslam Beg. Ishaq Khan vowed to honor the Geneva Accords and hold elections on schedule. Two judicial interventions brought more good news for protagonists of democracy. The Supreme Court upheld the Lahore High Court's decision in favor of a petition challenging Zia's dissolution of Parliament. However, with elections round the corner, both courts rejected the plea to restore the national assembly. A reference by the PPP against non-party-based polls was also accepted, paving the way for the first party-based elections after eleven years. Holding elections would be the easy part of the quest to restore democracy. Institutional imbalances deeply entrenched during the Cold War era threatened to make the transition to substantive democracy an exacting challenge.

The Princess of Larkana

There were emotional scenes as Benazir Bhutto hit the campaign trail days after giving birth to her first child, a son named Bilawal. In December 1987, she had married Asif Ali Zardari, a Sindhi landlord who liked partying and playing polo more than politics. Benazir's marriage and pregnancy led to predictions about the end of her political career. "I am wedded to politics," she told PPP supporters celebrating her wedding in a Karachi slum. "An arranged marriage was the price in personal choice I had to pay for the political path my life had taken," she wrote in her autobiography. "Was there a man in existence," she asked wistfully, who could accept that "my first commitment would always be to the people of Pakistan and not to him."[1]

Known as Pinkie to her family and close friends, the indulged rich girl who enjoyed reading penny dreadfuls and devouring chocolate mint ice cream and marrons glacés from London's Fortnum & Mason had come a long way from her days at Radcliffe and Oxford. Her steely determination through stints in jail during the sizzling heat of Pakistani summers had earned her respect and admiration. As the daughter of Zulfikar Ali Bhutto, a martyr in popular consciousness, Benazir carried the mystique of his charisma. "I am your sister," she yelled from a heavily decorated moving truck with her arms stretched to an adoring crowd waving the black, red,

Benazir Bhutto campaigning in Malir, Karachi. *The White Star Photo Pvt. Ltd. Archive.*

and green PPP flags.[2] Bibi, as she was known in popular parlance, "gives off white heat," a fervent supporter remarked.[3] Using her party's catchphrase "bread, clothing, shelter," Benazir promised to raise wages for workers and give land to the tiller in keeping with her father's principle of "Islamic socialism," adding her own charged slogan: "Martyrdom is our cause."

Elation at the crowds turning out to greet Benazir was offset by a nagging realization that without the tacit neutrality of the all-powerful army, state power would elude her grasp. She had begun ingratiating herself with the army even while Zia was alive. This alienated the PPP's left wing, already resentful of the neoliberal shift in her economic policies and pro-US stance. Unwilling to give quarter to ideological consistency, Benazir hailed General Beg's decision to keep the army out of politics and reassured the civil bureaucracy of her cooperation and disinterest in pursuing a politics of revenge. Her sole motivation was to return Pakistan to democracy through impartial elections.[4] None of her detractors were convinced. A former senior bureaucrat told Benazir that if she took Ishaq Khan's advice on how to run the government, she would "never regret her decision." Pakistan's soon-to-be prime minister confessed that she did not understand the workings of the bureaucracy and unlike her father was not personally acquainted with senior civil and army officials.[5]

The glamorous PPP leader, who was quite the darling of the international paparazzi, was clueless about the hornet's nest her potential rise to power had stirred up domestically. A favorite drawing room conversation was that the generals would let Benazir assume power once and then "wait patiently for her to trip over her own mistakes at the helm of a nation" that had "become virtually ungovernable" due to surging debt, a political culture of arms and drugs, and a surfeit of linguistic and sectarian strife.[6] Once intelligence reports predicted a PPP victory, the ISI stitched together the Islamic Jumhoori Ittihad (IJI), or the Islamic democratic alliance, consisting of the Pakistan Muslim League (PML) led by former prime minister Junejo, the National People's Party of Ghulam Mustafa Jatoi, the Jamaat-i-Islami, and the JUI. This conglomeration was intended to safeguard the army's interests in Afghanistan. A last-minute requirement for voters to show their national identity card at the polling stations disenfranchised nearly half of the eligible voters who did not possess the documentation that had been first introduced in 1973. This worked to the disadvantage of the PPP's support base in the rural areas, particularly among women. Zia's caretaker government was kept in place, resulting in misuse of the administrative machinery and the official media, to which opposition parties had no recourse.

Benazir tried minimizing her electoral shortcomings by forging alliances with big business and large landlord clans. She enraged party stalwarts by throwing open the PPP's doors to PML "turncoats," or *lotas*—a pejorative reference to a globular watering utensil that rolls and constantly changes hands. The IJI retaliated with a malicious campaign, accusing the Bhutto women of wanting to back down on the nuclear program under American pressure. Mian Nawaz Sharif, a Punjabi industrialist groomed by Zia's regime, predicted that "Islamic order and social justice" would "win the battle against those who want to make Pakistan a secular, socialist state."[7] Voters conducted their own political debates in congested urban neighborhoods, village gatherings, and the privacy of homes. In the words of one die-hard protagonist of democracy, neither preelection promises, bribes, or threats would sway voters who wanted to "break away from the dead past."[8]

Despite systemic rigging, the actual voting on polling day was peaceful. Several federal and provincial ministers lost their seats, and the Jamaat-i-Islami even with IJI cover was defeated. Backed by sections of the rising middle class in both rural and urban areas, the IJI gave the PPP a run for its money in Punjab. Junejo and Jatoi lost in Sindh, clearing the way for Nawaz Sharif of Punjab to lead the IJI. The PPP won 38.5 percent of the popular vote and ninety-three of the 205 seats up for grabs in a national assembly of 237 members. With 30.16 percent of the popular vote and fifty-five seats, the IJI took the steam out of the PPP's victory. Yet the PPP was the only party to win seats in all four provinces, lending substance to the popular slogan: "Chain of all four provinces, Benazir, Benazir." The PPP swept rural Sindh but lost several urban seats to the MQM while putting up a respectable showing in the NWFP, two provinces where it went on to form governments. In Punjab, the PPP came a close second to the IJI and expected to win over enough independents to rustle up a majority.

As leader of the largest party in the national assembly, Benazir was the logical candidate for prime minister. President Ishaq Khan delayed inviting her to form the government, leading to behind-the-scene activities by American diplomats. General Beg was opposed to Benazir taking office. He swallowed the bitter pill after she promised not to tinker with policies on Afghanistan, defense, and the nuclear program and agreed not to meddle with promotions in the army and civil administration or harass Zia's family. Although she denied charges that she had made any concessions as "absolute rubbish," Benazir was permitted to take over only after accepting conditions laid down before her on a take-it-or-leave-it basis.[9]

The gritty daughter of a proud father opted for the Machiavellian route to power. On December 2, 1988, during a historic swearing-in ceremony as the first elected woman prime minister of a Muslim country, Benazir saw the "sullen faces of the military generals, and the frightened faces of the civil bureaucracy caught between the old and new order."[10] Draped in the green and white of the national flag, she flustered supporters by promising continuity, tempering her stance to avenge dictatorship with democracy. Mohtarma, or respected lady, as Benazir insisted she be called, retained two members of Ishaq Khan's caretaker government, the foreign minister Sahibzada Yaqub Ali Khan and, briefly, also the finance minister Mahbubul Haq. Her closest aides, including the chief of staff at the prime minister's secretariat, the defense adviser, and defense minister, were retired army officers. Three of Pakistan's four provinces had retired generals as governors, of whom two were Zia's appointees.[11] For those who idolized her to a fault, this was the beginning of a long and painful journey of disillusionment.

Eager to form a government in Punjab, Benazir deputed her trusted aide Farooq Leghari to stop Nawaz Sharif from becoming chief minister. With independents on sale to the highest bidder, Sharif won by a comfortable margin. The bad blood between the PPP at the center and the IJI in Punjab made for an inauspicious start to a long-awaited transition to democracy. Benazir secured the parliamentary vote of confidence with 148 votes against fifty-five. But the PPP's uncertain majority in the national assembly was counterbalanced by the opposition's control of the senate. Once Benazir backed Ishaq Khan for president, the odds on her succeeding in office became longer. Zia's Islamization policies and authoritarian micromanagement of polity and economy had created a rough playing field. Linguistic and sectarian violence had poisoned social relations, especially in Sindh, where the MQM won thirteen seats in Karachi and Hyderabad. Sectarian, linguistic, and ideological hatreds were replicated in the media, where embedded ISI- and MI-backed journalists manipulated news for the establishment's benefit. Although Benazir showed political acumen by doing a deal with the MQM, the alliance was inherently unstable. The situation was no better in the NWFP, where the PPP formed a short-lived coalition government with Wali Khan's Awami National Party (ANP). Facing belligerent IJI opposition in Punjab, the young prime minister was left gasping for breath.

Benazir had expected to concentrate on addressing the grievances of the people upon assuming office. "I quickly realized I was wrong"; those who had "opposed my election, including the president, were bent on destabilizing me." Her mother was not far off the mark in noting that "Ali Baba may be gone, but the forty thieves remain."[12] The veiled reference was to Nawaz Sharif, whose family-owned steel business had soared during the 1980s to become one of the wealthiest industrial houses in the country. In his student days, Nawaz had been an admirer of Zulfikar Ali Bhutto but became a bitter opponent after his family's Ittefaq steel mills were nationalized. Military rule proved to be a blessing for the House of Sharifs. The clan's spectacular ascent was a quintessential example of the Zia regime's indulgence of crony capitalism. Huge loans given to a favored few at implausibly low interest rates were never recovered, damaging an overregulated banking system and wrecking the economy. While a small circle raked in millions of dollars, the exchequer was pushed to the verge of collapse. Excessive borrowing at high interest rates produced a bulging domestic debt of over $19 billion. Revenue receipts outstripped current expenditure by a huge margin as the upper and middle classes continued to evade direct taxation. The fiscal deficit stood at 8 percent of the GDP while the untaxed informal economy was the size of almost a third of the GDP. Social sector funds had to be slashed to meet rising debt-servicing payments and finance the defense budget, which together accounted for over 80 percent of current expenditures.

These bare statistics signposted the national priorities of a country with one of the world's lowest literacy rates at 26 percent, deplorable mortality rates, the highest birth rate (3.2 percent) in South Asia, and over a quarter of the population unemployed. Benazir inducted seventy ministers and advisers into her cabinet, making it the largest ever in Pakistan's history.[13] Distracted by the rich pickings, PPP ministers proved inadequate to the task of governing the country. An uncooperative and hostile bureaucracy delighted in exposing the inexperience of a federal cabinet lost in Islamabad's murky gangways of state power. This was grist to the IJI's propaganda mill attacking the PPP government's corruption, incompetence, and immorality. The one that stuck like a limpet was the nickname "Mr. Ten Percent" for Asif Zardari—a derisive reference to Benazir's husband taking a cut in business deals requiring government approval.

Political standards hit new lows with the IJI's gendered harangues against Benazir. A chauvinistic Urdu press accused her of treason after she parleyed with her Indian counterpart, Rajiv Gandhi, in 1988 at the fourth summit of the seven-nation South Asian Association for Regional Cooperation (SAARC) in Islamabad. The agreements inked by the two prime ministers merely formalized earlier decisions not to attack each other's nuclear installations, to encourage cultural exchanges, and to end double taxation in trade and commerce. The cause of the brouhaha was Benazir's decision to give New Delhi a list of Sikh militants on the ISI's payroll and stop assistance to insurgents in Indian Punjab. Journalists planted by the ISI led the media charge, giving a fillip to the IJI's campaign of disinformation and half-truths about the PPP leader. The controversy over Salman Rushdie's *Satanic Verses* also threatened to damage Benazir because her autobiography *Daughter of the East* had been printed by the same American publisher. After countrywide protests by Islamist parties led to five

deaths, the prime minister banned Rushdie's book for its offending por-
trayal of the Muslim prophet and his wives. This failed to deter the right-
wing opposition from targeting not just Benazir but all women with their
misogynist rhetoric. Nawaz Sharif publicly asked IJI parliamentarians to
sing the popular war song "War Is No Game for Women" in the national
assembly.[14]

Benazir's dismay at losing the politically weightiest province was mild
in comparison to the disappointment of Zia's acolytes at not retaining
power at the center. There was no precedent of a Pakistani center facing an
opposition government in Punjab. The Punjab government's refusal to
obey the center's directives on the posting of senior federal civil servants
pulled the judiciary and the presidency into the political fray. Rankled by
Punjab's unilateral assertion of independence from the center, the president stepped up pressure on Benazir, making it impossible for her to run
the government. A wily bureaucrat who knew his way through the labyrinth of state power, Ishaq rejected the prime minister's advice on key
appointments and worked to undermine her position politically in the
NWFP and Sindh. If the federation wore a strained look, the state's ongoing support for Islamic militancy augured poorly for Benazir's government. Sectarian mosques dotting the urban and rural landscape gave impetus to the IJI's negative politics. At a convention in Rawalpindi, 2,000
clerics unanimously agreed that Islam prohibited woman's rule and vowed
to dislodge Benazir. But it took an international crisis before the president
could sack an elected prime minister.

In May 1989 Benazir made the tactical error of appointing a retired
general as head of the ISI. This put the country's premier intelligence
agency outside GHQ's pale, infuriating the army chief and his cohorts,
who resented seeing a retired colleague bagging a key position in the hier-
archy.[15] Taking advantage of her low credibility with the generals, the
president began stalling Benazir's policy recommendations. Relying on
her considerable international stature, she still hoped to turn things
around. Unfortunately, her populist gestures often misfired. The decision
to commute all death sentences, hailed by international human rights
groups, let hardened criminals escape the noose. Lifting the ban on student and labor unions was a mixed blessing, given the Jamaat-i-Islami's
strong presence in these organizations. Nominal steps to redress injustices
done to women by Zia's regime were symbolic; the offending legislation

Benazir Bhutto at a public rally in Lahore. *The White Star Photo Pvt. Ltd. Archive.*

remained on the statute books. The national assembly had difficulty maintaining a quorum. Other than annual budgets, not a single piece of legislation was passed.

If it had just been a case of structurally induced paralysis in a military-dominated state, Benazir's first tenure in office could be brushed aside as a nonevent. But the IJI's venomous propaganda charging PPP ministers and, above all, Asif Zardari with massive corruption did irreparable damage to the Bhutto name. For all the songs about blood and martyrdom, the swindling of millions from the national treasury stuck in popular imagination. Stashing money in Swiss bank accounts and dubious offshore financial institutions was an old trademark of Pakistan's ruling elite. An ingrained national pastime cannot exonerate Benazir of sanctioning kleptocracy. Having aroused popular expectations, she was now reaping the blowback of Zia's monetization of politics and her own opportunistic electoral alliances. Forced to implement austerity measures as part of the IMF's structural adjustment program, her government could not earmark resources for development projects to satisfy the PPP's support base. With her own parliamentarians threatening to defect unless paid off in cash or kind, Benazir spent more time dousing internal party revolts than offsetting the opposition's tirade by settling into some sort of a rhythm to govern a divided and disillusioned country. The people's poet said it all in a few flourishes of the pen:

> Nothing has changed for the poor
> Only ministerial fortunes have changed.[16]

Constrained by the strategic imperatives of a military-dominated state, Benazir could do nothing to alter Pakistan's hazardous course in Afghanistan and, after late 1989, also in Kashmir. To make up for her domestic misfortunes, she welcomed a stream of guests from Washington. This raised the suspicions of the president, who kept the nuclear program "under close lock and key" and began "guarding the box like a ferocious watchdog."[17] During the 1980s, US strategic goals in the region had outweighed criticisms of Pakistan's nuclear policy. With the Soviets withdrawing from Afghanistan, it was no longer prudent for Washington to look the other way while Islamabad raced ahead to attain nuclear capability.

During her first official visit to the United States on June 6, 1989, CIA officials tartly warned Benazir of serious consequences if she did not roll back the nuclear program.[18] Under the Pressler Amendment, American aid would cease if President Bush failed to assure Congress that Pakistan was not developing nuclear weapons. By pledging her commitment to nonproliferation and opposition to a nuclear arms race in South Asia, Benazir kept the aid flowing for a bit longer. American officials knew from an intelligence report that India was poised to test a hydrogen bomb and that Pakistan was making giant strides toward building a nuclear weapon for deployment with F-16 fighter aircraft.[19] In the aftermath of Benazir's visit, President Ishaq Khan came under intensified American diplomatic pressure to rein in Pakistan's nuclear ambitions. Benazir had concurred with President Bush that Afghanistan needed a political solution based on an agreement between the Soviet-backed regime in Kabul and rebel groups supported by Pakistan and the United States. General Beg had grandiose ideas about Islamic power and wanted to extend the logic of strategic depth in Afghanistan to wrest Kashmir from Indian control. When a popular insurgency erupted in Kashmir, Benazir asked the army and the ISI not to push militants returning from Afghanistan across the line of control.[20] Her directive was ignored.

In an operation code-named "Midnight Jackal," two ISI operatives were caught plotting to topple Benazir's government with the help of dissident PPP parliamentarians. Large sums of money exchanged hands. The source of the funding was even more controversial than the objective, with some pointing to Saudi Arabia and, more specifically, to a still little-known figure named Osama bin Laden. On October 23, 1989, the IJI-led opposition moved a no-confidence motion, charging the government with incompetence and corruption. Members of Parliament were herded to remote destinations and locked up in hotels to prevent the other side from buying them off. Newspapers were awash with tales of blackmail and bribery, further tarnishing the image of electoral representatives. Although Benazir survived the no-confidence motion, the ugly episode left most Pakistanis in what one editor aptly described as "crisis fatigue." Disgusted by the political shenanigans of their representatives, they wanted the political parties to settle down and start solving Pakistan's problems.[21]

Benazir's government lasted for another eight months without much to show for itself. Instead, she made history by giving birth to her second child while in office, lending credence to the opposition's charge about her unfitness to govern. With a popular insurrection in Kashmir raising the specter of another Indo-Pakistan war, Benazir's presence at the helm was abhorrent to the generals, who saw her as the daughter of a man responsible for breaking up the country. Reacting to a press comment that GHQ had hijacked foreign policy, an impatient army chief swaggered, "we have bigger things to hijack, if we want to."[22] As the sinews of war built up in the early summer of 1990, Benazir borrowed her father's famous phrase and threatened a thousand-year war with India. General Beg for his part accused India of subversive activity in Sindh, where escalating violence and a wave of killings led the federal government to ask the army to intervene. An Urdu speaker, the army chief disapproved of the PPP's handling of Sindh and thought his men were needed more urgently at the Indian border. Benazir's refusal to countenance martial law in Sindh brought her relations with the army to breaking point. Seeing their opportunity, the IJI-led opposition called for the dismissal of the PPP government in Sindh. MQM's support of the IJI stratagem aggravated tensions between Urdu speakers and Sindhis. To fast-track the PPP out of power, the IJI resorted to the old Islamist trick of demanding the enforcement of the sharia. IJI-sponsored sharia conferences declared democracy to be "the shroud for our religion."[23] Benazir's opposition to the bill was used to attack her for being anti-Islamic.

By the end of July 1990, President Ishaq in consort with the army high command had decided to dump Benazir under article 58 (2b) of the constitution. In a fortuitous turn of the wheel, Saddam Hussein's invasion of Kuwait on August 2 took the international gaze off the derailment of an elected government in Pakistan. Summing up her amateurish tryst with state power, which elicited comparisons with Alice in Wonderland, a "blissfully ignorant" Benazir dismissed rumors of her sacking as "clumsy propaganda."[24] On August 6, when the din became awkwardly loud, she called the president, who confirmed the news and tersely told her to listen to his address to the nation. It was a cruel and humbling experience for a politician who took pride in her understanding of realpolitik. She had made no contingency plans and now faced the ignominy of being tossed to the winds.

President Ishaq Khan accused the PPP government of unconscionable corruption and maladministration. Benazir was charged with illegally distributing 545 prime residential plots in the federal capital to PPP ministers and parliamentarians at below-market prices. Cases of graft and illegal favors in awarding government contracts were brought against her in quick succession.[25] Calling the charges politically motivated, Benazir petitioned the Supreme Court against her dismissal. Appearing personally to argue her case, she did not deny the corruption charges so much as complain about the preferential treatment meted out to her IJI opponents, who were no saints when it came to using high office for personal gains. The Supreme Court upheld the president's decision but had no legal basis to prevent Benazir from contesting the elections.

Maligned by an establishment-backed opposition, Benazir was mauled at the polls. After engineering her dismissal, General Beg appointed the director general (DG) of MI Major General Asad Durrani as DG of the ISI. In what came to be known as the Mehrangate Scandal, Beg obtained Rs.140 million from Yunus Habib, owner of Mehran Bank, for distribution by the ISI as political bribes and election funds to those opposing the PPP. Durrani later revealed the names of the beneficiaries. The president showed his complicity by exhorting voters on the eve of elections not to vote for un-Islamic parties. In October 2012, the Supreme Court upheld Air Marshal Asghar Khan's appeal against electoral irregularities in 1990 and the illegal distribution of money to politicians by the ISI. It was a belated recompense for the PPP. Benazir's spirited refrain during the campaign was that she would redeem her honor. Blatant electoral manipulation by the president, a biased army chief, and the opposition caretaker government's misuse of the administrative machinery combined to deny her that satisfaction. She wept on hearing the results. The nine-party IJI won 105 seats and its allies another fifty while the PPP-led Pakistan Democratic Alliance was reduced to a rump of forty-five, less than the half the count in the 1988 elections.

In a revealing indication of emergent political trends, the PPP was vanquished in Punjab. By diluting her party's populist policies, Benazir changed the PPP's leftist image to that of a "feudal"-dominated rural party. She had broken with the "Old Bolsheviks" of the PPP to woo the middle classes. Her inability to win the targeted vote heralded a new era in which the Pakistan Muslim League (Nawaz) (PML-N) appealed more to Punjab's conservative urban middle classes drawn from military, industrial, and commercial backgrounds. Losing in a province containing nearly two-thirds of the vote bank was shattering. Provincial elections showed the extent of the PPP's obliteration in Punjab. In a 240-member provincial assembly, it secured a paltry ten seats against the IJI's impressive 211. No less disconcertingly for the princess of Larkana, the PPP failed to win a majority in her own home province. Ishaq Khan brokered an IJI–MQM government in Sindh headed by Jam Ali Sadiq, an unscrupulous politician who had served as Benazir's adviser. Completing the sweep, the IJI also formed coalition governments in the NWFP and Balochistan.

A Man of Steel?

The IJI celebrations were tempered by the gnawing realization that the PPP was still not out of political contention. Left trailing in the seat count by a long margin, the PPP secured 36.8 percent of the popular vote—less than one percent short of the IJI's winning share of 37.4 percent. These figures would come to torment the IJI at the next electoral joust. For now, Nawaz Sharif had to find a way to get around the structural imbalances that led to the implosion of Benazir's government. Wrangling between the two main parties after the 1988 elections had left the Eighth Amendment unscathed. Two years later, the president was in a much stronger position. If the president's constitutional powers made a sham of parliamentary government, Pakistan's economic malaise stunted Sharif's probusiness policies.

An initially smoother relationship between Nawaz Sharif and the crusty "baba," or old man, as Ishaq came to be known, was possible because of their joint investment in keeping the PPP out of power. A less well-acknowledged factor was the old boys' networks that kept the creaky rungs of the establishment well oiled. Another reason for Nawaz Sharif and Ishaq Khan to work in relative harmony was their shared views on Kashmir. Ultimately, it was the suspension of American aid in the amount of $564 million that prompted the two civilian pillars of the troika to come together in national defiance. On October 1, 1990, after President Bush's refusal to certify that Pakistan did not have nuclear weapons, Congress invoked the Pressler Amendment, cutting off all American aid for civilian and military projects in 1990–91. Military supplies were suspended, mothballing the delivery of F-16s for which Pakistan had started making payments and rupturing relations between the two militaries for over a de-

Muhajir Qaumi Movement–Pakistan Muslim League (Nawaz) alliance, Altaf Hussain with Nawaz Sharif, Begum Abida Hussain, and Ghulam Mustapha Jatoi at a public meeting in Karachi, December 1988. *The White Star Photo Pvt. Ltd. Archive.*

cade. The American decision was presented to the electorate by the IJI as evidence of Benazir's Zionist connections.

The truth was more nuanced. US–Pakistan relations depended on Washington's global preoccupations with communism or nonproliferation, not on any intrinsic value it attached to relations with Islamabad. Since the 1980s, Pakistan's importance to American strategic interests in Afghanistan had prevailed over criticism of its nuclear program. The Soviet withdrawal reduced Pakistan's strategic value for the United States, now more preoccupied with Saddam Hussein in the Gulf and communism's collapsing citadel in Eastern Europe. From being the "most-allied-ally" of the 1950s to the staging post of "jihad" against the Soviets in the 1980s, Pakistan along with the rest of South Asia had by the early 1990s slipped, in the words of one American analyst, to "near the bottom of our priorities." Although Washington could never consider Pakistan a "negligent quantity in any geopolitical calculation," the high level of aid provided over the past decade was unsustainable. But a complete break was inadvisable. Pakistan had allied with the United States in the 1950s only because it had failed to muster support from the Muslim countries against India. Islamabad had since diversified its foreign policy and strengthened ties with China. Continued access to US weaponry was still critical to the Pakistani military. All the mainstream political parties recognized this and professed the need for continued ties with America. This could change if anti-American elements increased their profile, a distinct possibility if the tenuous transition to democracy was disrupted by another military takeover. The wisest course for America was to strengthen Pakistan's democratic transition by increasing economic assistance for popular civilian programs.[26]

By suspending economic and military aid to their Cold War ally, American legislators won applause from the pro-India lobby on Capitol Hill and a mostly Pakistan-wary US media. The suspension of aid was a critical turning point in relations between the United States and Pakistan whose adverse effects would linger for the next several decades. Overcommitted in Afghanistan to the grave detriment of internal political stability, the army and its octopus-like intelligence networks no longer had reason to be pliable instruments of America. Suspicious of Indian designs in Afghanistan and with Kashmir on the boil, GHQ set out to pursue its own regional security interests. This entailed sponsoring a low-intensity proxy war against India in Kashmir and backing favored rebel groups in Afghanistan fighting to gain control after the withdrawal of the last Soviet troops in February 1989. Nawaz Sharif endorsed the army's agenda despite the American threat to declare Pakistan a "terrorist" state. His dashes to key Muslim capitals, notably Riyadh, and tough talk about national self-reliance struck the right chords with the senior echelons of a post-Zia army that took its Islamic war cries seriously.

The only hitch in an otherwise ideal situation was an irrepressible army chief who liked being in the limelight. Playing to radical Muslim opinion on the streets, General Beg opposed supporting a US-led invasion of Kuwait but agreed to send 11,000 Pakistani troops to defend places of Muslim religious worship in Saudi Arabia. Relying on intelligence hard-liners, he predicted that the United States would get a bloody nose if it attacked Iraq. In a pointed reference to the nuclear program, he spoke smugly of Pakistan's ability to build an effective and visible deterrent. Eying a quick launch into politics after his retirement, the voluble army chief elaborated on the doctrine of strategic depth and the imperative of "strategic defiance" by combining forces with Iran and Afghanistan in a future war against India. With Beg shooting from the hip and pushing for greater military oversight in foreign affairs, rumors of a coup were back in season.

The appointment of the Sandhurst-trained Lieutenant General Asif Nawaz as army chief gave respite to the moderate prodemocracy lobby. Other contenders had included General Hamid Gul, who was Beg's choice and close to Sharif but whom the American ambassador to Pakistan, Robert Oakley, ruled out by calling him "Saddam Gul."[27] Asif Nawaz's elevation raised hopes of an end to the army's political adventurism. These expectations were dashed by the structural deformities in the distribution of civil–military power. Asif Nawaz had not been the choice of the prime minister, who retaliated by appointing a rabid Islamist, Lieutenant General Javed Nasir, as DG of ISI. This angered Asif Nawaz. It would only be a matter of time before an intrinsically unstable power equation fell apart. Nawaz Sharif had kicked off his term with a business-friendly economic agenda. Economic liberalization and relaxation of controls improved capital inflows but could not jumpstart a stagnant and debt-ridden economy. IMF and World Bank–directed efforts to expand the state's abysmally restricted revenue net provoked protests across the board. By the summer of 1991, labor unrest and business outrage at newly proposed taxes had taken the wind out of Sharif's economic reforms. Inflationary pressures alienated the middle classes while a spurt in kidnappings, murders, bomb blasts, and bank robberies in Sindh frightened off potential foreign investors. Sharif's spiraling woes led to opposition demands that the president dismiss the prime minister.[28]

Within months of taking office, the IJI was faced with a damaging cooperative banking scam involving an estimated $420 million. Stories of embezzlement, nepotism, and bad investments led to a run on deposits, forcing the closure of dozens of cooperatives. Sixteen key leaders of the ruling party and the prime minister's own family members and business group were involved in the scandal. Some of those charged with wrongful profit at public risk included members of the president's family. Although Sharif returned the loans given to the Ittefaq group, a gleeful Benazir assailed him for misusing office for personal gain. More impressive in opposition than in power, she went to town blackening her rival's name in a publication titled *The Plunder of Pakistan*.[29] However, with Ishaq Khan backing Sharif, the political fallout of the cooperative banking fiasco did not bring down the government. The sop of a diluted Sharia Bill in May 1991 helped neutralize the religious lobby.

Nawaz Sharif had been a prime beneficiary of Zia's military dictatorship. But even with the right political credentials, Islamic orientation, and gender, Sharif could not resolve the contradictions between an elected government and a political economy of defense. Eleven years of Zia had entrenched the military more firmly in the national economy. The military-run industrial conglomerate dubbed "Milbus" had an annual turnover in 1991 of almost half a billion dollars. From small arms and ammunition to banking, automobiles, telecommunications, breakfast cereals, cooking oil, and even bakeries, there was virtually no sector of the economy in which defense personnel had not established a business interest, whether collectively through military welfare organizations or individually as private entrepreneurs. Led by the army's Fauji Foundation, all three services have substantial investments in welfare trusts geared to benefit retired senior personnel. Headed by retired officers, the military's welfare foundations are a key source of patronage for the service chiefs. The welfare foundations get preferential access to state resources and are not subject to the same public transparency laws as private companies. No less lucrative is the armed forces' 10 percent share of all state lands. These are parceled out to military personnel according to rank, with the most junior officers getting thirty-two acres and those above major-general rank acquiring as much as 240 acres. This has given the military an important stake in the agricultural sector and boosted the formation of a loyal rural middle class. However, it has been in urban real estate that senior personnel of the defense services have made the most money.[30]

For a businessman politician, the prime minister was something of a romantic at heart. Egged on by a domineering father, Mian Muhammad Sharif, whom he called "Abaji" (father), Nawaz Sharif harbored illusions of Mughal grandeur. Politically motivated acts of generosity, bribery in more mundane jargon, were considered by the Sharif patriarch as the most effective way of negotiating the levers of state power. To overcome the problems posed by the military's expansive corporate interests in the political economy and to dispense state patronage, a brand new fleet of BMWs was distributed to a select group of generals. Perturbed by reports of Nawaz Sharif trying to buy the loyalties of his senior officers, the army chief went blue in the face when the prime minister handed him the keys to a sparkling new BMW with the comment that the general's car, a Toyota, did not befit his dignity.[31] Relations between the two remained in disrepair over a range of issues—the military crackdown on the IJI's MQM allies in Sindh, army appointments, defense contracts, and the use of urban real estate to compromise corps commanders—until Asif Nawaz died of a heart attack in December 1992.

Saved by the bell from a mortifying clash with the most powerful man in the country, Nawaz Sharif landed himself in a withering struggle with Ishaq Khan over the appointment of the next army chief. After the president appointed a fellow Pathan, Lieutenant General Abdul Waheed Kakar, as the new army chief, the prime minister decided to scrap the Eighth Amendment. Needing a two-thirds majority in the national assembly, Nawaz Sharif reached out to Benazir, appointing her chairman of the parliamentary Foreign Relations Committee. Asif Zardari, imprisoned on kidnapping and extortion charges in 1990, was released from prison after twenty-seven months. On February 24, 1993, Sharif made the tactical mistake of announcing his intention to curb the president's powers. By then, Ishaq Khan's troubleshooters were working to torpedo the rapprochement between the two main parties. When Mohammad Khan Junejo, president of the PML, died in March, Sharif snapped up the position, enraging other potential contenders. By early April, seven ministers in the federal cabinet had jumped ship, and nearly half the parliamentarians were ready to ditch Sharif. After playing both sides, Benazir struck a deal with the president. The game was up for Nawaz Sharif, but not before the enactment of a typically Pakistani twist to a seamy political saga.

On April 18, 1993, within hours of the embattled prime minister calling the presidency a "den of conspirators," an indignant Ishaq Khan dismissed Sharif, dissolved the assembly, and announced elections on July 14. A caretaker government headed by the Baloch leader Balakh Sher Mazari was appointed. The PPP joined the federal cabinet with Benazir's discredited spouse holding a ministerial position, demonstrating that anything is possible in Pakistani politics. For the third time in less than a decade, an elected prime minister and assembly had been sent packing on identical charges—corruption, nepotism, and maladministration. However, unlike his two Sindhi landlord predecessors, Sharif was a Punjabi businessman who had fallen foul with two Pathan pillars of the troika. Nawaz Sharif was accused of subverting the constitution, lowering the prestige of the armed forces, persecuting political opponents, intimidating journalists, lacking transparency in his privatization policies, and breaching the rules of the civil administration. In contrast to the tame public reception to earlier prime ministerial sackings, Sharif's business supporters in Lahore and Karachi registered their protest by closing down shop for a day.

On May 26, in a historic judgment an eleven-member bench of the Supreme Court headed by Chief Justice Nasir Hasan Shah voted ten to one in favor of Sharif's petition challenging his dismissal and the dissolution of Parliament. It was an astonishing volte-face considering the Supreme Court's rulings against similar petitions in 1985 and 1990. The lone dissenter, Justice Syed Sajjad Ali Shah from Sindh, noted glumly that although two Sindhi prime ministers had been sacrificed at the altar of article 58 (2b), the scales had been turned for a Punjabi prime minister. More than Sharif's provincial affiliation, the army chief's neutrality encouraged the judges to stand up to the president. Electoral irregularities in 1990, turf wars with the prime minister, and scandals involving family members had sullied Ishaq Khan's reputation. Pakistan's conspiracy crunchers had their own explanations. Even as the judiciary was applauded for its courageous stand, some of the learned judges were alleged to have received payoffs from the Sharifs.

Jubilation over Nawaz Sharif's reinstatement among Punjabi businessmen and traders was short-lived. An unrepentant Ishaq Khan was intent not only on completing his term in November but also on unseating the prime minister again by dissolving the provincial governments and calling elections. During the interregnum between the IJI government's demise and resurrection at the center, Punjab had been lost to the PPP. Facing hostile governments in all four provinces, Nawaz Sharif could survive a renewed presidential assault only by regaining control over his home province. As his supporters and opponents battled it out in Punjab, opposition parties called for the dissolution of the assemblies in the other provinces. When an infuriated Nawaz Sharif moved to impeach Ishaq Khan, General Kakar intervened to put an end to six months of disgraceful political intrigues.

Matters came to a head when Benazir threatened to lead a long march to the capital unless elections were called. Under the terms of the agreement brokered by the army chief, both Ishaq Khan and Nawaz Sharif resigned from office on July 18 after agreeing to dissolve the national assembly and calling general elections. Caretaker governments consisting of technocrats, retired bureaucrats, judges, and military officials were slotted in at the center and the provinces. The man chosen as interim prime minister was Moeen Qureshi, a former senior vice president of the World Bank, who had lived abroad for decades, oblivious of the grisly undercurrents of Pakistani politics. Other than holding elections under the army's supervision, Qureshi's main task was to facilitate delivery of a stalled aid package totaling $2.1 billion. He accomplished both and more—stabilizing the country's foreign exchange and fiscal problems, imposing a small tax on agricultural incomes on farms above sixty acres, enforcing tax collection, and going after the more outrageously crooked among the superrich. The measures were popular, leading cynics to say that Pakistan needed nonelected interim governments for extended periods and elected governments for shorter durations.

On October 6, 1993, a mere 40.54 percent of the electorate trooped to the polling stations under the gaze of 150,000 security personnel. With Sharif out of favor, Benazir's return to power was a foregone conclusion. In Pakistan's monetized and weak political party system, candidates solicit tickets from the party most likely to win. But as the ISI's wizards intended, no party won a clear majority. The PPP secured eighty-six seats in an assembly of 207 and Sharif's PML-N won seventy-two. In a reversal of the 1990 elections, the PML-N polled 39.7 percent of the popular vote to the PPP's 38.1 percent, underscoring Nawaz Sharif's emergence as a popular leader in his own right. The Jamaat-i-Islami broke with the PML-N, splitting the conservative vote in fourteen closely contested constituencies, while the MQM's decision to sit out the national elections allowed the two mainstream parties to pick up six seats each in Karachi, with one going to the Pakistan Islamic Front. The national pattern repeated itself in provincial elections three days later, with the PPP and the PML-N taking the lion's share of the vote. The PML-N emerged as the largest single party in Punjab, but the PPP's preelection alliance with Junejo's PML-J gave it control over the province that mattered most in the federal power equation. The PPP also assumed power in Sindh but lost out in NWFP, where it won the largest haul of seats, and also in Balochistan, where it was bested by a PML-N and ANP alliance.

A Second Chance

With support from smaller parties and independents, Benazir rustled up 121 votes against Nawaz's seventy-two to become the country's prime minister a second time. A sweet vindication, it was also something of a milestone in the history of women in the Muslim world. Khaleda Zia had been prime minister of Bangladesh since 1991. With Benazir's victory soon after Tansu Cillar's election as prime minister of Turkey, women were ruling a quarter of the world's billion Muslims. A page turned in Pakistani history as well when Ishaq Khan bowed out of the presidential race and the PPP's Farooq Leghari won comfortably. For the first time since 1977, the president and prime minister belonged to the same party and so the prognosis for a smoother functioning of government looked more promising than in 1988 or 1990. A jump of 221 points in the Karachi Stock Exchange reflected business optimism. Benazir raised expectations by stating that the Eighth Amendment had become redundant and she would move to repeal it in due course. GHQ was unwilling to countenance clipping presidential powers that gave it indirect control over the political process without the trappings of responsibility or accountability.

With the Eighth Amendment in place, nothing could stop the armed forces asserting themselves against an elected government. Benazir made her peace with the martial state by accepting its diktat on Afghanistan, Kashmir, and the nuclear issue. GHQ used the prime minister's high global profile to internationalize Kashmir, further its objectives in Afghanistan, and persuade Washington to lift military and economic sanctions. If by attracting foreign investment, the PPP government could boost a sluggish national economy, so much the better. Benazir spent almost half of her second term touring foreign capitals advocating causes dear to the military. But nothing could dilute the resentment of misogynist army officers about saluting a woman head of government. Her conspicuous presence on the international stage was a hindrance to addressing a formidable set of problems: linguistic and sectarian discord, antsy generals, overbearing drug lords, a glut of illegal arms, the collateral damage of the Afghan war, and an ongoing spat with Washington and New Delhi over the nuclear program and Pakistan's backing for the insurgency in Kashmir.

The PPP government's tenure depended on coalition partners who wanted favors inconsistent with the stability and transparency demanded by the electorate and the generals. Accused of being haughty and insuffer-able in office, Benazir was cautious in her choice of senior appointments and opted for a slimmer cabinet. She retained the finance portfolio, aware that her grip on state power required disbursing money and patronage of which there was not enough to go around. A realist willing to compro-mise on principles for political ends, Benazir relied increasingly on Asif Zardari in a stultifying male-dominated society. Accusations of greed, corruption, and high-handedness resurfaced with a painful new twist. Agitated by Zardari's financial misdeeds and his growing clout in party matters, Nusrat Bhutto openly sided with her son, Mir Murtaza Bhutto, in exile for the past sixteen years. Murtaza had been convicted in absentia by a military court in 1981 for the hijacking of a PIA plane.[32] He denied responsibility and suggested the incident was staged by Zia's regime to blacken the Bhutto name. Devastated by the tragic death by poisoning of her youngest son, Shahnawaz, in the south of France during the sum-mer of 1985, which the Bhutto family blamed on Zia's agents, Nusrat wanted her only surviving son to return home. Once the PPP assumed office in 1988, she expected Benazir to pardon Murtaza and facilitate his return. This overlooked the structural realities of Pakistan's power con-figuration. Benazir blandly stated that Murtaza had to clear the terror charges before being rehabilitated in the PPP.

This sowed the seeds of a bitter family wrangle. Murtaza pilloried his elder sister for letting her playboy husband stain their father's legacy by indulging in corruption at the cost of loyal party workers. Mrs. Bhutto's projection of Murtaza as the male heir to her martyred husband's political legacy miffed Benazir, who feared her younger brother would split the PPP. When Murtaza decided to contest the 1993 elections in absentia, Benazir easily prevailed over his makeshift campaign. Murtaza contested two seats, losing one but winning a Sindh assembly seat from the family's ancestral home in Larkana. He owed the victory to Nusrat Bhutto's emotional cam-paigning and effective use of the metaphor of blood while holding Murta-za's three-year-old son—named Zulfikar Ali Bhutto Jr.—like a prized tro-phy. On November 3, 1993, Murtaza returned from Syria to a hero's welcome, only to be imprisoned on charges of terrorism and sedition carrying the death penalty. Though he was more of a loose cannon than a political threat, the family quarrel left Benazir more isolated and paranoid.

She came to depend more on her husband. For a latecomer to politics, Zardari was streetwise and ruthless. Benazir was impressed by his political instinct and ability to deliver results. The first couple lit more forest fires than all the fire brigades at their disposal could put out. It was a tragic case of success gone wrong due to willful neglect of the harsh realities facing ordinary people, who were getting poorer by the day while their representatives fattened their own pockets. And so for the second time around, Benazir started her three-year stint in office with a bang, only to get embroiled in byzantine intrigues, and went out with a deadening whimper. Unlike the first occasion, when her downfall was scripted by the intelligence agencies, Benazir had a hand in her political undoing the second time round. Mistaking the illusion of power for real strength, she moved to dislodge her mother as cochair of the PPP and got elected as party leader. Nusrat Bhutto retaliated by accusing her daughter of "matricide" and referring to her as Mrs. Zardari. Backing her son's bid to take over the PPP in Sindh, Nusrat claimed that her husband never wanted Benazir to lead the party. The "battle of all mothers," as the family feud was called, took an ugly turn with Mrs. Bhutto calling Benazir a dictator and a liar. "Every action my mother takes against me hits my heart like a bullet" was the prime minister's muted complaint.[33]

An inclination to amass power was an occupational hazard of ruling Pakistan. Well ensconced at the center and with a loyalist as president, Benazir needed to start delivering on her promises to the electorate. Instead, she asked Leghari to use his emergency powers to dismiss the opposition government in the NWFP, where the PPP was the largest single party. After a bruising two-month legal and political battle that embittered relations between the federal government and the opposition, the PPP came to power in the NWFP. An outraged Nawaz Sharif staged a walkout from Parliament to protest the PPP's undemocratic methods and flagrant abuse of power. A belligerent PML-N campaign backed by the business community to paralyze the government ensued. The money and the street muscle of the political parties were expected to do the rest. As the clamor against the PPP's misrule grew shriller, Benazir did what her predecessors had done before—stuffing the judiciary with preferred appointees, including former PPP activists. She also refused to honor the constitutional provision calling for the separation of judicial and executive powers by taking away the magisterial powers of deputy commissioners. The lone dissenter in the judgment against her government's restoration in 1990, Sajjad Ali Shah, was selected chief justice in violation of the judiciary's tradition of seniority. Tinkering with judicial appointments was a prelude to booking several opposition politicians on charges ranging from the illegal possession of a rifle, ironic in a gun-saturated country, to varying degrees of corruption. Members of the Sharif family were implicated in over a hundred cases of fraud and embezzlement, forcing Nawaz's younger brother Shahbaz to seek refuge in cosmopolitan London.

As the democratic gloss gave way to a creeping authoritarianism, Benazir lost credibility and popular support, making her an easier prey for the opposition. Accused of being the Pakistani face of the West, she had made her peace with the keepers of state power by dressing down her image as a Western-educated woman from one of Pakistan's most influential landed families. Her critics scoffed at her concessions to religious conservatism— wearing a head covering and refusing to shake hands with men—dismissing the gestures as hypocritical. Tactical compromises did not mean scaling back on her liberal ideas, far less losing sight of the broader context within which Pakistan had to operate in the international community. So while her judicial appointments—as many as twenty at a stroke of the pen in April 1994—were politically motivated, they also aimed at countering the bigoted narratives of Muslim identity that were being brandished by Islamic propagandists.

If declaring Ahmadis a non-Muslim minority against their will tore into the foundations of equal rights of citizenship, the blasphemy laws against anything derogatory toward the Prophet of Islam killed the spirit of civility. Pakistan's blasphemy laws are derived from sections of the colonial Penal Code of 1860 aimed at safeguarding religious sensibilities. The number of blasphemy cases, significantly enough, rose in direct proportion to the incremental stringency of the laws. There were only a handful of such cases until 1984, when Zia barred Ahmadis from using Islamic terminology and made blasphemy punishable with life imprisonment. Nawaz Sharif's government did one better in 1992 by changing the punishment for blasphemy into a mandatory death penalty. Accusations of blasphemy against non-Muslims, more often than not, provided a moral cover for settling personal scores and localized power struggles. No one was safe from the charge in Islamic Pakistan. Most blasphemy cases were against Muslims, followed by Ahmadis and Christians. Zealous mobs often settled the matter extrajudicially, beating the accused to death for allegedly defiling pages of the Quran or referring to Prophet Muhammad in a deprecatory way. In April 1994, the Lahore High Court extended the scope of the blasphemy laws to all the prophets mentioned in the Quran, including Jesus, underlining the superior judiciary's bias toward religious extremists. As Muslims firmly reject Christ's divinity, the ruling potentially endangered the lives of Pakistan's 1.2 million Christians.

In February 1995, two Christians were sentenced to death on dubious charges of blasphemy. One of the accused, Salamat Masih, was thirteen years old. Pakistan was a signatory to the UN convention prohibiting capital punishment for anyone under sixteen. When a shocked Benazir promised to amend the blasphemy laws to prevent people being falsely accused, she was charged with contempt of court by the religious right. Two judges saved the day for her, one a former member of the PPP and the other a sympathizer, who heard the appeal before the Lahore High Court against the death sentences. Before the court ruling, an angry mob shot dead the older of the two Christians accused of blasphemy near the premises of the Lahore High Court. The boy was acquitted and the defense lawyer Asma Jahangir, an internationally reputed human rights activist, arranged for his asylum in Germany.

Benazir's liberal credentials survived and her judicial appointments were partially vindicated. But the price paid was high. A united front of twenty-one religious parties and the PML-N blasted her for being an agent of the West. The accusation amounted to a death sentence in a country where well-armed and battle-hardened religious militants outnumbered poorly trained and barely equipped policemen several times over. Benazir was aware of the links between homegrown religious militancy and the army's double-barreled proxy wars in Afghanistan and Kashmir. In the fall of 1995, she survived a coup attempt in which thirty-six officers were charged with plotting an Islamic revolution. Right-wing parties and sections of the Urdu press assailed her for extraditing Ramzi Ahmed Yousef, a Kuwaiti of Pakistani descent, accused of plotting the World Trade Center bombing of 1993, who had earlier tried assassinating Benazir. The Americans reciprocated by giving Pakistan a onetime waiver from the Pressler Amendment, resulting in $368 million worth of arms for the military. This came at a time when the ISI had raised the stakes in Afghanistan by creating the Taliban, a ragtag army recruited from Afghan refugee camps and trained in Deobandi madrasas run by the JUI in NWFP and FATA. Her robotic support of the extremist Afghan militia at interna-

tional forums and the prominent role played in its formation by her interior minister, General Naseerullah Khan Babar, led to the coining of the
phrase "Benazir's Taliban." She shrugged aside the attribution as unfair
since her government differed with the Taliban's quaint Islam, particularly its illiberal attacks on women's freedom. Constrained by her alliance
with the JUI faction of Maulana Fazlur Rahman, Benazir recoiled from
tackling the menace of religious militancy. Her indecisiveness toughened
the resolve of Islamist groups whose supporters thronged mosques where
loudspeakers exhorted believers to wage jihad against a government led
by a Westernized woman. Tribesmen in the North-West Frontier were demanding the imposition of the sharia, killing local officials and kidnapping politicians to press the government to act.

Capitalizing on the situation, Nawaz Sharif brushed up his alliance
with the MQM, which was demanding provincial status for Karachi and
threatening to shut down the country's only port city, with 45 percent
of the industrial units. With its teeming population, stark differences
between rich and poor, ramshackle to nonexistent social services, and a
gun-saturated culture, the city's ordered misery was a perfect staging
ground for a campaign to oust the government. The government crackdown was brutal, inspiring comparisons with Belfast and, more frighten-
ingly, with Beirut of the 1980s. An estimated 3,000 perished, mostly MQM
supporters. Benazir called it an operation against terrorists and drug bar-
ons. Crime and politics were intimately meshed in the urban wilds of Karachi. It was no longer a war between Urdu speakers and Sindhis but increasingly political and religious in character. The army action since June
1992 had split the MQM into two warring factions. Sectarianism reared its
head in Karachi for the first time in July 1994, when masked gunmen
killed six people after attacking a busload of Shias. In March 1995, the assassination of two American consular officers gave an international dimension to the city's law-and-order problems. Unwilling to get trapped in
the urban quagmire, the army announced its withdrawal in December
1995, protesting the refusal of two successive governments to give it decisive powers to tackle terrorism. Benazir's best bet, the generals advised
her, was to reach a political settlement with the MQM.

Negotiations were resumed with the MQM leader Altaf Hussain, in exile in London since 1992 to escape murder charges. Karachi's blood-soaked
streets had left several hundreds dead, maimed, and uprooted, dimming

the prospect of a political reconciliation. Hussain set tough conditions for an agreement. As Pakistan's financial hub and source of 40 percent of federal revenues, what happened in Karachi affected the entire country. A surprisingly robust economy was the only hopeful sign in the city's woeful tale of murder, mayhem, and mutilation. Paradoxically, this was also why the battle for Karachi was being fought with such intensity. To save her home city, Benazir encouraged public and private investment in the energy sector to ease the chronic shortage of electricity and attract new business ventures. Paramilitary troops replaced the army, and the situation was brought forcibly under control. An artificial peace only prolonged the strife. Without a political accommodation between Karachi's warring groups and a concerted drive against the city's powerful mafias, even the most generous incentives to do business in Pakistan's commercial center could not attract investors.

Despite the government's claims to have increased foreign investment and improved the balance of payments, the macroeconomic indicators were not reassuring. Pakistan remained one of the lowest directly taxed countries in the world, forcing the government to borrow at high commercial interest rates to service a burgeoning national debt of almost $30 billion that absorbed over 60 percent of government revenues. The devaluation of the rupee increased the burden of debt payments. Inflation ballooned to an all-time high of 12 percent. Industry was hit by recession, and businessmen were furious with the federal government's IMF-dictated austerity budgets. The banking system was reeling under the cumulative effect of bad debts that had grown to a whopping Rs.130 billion by 1996 from Rs.13 billion in 1984 and Rs.84 billion in 1990. Most of the debts involved government and opposition politicians, their relatives, and business associates.[34] Systemic corruption neutralized the corrective measures that the federal government was prepared to take, leaving the culprits secure in the knowledge of eventually walking free. Zardari, now known as "Mr. 20 percent," was believed to be working with Benazir on most of his moneymaking ventures ranging from submarines to fighter aircraft and power-generating plants. By now, all the major public sector financial institutions were headed by Zardari's chums.

The generals provided the president with incriminating evidence of misappropriation of public funds and expressed misgivings about the government's failure to evolve a national consensus on Afghanistan, Kashmir, and the nuclear issue. Kabul had fallen to the Taliban. Notwithstanding her tireless efforts to defend Pakistan's Afghan policy, Benazir was seen as a hindrance to the army's aggressive forward policy. By contrast, there was active sympathy for the Taliban among the opposition parties, notably the JUI and the Jamaat-i-Islami. This partly explains why the announcement of the national budget for the fiscal year 1996–97 occasioned a well-orchestrated public campaign against the IMF-enforced stringencies. Revisions of the budget began almost as soon as it was passed. The IMF withheld the $80 million third tranche of its standby loan once the government tried wriggling out of the conditionalities. Moody's downgraded Pakistan's credit rating, setting off panic alarms. Without external funds, the possibility of Pakistan defaulting on its debt payments was no longer a matter of speculation.

Compounding her government's difficulties, Benazir provoked a row with her chosen chief justice, Sajjad Ali Shah, by refusing to comply with the Supreme Court's ruling to remove twenty high court judges she had appointed out of turn. Her troubles with the judiciary together with a resurgence in sectarian violence and a deepening economic crisis led GHQ to intensify pressure on the president to act against government corruption. Leghari warned Benazir of the dangers she was courting by alienating the judiciary and giving her spouse a wide berth. With Pakistan on the verge of declaring bankruptcy, the press was abuzz with news of the first couple purchasing a twenty-room neo-Tudor mansion worth $8 million in a 365-acre lot in the London suburb of Surrey. Rejecting the accusations, Benazir brought her husband along with fourteen others into the cabinet in early August. At his insistence, Zardari was given the environment and investment portfolio. As her credibility wilted at home and abroad, people expected the president to dismiss the government. But the lethal blow against Benazir was administered before Leghari's anticipated move under the Eighth Amendment.

On September 20, 1996, Murtaza Bhutto was killed in a police ambush outside his residence along with seven members of his entourage. The cold-blooded murder of the prime minister's estranged brother by a Karachi police force controlled by the PPP's government in Sindh led to innuendos about Zardari's hand in the assassination, a charge later voiced by Murtaza's Lebanese-Syrian wife, Ghinwa, and his daughter, Fatima.[35] The top city cops and the provincial chief minister were close to Zardari. PPP officials implicated themselves by being overly defensive and justifying the police action, noting that no one was above the law. Murtaza had been defying state authority by moving around the city with armed supporters, some of whom the ISI alleged had received training from India's premier intelligence agency, the Research and Analysis Wing (RAW). Hours before his tragic death, Murtaza at a press conference denied the charge and dismissed accusations of his involvement in a spate of bomb blasts that had recently hit Karachi.

"Hang Benazir" and "Zardari is a killer" were the slogans that greeted the visibly bereaved prime minister as she arrived at the Bhutto family's mausoleum at Garhi Khuda Baksh to join her ailing mother and devastated younger sister, Sanam, beside Murtaza's rose-strewn grave. In a press statement, Nusrat Bhutto, earlier quoted as blaming Benazir and Zardari, described her son's murder as "a deep rooted conspiracy against the Bhutto family." In slaying Zulfikar Ali Bhutto's only surviving son, the murderers had killed a part of her, Benazir, and Sanam.[36] This display of family solidarity in a moment of intense grief gave the floundering prime minister an emotional reprieve. But even before the rose petals withered on Murtaza's freshly dug grave, political insiders were describing the murder as a masterstroke by the spy agencies and predicting the end of Benazir. The death of the policeman, Haq Nawaz Sial, who shot Murtaza pointed to a plot at the highest level of the state. There were reports of Sial's widow suddenly acquiring a large sum of money. Accusing hidden forces of wanting to eliminate the Bhuttos from Pakistani politics and implicitly blaming Leghari and the intelligence agencies, Benazir absolved the two police chiefs who had led the operation of responsibility. Countering suspicions of the involvement of the army's intelligence agencies, Ghinwa Bhutto alleged that the incident was planned and executed on Zardari's orders by criminal elements, senior police officials, and the Intelligence Bureau.

The Pakistani state's ponderous investigative capacities ensured that the mystery of Murtaza's death was never solved. Even her supporters admitted that Benazir had lost the moral legitimacy to rule. Leghari rubbed salt into the wound within hours of Murtaza's funeral by asking the judiciary to clarify his powers in relation to the prime minister in the appointment of senior judges. A few days later he moved Parliament to amend the law for the establishment of an independent judicial commission to try corrupt officials and politicians. Within weeks of Murtaza's assassination, Leghari at the army's insistence had practically taken over the country's foreign, economic, and financial policy. The differences between two elected pillars of the troika were now beyond bridging.

"Kill a Bhutto to get a Bhutto," was Benazir's poignant depiction of the conspiracy. They want me "to collapse and quit," she told *The News*, "but I won't let them succeed in their nefarious designs." She had no idea "whether they are going to hit me next, my husband, my children, my mother, or Murtaza's children."[37] Even after her relations with Leghari had been bent out of shape, political analysts did not foreclose a reconciliation that could save Benazir a second humiliation. For this miracle to happen, she needed, in the words of one astute commentator, to curb her instinct to tilt at windmills.[38] With the army's backing, Leghari fired Benazir and dissolved the national assembly close to the midnight hour on November 5, 1996. Elections were slated for February 3, 1997. A six-page presidential proclamation censured the dismissed prime minister for condoning corruption, failing to curb extrajudicial killings in Karachi, undermining the judiciary's independence, and making unwarranted allegations of his personal involvement in Murtaza's death. Later the four provincial governments were also dismissed. A caretaker government was appointed at the center headed by a former PPP leader, Malik Meraj Khaled, an assortment of technocrats, and relatively untainted politicians. The provinces, too, were placed under interim setups. Several PPP leaders were arrested within hours of the dismissal, including Zardari, who was booked for Murtaza's murder and various corruption cases.

Independent-minded PPP sympathizers were more relieved than sorry to see the back of a leader on whom they had pinned their hopes in vain for a second time. There were rapturous celebrations by the opposition. MQM supporters danced in the streets of Karachi, firing their automatic rifles in a display of power. Fireworks lit the skies in Lahore as joyous PML-N supporters distributed traditional sweetmeats. A recession-hit business community responded ecstatically. The Karachi Stock Exchange, a political weather vane that had risen by 3 percent just on rumors of the sacking, rallied 150 points in approval of the presidential action. There was cautious optimism among domestic and foreign investors that the dismissal would end political uncertainty and result in a concerted anticorruption drive. Leghari was able to carry out the coup only after agreeing to soften the law against defaulters of public loans. The concession was crucial in getting support from the Sharif brothers, both of whom faced potential electoral disqualification under the existing laws on bank defaulters. Removing one set of corrupt politicians with another equally culpable group was hardly conducive to cleaning up politics. So although constitutional, the reasons for Leghari's action reflected the establishment's low opinion of elected representatives. Benazir was Pakistan's fifteenth prime minister and the tenth to be dismissed. The president had invoked the same powers and used the same reasons for the fourth time in eleven years to sack an elected prime minister and dissolve Parliament.

As in the past, public opinion initially welcomed the decision, naively seeing it as an opportunity to check political corruption and stem the rot in state administration. But key differences from earlier decades underline the significance of Pakistan's so-called lost decade of democracy. Protagonists of democracy may have been on the back foot after the harrowing spectacle of three nonperforming elected governments since Zia's death, but they vastly outnumbered those who believed authoritarian rule was the only answer to Pakistan's manifold ills. Democracy for the common citizen working long hours to eke out a living was not an empty slogan as it was for most politicians. People expected their representatives to perform and deliver on promises more than ever before. A voluble, if not completely free, media adeptly performed its task by publicizing the people's disillusionment with nonperforming and greedy politicians. Skeptics casting doubt on the reality of the people's sovereignty were overly hasty in calling accountability the "sad Pakistani synonym for the notion of revolution."[39] Unprincipled politics from 1988 to 1996 had not discredited the ideals of democracy. The cry for elections had dominated the democratic discourse during the Zia era. After a decade of shoddy attempts to institute electoral democracy, good governance and accountability were the new buzzwords in national political discourse—a merciful advance on the dire technocratic maxims of the military authoritarian state. Judicial activism was another significant feature of the years following the end of military rule in 1988. If the legislative arms of the state were still beholden to executive authority, the judiciary's assertiveness and growing public credibility replaced the troika with an even more uneasy power quartet. Would the Supreme Court duplicate its May 1993 action and restore the sacked PPP government and defunct national assembly?

Benazir Bhutto certainly hoped so. Dismissing the president's charges as "false and malicious," she resolved to fight the charges in court.[40] She regretted that an elected government was plucked out of office so that interim governments stuffed with imported technocrats could sign agreements with the IMF increasing the tax burden and pushing up prices. Her truculence in asking what was so special about Nawaz Sharif that the courts had overturned the presidential order provoked charges of rank provincialism. She had a point. Unless the superior judges gave a consistent ruling on the president's powers under section 58 (2b), the judiciary's integrity as the recently empowered pillar of the state was open to questioning.

Before the polls on February 3, 1997, the Supreme Court validated the presidential order by a majority of six to one. Benazir now had the unenviable choice of boycotting the elections or leading an ill-prepared PPP into a competition she was likely to lose. Her only consolation was the egg on Leghari's face. None of the crooks identified by the president and the caretaker government were convicted prior to the elections. Even the army was baffled about the purpose of ousting Benazir. Expecting a renewed bout of presidential and prime ministerial squabbling, the generals pressed for a constitutional role in politics on the Turkish and Indonesian model. A military advisory council was deemed essential because the police and judiciary were susceptible to political influence. So Leghari created a National Defense and Security Council headed by him and four senior most officers to keep politicians under the gun. The generals were hardly the best exemplars of a stable Pakistan, which required a reduction of their influence and not its institutionalization.

A Wasted Mandate

Benazir's indecision on whether to contest the elections, pending the judicial review of the presidential action, deflated party workers. So did her tactic of making Leghari and not the PML-N the focal point of attack. Besides the PML-N, the projected winner, other contenders included the cricketing legend Imran Khan, who had captained the Pakistani team to its only World Cup victory in 1992. Reprimanding the mainstream parties for their corruption, the cricketing icon urged voters to give his Pakistan Tehrik-i-Insaaf (PTI), or justice party, a chance. While making accountability central to the political discourse in the run-up to the polls, Imran mistook his popularity on the cricket green for the will-o'-the-wisp of the electoral arena. Pakistan's Mr. Clean failed to win a single seat from the half a dozen he rashly contested.

By contrast, the not-so-clean PML-N romped home with 134 out of 217 seats in the national assembly, defeating the PPP, which ended up with just nineteen seats. A major reason for the PPP's drubbing was that a section of its supporters stayed home on election day, angered by stories of the Surrey mansion and the luxurious lifestyle of Zardari's polo horses, who were said to be lavishly fed and kept in air conditioned stables at the prime minister's house. Tired of politicians taking turns in looting the public exchequer, the 1997 elections saw the lowest ever turnouts, with estimates ranging from a mere 26 percent to 35 percent. The PML-N secured a two-thirds majority in the national assembly, 90 percent of the seats in the Punjab assembly, and a near majority in the NWFP. Nawaz Sharif's re-election as prime minister on February 18 represented a victory for newly assertive urban and rural middle classes in what were still primarily landlord-dominated politics. No party secured a majority in either Sindh or Balochistan. The PPP won rural Sindh while the MQM retained its hold over the urban areas and formed a coalition government with the PML-N. A mishmash of parties in Balochistan led to the baton being passed to Akhtar Mengal, the leader of the Balochistan National Party (BNP), which won nine out of forty seats in the provincial assembly. This gave the PML-N a stranglehold at the center and three out of four provinces.

Nawaz Sharif's historic mandate was liable to turn into an albatross unless he plugged the leaks in an increasingly dysfunctional state. Excessive presidential powers and the institutional dominance of the military and the bureaucracy were not the only source of worry. Institutional disarray at all levels of government had assumed epic proportions, magnifying the structurally rooted problems of coordination and delivery. If autocratic rule and an exclusive reliance on patronage networks had eroded the functioning of government institutions and aggravated the plight of many, successive elections also raised expectations. People wanted improvements in their meager livelihoods, basic social services, and a stop to the pilfering of the state exchequer by the captains of corruption. A dozen Pakistanis were known to have made enough illicit money since the start of the Afghan war to repay half the nation's foreign debt.[41] Outrage at the ostentatious lifestyles of the rich, famous, and corrupt was widespread. These were cautionary signs for Nawaz, who started by holding out an olive branch to the opposition while undertaking to persist with the accountability drive.

Real accountability meant rocking the boat and losing office in quick time. To stay in power, Nawaz Sharif turned his guns on the bureaucracy, leaving his supporters among the political hordes, defaulting businessmen, parasitical landed classes, and an army of tax evaders to savor their ill-gotten gains. His inclination to govern like a grand Mughal made compromises unavoidable. When Nawaz appointed his younger brother Shahbaz as chief minister of Punjab, his own supporters saw it as reposing too much power in the Sharif family and weakening both the party and the legislature. In a context where the president and the army chief were the actual wielders of authority, the urge to amass power was an inescapable trap. Within weeks of assuming office, Nawaz Sharif was locked in a tussle with the president over appointments and transfers of civil officials, delaying the implementation of his economic reforms.

A onetime bureaucrat, Leghari had developed ambitions of micromanaging Pakistan. After sacking Benazir, he appointed former batchmates to top positions in the bureaucracy to keep close tabs on the new government. In a clear indication of the president's intentions, the caretaker government announced the National Finance Commission (NFC) award—the handiwork of civil bureaucrats—just days before the PML-N was to take office. An enormously divisive political issue, the NFC allocated the share out of financial resources between the center and the provinces on the basis of population. No population census had been held in Pakistan since 1981 because of opposition from vested interests. The NWFP was the only province that wanted a census despite the presence of a large number of Afghan refugees. Punjab, Sindh, and Balochistan were opposed, fearing that demographic shifts caused by increasing urbanization over the past decade and a half would reduce their share of federal financial resources and government jobs. Karachi's allocation of federal resources was based on the 1981 census, which recorded its population as just under 5.5 million. By 1997, the city's population was an estimated 12 million. Besides the practical need for a population census, a provincial consensus on the apportioning of the federation's resources was critical for the success of

Nawaz Sharif's ambitious economic regeneration program conveyed by the catchphrase "repay debts, restore national dignity" to put Pakistan back on the road to self-sufficiency and prosperity.

With an external debt of $34 billion, nearly half the GDP, $4.5 billion annually was required for debt servicing, which accounted for 40 percent of the federal budget. The trade deficit was at an all-time high of $4.5 billion, creating serious balance-of-payments problems. For two decades, the tax revenue to GDP ratio had remained stationary at 13 percent to 14 percent, making it impossible to service the debt without borrowing from commercial banks at high interest rates. The alternative of IMF loans meant hiking the costs of utilities and tightening the government's belt. Cutting the defense budget was not an option. So development expenditure—a mere 3.4 percent of GDP—was slashed by 19 percent during 1996–97. Industrial output grew by a paltry 3 percent. Unemployment among the youth assumed dangerous proportions while the rate of inflation was 20 percent.[42] Destitute families had to send their children to local madrasas, where they were fed and clothed and given toxic doses of propaganda against rival Muslim sects, Indian hegemons, American imperialists, and Israeli Zionists. These madrasas received millions of rupees of state-collected *zakat* funds, but only a select few provided military training for the "jihad" in Afghanistan and Kashmir.

Reviving the economy without tackling militancy and meeting the demands of the smaller provinces for more resources and autonomy was an act of whistling in the wind. These hard truths were not hidden from a businessman-cum-politician who supported centralization and GHQ's provocative policies in the region. Making dissimulation his strategy, Sharif made peace gestures toward Delhi and tried assuaging Washington's alarm at Pakistan's intrusive regional policies by appealing to the Taliban to close down terrorist camps. At the same time, he extended support for the military's Afghanistan and Kashmir adventures as well as the nuclear program. The inability to connect the army's regional policies with internal security was to cost Sharif on both the economic and the political front. Without new investments, there was no prospect of sustained economic recovery or of averting the social discontent that was manifesting itself in an explosive blend of sectarian and linguistic hatreds.

In his first major policy decision, Nawaz Sharif announced a foreign debt retirement scheme to raise a billion dollars from overseas Pakistanis through donations and above-market interest rates on foreign exchange deposits. Local citizens were asked to contribute to the fund. The play on patriotism elicited a positive reaction from some nonresident Pakistanis and, most touchingly, the lower classes at home. The better off remained apathetic. Without help from Pakistanis at home and abroad, talk of breaking out of IMF and World Bank shackles amounted to moonshine. Businessmen and urban middle classes cheered Nawaz Sharif's tax breaks and the lowering of customs duties, but these measures pushed up the budgetary deficit over the targeted 4 percent of the GDP agreed on with the IMF.

Taking advantage of his parliamentary majority, Nawaz decided to preempt Leghari from obstructing his probusiness plans by striking down the clauses of the Eighth Amendment that affected his tenure in office. He won support from his coalition partners and the PPP to repeal a law that had seen three different presidents sacking four elected governments at roughly thirty-month intervals. On April Fool's Day, the Thirteenth Constitutional Amendment Bill was unanimously passed by both houses of Parliament at lightning speed. The Eighth Amendment had made forty changes to the 1973 constitution, including the incorporation of the Hudood and blasphemy laws as well as several clauses impinging on fundamental rights and parliamentary supremacy. The Thirteenth Amendment left these and other objectionable laws untouched, focusing exclusively on the presidential and prime ministerial equation. Only four clauses of the Eighth Amendment pertaining to the president's powers to dismiss governments, dissolve elected assemblies, and appoint service chiefs and governors were repealed. Putting on a bold face, Leghari promptly gave his approval, maintaining he had always favored the repeal of the Eighth Amendment. The downside to the speediest passage of a constitutional amendment in Pakistan's history was the lack of any debate in Parliament on the implications of the move. This was a surprising oversight since the Eighth Amendment had served as a safety valve against military intervention. The Thirteenth Amendment merely strengthened Nawaz's hands. It did not correct imbalances between state institutions or place checks on the prime minister's executive authority to lend substance to the slogan of parliamentary sovereignty.

Looking for a role closer to an elected dictator, Nawaz next moved Parliament to adopt the Fourteenth Amendment, debarring members from defecting and effectively preventing PML-N parliamentarians from expressing dissent. The absence of internal party democracy and accumulation of unchecked personal powers troubled the generals. Without the president's restraining powers on the elected government, the army high command had to rethink its post-1985 tactic of controlling politics indirectly. Even if successive presidents used the Eighth Amendment subjectively and not as a check or balance, the elimination of article 58 (2b) followed by the Fourteenth Amendment placed the prime minister in a seemingly impregnable position, leaving disaffected generals with no option but to resort to direct military intervention.

Military rulers were not fashionable in the post–Cold War world and could prove fatal for a country on life support from international monetary agencies. The army chief, General Jehangir Karamat, was a democrat in khaki. Breaking with his predecessors, Karamat did not balk at Sharif's decision to curtail the president's powers or object when the military advisory committee set up by Leghari was not given constitutional status. The army's expectations of an economic regeneration, vital if it was to continue holding up the standard against India, explains its willingness to accommodate the steps taken to restore parliamentary democracy. With their vast stake in the national economy and direct control over one-third of the industrial sector, the senior echelons of the armed forces had cause to rejoice at the new government's probusiness agenda. This could change under a new army chief, particularly if Sharif failed to jump-start the economy and stabilize the fiscal situation to alleviate pressures on the defense budget, which had been pared down by 10 percent.

In the event, it was the judiciary's budding independence and activism that sent the prime minister's team into a tailspin. The government's constitutional amendments and assumption of special powers to combat law-and-order problems were challenged in the courts as violating fundamental rights. A savvy politician would have kept relations with the judiciary in good repair. Nawaz refused to honor the judicial verdict giving the chief justice the right to appoint senior judges. With presidential backing, the chief justice stood his ground on judicial appointments and entertained petitions against the two constitutional amendments and the new antiterrorism act. The Fourteenth Amendment was suspended, enraging Nawaz Sharif, who called it a violation of parliamentary sovereignty. His strong language against the chief justice resulted in him being booked for contempt of court. When Leghari refused to oblige Nawaz by agreeing to replace the chief justice, the federal cabinet voted to impeach the president. But the PML-N did not have the numbers in Parliament for the impeachment. After the army chief intervened, Nawaz dropped the idea of impeaching Leghari in return for a week's reprieve on the cases pending against him in the Supreme Court. The PML-N master fixers used the time to engineer a split in the higher judiciary, a first in Pakistan's innovative history of intrigues. A three-member bench of the Supreme Court in Quetta passed an interim order restraining Justice Sajjad Ali Shah from functioning as chief justice as he had been appointed out of turn. This sparked off a tragicomic drama of the absurd, with the judiciary divided along political lines.

On November 28, 1997, PML-N supporters led by government ministers stormed the Supreme Court as a heavy police contingent looked on helplessly. The mob broke into the courtroom where Justice Shah was hearing the contempt case and made an abortive attempt to take the chief justice into custody. The emergence of two rival Supreme Courts made a perfect mockery of constitutional government even by Pakistani standards. Presiding over a three-member bench, Justice Shah upheld the petition against the Thirteenth Amendment and restored the president's powers to sack the prime minister and dissolve assemblies. A rival ten-member bench promptly shot this down. The constitutional crisis ended with Leghari's resignation once the army chief combined khaki with mufti to mediate a two-month conflict between the judicial, executive, and legislative arms of the state that had cost a wobbling economy an estimated $2 billion.

Encouraged by his success in chastening the president and the chief justice, Nawaz Sharif selected retired justice Mohammad Rafiq Tarar, a Sharif loyalist and fellow Punjabi, as the PML-N presidential candidate. This undermined one of the few political conventions honored in Pakistan of ensuring that the president and prime minister have different regional backgrounds. Known for his Islamist leanings and chauvinistic ranting on India, President Tarar was a rubber-stamping clerk for the Sharifs. The Supreme Court headed by the new chief justice, Ajmal Mian, validated both the Thirteenth and the Fourteenth Amendments, giving the prime minister untrammeled powers over the executive and the Parliament. Accustomed to making decisions based on personal loyalties, not the rule of law, Nawaz could not fathom the institutional dynamics of either the judiciary or the army. He had already antagonized the third non-elected institution of the state by targeting the bureaucracy in his accountability drive. Once the mystique of his electoral mandate wore off and his regional political alliances fell apart, Nawaz Sharif was left to plough a lonely furrow, much like the lesser Mughals whose predecessors he tried emulating. A gagged political party could not muster the courage to warn their leader of the perils he was courting by simultaneously enhancing his own power and the Sharif family's financial portfolio.

While Nawaz Sharif was busy trying to consolidate his hold over state power, Pakistan was losing ground in the international arena to a newly liberalizing and economically resurgent India. The end of the Cold War had diminished Pakistan's importance for the United States, notwithstanding Washington's concerns about its nuclear program and role in exporting terrorism and drugs. Pakistan's support for the Taliban was a major irritant for the United States, interested in a peaceful Afghanistan to capitalize on the oil wealth of the Central Asian states. But it was Washington's willingness to appease India by keeping Kashmir off the UN's agenda that most perturbed the Pakistani military high command. The tactic of pushing battle-hardened militants from Afghanistan across the LOC to wage a low-intensity war against Indian security forces in Kashmir was designed to keep the subcontinent's most contentious dispute in the international gaze. Proceeding with the nuclear program regardless of American rebukes and threats of international sanctions was the other link in the military's efforts to offset India's growing international clout.

On April 6, 1998, Pakistan successfully test fired an intermediate-range missile with a range of 1,500 kilometers. The missile was named Ghauri, after the twelfth-century Turkish invader whose foray into India led to the establishment of the first Muslim dynasty in Delhi. In a clear message to India, which had an arsenal of missiles named Prithvi, Trishul, and Agni, Pakistan's controversial nuclear scientist, Dr. Abdul Qadeer Khan, announced that a 2,000-kilometer-range Ghaznavi missile was in the offing. New Delhi's right-wing Hindu nationalist BJP-led government was not rattled by the show of Pakistani military might so much as by the choice of names of medieval Muslim invaders, Ghauri and Ghaznavi. India's nuclear tests were not Pakistan specific. George Fernandes, the Indian defense minister, stated that the main potential threat to India came from

China and not Pakistan. India had reached the technological threshold for nuclear testing by the summer of 1995. The Congress government of Prime Minister Narasimha Rao chose not to proceed with the tests after American intelligence satellites blew the Indian cover. India and Pakistan had refused to sign the Nuclear Nonproliferation Treaty (NPT) for discriminating against countries that did not already possess nuclear capability. Since 1996, Washington had been pressing New Delhi and Islamabad to sign the Comprehensive Test Ban Treaty (CTBT), prohibiting nuclear tests. While India stood its ground, Pakistan might have extracted long-term economic and strategic benefits by taking an independent stance and signing the treaty. By linking the signing of the CTBT with India's compliance to the treaty, Pakistan made itself redundant in the US-initiated Western negotiations with New Delhi.

The BJP government's primary motivation for conducting five nuclear explosions in the Pokhran desert in the second week of May 1998 was to extract maximum political mileage at home by exhibiting India's national pride globally to gain de facto entry into the elite nuclear club of the most powerful nation-states. With the nuclear tests announcing its arrival on the global stage, India could use the CTBT bait to ask for a UN seat on the Security Council, to neutralize the Kashmir dispute, and to attract billions of dollars of US investment in critical sectors of its economy, in addition to seeking the transfer of supersensitive defense technology. A secondary objective in going public with India's nuclear capability was to flush out Pakistan's program into the open at a time when Islamabad was struggling to keep afloat financially. As early as 1983, Pakistan had cold tested a nuclear device and followed it with several others. If Pakistan emulated India, as was expected, the weight of international sanctions would cripple its economy, leaving it vulnerable to international pressure, and ease India's discomfort in Kashmir.

Pakistan's poor economic condition encouraged the American president to dissuade Nawaz Sharif from going down the Indian path. Clinton offered to repeal the Pressler Amendment, deliver the F-16s paid for by Pakistan, and negotiate a substantial aid package worth billions of dollars. An ultranationalist politician who had his hand on the popular pulse, Sharif was undeterred by fears of economic collapse or international isolation. He decided to match the Indian tests the moment the news was conveyed to him. In a tactical maneuver, the army chief asked the prime minister to let his economic team take a comprehensive view of the re-percussions before ordering the tests. This was designed to extract a firm assurance from Nawaz Sharif that the economic crunch in the wake of the tests would not prompt additional cuts in the defense budget, leading to a decrease in the armed forces' operational capacity, particularly in Kash-mir. General Karamat got the assurance.[43]

Within five days of India's second set of tests on May 13, Nawaz Sharif had given the go-ahead. By then preparations were under way in the re-mote Chagai Hills of Balochistan. It took another fortnight before Paki-stan conducted five nuclear explosions on May 28, in a tit-for-tat with In-dia. A sixth test two days later matched India's six explosions, including the one in 1974. Appearing on national television the prime minister proudly declared: "Today we have settled the score with India."[44] A na-tional emergency was enforced as a precaution against Indian retaliation. Acclaimed as a national hero, and in some quarters as the new Muslim Saladin, Nawaz Sharif was thrilled with his newfound popularity. The high economic price Pakistan paid for the explosions almost seemed worthwhile. American-led international sanctions and the suspension of external funds vital to service the debt caused an economic meltdown. Nawaz Sharif lost face with nonresident and resident Pakistanis, whose dollar deposits worth $11 billion were frozen by the State Bank of Pakistan in exchange for the equivalent rupee amount at an overvalued official ex-change rate. The rupee plunged, creating a 25 percent differential between the official and market exchange rates.

Unfazed by the chorus of international condemnation and the shatter-ing blow to the tenuous livelihoods of many of his compatriots, Nawaz Sharif gloated in the glory of becoming the prime minister of the world's only Muslim nuclear state. As the self-styled leader of the ummah, Sharif had no pangs of conscience dashing off to Saudi Arabia and other oil-rich Muslim countries to seek money to service Pakistan's bulging foreign debt. The East Asian economic crisis of 1997 had taken a toll on the invest-ments and oil income of these Muslim countries. All Sharif could get was a $2 billion credit to cover Pakistan's annual oil imports. With the threat of default looming, his government took comfort in the dictum that no one wanted to see a nuclear state going bust in a dangerous corner of the world. This had large consequences for how postnuclear Pakistan per-ceived itself, the neighborhood, and the broader international system. The illusion of Pakistan's newfound prestige was at odds with the reality of its limited bargaining position due to the desperate economic situation. This was underlined by the American decision in August 1998 to use Pakistani air space to fire seventy cruise missiles on Osama bin Laden's training camp in Afghanistan without informing the government or the military high command until the operation was under way. Although the Al Qaeda leader escaped unharmed, many of those killed were Pakistani nationals. This was evidence, if it was needed, of the ISI's complicity with the Al Qaeda training networks operating out of Afghanistan.

The allure of Pakistan's emergence as a nuclear power wore off quickly. There were street demonstrations against spiraling inflation and rising unemployment. Sharif's problems mounted with renewed violence in Karachi between two warring factions of the MQM and trigger-happy paramilitary forces that left a gruesome trail of blood and gore. The federal government proposed setting up military courts to deliver "speedy justice" to culprits arrested by a corrupt and politically manipulated city police that was more a part of the problem than a solution to Karachi's ills. Meanwhile, there was growing violence against Christians and Shias by armed Sunni groups across Pakistan. In these troubled times, Nawaz decided to railroad the Fifteenth Constitutional Amendment bill through Parliament, making the Islamic sharia the supreme law of the land. His admiration for the strict "Islamic justice" practiced by the Taliban alarmed liberals and put off potential donors and investors. With Pakistan teetering on the edge, the prime minister tried enlisting the army's help in enforcing law and order and running the civil administration. The army chief resisted directing his men to nab electricity thieves and corrupt officials pocketing government salaries for nonexistent teachers in thousands of "ghost schools" throughout Punjab.

On October 5, 1998, while speaking at the Naval Staff College in Lahore, General Karamat proposed a National Security Council to lend stability to the political system. The idea had been around for ages. Livid at the army chief for refusing to comply with his requests, Nawaz Sharif considered the remarks an uncalled-for intervention in civilian affairs and demanded an explanation. Karamat said that he had proposed nothing new and politely stepped down. There was indignation in the army over General Karamat's humiliation. Less than two years since returning to office, Nawaz Sharif had become one of the most powerful prime ministers in

Pakistan's history. He had removed practically all the potential hurdles within the institutional power structure that could prevent him completing his second term in office.

All that Nawaz Sharif now needed was to choose the right person as the next army chief. He preferred Lieutenant General Ziauddin Khwaja, a fellow Kashmiri and Punjabi, but also lowest on the seniority list. Opting not to further rankle the army, Sharif selected Lieutenant General Pervez Musharraf, an Urdu speaker whose family had migrated from New Delhi to Pakistan after partition. The appointment entailed superseding three officers. Musharraf's superiors in the service did not consider him fit for the office of army chief, a view corroborated by the ISI and other intelligence outfits.[45] Nawaz Sharif opted for Musharraf because he lacked a natural constituency within the army.

The presumption that an Urdu speaker would be less likely to assert his authority over a Punjabi and Pathan army was misplaced. A flamboyant and gutsy figure, General Pervez Musharraf had led a newly raised elite Special Services Group Commando battalion in an unsuccessful assault on Indian Army positions on the Siachen glacier in 1987. The death of several of his men galled Musharraf, who shared the army's dismay at losing Siachen to India in 1984. Soon after becoming army chief, Musharraf in collusion with a handful of senior officers decided to take the Kargil heights from Indian control. The best time for this was in the dead of winter, when the Indians evacuated their forward posts to escape the bitter cold. Nibbling at territory along the LOC separating the two parts of Kashmir was an activity both sides engaged in as a matter of course. By capturing the Kargil heights, Pakistan could threaten India's main supply route linking Srinagar to Dras and Leh in Ladakh. This would partially offset the strategic loss of the Siachin glacier and serve notice to India.

Similar proposals had been floated before and shot down, twice on Benazir's watch, because of concerns about Indian retaliation across the international border and a global outcry against Pakistani aggression. With the nuclear umbrella in place, the masterminds of the proposed operation across the LOC were confident that New Delhi would avoid provoking an all-out war. This clinched it for Nawaz Sharif, with whom Musharraf cursorily broached the matter sometime toward the end of 1998 and January 1999. The timing and details communicated to the prime minister remain controversial. Musharraf vehemently refuted Nawaz Sharif's claim that Sharif had no knowledge of the operation. An army chief acting unilaterally poses serious questions of legality, while the prime minister's complicity in the Kargil episode raises concerns about his credibility, months after the two nuclear rivals had signed an agreement in February 1999.

In a rare gesture from an Indian leader, Prime Minister Atal Behari Vajpayee had inaugurated a bus service between the two countries across the Wagah border near Lahore. Improved people-to-people contacts, commercial transactions, and intellectual exchanges could have been the upside to Pakistan and India coming of nuclear age. The spirit of the visit was vitiated by the refusal of the generals to greet the Indian prime minister at Wagah. The story of the Kargil war has been slowly unfolding on both sides of the border. Army circles jumped to the conclusion that the Lahore declaration signed by Nawaz Sharif and Vajpayee omitted reference to Kashmir. Actually, the agreement mentioned Jammu and Kashmir as one of the outstanding matters needing resolution. The reason for the unease, certainly on the army chief's part, was that the military incursion was already under way by the time Vajpayee stepped on Pakistani soil. As one of the key brains behind the Kargil operation, Musharraf had calculated that territory gained through the incursion would strengthen Pakistan's hand, internationalize the Kashmir issue, and bring the Indians to the negotiating table.[46]

Within days of Musharraf becoming army chief in October 1998, some 200 troops from the Northern Light Infantry crossed the LOC into Kargil. Later more were pushed in, bringing the figure to about 1,500. They were expected to occupy eight to ten Indian check posts along the LOC. Finding no Indian troops for miles on end, they opportunistically took 153 posts and pickets spread over five sectors, of which three were around 300 square kilometers and two around 200 square kilometers.[47] The intended incursion had become an invasion. A tactical masterstroke in a war game, it was a strategic disaster in real time. Knowledge of the operation, code-named Koh-i-Paima, was confined to just seven of the army's top guns. With the other two service chiefs and the intelligence agencies in the dark, there was no discussion on the wider strategic, political, or economic implications of the thrust. If Nawaz Sharif knew about the operation, he was not kept abreast of its actual progress. The lack of institutional coordination at the highest echelons of the state dealt a devastating blow to Pakistan's already shaky international image.

The Indians were caught napping but had the weight of international opinion on their side. In April some shepherds reported suspicious activity along the Kargil hilltops. By then the offensive had begun. Although the Indian Army started retaliatory moves by May 9, it was not before mid-May that Indian media reports revealed the full extent of the incursion. The initial shock and horror in India turned into media-staged national hysteria at Pakistan's betrayal of trust within months of the Lahore Declaration. While undertaking to oust the intruders, New Delhi started an effective diplomatic campaign. As international condemnation of Pakistan's reckless action poured in, Islamabad was at its dysfunctional worst. Distrust between the civilian and military arms of the state left the PML-N government's star players clueless on how to respond to an operation carried out by their own army. The Indian government leaked transcripts of Musharraf's phone conversation with his chief of general staff, Lieutenant General Mohammad Aziz Khan, discussing ground operations and tactics to fend off the storm New Delhi was kicking up internationally.

Nawaz Sharif privately told Vajpayee that he had not authorized the intrusion. Although kept in the dark about the actual progress of the Kargil operation, the army did brief the prime minister on Kashmir. During one such meeting in late January, the issue of breaching the LOC was raised with Nawaz Sharif from a tactical but not a political or diplomatic angle. The army gave the first full briefing on Kargil to the prime minister on May 16, 1999. Instead of criticizing the infiltration, Sharif adopted the army chief's agenda of using Kargil to internationalize Kashmir as his own. Consequently, the prime minister lost face in Western capitals without gaining any political mileage at home. President Clinton told Nawaz Sharif that the incursion was plain stupidity and connecting Kargil with Kashmir out of the question. Nothing short of a complete pullout by Pakistan would do. Even the Chinese withheld diplomatic support. Only Saudi Arabia and the United Arab Emirates stood by their internationally isolated brotherly country. Sharif's denials that the intruders were Pakistani army regulars made things worse. Institutional dissonance and a thick web of distrust and intrigue left civil officials floundering and lying through their teeth. This allowed the Indians to put forward a coherent case against Pakistani aggression with a view to permanently defusing the Kashmir issue. Most effective was New Delhi's tactic of telling the Americans that they were prepared for an all-out war unless Pakistan carried out an immediate and unconditional withdrawal. Intelligence reports by the American CIA pointed to the danger of nuclear exchange between the two nuclear rivals, sending the White House into top gear to stop that deadly prospect.[48]

By mid-June the presumption of the Kargil planners that India would not be able to overturn the military gains had proven incorrect. Despite suffering heavy causalities, the Indian military continued chipping away at the advantage gained by the intruders. Pakistan's policy of plausible deniability meant that the supply lines to the troops pushed into Kargil could not be sustained. As India began ratcheting up the military pressure, Pakistani Army regulars were left to fend for themselves in subzero temperatures and a hail of enemy firepower. Both the air force and naval chiefs warned Nawaz Sharif of the possibility of an all-out war, with India imposing a blockade of Karachi. The army chief disagreed, claiming Pakistan had got the better of India, and asked Sharif to use Pakistan's military advantage in the Kargil heights to negotiate an honorable exit.[49] From General Musharraf's restricted angle of vision, an honorable exit meant a quid pro quo from India on Kashmir, not the unilateral withdrawal the prime minister was contemplating.

Once a hurried visit to Beijing and secret back-channel diplomacy with New Delhi got nowhere, Nawaz Sharif turned to Washington with the army chief's tacit approval. The American president was keen to use his mediation in the Kargil crisis to win New Delhi's confidence and open a fresh chapter in Indo-US relations. The White House's exchanges with the Pakistani prime minister were closely choreographed with the Indians. Once Nawaz Sharif agreed to order an unconditional withdrawal, Clinton invited him to an unprecedented meeting with him on American Independence Day. As he boarded the flight to Washington, Sharif was less worried about getting an earful from the US president about Pakistan's indiscretion than the political fallout of the decision to withdraw and the army chief's likely reaction. Although informed of the visit at the last minute, General Musharraf thought American mediation could get Pakistan a better deal from India. However, unlike the civilian leadership and the other two service chiefs who questioned the wisdom of the incursion, Musharraf believed Pakistan could hold its ground in Kargil and not cave into American pressure.

On July 4, 1999, an ill-prepared and distracted Sharif met a well-briefed Bill Clinton to discuss the modalities of ending a crisis that threatened the world with a nuclear catastrophe. Cornered and outwitted, Sharif agreed to an unconditional withdrawal without extracting a guarantee for the safe passage of the retreating troops, a shocking omission but one consistent with the Pakistani refusal to own the intruders as their army regulars. The joint declaration after the meeting effectively conceded that the Kargil operation was a blunder. Other than a personal undertaking from Clinton to try and resolve the Kashmir dispute, the Americans made no formal commitments to Pakistan. Rather, it was Sharif who promised help locating Osama bin Laden after being roundly berated by Clinton on the ISI's role in propping up the Taliban and implicitly Al Qaeda as well.

For a man dreaming of completing not one but two terms in office, the dash to Washington with his family in tow only to return empty-handed was tantamount to an attempted suicide that almost succeeded. Misled by the false claims of the official propaganda machinery, public opinion was utterly befuddled by the unannounced Washington visit and its unwholesome results. The opposition attacked Sharif for selling out, with some accusing him of treason. General Musharraf and his co-associates in the Kargil saga were enraged. Nawaz Sharif had squandered the military advantage in Kargil to avert an improbable nuclear war cooked up by American security hacks. As tensions between the army chief and the prime minister reached fever pitch, the Clinton administration on September 20, 1999, warned against any unconstitutional change in Pakistan. Seeing this as his security cover, Sharif committed the ultimate folly of sacking the army chief. He enlisted the help of the Quetta corps commander and his Kashmiri clansman, Lieutenant General Ziauddin Butt, who was then the DG of ISI. Musharraf retaliated by sacking the Quetta corps commander. The government started a vicious media campaign against the army chief's insubordination and recklessness. In a diversionary move, Nawaz Sharif gave Musharraf the added responsibility of chairman of the Joint Chiefs of Staff.

Just as relations between GHQ and the elected government seemed to be returning to normal, the prime minister decided to dismiss Musharraf without consulting the cabinet or his younger brother. The announcement of General Ziauddin's appointment as the new army chief on PTV prompted a countercoup by GHQ while Musharraf was on a plane returning from a visit to Sri Lanka. Nawaz Sharif was helpless as troops surrounded PTV studios and his official residence in Islamabad. In an episode that vies with the best Hollywood political thriller, Sharif and his aides tried preventing the PIA commercial plane carrying Musharraf from landing at Karachi Airport. In an indication that contingency plans for a coup existed, the corps commander of Karachi in coordination with GHQ scotched this hazardous plan, and the drama ended with the plane landing at its destination.

Nawaz Sharif had only himself to blame for not getting the full measure of his own army. Removing the army chief without the GHQ's backing was dim-witted. From the famed historic mandate to his heroics against the president and the judiciary to the pitiful display of political and diplomatic acumen during Kargil and the comical attempt at dismissing an army chief, the prime minister had slipped up far too many times to escape the retribution that awaited Pakistani civilian leaders who crossed the red line with the military establishment. Some but not all of the swings of the political pendulum between 1988 and 1999 were the handiwork of the army's top brass. The army chief's triumph over a prime minister commanding a decisive majority in Parliament showed that the balance of power was still weightier on the side of the preeminent nonelected institution of the state. Yet Pakistan under military rule in October 1999 was a different country from the one Zia-ul-Haq had captured in July 1977. The decade following his death in 1988, too easily dismissed as the "lost decade," had seen the crystallization of new political dynamics—an active judiciary, a struggling if vocal media, and a polarized but more conscious civil society—that was altering the civil–military equation in significant new ways. Just how much would become apparent as Pakistan succumbed to a fourth brush with military rule.

NINE

A GEOSTRATEGIC RIDDLE

ON OCTOBER 16, 1999, THE *ECONOMIST*'S COVER STORY "Oh Pakistan" showed a *shalwar kameez*–clad Nawaz Sharif sitting next to a uniformed General Pervez Musharraf sharing a thought bubble: "You Are Fired!" Military coups had become a rarity in the world by the end of the twentieth century but, as the British weekly noted, for Pakistanis there was something familiar about General Musharraf's coup. The takeover had followed the script for the state of martial rule pioneered by General Ayub Khan and fine-tuned by Generals Yahya Khan and Zia-ul-Haq. On October 12 soon after the announcement of Musharraf's dismissal as chief of army staff on national television, the screens went black, then martial music erupted against the backdrop of soldiers marching in patriotic earnestness. As was standard, no tears were shed for the sacked prime minister and his corrupt government. No street demonstrations were held to protest the fourth bloodless coup by an army that had ruled the country for twenty-five years during the fifty-two years since independence. Without endorsing the military seizure of power, the *Economist* thought Nawaz Sharif's departure from the scene might turn out to be for the better. Everything depended on General Musharraf, who had "the power to make his country a better place, or to destroy it."[1]

The *New York Times* editorial "Dangerous Coup in Pakistan" was more forthright in denouncing the intervention, calling it a "cause for alarm in South Asia and the rest of the world." A newly armed nuclear power with a history of wars and internal upheavals, Pakistan's relapse into military rule under General Musharraf, who had so recently shown an inclination to be confrontational with India, had again made the subcontinent "one of the most dangerous places in the world." Whatever the faults of the sacked civilian government, the coup had no justification. Democracy had to be restored in Pakistan at once. The United States needed to work with China and Saudi Arabia to ensure that Musharraf and his top generals did not embark on another military misadventure against India. There were simply "no military solutions to Pakistan's problems."[2] The editorial line mirrored the Clinton administration's adverse reaction to a coup it had tried preventing. On September 20, 1999, officials of the State Department, the Pentagon, and the National Security Council had issued four separate statements warning the army against taking any extraconstitutional step. Such unprecedented backing by Washington for a civilian government in Islamabad was not without its quid pro quo. Committed to capturing Osama bin Laden before leaving the Oval Office, Clinton wanted Nawaz Sharif's help in getting the Pakistani Army to stop supporting the Taliban and instead use its intelligence networks to locate bin Laden.[3]

Fearing a military coup, the Pakistani prime minister was only too willing to oblige. A week before the drama that led to the overthrow of the PML-N government, both the Sharif brothers publicly condemned the Taliban, leading to speculation that "the government was pushing an American agenda in the region."[4] This fueled resentments in GHQ and was one of the less well-publicized reasons for the coup. As a liberal-minded columnist of an English daily put it, the Sharifs responded to their mounting internal problems by becoming "the greatest lackeys of the Americans that we have ever had." They had beaten Benazir Bhutto "hollow" in this shameful race and "bartered national self-respect in a bid to seek American support."[5] With even prodemocracy liberals applauding Sharif's fall, the coup was a major setback for the American drive to find the Al Qaeda leader. Anticipating the problems ahead, a State Department spokesman tartly said that the United States wanted the immediate restitution of democracy in Pakistan and would not "carry on business as usual" with the military regime.[6]

International disdain greeted the army coup. Even China reacted cautiously, veiling its concern about the specter of "Talibanization" by noting that the two countries were "friendly neighbors" and the situation in Pakistan was being watched carefully. The Chinese had been annoyed to discover links between the ISI and Islamic Uighur militants in Xinjiang. "We need a Khomeini-style or Taliban-style campaign to cleanse society," a Pakistani shopkeeper was quoted as saying in the economic daily *Zhongguo*

Jingji Shibao brought out by the Chinese State Council's Development Research Center. More worrying, the paper noted, was the growing influence of "fundamentalism" in the Pakistan military. Russia feared that closer military cooperation between Pakistan and the Taliban would increase tensions in its southern regions, including the Caucasus. Moscow had intelligence reports about Chechen envoys visiting Afghanistan to buy Stinger anti-aircraft missiles and receiving four of them "as a gift." Voicing its own unique concerns, Iran instead rebuked the West for backing Pakistan and the Taliban regime. One Iranian newspaper asked rhetorically whether the military regime would end Pakistan's international isolation by suspending support for the usurpers of power in Afghanistan. Taliban-ruled Kabul described the coup as Pakistan's internal affair and expressed a desire for good and friendly relations with each successive government in Islamabad.[7]

Of the regional neighbors, India had most reason to be alarmed. The main architect of the Kargil operation had taken control of Pakistan. Deeply suspicious of Musharraf and unwilling to take any risks, the government of India set the ball rolling for military exercises to test the combat fitness of its army along the western border with Pakistan. At the same time, New Delhi mounted an effective diplomatic offensive to force Musharraf to back off. It did not have to work too hard. At UN headquarters in New York, there was deep consternation. A few weeks before the change of government in Pakistan, the United Nations Drug Control Program had reported that Afghanistan produced 4,600 metric tons of opium, a figure that was three times higher than the combined world production of the drug. As far as the UN was concerned, Afghanistan under the Taliban was the "biggest narcopower in the world."[8] With the Pakistani military high command now in a position to back the Taliban without any hindrance from a civilian setup, there was nothing to stop the export of opium from Afghanistan.

Amid grave misgivings in the neighborhood and the world at large, Pakistan slipped into another phase of military rule. If the script was familiar, the geostrategic context had dramatically changed. The Cold War was over for the rest of the world, but its enduring legacies were only too visible in Pakistan. Past military interventions and misgovernance by unstable and short-lived civilian governments had deeply polarized politics and damaged the economy, with perilous effects on the exercise of state authority. Decades of centralization had fragmented state institutions that were now more susceptible to political influences and outright capture at the regional and local levels by interweaving networks of sectarian and criminal militias. The implications of these existential threats were largely lost on the military high command, the main stakeholder of Pakistan's increasingly dysfunctional centralized state system. Wedded to an India-centered national security paradigm, the military high command was single-mindedly committed to pursuing their strategic objectives in Afghanistan. The United States had assisted Pakistan in attaining a viable defense against its premier enemy and in the process strengthened the army and its intelligence services, which now posed the biggest obstacle to American objectives in the region. Instead of propping up military dictatorships around the world to contain communism as they had during the Cold War, the Americans were now more interested in forging a strategic and economic partnership with the rising regional giant India.

On the eve of the twenty-first century, authoritarian Pakistan was an international pariah for supporting the Taliban regime and initiating the Kargil incursion. A nearly moribund economy and widespread corruption and insecurity of life and property had demoralized the citizenry. The blowback of the Afghan war had reared a thriving arms and drugs economy run by criminal mafias protected by state officials and politicians. Pakistan's growing urban landscape was dotted with mosques and madrasas. The products of religious seminaries offering extreme and militant versions of Islam were either recruited to fight "jihad" in Afghanistan and Kashmir or turned into killing machines by would-be religious ideologues battling rival sectarian communities. Confronted with intense internal and external pressures, Pakistan needed deft and swift handling on several contradictory fronts. By placing himself in the line of fire, had General Musharraf bitten off far more than he could chew? As before, the fate of a military dictator would be shaped by developments beyond Pakistan's borders. In Musharraf's case, September 11, 2001, would prove to be the decisive turning point in determining the longevity of his regime.

Martial Law in All but Name

A villain to the outside world, the fifty-six-year-old Musharraf projected himself as the savior of Pakistan. The general was no intellectual, though he liked reading the speeches of Abraham Lincoln.[9] He also idolized

Mustapha Kamal Ataturk and was a Turkophile. In his first address to the
nation telecast by state television at 2:50 a.m. on October 13, 1999, Musharraf warned religious extremists not to exploit religion for political ends
and made it clear that Nawaz Sharif had been ousted to stop further attempts to politicize and destabilize the army. "Despite all my advice," the
mustached and bespectacled commando in a camouflage uniform bewailed, "they tried to interfere with the armed forces, the last remaining
viable institution in which all of you take so much pride and look up to at
all times for stability, unity, and integrity of our beloved country."[10] If this
was an ironic invocation of the military's aid to civil power, Musharraf
was against ruling under martial law, having observed its detrimental effects on the army and the civil bureaucracy. Under his watch, army officers would not be superimposed on civil bureaucrats but would work
alongside them. Whether such a hybrid system of civil–military authority
could correct the infirmities of a compromised and inefficient administrative machinery remained to be seen.

After consulting with the old constitutional wizard Sharifuddin Pirzada,
Musharraf on October 14 used the cover of a hurriedly drafted Provisional
Constitutional Order (PCO) to announce the continuation of the "state of
emergency" proclaimed at the time of the nuclear tests on May 28, 1998. It
was Pakistan's eleventh constitutional framework. Musharraf took over as
chief executive, a position equivalent to the prime minister, and ostensibly
a "humanised substitute for chief martial law administrator."[11] Sharif's
loyalist president Tarar, a symbol of Islamic fundamentalism for the outside world, was told to remain in office and act in accordance with the
chief executive's advice. Members of the judiciary were also asked to continue, even though orders of the chief executive could not be challenged in
the courts. What was novel about the state of martial rule operating
under emergency powers in the fall of 1999 was the decision not to enforce press censorship. A remedy of necessity not to be confused with
democratic intent, it was designed to maximize the flow of information
to avoid the fatal public isolation of Zia's regime. Countering the growing
reach of Indian television channels in Pakistan, as became evident at the
time of the Kargil conflict, was another reason to relax controls on the
media. With General Musharraf above the law, the constitution in abeyance, and elected assemblies suspended but not dissolved—foreclosing
the prospect of elections within the prescribed ninety days—there was

no question that Pakistan was for all practical purposes under martial rule.

Like Zia, who capitalized on the cry of anti-Bhutto forces for "the system of the Prophet of Islam," Musharraf seized on the popular demand for "accountability." Giving credence to his regime's determination to wage war on corruption, Musharraf established a National Accountability Bureau (NAB) with power to send defaulters to jail for fourteen years and confiscate the assets of other offenders. Two days before the deadline set by Musharraf for the return of outstanding debts owed to the banks, the NAB announced its first catch of thieves. The list named 320 individuals, including several big fish like Nawaz Sharif, his younger brother, and other members of his family. Also named was Benazir Bhutto, who was in self-imposed exile in London to avoid serving a five-year term for a previous conviction. Anwar Saifullah, who conducted the accountability campaign under Nawaz Sharif, was among those arrested. Ordinary Pakistanis were delighted to see the high and mighty booked for their crimes. Musharraf had caught the pulse of a vocal section of the population disgusted with the sordid tales of corruption in state institutions.

Apart from corruption cases, the regime's other main propaganda card was the hijacking and kidnapping case against Nawaz Sharif. This sought to absolve the army's action and spotlight the machinations of a financially tainted and reckless politician. In his memoirs, Musharraf dismisses speculations that Nawaz Sharif's overthrow was preplanned by the army. The "countercoup" was prompted by the prime minister's inexplicable urge to "commit political suicide." Musharraf recounts instances of Sharif's imprudence and high-handedness, including an attempt to remove two major-generals whose loyalty Sharif suspected. Equally damning is the story of the illegal detention of the editor of the Lahore weekly *Friday Times,* Najam Sethi, whose searing critiques so rattled the Sharif brothers, they retaliated by framing him for treason.[12] It is difficult to sympathize with a politician who had brought about his own downfall for a third time in less than a decade. Nawaz Sharif's decision to fire the army chief before securing the loyalty of the corps commanders exposed his flawed judgment. A successful coup in Pakistan was impossible without the support of the Rawalpindi corps commander, whose 111th Infantry Brigade was responsible for the security of the president and the prime minister. At the time of the 1999 coup, the brigade was under the command of a Musharraf loyalist, Lieutenant General Mahmud Ahmed. Yet there was a familiar orchestrated ring to the propaganda unleashed against the former prime minister for his guilt in the hijacking of the PIA plane carrying Musharraf and 198 passengers from Colombo to Karachi.

In a high-profile courtroom drama, a special antiterrorism court headed by a civilian judge tried Nawaz Sharif and his co-accused on charges of treason for endangering the life of the army chief and other passengers by preventing the plane from landing at Karachi Airport. If proven guilty, the defendants could face the death penalty. Sharif's trial revived memories of another military era in which an elected prime minister was sentenced to death by hanging. There were calls for a fair trial from all over the world, with the Clinton administration appealing to the military junta to observe Nawaz Sharif's legal rights.[13] This became unlikely once Musharraf moved to confirm the judiciary's compliance. To preempt an adverse court decision, members of the superior judiciary were suddenly asked to take a fresh oath of office binding them to act in accordance with the proclamation of emergency and the PCO. The oath effectively made the judges subservient to the army chief instead of the constitution. In a sign of the judiciary's growing self-assertion, Chief Justice Saeeduzzaman Siddiqu refused to take the oath.

On April 6, 2000, a verdict of guilty was announced against the former prime minister by a judge who had taken the oath on the PCO. In view of the unusual circumstances surrounding the hijacking and terrorism charges, Nawaz Sharif was not given the death penalty but sentenced to two concurrent life terms, one for hijacking and the other for terrorism. The six co-accused were all acquitted. Sharif's lawyers filed an appeal while the prosecution asked for a reconsideration of the sentence on the grounds that a death penalty was more appropriate. Meanwhile, on May 12, a twelve-member bench of the Supreme Court, working under the constraints of the PCO, unanimously justified the military coup. The ruling gave Musharraf power to amend the constitution but, in a departure from previous rulings on the legality of military coups, set a time limit of three years for the regime to achieve its agenda.

Before the court could decide on Nawaz Sharif's appeal, hectic behind-the-scenes diplomatic activity took place between Islamabad and Riyadh that was overseen by Saad Hariri, the son of the Lebanese prime minister Rafiq Hariri. The Clinton administration is said to have facilitated the negotiations through Prince Bandar, the Saudi ambassador in Washington.[14] A deal was clinched that saw the former prime minister and seventeen members of his family flying off to Saudi Arabia in December 2000. The dramatic news stunned Pakistanis; they had seen some extraordinary twists in their politics, but this put the best writers of political thrillers into the shade. Pleading poor health, Nawaz Sharif forfeited more than $10 million of his property and accepted a period of extended disqualification from politics to go into opulent exile as a guest of the Saudi royal family. In preferring comfort to martyrdom, Nawaz Sharif was seen to have dishonored Pakistan, leaving his close associates unnerved and dejected. Musharraf's supporters were equally confused and disappointed. After announcing an uncompromising accountability drive, Pakistan's Mr. Clean had let the biggest fish off the hook.[15]

The contradictions between Musharraf's reformist objectives, his stolid embrace of the national security paradigm, and his simultaneous promise to restore "true democracy" based on thorough accountability were irresolvable. His dilemma was self-made. If he had wanted to reform the mess left by earlier governments, Musharraf could have used his overarching powers like any other military ruler. But he wanted to be a political player and, consequently, in trawling for support had to make compromises that severely damaged his credibility. The giddy hopes that had accompanied his ascent to power turned into muffled discontent. The pace of the promised reforms was slow and uneven. By September 2000, the well-respected NAB chairman, General Syed Mohammad Amjad, had been replaced, and the push for accountability had lost impetus. A well-advertised drive for deweaponization also had to be aborted, as was an attempt to reform the blasphemy law after religious hard-liners objected. Expecting the army to act quickly on the reform front, people were disheartened by the regime's inaction and retraction. There were murmurs for the restoration of democracy and, more forebodingly, statements by the Jamaat-i-Islami leadership that Pakistan should sever ties with America. By the end of his first year in office, most thinking people had lost faith in Musharraf's sincerity. He had neither halted sectarian killings nor stood up to the Islamist groups. Soaring inflation caused by rising oil prices had badly hurt consumers, particularly those living from hand to mouth. As the military regime moved to introduce a range of stringent measures demanded by the IMF to extend the country's fiscal resources, more and more people would come to blame Musharraf for their sufferings. The policy of selling public companies to private buyers put a squeeze on jobs. Unemployment and disenchantment was growing amid unabated sectarian killings, reversing the steps being taken to rejuvenate both the economy and national morale.

The failure that rankled most in the minds of moderate opinion was Musharraf's inability to restore Pakistan's image in the international community or normalize relations with its regional neighbors. It was not uncommon at the time to hear educated Pakistanis say that they were prepared to forgive Musharraf's coup if he put the economy back on track and made peace with India. But this required a complete strategic rethink of the national security paradigm, which did not suit the immediate purposes of the military command. Pakistan's pro-Taliban policy was an obstacle to reviving the country's global image. Relations with Tehran, which supported the Tajik and Uzbek–led Northern Alliance fighting the Pathan Taliban, had never been worse. More ominous was the Musharraf regime's continued support for militants fighting Indian security forces in Kashmir, which kept relations with New Delhi at an edge.

The two estranged nuclear neighbors had come to serious blows in the aftermath of the hijacking of an Indian Airlines plane on December 24, 1999, en route from Kathmandu to New Delhi. There were 175 passengers and eleven members of the crew on board. After stopping briefly in Amritsar, Lahore, and Dubai—where twenty-seven people were released in exchange for fuel and food—the plane landed in Kandahar—the power base of the Taliban leader Mullah Omar. The hijackers, who stabbed one passenger to death and left his body in Dubai, threatened to blow up the plane unless Maulana Masood Azhar, a Pakistani leader of the Kashmiri separatist group Harkat-ul-Mujahidin (HUM) who was imprisoned in India, was freed. They also wanted the release of thirty-five other prisoners, mostly Pakistanis, a ransom of $200 million, and the handover of the body of a slain Kashmiri separatist leader. In a first in the arena of global diplomacy, the Taliban mediated India's negotiations with the hijackers, who dropped their demands for ransom. In a humiliating setback, the BJP government in New Delhi agreed to exchange three high-security prisoners, including Masood Azhar, for the safe return of the plane and its passengers. The drama ended on New Year's Eve with the passengers and crew released and flown to New Delhi. The five hijackers and three released militants were given ten hours to leave Afghanistan, which they did by taking a Taliban member as hostage and releasing him after crossing the international border at Quetta.[16] Pakistan welcomed the end of the hijacking and praised the Taliban for their mature handling of a delicate situation. They had shown humanitarian concern for the passengers and demonstrated their opposition to terrorism.

An explicit call for an end to the international isolation of the Taliban was drowned by Indian accusations of Pakistan's involvement in the hijacking. New Delhi soon identified the five hijackers as members of the Harkat-ul-Ansar, an organization on the American list of terrorist organizations which had renamed itself HUM. Disclosing the ISI's links to the hijackers, the Indian home minister L. K. Advani accused Pakistan of engineering the hijacking, eliciting a sharp denial from Islamabad. In a statement in Karachi a few days later, Masood Azhar confirmed that he and the other two militants had crossed over to Pakistan. However, he refuted Indian claims that the hijackers were Pakistani, maintaining that they were Indian and had returned to India.[17] Azhar went on to launch a new militant organization, Jaish-i-Muhammad, which was directly involved in Kashmir. Pakistan narrowly escaped being declared a terrorist state by the United States after India presented detailed evidence of the ISI's complicity in the hijacking. Prime Minister Vajpayee was actively canvassing world leaders to name Pakistan a rogue state, and the Indian Army was conducting an elaborate military exercise called Vijay Chakra on the country's western border. But there was no smoking gun to establish that Musharraf's government had staged the hijacking.[18] American officials admitted that while they had no hard evidence to implicate Pakistan, there was no doubt that HUM had carried out the hijacking.[19] Indo-Pakistan relations remained in disrepair until the summer of 2001, when Prime Minister Vajpayee invited Musharraf for talks in Agra.

New Delhi's volte-face was attributed to gentle American prodding. Pakistan had drifted away from the US camp to such an extent that Musharraf had initially refused to have anything to do with the search for Osama bin Laden. "We have nothing to do with that issue," he had brusquely said at his first press conference, adding that the Taliban knew best what to do with Osama and the American demand.[20] While keeping channels open with the Americans, Musharraf remained uncooperative even after the hijacking incident led to an international outcry against Pakistan for harboring terrorists. He refused to ban HUM, fearing street demonstrations by Islamist parties, who would accuse him of selling out to America. Another reason for hesitation amid pressure from Washington to take action against HUM was its close connection with two of his most powerful generals—Lieutenant General Mohammed Aziz Khan, the chief of general staff; and Lieutenant General Mahmud Ahmed, DG of the ISI. Both men had been instrumental in the October 1999 coup, while General Aziz Khan, an inhabitant of Azad Kashmir, was a key player in the Kargil adventure. The Americans believed Musharraf was facing an internal challenge from Aziz Khan and Mahmud Ahmed.[21] It is unclear whether this was a planted impression. In the months to come, Musharraf would point to dangers from within the junta and Islamic militants to his own secular moderate position to gain some leverage with the United States. Washington's decision to refrain from adding Pakistan to the 1993 list of seven terrorist states—Cuba, Iran, Iraq, Libya, North Korea, Sudan, and Syria—gave Musharraf critical breathing space to consolidate his hold over the army and improve his chances of making a positive difference on the domestic front. He had successfully neutralized the opposition and was in the process of trying to build his own political base through the time-honored device of military regimes holding local body elections before those for the national and provincial assemblies.

President Clinton was scheduled to visit India in the spring of 2000, with brief forays into Pakistan and Bangladesh. The president's stop in Pakistan was put on hold, pending Islamabad's response to the American demand to rein in the militants, ease tensions with India, and restore democracy. A flurry of diplomatic activity led to Musharraf giving an assurance to cooperate with the United States on terrorism and nonproliferation. With senior administration officials in Washington advising engagement over diplomatic ostracism, Clinton came to Pakistan for four hours after being royally treated in India for five days. The American president's visit was an important milestone in the history of Indo-US relations. By comparison, his "doormat visit" to the erstwhile Cold War ally brought the formal distancing of the two countries out into the full glare of public scrutiny. There had been a militant attack on a Sikh village in Kashmir that left thirty-four dead while the president was being regaled in India. Clinton arrived clandestinely in a decoy plane after his personal plane landed at the military airport in Islamabad with a load of FBI men.

In a remarkable display of American security paranoia at outlandish expense, the US Secret Service occupied the Pakistani capital for the day. In the memorable words of Robert Fisk, the correspondent of the *Independent,* Islamabad was turned into "a city without a people in a country without a voice." Pakistanis were incensed at the ease with which their national capital had been taken over by American security agents. Fisk thought there was "something almost sinister about President Clinton's cortege, his long, sleek limousine swishing at 60 mph down the empty autobahn."[22]

Making for a sharp contrast to the adoring crowds that had greeted Clinton everywhere in India, the streets of Islamabad were empty. In a televised address to the people of Pakistan, a first by a foreign leader, the American president called for the restoration of democracy; a peaceful resolution of the Kashmir problem; the diversion of resources from nuclear and other military programs for development purposes; and a signing of the CTBT. Pakistanis could either continue to stir trouble in the region by sponsoring Islamist groups and court an economic collapse or ensure "economic security and peace." The climax of the speech came with a warning to Pakistanis of the comeuppance of people who try "redrawing borders with blood." What Clinton overlooked was that the problem in Kashmir was about not people trying to redraw borders with blood but the forcible imposition of borders where ties of blood spill across any artificially created frontiers. His solution to the Kashmir dispute of restraint, respect for the line of control, renunciation of violence, and renewal of talks with India left out the all-important fifth "R"—a resolution of this long-standing problem.[23]

Substantively, Clinton said nothing Pakistanis had not heard before. What they wanted was some reassurance from the leader of the most powerful nation on earth that redirecting energies to "regional peace" would bring Pakistan solid post–Cold War dividends. The new American agenda in the region, emphasizing stronger economic and strategic ties with India, seemed to leave them out of the reckoning. As some Pakistanis had feared, Clinton's touchdown in Pakistan only gave legitimacy to Musharraf and did not improve the chances of democracy being restored. In his meeting with the Pakistani leader, Clinton focused on Osama bin Laden and Al Qaeda's terror network. Musharraf, pressed by Clinton to use his influence on Mullah Omar to uncover bin Laden, promised to help

but warned that he could not afford to alienate the Taliban. Pakistan was
facing "so many threats" that it was "impossible to press this issue now."
Musharraf said he was "in a precarious position" and very overstretched.
The Americans offered him nothing "other than the blessing of a presidential visit, which he now had in his pocket."[24] In April 2000 the US State
Department's annual report assessing efforts to combat terrorism for the
first time identified South Asia as a major center of terrorism. Afghanistan and Pakistan were accused of providing safe haven to international
terrorist groups motivated by Islamic ideology and financed by drugs trafficking, crime, and illegal trade. While Afghanistan was not added to the
list of terrorist states because Washington did not recognize the Taliban
government, Pakistan was presented as "a friendly state that is trying to
tackle the problem."[25]

Sensing his opportunity, Musharraf considered visiting Kabul to personally deliver the American message on Osama bin Laden to the Taliban.
The DG of the ISI, General Mahmud, objected and advised sending the
interior minister Moinuddin Haider instead. With the Pakistani intelligence services thoroughly entangled with the Taliban, the search for bin
Laden threw up no fresh leads. Nor was there any lessening of Pakistani
involvement in Kashmir. In June 2000 a cease-fire declaration by the
Hizb-ul-Mujahidin, the largest militant organization in Kashmir and the
armed wing of the Jamaat-i-Islami, at the ISI's behest was withdrawn on
General Aziz's insistence.[26] Internal disagreements within the regime ensured that Musharraf's public condemnations of religious militancy made
little headway other than a crackdown on sectarian outfits that were undermining the regime's efforts to restore investor confidence. The Americans
considered the bearded General Aziz a danger and pressed for his removal. So Musharraf reshuffled the army command, appointing Aziz
corps commander of Lahore, by no means a demotion, and making Lieutenant General Mohammad Yusuf the chief of general staff.[27] In early
2001, Pakistan lost face when the Taliban ignored Islamabad's missives for
restraint and proceeded, to the horror of the entire world, to destroy the
Bamiyan Buddhas. Instead, Mullah Omar sent a letter to Musharraf urging him to enforce Islamic law in Pakistan. The limits of the army's control over the Taliban, however, can best be gleaned from the Taliban's emphatic refusal to concede the demand of their ISI handlers that they accept
the Durand Line as the international frontier with Pakistan.

If there was an upside to Clinton's visit, it was Islamabad's continued engagement with Washington, whose benefits materialized with the victory of George W. Bush in 2000. During the election campaign, the future American president could not remember Musharraf's name but ventured the opinion that the general was doing a good job in Pakistan. With a Republican administration in office, the question of Pakistan's democratic credentials was no longer an issue. The shift in Washington coincided with a thaw in relations between the two subcontinental neighbors. Pakistan's assistance in response to a devastating earthquake in Gujarat, and persistent American pressure, saw New Delhi softening its stance. A monthlong cease-fire announced by Prime Minister Vajpayee in November 2000 was extended after Pakistan ordered its troops to exercise restraint along the LOC. In keeping with Musharraf's stated concern for dialogue with India, Islamabad no longer insisted on being included in talks between New Delhi and the political leadership of Jammu and Kashmir.

On May 24, 2001, India invited Musharraf for talks, which he accepted. Days before leaving for the two-day summit in Agra between July 16 and 18, the general removed Tarar from office unceremoniously and elevated himself to the position of president. The more discerning among the Pakistani intelligentsia denounced the decision as unconstitutional. They could see that Musharraf was beginning to enjoy power a little too much. This brought a sharp retort from official circles. The general needed the presidential office to extract maximum advantage from his Indian visit. While Musharraf dazzled the Indian media with his capacity to talk endlessly, the seventh Indo-Pakistan summit in fifty years failed just like the others because neither side was prepared to make concessions that would require altering their respective national security paradigms. In a public relations exercise that hinted at GHQ's impress, the presidential entourage had a large representation of right-wing journalists known for their hard-line position on India. Their counterparts in India had a strong advocate in the government, the home minister L. K. Advani, who scuttled the agreement between Musharraf and Vajpayee. The summit ended without an anticipated joint declaration. But in the aftermath of the summit, India and Pakistan saw some wisdom in exerting more energy on resolving their differences through backdoor channels than engaging in counterproductive verbal warfare through the media.

A Changed World: The Aftermath of 9/11

Relations between the two nuclear neighbors were finely poised when the attacks of September 11, 2001, on America radically transformed the geopolitical situation. Washington's political pundits had already named South Asia "the most dangerous place in the world" and proceeded to paint hair-raising scenarios of a holocaust more deadly than any that had visited the planet. These recalled images of American and Soviet warheads descending like "burning stars" on the divided subcontinent in Manto's sardonic piece on the risks of nuclear warfare written in the early 1950s.[28] The only twist now was that Indian and Pakistani nuclear warheads threatened the unthinkable. After the attacks on the World Trade Center and the Pentagon, the looming dangers of war between India and Pakistan over Kashmir, far from receding into the background, assumed more dangerous proportions. After the failed summit at Agra, the two countries remained mired in mutual suspicion and recriminations over Kashmir. Prior to the tragic events of 9/11, there was some comfort in the knowledge that mutually assured destruction would deter any madness on the part of either of the two nuclearized countries. But with the United States itself touting the doctrine of preemptive action as a legitimate weapon of self-defense, none of the old certitudes about deterrence gave cause for equanimity.

Before the fires encircling the Twin Towers in New York had gone out, Pakistan had been catapulted to center stage of America's global policing enterprise for a second time in just over two decades. But there was a massive difference in context. The decision to join hands with America against the Soviet invasion of Afghanistan had the support of the army and the people, a combination that gave an unpopular military ruler the opportunity to buttress his position in power. More than two decades later, the Pakistani Army and its intelligence network were knee-deep with a Taliban regime in Kabul that was sheltering Osama bin Laden. Any successful American drive against Al Qaeda in Afghanistan required Pakistan's help. However, Washington was unsure whether the commando-turned-president would willingly alter his regime's pro-Taliban policy to bring bin Laden and his top associates to justice. Musharraf was in Karachi presiding over a meeting at the Governor's House when Secretary of State General Colin Powell called to convey President Bush's artless message:

"You are either with us or against us." Musharraf took it as an ultimatum, an impression General Mahmud Ahmed, who was in Washington at the time, confirmed. Richard Armitage, the deputy secretary of state, alleg-. edly told the DG of the ISI that if Pakistan opted for the terrorists, it "should be prepared to be bombed to the Stone Age."[29] Although denying he ever used these words, Armitage conceded that he resorted to strong language to convey the point to the Pakistani intelligence chief.[30]

Much speculation has surrounded Musharraf's decision to support America's ill-phrased "war on terror." According to him, he made his choice based on "self-interest and self-preservation" because "Pakistan always comes first." Not supporting America would unleash the fury of the world's sole superpower on Pakistan. "If we do not join them," Musharraf asked himself, "can we confront them and withstand the onslaught?" The answer was no. The Taliban were not worth destroying Pakistan. Their "misplaced messianic zeal," fired by "half baked, obscurantist clerics," went against the grain of the Islam practiced by the majority of Pakistanis.[31] These ennobling words written with the benefit of hindsight mask the resistance he had to overcome among his corps commanders to meet the US demands. "Trust me," Musharraf said on national television, while confirming that Americans had asked to use Pakistani air space and intelligence to locate Osama bin Laden. If the government did not cooperate with the Americans, India would exploit the situation and accelerate efforts to get Pakistan declared a terrorist state. New Delhi had already offered to let the United States use India's air bases for the expected strikes against Afghanistan. With Uzbekistan and Tajikistan dragging their feet on the question of assistance, Pakistan was by far the best choice as a staging ground for the American war. Musharraf's formal announcement to give the United States logistical support for a possible military thrust in Afghanistan provoked demonstrations by an array of Islamist groups operating under the aegis of the Pak-Afghan Defense Council in dozens of Pakistani cities calling for "jihad" against America. But they were nowhere near as massive or threatening in intent as the sound bites of Islamist narratives against US imperialism highlighted in the international media.

Kabul snubbed Islamabad by refusing to give up Osama. So choosing America over the Taliban was not too difficult. But rolling back the carpet the Pakistan military had itself laid out for all manner of religious

extremists at home was easier said than done. Having raised its bands of
Islamic extremists in pursuit of its regional security interests in Afghanistan and Kashmir and also domestically, the Pakistani military
establishment found itself in an impossible quandary. For all the skeptics,
the angry anti-American demonstrators, and the forked tongues charging
Musharraf with treachery, there were also other Pakistani voices who,
because they had seen their lives disrupted by sectarian strife, economic
stagnation, and endless political instability, saw the new alliance with the
United States as an opportunity to claw the country back from the jaws of
the religious nutcracker. Through the distorting eye of the media, the only
upholders of the American cause in Pakistan naturally appeared to be
baton-wielding police forces and armored vehicles.

That by joining Washington's "war on terror" they could be sacrificed
in the process was a very real fear for most Pakistanis. They had no love
for the Taliban, far less for Al Qaeda, but they seriously questioned America's reliability. A fourth US betrayal in a row seemed to be on the cards.
The other three betrayals occurred when the United States suspended
critical military assistance during the 1965 war; failed to prevent the disintegration of Pakistan in 1971; and then, following the Soviet withdrawal,
left Pakistan to wrestle alone with the problem of refugees, a parallel arms
and drugs economy, and, above all, the poisonous legacy of the Afghan
"jihad" in the form of religious zealotry.[32] Musharraf had a lot of convincing to do. Once sympathy for the September 11 attacks had been replaced
by revulsion at American carpet bombing of Afghanistan, even sections
of the liberal intelligentsia questioned the wisdom of allying with the
United States. For a country prone to conspiracy theories, the media was
rife with commentary refuting the American narrative on the 9/11 attacks.
Reports of Pakistanis being targeted in the United States by law agencies
fueled anger and fanned belief that the attacks on the World Trade Center
and the Pentagon were an inside job or an Israeli conspiracy to malign
Islam. Pakistan's negative profiling in the United States even after Musharraf had extended logistical help provoked a barbed reaction from one
columnist. Not a day went by when Washington did not threaten "punitive measures" against Pakistan. On days when no adverse statement was
forthcoming, some US think tank or the other published a report condemning Pakistan as the "worst of the worst," a phrase attributed to the
CIA.[33] More measured observers noted that as a victim of terrorism,

Pakistan needed to take a stand against transnational terrorist networks in its own interests and not simply as a derivative of American interests in the region.

Instead of welcoming its estranged neighbor's decision to turn over a new leaf, New Delhi resented Pakistan's elevation to the position of Washington's key strategic partner. The Indian media directly implicated Pakistan in the attacks on America. Based on an interview with a representative of the Northern Alliance, whose leader Ahmad Shah Massoud was assassinated two days before 9/11, the anti-Taliban Afghan opposition blamed the "Laden-Taliban-ISI triangle" for the attacks.[34] These charges embittered the public discourse in Pakistan, with hard-liners blasting India for its belligerence and rigidity on Kashmir. There could be no one-sided concessions to India on trade or Kashmir without a matching willingness on New Delhi's part to bury the hatchet. Pakistan's pro-Taliban policy had been predicated on the military acquiring strategic depth against India. That policy was now in shambles. The staggering impact of the 9/11 attacks on global politics had created a unique historical conjunction. A balanced understanding of subcontinental history, devoid of narrowly construed national strategic interests, might have started a fresh chapter in relations between the two regional rivals. With Indo-Afghan trade dependent on movement through Pakistani territory, there were powerful economic reasons for New Delhi to make it plain that it had no wish to aggravate Islamabad's security dilemmas by joining Afghanistan in a pincer movement—the ultimate nightmare of the Pakistani military establishment. In its eagerness to capitalize on Pakistan's discomfiture over its failed policy vis-à-vis the Taliban, especially the ISI's complicity in promoting terrorism in Afghanistan, India missed a unique opportunity to redefine the old and tired paradigm of Indo-Pakistani security perceptions.

The overthrow of the Taliban regime and the installation of a government headed by the Pakhtun leader Hamid Karzai flustered pro-Taliban elements in the Pakistani Army. Karzai had studied in India and initially supported the Taliban. After the Taliban assassinated his father in Quetta, in which he detected an ISI role, Karzai joined hands with Massoud's Northern Alliance. The DG of the ISI, General Mahmud Ahmed, spearheaded internal resistance to the official change of policy toward the Taliban. The ISI was a hub of pro-Taliban sentiments. Pakistani Army personnel

326 THE STRUGGLE FOR PAKISTAN

were fighting alongside the Taliban. As the Americans discovered to their surprise, Taliban resistance melted away the moment Musharraf ordered the withdrawal of their Pakistani handlers. Two days after America started cluster bombing the hapless Afghans, Musharraf ousted Mahmud as DG of the ISI. There have been allegations that the move became unavoidable once India supplied evidence to the Americans confirming links between the World Trade Center hijackers and the ISI chief. The go-between was Ahmad Omar Sheikh, a British national and a graduate of the London School of Economics, who was one of the three militants released by India after the Kandahar hijacking. Sheikh had allegedly wired $100,000 to Mohammad Atta, one of the nineteen hijackers, at the behest of the Pakistani spymaster.[35] Mahmud's removal did not end Musharraf's troubles. Several of the operatives maintained personal ties with the Taliban. General Hamid Gul, the voluble former DG of the ISI, lashed out at the United States for treating Pakistan's premier intelligence agency as "a mercenary force" to be "shared or rented out to other countries." American officials accepted that such attitudes were a result of the decade-long disruption in relations with the ISI in the aftermath of the Soviet withdrawal from Afghanistan. "You left us in the lurch," Shamshad Ahmad, Pakistani ambassador to the UN, said to the *New York Times,* with "an influx of refugees, the drug and gun running, a Kalashnikov culture."[36]

Being the least trustworthy nation in the world from the American perspective and an indispensable ally in the war of retribution in Afghanistan was a paradox that defies simplistic explanations. As American military officials would later admit, they could not expect Pakistanis to break ties with the Taliban they had cultivated as strategic assets for seven years. But operational cooperation from Pakistan had to be obtained in order to ensure a terrorist-free post-Taliban Afghanistan. So Washington lifted the sanctions imposed on Pakistan after Musharraf's coup and prepared a huge package worth billions of dollars of military and economic assistance as a reward for support against terrorism. Consisting of extensive debt rescheduling, grants extended over several years, and trade benefits, the Bush administration's package for Pakistan made it the third largest recipient of American aid after Israel and Egypt. There were other more remarkable inducements. On November 21, 2001, the United States halted airstrikes on Kunduz to allow Pakistan's military planes to airlift more than 1,000 Pakistani soldiers and agents who had been fighting alongside the Taliban and Al Qaeda in the besieged city. The ISI is known to have used the opportunity to fly out senior Al Qaeda members as well as Chechens, Uzbeks, and Afghans considered to be strategic assets.

Even as President Bush ritualistically lauded Pervez Musharraf for Pakistan's exemplary role in the "war on terror," the ISI was relocating the Taliban in parts of Balochistan and the federally administered tribal areas of the northwest. The Americans failed to capture Osama bin Laden, who escaped from the Tora Bora mountains into FATA. There bin Laden and his entourage bought refuge in exchange for substantial sums of money. The emergence of Pakistan's northwestern tribal borderlands as terrorism central introduced a deadly new strain into the situation that was to come back to haunt Musharraf.[37] Ignoring the official change of policy, the ISI stiffly rejected the need for a paradigm shift in their strategic doctrine. Incensed by India's close ties with Hamid Karzai's government, they distrusted America, which would eventually have to quit Afghanistan, leaving Pakistan to deal with the dregs of war. This placed Musharraf in a Catch-22. He could not alienate the army, far less the ISI. So he struck the devil's bargain. While handing over Arab members of Al Qaeda to the Americans, the ISI unofficially continued supporting the Afghan Taliban through a "rogue" network of former employees and personnel of the army and the Frontier Constabulary. There was no question of abandoning the policy in Kashmir. So while taking steps to clamp down on sectarian groups, Musharraf turned a blind eye toward militant organizations like the Lashkar-i-Tayyiba that were fighting in Kashmir. He was more straightforward when it came to arresting politicians. Maulana Fazlur Rahman, the leader of the pro-Taliban Deobandi JUI-F, and Qazi Hussain Ahmad of the Jamaat-i-Islami were hurled into jail on charges of inciting mutiny in the armed forces.

The inherent incompatibility between Musharraf's cooperation in the "war on terror" and support for the Afghan Taliban and militant groups fighting in Kashmir was soon exposed. Just as he appeared to be digging in his heels to break the military–mullah nexus, relations with India took a critical turn for the worse. On December 13, 2001, five heavily armed militants attacked the Indian Parliament in New Delhi. None of the elected members were harmed. In a grim half-hour battle outside the hastily closed doors of the Indian Parliament, twelve people were killed, including the militants, and eighteen suffered injury. Pakistan promptly condemned the attacks. Suspicions fell on the Lashkar-i-Tayyiba and Jaish-i-Muhammad, the two Al Qaeda–linked Pakistani militant groups fighting in Kashmir. The attack was similar to the one on the Jammu and Kashmir legislative assembly two and half months earlier for which the Jaish had claimed responsibility. Although India did not initially link Pakistan with the attacks, the setback to American efforts at balancing the two nuclear neighbors in the interests of the war in Afghanistan was all too apparent. Washington responded by increasing pressure on Musharraf to accelerate the process of curbing extremism. India reacted by amassing troops on its western border, forcing Pakistan to consider pulling its forces along the border with Afghanistan—just what Al Qaeda and its associates wanted.

The US need for Pakistan's operational support for the war in Afghanistan averted the possibility of armed conflict between the two nuclear powers in the subcontinent. India backed off, allowing Musharraf to continue his high-wire act. The American view of the situation was well summed up by a *New York Times* correspondent in a story headlined "U.S. Interests Trump Hypocrisy on Pakistan." After so many wrong steps in its history, Pakistan had taken "a right one." But it was faced with "maximum danger" and had to curb the homegrown terrorist networks to forestall the threat posed by battle-hardened pro-Taliban Pakistanis returning from Afghanistan. Under the circumstances, "whatever the stench of blood in Islamabad, we Americans must hold our noses and do all we can to help General Musharraf hold his course."[38]

Musharraf First!

Presenting himself as the final frontier between "enlightened moderation" and "Talibanization," the spunky commando who had a taken a shine to the media turned his full attention to using it successfully to prolong his stay in power. Taking full advantage of the shift in the geostrategic situation and his newfound rapport with the Americans, he moved to consolidate his position as president in the well-trodden path of military dictators. Facing intense internal and external pressure, Musharraf had accepted the Supreme Court's ruling setting a time limit for his regime and announced elections in early October 2002. After consulting the military manual on how to rule Pakistan, he called local body elections before those for the national and provincial assemblies. Only candidates cleared by the military were permitted to contest. The ISI handpicked candidates for the position of Nazim (mayor) in the more sensitive districts. The military regime's devolution plan, ending a 150-year-old scheme of local government, threw an already compromised system of district administration into confusion.

General Musharraf's intention to reinvent himself as a politician had been clear ever since Nawaz Sharif's surprise exile to Saudi Arabia. Determined to prevent the two main political parties from returning to power, in January 2002 he banned political parties from electing a leader for more than three terms. His target was Benazir Bhutto, who had been elected leader for life four years earlier. Intent on ruling Pakistan, Musharraf decided to hold a national referendum in late April 2002 seeking an extension of his term as president for five years. Lawyers denounced the referendum idea as unconstitutional as presidential elections could not bypass Parliament. Musharraf kicked off a twenty-city whistle stop tour in Lahore at the Minar-i-Pakistan (Tower of Pakistan), where the Muslim League had adopted the resolution that came to be known as the "Pakistan demand." Pakistanis had to decide on referendum day "whether you want to give Pakistan back into the hands of the same looters."[39]

The referendum was a blot on the general's otherwise well managed self-promotion campaign. According to official figures, which were hotly disputed, the referendum resulted in a high turnout and a 97 percent "yes" vote. The political wing of the ISI had stuffed the ballot boxes and ordered government servants to vote. An embarrassed Musharraf publicly apologized for the rigging and shifted the blame for the fiasco onto the head of the ISI's political wing, Major-General Ehtesham Zamir, who had suggested the idea of a referendum. The truth was different. Musharraf knew that a future Parliament could very well refuse to support the amendments he had made to the constitution to validate his actions. This would leave him in a precarious position, possibly facing charges of treason. The referendum had delivered him a pyrrhic victory. He was now embroiled in a personal struggle for survival, a course that only pulled him deeper into the quicksand of Pakistani politics.

With the PCO-bound judiciary and the White House on his side, Musharraf marched ahead to safeguard his position against any potential electoral gains by the opposition parties. On August 21, 2002, a Legal

General Pervez Musharraf. *The White Star Photo Pvt. Ltd. Archive.*

Framework Order (LFO) was issued containing a succession of highly controversial amendments on which the general had solicited public opinion in July. Led by the legal community, there was impassioned opposition to the proposed amendments. Unfazed, Musharraf restored the Eighth Amendment, giving him power as president to dissolve an elected assembly. He predictably also extended his term in office, assumed the power to appoint judges of the Supreme Court, and, most contentiously, gave the military a formal role in governing the country. A clause was added to the constitution providing for the establishment of a National Security Council (NSC) that effectively institutionalized civilian subordination to military authority. An unabashed move to perpetuate himself in office, it was justified by Musharraf on the grounds that the army had to be brought into the political system in order to keep it out. No one was convinced beyond his immediate circle of advisors. It was precisely because the military had never been out of the political system that Pakistan was in such a state of disrepair.

Loudly protesting Musharraf's daylight assault on democracy, the main opposition parties began preparing for the October elections in earnest. Benazir got herself reelected as PPP leader, but there was a ban on parties whose office holders had been convicted and so a new party called the Pakistan People's Party Parliamentarians (PPPP) was formed. The PML-N selected Shahbaz Sharif, Nawaz's younger brother and former chief minister of Punjab, as leader. In September 2002, Nawaz officially withdrew his candidacy in an expression of solidarity with Benazir. By putting both Nawaz and Benazir out of the reckoning, Musharraf had won half the battle before a single ballot had been cast. Extraordinary steps were taken to tilt the electoral system against the two mainstream parties. Electoral constituencies were delimited so that fewer votes fetched more seats, benefiting smaller and Islamist parties that could be made to support the regime. Legislative candidates were required to possess a bachelor's degree—an astonishing provision in a country with one of the lowest literacy rates in the world. In a major concession to Islamist parties, madrasa graduates were deemed to meet the degree qualification. Candidates were required to disclose their financial records, attest to Jinnah's declaration of Pakistan as a democratic state based on Islamic principles of social justice, and, to confuse matters, also commit themselves to upholding the country's sovereignty and Islamic ideology.

The regime's social engineering prior to the polling date on October 10, 2002, gave an electorate of 72 million a very limited right of choice. Regardless of how the votes were cast, the authoritarian system would remain intact, with President Musharraf and the Pakistani Army calling the shots through the NSC. Preelectoral maneuvering and ballot rigging, all under the watchful eye of the ISI's political wing, threw up a divided Parliament—a perfect recipe for giving military rule a civilian face and continuing with much-needed reforms, especially on the economic front. With a few exceptions, all the politicians Musharraf had been vilifying as corrupt were back in Parliament. A breakaway faction of the PML-N took the acronym PML-Q for Quaid-i-Azam and became the king's party. As expected, the PML-Q won the largest number of seats, but with seventy-seven members in an assembly of 272, it did not have the numbers to form a government on its own. PPPP with sixty-two seats came second and resurrected itself in Punjab by winning sixty-three seats in the provincial assembly, a remarkable achievement for a party the ISI had done so much to undermine. The main beneficiary of the regime's preelectoral manipulations was the Muttahida Majlis-e-Amal (MMA), an alliance of six Islamist parties, which secured forty-five seats. It was the biggest ever electoral victory for religio-political parties, ironically under a military ruler who had recently jailed two of the top leaders of the MMA for sedition. The PML-N was the biggest loser in Musharraf's electoral game, mustering only fourteen seats in Parliament and being reduced to a rump in its power base of Punjab, where the PML-Q won an absolute majority.

With the election results pointing to a coalition government at the center in which the Islamist parties would have substantial influence, there was renewed concern in Washington about extremists gaining control of nuclear Pakistan. In February 2002, Daniel Pearl, the *Wall Street Journal*'s correspondent in Mumbai, had been abducted in Karachi while he was investigating links between Richard Reid, the "shoe bomber," and Al Qaeda. After a tortuous ordeal, militants working under the notorious Ahmad Omar Sheikh beheaded Pearl. In July 2002, Sheikh was sentenced to death by hanging. The sentence has yet to be carried out. After Pearl's brutal murder, Pakistan's negative image took a turn for the worse. Slating the administration for propping up a country that had given nuclear technology and possibly uranium to North Korea, a columnist of the *Washington Post* labeled Pakistan the "most dangerous place on earth" and the "base from which nuclear technology, fundamentalist terrorism and life-destroying heroin are spread around the globe."[40] Having fallen into the habit of defending Pakistan's embattled president since September 11, officials of the Bush administration welcomed the 2002 elections as a milestone in an ongoing transition to democracy. The European Union's observers took the opposite view, dismissing the elections as a farce not worth anyone's democratic salt. While there were good reasons to question the democratic character of the elections, what really concerned European capitals were the implications of a pro-Taliban government in Pakistan for the US-led NATO war in Afghanistan, and particularly in the NWFP, where the MMA won an emphatic victory.

Those accustomed to instantaneous modes of analyzing contemporary politics attributed the victory of pro-Taliban parties to the wave of anti-Americanism sweeping Pakistan. A more historically grounded analysis of the 2002 elections, however, only confirmed the giddy fluidity of Pakistani politics and the many surprises they were capable of throwing up. The MMA's feat has to be seen in perspective. It was only during the 1970 elections that the religio-political parties showed any spread of support. With Yahya Khan's regime playing the Islamic card, they together polled 22 percent of the popular vote but were too divided to translate the gains into healthy seat tallies in the national assembly. While the ISI had now resolved that difficulty, the MMA's total share of the popular vote was still negligible. This meant that the MMA with about 11.1 percent of the popular vote and tribal representatives from FATA, who invariably voted for the government of the day, held fifty-two seats in the national assembly. The PML-N, with a slightly larger vote bank of 11.23 percent, had fourteen. Ironically, it was the PPPP, the lone party supporting Musharraf's pro-American policies, that won the highest number of popular votes, 25.01 percent, with the PML-Q trailing at 24.81 percent. After the inclusion of reserved seats, the MMA's seat count increased to fifty-nine; the PML-N's to eighteen; the PPPP's to eighty with the PML-Q commanding the lion's share of 118 seats in an assembly of 342.[41]

An overemphasis on ideological factors and the anti-Americanism of the Pakistani electorate misses the point. The ideological split was underplayed in the 2002 elections with all the parties—including the PML-Q—making a big play of putting an end to military rule and restoring democracy. Taking advantage of pro-Taliban sentiments among Pathans in

NWFP and Balochistan, the MMA did invoke the divine writ and pronounced hellfire on Musharraf for letting American troops on Pakistani
soil. The lesser fry in the six-party alliance celebrated victory by championing a variety of Islamic causes, such as banning cable television and
music, closing down video stores, making the hijab compulsory, and dismantling coeducational institutions. But despite its good showing in national and provincial elections, the MMA's success had not ushered in an
Islamic revolution to justify writing off Pakistan as a moderate and responsible member in the international comity of nations. At the same
time, there was no reason to be overly sanguine about the consequences of
the MMA's success. With their strength well reflected in the Senate, the
Islamists would now press for the passage of a series of retrograde pieces
of social legislation targeting women and minorities.

It was in some ways an ideal outcome for Musharraf. He could now
point to the MMA's strength in a divided Parliament to resist American
pressure for unilateral action on the foreign policy front. His only difficulty was that the newly elected opposition members of Parliament were
dead set against approving the 297 ordinances he had issued in the last
three years. So the regime opened negotiations with the MMA and after
almost a year of tough bargaining won over enough of its members with
promises and inducements to help Musharraf extend his term as president
until 2007. In the meanwhile, a fragile coalition government led by the
PML-Q and dissident members of the MMA was established. It took in-
tensive horse-trading by the ISI acting in unison with the accountability
bureau, NAB, to tear away enough opposition parliamentarians to secure
the election of the PML-Q's Zafrullah Jamali as Pakistan's first Baloch
prime minister. The NAB withdrew charges against members of Parliament crossing over to the government side, driving another nail into the
coffin of the regime's anticorruption campaign. In December 2003, in exchange for Musharraf agreeing to seek a parliamentary vote of confidence
in his presidency and resigning as chief of army staff by December 2004,
the MMA accepted an amended version of the Seventeenth Amendment
Bill. This gave retrospective validity to Musharraf's actions after the coup
and effectively reenacted the reviled Eighth Amendment.

In January 2004, after securing a vote of confidence, Musharraf moved
to further entrench the military's role in politics. Amid wails of protest
from opposition benches, Parliament in April reversed a long-standing

political consensus against institutionalizing the military's role in politics by approving the creation of the NSC. The NSC was structured to guarantee presidential control of its proceedings and decisions. Musharraf's consolidation of power was matched by growing authoritarianism, making a travesty of his claims to be establishing a real democracy. At the end of 2004, he reneged on his promise to relinquish the post of army chief, making it the cause célèbre of Pakistani politics. Musharraf was ridiculed for his attachment to the military uniform and dubbed Busharraf. The more wicked coined cheeky jibes, including one based on a hugely popular Hindi film song "Choli ke Peechay Kyaa Hae" (What's Behind the Blouse), inquiring what the general was hiding behind his uniform. Even the otherwise obliging Prime Minister Jamali was driven to criticize the military's role in politics, leading to his unexpected resignation in July 2004. Chaudhry Shujaat Hussain, leader of the PML-Q, was appointed as an interim successor until the election of the finance minister, Shaukat Aziz, to the national assembly. Despite an opposition boycott, the Citibank executive, whom the wits promptly nicknamed Shortcut Aziz, was sworn in as the new prime minister and told to retain the finance portfolio.

No amount of tampering with the constitution and the electoral system could release Musharraf from the dangers of religious extremism, which showed no signs of abating. There were growing incidents of sectarian violence by Sunni militant groups, protesting Pakistan's alliance with the United States. The regime's crackdown on sectarian groups failed because they were intrinsically linked with the militant networks cultivated by the ISI over the past two decades in pursuit of the army's strategic doctrine in the region. In December 2003, Musharraf twice narrowly escaped assassination attempts in Rawalpindi, raising questions about police and army personnel helping the militants. He survived three more attempts on his life, grimly reminding the citizenry that no one in Pakistan was completely safe. The attacks were connected with Musharraf's overtures to India on Kashmir, which inflamed not only the militants and his own army but also many ordinary Pakistanis, who thought it amounted to a national betrayal. Living dangerously may have come easily for a commando, but his willful disfiguration of the constitution to plant a khaki democracy was even more liable to implosion than the controlled democracy of General Ayub Khan.

An Impossible Balancing Act

Once the Americans attacked Iraq in March 2003 and lowered their perception of the threat emanating from Afghanistan, the ISI had little difficulty persuading Musharraf that the country's self-interest lay in keeping
lines of communication open with the Taliban. Contacts were also revived
with some of the ISI's former allies among the Afghan warlords. Several
Al Qaeda operatives were handed over to the Americans, but not the elusive Osama bin Laden. Musharraf's response to American iterations to do
more was to point to India's growing entanglement in Afghanistan and
the menace this posed for an already delicate situation in the NWFP and
Balochistan. He urged Washington to use its influence on New Delhi to
help resolve the Kashmir dispute in return for abandoning support for
militants fighting Indian security forces in the valley. For this ploy to
work, both the Americans and the Indians needed hard evidence of his
ability to deliver. So Musharraf ordered the ISI to stop pushing militants
into Kashmir, enraging his army and right-wing opinion in Pakistan,
most notably in Punjab, where there was substantial support for the
Lashkar-i-Tayyiba's Kashmir operations among small traders and shopkeepers. In a first for a Pakistani leader, Musharraf also indicated that he
was prepared to drop the official insistence on the implementation of UN
resolutions on Kashmir if alternative solutions acceptable to all parties
could be found.

In late 2003, India reciprocated by publicly admitting that the rate of
militant cross-border incursions into Jammu and Kashmir had declined
considerably. The softening of tone between the two neighbors set the
stage for talks between Musharraf and Vajpayee in January 2004 at an
unexpectedly productive meeting of the SAARC in Islamabad. In a joint
declaration, the two countries undertook to start a "composite dialogue"
to settle all outstanding bilateral issues through regularly scheduled meetings related to various issues, including Kashmir. Musharraf's readiness
to address outstanding matters between the two countries without insisting on the prior resolution of the Kashmir conflict drew the fire of the
opposition parties, who attributed the stance to American influence. Even
liberals were suspicious of Musharraf's unilateral proposals and joined
the MMA in calling for matching concessions from India. Kashmir as
ever was a Janus-faced issue in Pakistani politics and public discourse.
Peace with India based on a political solution acceptable to Kashmiris

had now replaced the popular demand that Kashmir be handed over to Pakistan.

Relations between India and Pakistan continued to improve despite the unsettled nature of the situation in Kashmir. The two sides held talks on a proposed gas pipeline between Iran, Pakistan, and India in the face of strong US opposition. They also discussed the distribution of irrigation water, an issue inextricably linked to Kashmir. The US–India nuclear co-operation agreement in June 2005 delivered a clear message. If Pakistan continued to cooperate with America and made peace with India, it too might one day be rewarded with the generous technological and economic concessions given to its premier enemy. As a confidence-building measure, the border of divided Kashmir was opened to bus services and civilian traffic in April 2005. This affirmation of Indian prime minister Manmohan Singh's vision of making borders that cannot be changed irrelevant was disrupted in October after a massive earthquake devastated Kashmir and parts of northern Pakistan. The bus service was not restored, indication of the resistance within Indian and Pakistani officialdom to the idea of porous borders in Kashmir. This played into the hands of militants associated with Al Qaeda, who wanted to push India and Pakistan into a war in order to relieve pressures on their activities on the western front with Afghanistan.

In July 2006, seven bomb blasts on trains in Mumbai killed more than 200 people and injured several hundreds. The city police blamed the Lashkar-i-Tayyiba and the Students Islamic Movement of India for the attacks. With America advising restraint, the Mumbai bombings did not prevent Manmohan from holding private talks with Musharraf in September during the Non-Aligned Movement Summit in Havana. These exchanges produced nothing substantive by way of a breakthrough on any issue, though there was some welcome positive rhetoric on Kashmir from both sides. At a practical level, Pakistan moved to improve trade with India and to facilitate exchanges between business groups in both countries. It also continued to eagerly work to find agreement on the Iran–Pakistan–India gas pipeline but met with a reversal when Washington prevailed on New Delhi to replace the minister of petroleum Mani Shankar Aiyar, who was a strong advocate of the proposed project.

While getting in stride with India, Musharraf continued to slip on the domestic front. Dependent on the MMA's support, he could not surmount their determined opposition to reform the madrasas, with the result that

sectarian strife remained unchecked. An underpaid and demoralized police force made itself conspicuous by its absence from the crime scene at
the wrong time. No such leniency was in evidence when it came to human
rights organizations. In May 2005, a gutsy display of solidarity for women
victims of violence at a symbolic mixed-gender marathon in Lahore called
by the internationally acclaimed human rights activist Asma Jahangir was
attacked by the police. While silencing the liberal and moderate voices he
was purportedly saving from the extremists, Musharraf was turning a
blind eye on the activities of militant groups nestled with Al Qaeda in the
wilds of FATA. If additional proof was needed of his failure to practice
what he preached, power was conceded to tribal leaders in Balochistan
when the cause of a moderate democratic Pakistan demanded strengthening the educated middle classes in the province. Far from showing
"enlightened moderation," Musharraf agreed to let conservative and patriarchal village *panchayats* (local governments) wield enormous power
to the grave detriment of rural women all over Pakistan. When a calami-
tous earthquake killed 73,000 and left millions homeless in northern
Pakistan, civil society relief organizations were relegated to the sidelines
in favor of relief operations carried out by the Lashkar-i-Tayyiba and the
army.

In playing both sides of a risky political game, Musharraf was running
out of allies. The king's party could not halt his plummeting popularity.
Furious with him for breaking his solemn pledge to give up his uniform,
the MMA refused to have any truck with the regime. Neither did the two
mainstream parties whose exiled leaders instead signed a charter of democracy in London in May 2006 demanding the restoration of the 1973
constitution. While criticizing Musharraf on every front, including his
handling of relations with India, Nawaz Sharif and Benazir Bhutto were
careful to express their support for the alliance with America. The PPP
leader was particularly vocal in condemning religious extremism. From
the American viewpoint, Musharraf needed to be rescued from the pack
of killjoy clerics, who were instituting their brand of Islam in the NWFP
and giving vent to the "Talibanization" of a strategically vital region. So a
channel of communication was established between Benazir and Musharraf to work out a power-sharing arrangement that was applauded and
condemned in a Pakistani media reflecting the political polarization in
the country.

The July 2005 bombings in London gave Musharraf the pretext to apprehend 300 militants in Pakistan in defiance of the MMA's call for nationwide protests. In the next twelve months, there was a sharp rise in violence across Pakistan. Apart from attacks on the central government and American installations by militants, there was a heightening of sectarian tensions. Christians were periodically targeted. Intertribal rivalries in the NWFP and Balochistan fostered by government agents had morphed into a full-blown insurgency. In Balochistan, tribes opposed to the central government's military encroachments attacked public installations and murdered three Chinese working on the government-initiated development of the Balochi port of Gwadar, as a gateway to Afghanistan and Central Asia. The foundation for the construction of a deep seaport at Gwadar, described as China's "pearl in Pakistani waters," was laid shortly after 9/11 and the arrival of US forces in Afghanistan. Balochi nationalists resented being overlooked in the deal and were enraged by the sale of prime real estate in Gwadar to military and civil officials and their friends among wealthy Pakistanis in other parts of the country. The situation deteriorated alarmingly in August 2006, when Nawab Akbar Bugti, the leader of the Bugti tribe and a former governor of the province, was killed in a clash with government forces. There was a spontaneous burst of strikes and civil unrest in Balochistan and an explosion of condemnation across Pakistan. Musharraf poured salt on the wounds by congratulating the secret intelligence chief who carried out the ground and aerial operation. In December 2005, Musharraf had survived a rocket attack when he visited the Bugti areas. Rockets were also fired at the location where he was staying in Quetta. Akbar Bugti's death marked the beginnings of an insurgency in Balochistan led by his grandson, Brahamdagh Khan Bugti, from exile in Kabul. Musharraf's warning to the Baloch insurgents—"don't press us," or "you won't even know what has hit you"—invoked the rhetoric of another military regime in 1971.

If Balochistan was spinning out of control, tens of thousands of army personnel in search of Al Qaeda fighters were regularly fighting pro-Taliban militants in the autonomous northwestern tribal areas. The army was unwilling to fight its people. Demonstrating a lack of resolve, if not actual weakness, Musharraf in September 2005 sanctioned an agreement with militants in North Waziristan, reducing the Pakistani military presence there in exchange for an end to cross-border movement and attacks on government forces. Washington reacted to the Waziristan Accord, as the agreement came to be known, with great consternation. Islamabad had been making similar agreements with tribal militants since 2004. Not only were these easily broken, but they had also given the militants time to regroup and give the army a bloodier nose. In the meantime, the traffic across the border continued to threaten the US-led NATO forces in Afghanistan. Some American officials privately suspected Musharraf of furtively siding with elements waging war against US forces in Afghanistan. His unbending stance toward Baloch nationalists and velvet glove approach toward wayward Pathan tribesmen in league with Al Qaeda is explicable only if seen from the army's perspective. Making for a contrast with his inflexible attitude toward the Baloch, Musharraf was all for appeasing the Pathans. Apart from their strategic importance for the war in Afghanistan, Pathans, unlike the Baloch, were well represented in the army.

Consequently, Balochistan remained a festering sore throughout the remaining years of Musharraf's rule. The graph of violence across Pakistan began rising after the end of 2006 before hitting a new peak in mid-2007 with a series of suicide bombing attacks. A disquieting new trend was the spread of sectarianism in the federally administered northern areas (FANA) of Gilgit and Baltistan, which had long been denied autonomy and basic political rights. The military's on-again, off-again operations in FATA incensed Kabul and led to Washington strongly admonishing Musharraf for failing to stop the tribal militants from conducting their pro-Taliban operations in Afghanistan. Village councils with the tacit approval of the regime pronounced death on a thousand women in 2006–7 in the name of "honor killings," sending tremors throughout the world at the prospect of Pakistan's sliding into a Taliban style of government. Musharraf cut a sorry figure internationally when he defended his regime's stance on Mukhtaran Mai, a thirty-three-year-old gang-raped victim of an honor vendetta ordered by a village council in 2002. She contacted human rights groups and spoke out against the rapists. Irritated by the international publicity given to the case, Musharraf said in an interview to the *Washington Post* in September 2005 that "A lot of people say if you want to go abroad and get a visa for Canada or citizenship and be a millionaire, get yourself raped." He denied making the remark, but audiotapes of the interview established otherwise.[42]

Musharraf's attempts to ride two horses at the same time severely damaged his international credibility just as his domestic authority was under challenge from an array of forces. This added to the sense of opportunity among those emboldened by years of ISI direction and beneficence. The Lal Masjid in the heart of the nation's capital had been a nucleus of militant traffic ever since the war against the Soviets. Built in 1965, the expansive mosque-seminary complex—named after its red walls and interior—was headed by Maulana Muhammad Abdullah, a close associate of General Zia-ul-Haq. With thousands of seminary students and a vast clientele that included influential political personalities, both civil and military, the Lal Masjid exerted enormous influence. After Abdullah's assassination in 1998, his two sons, Abdul Aziz Ghazi and Abdul Rashid Ghazi, took control of the mosque and turned it into a fount of opposition to the government. In 2006, Abdul Aziz issued a fatwa stating that army personnel fighting the Taliban would be denied a Muslim burial. The Lal Masjid administration published fifty preliminary guidelines for the enforcement of the sharia in Pakistan.[43] Abdul Aziz threatened to let loose a brigade of suicide bombers if the government impeded the imposition of the sharia. In an open revolt against the government, the two brothers formed a cultural police brigade. Stick-wielding burka-clad women belonging to the Lal Masjid's Jamia Hafsa joined students at the adjacent men's seminary to threaten ordinary citizens with hellfire.

The situation boiled over in June 2007, when students at Lal Masjid took seven Chinese and two Pakistanis hostage from a massage parlor and accused them of running a brothel. Similar incidents had occurred over the past several months without any response from the government. On this occasion, the government acted swiftly to avoid a diplomatic incident. The Chinese were released, but Musharraf's international standing was left badly tarnished. If he could not control extremism in his own capital, how could he combat terrorists in the northwestern badlands? There was uproar against governmental inaction that the electronic media exploited to its advantage. By the time Musharraf came around to ordering an army operation, the entire country was transfixed by the Lal Masjid drama unfolding on their television screens. In a bizarre twist that lent symbolism to the bitter standoff, Abdul Aziz Ghazi was caught escaping in a burka on candid camera. Televisions channels competed with one another to provide equally exciting newsbreaks. Abdul Rashid Ghazi was heard speaking to a senior government official on television while the siege was under way. The reassertion of state power was brutal, leaving nearly 200 dead, including Abdul Rashid, who was prevented from surrendering by his followers. In an about-face, the media that had been clamoring for state action against the Lal Masjid nuisance now accused the government of atrocities. This shift in tone occurred when several news channels gave live coverage to Rashid's funeral as they would a national hero. Far from bolstering Musharraf's regime, the Lal Masjid episode led to a distinct worsening of the security situation. An intensification of anti-government feelings among pro-Taliban and radical quarters led to retaliatory attacks in Islamabad, the NWFP, and other parts of the country.

Abrupt shifts in mood were not untypical of a country that was wrestling with religious extremism and military authoritarianism. As the ides of March approached, Musharraf was increasingly worried about his presidential term ending in the fall of 2007. So he decided to get rid of Chief Justice Iftikhar Mohammad Chaudhry, who seemed unlikely to approve his second term as president. On March 9, 2007, Justice Chaudhry was summoned to Army House in Rawalpindi and in the presence of five army generals, including the DG of the ISI, General Ashfaq Parvez Kayani, asked to resign. In a first for Pakistan's jaded judicial history, the chief justice refused and so was dismissed on charges of misconduct. Chaudhry had irked the regime with his independent stand on several cases, including human rights violations in Balochistan and a petition against the privatization of the Karachi Steel Mills that implicated Prime Minister Shaukat Aziz. Bar associations across Pakistan erupted in nationwide protests and were backed by opposition parties and civil society groups, demanding the restoration of the chief justice. The decades-old tradition of democratic protest against military authoritarianism in Pakistan proved to be alive and well.

News reports throughout the world showed, instead of gun-wielding militants, endless lines of black-coated lawyers, men and women, protesting the assault on the judiciary. Against the battle-scarred urban landscape of Karachi, the lawyers' movement clashed with government supporters on May 12, 2007, resulting in the death of forty-one people. There was outrage at what was seen as a deliberate attempt by Musharraf to use the MQM, with whom he had forged an alliance in December 2003, to foil the lawyers' movement for the independence of the judiciary. At the rudder of a sinking ship, Musharraf had responded as the dictator he really was rather than the honest democrat he pretended to be. In a series of poorly thought-out moves, his government suppressed the media by invoking the Pakistan Electronic Media Regulatory Authority (PEMRA) Ordinance of June 2007. Under the ordinance, the government could take unilateral action against television channels, confiscate their broadcasting equipment, and seal the premises. Aimed at pricking the bubble of the lawyers' movement, which key media houses were actively supporting, these measures were immediately contested in the courts. The government had referred the case against Chaudhry to the Supreme Judicial Council, which in July ruled the suspension unconstitutional and reinstated the chief justice.

With Musharraf in serious trouble, the media was rife with speculation about the possible return of Benazir Bhutto and Nawaz Sharif. In August 2007, the Supreme Court ruled that Sharif was entitled to return, regardless of the terms of his exile. When the former prime minister arrived in Islamabad the next month with a party of jubilant supporters, he was summarily sent back to Saudi Arabia by the government. As was now becoming the norm in Musharraf's Pakistan, a legal challenge was filed against the deportation. Benazir stood a better chance of being permitted to stay in Pakistan because she was negotiating with the regime. Despite misgivings in PPP circles in Pakistan, she was prepared to cooperate with Musharraf if he resigned as army chief and withdrew corruption charges against her and key associates. Musharraf needed the PPP's tacit support, not their leader's obtrusive presence. So on October 5, 2007, he passed a controversial National Reconciliation Ordinance (NRO), granting Benazir and other politicians immunity from prosecution under charges brought against them between 1986 and 1999. The next day Musharraf was resoundingly reelected president for another term by outgoing assemblies at the center and the provinces. Lending a semblance of legitimacy to an otherwise sham presidential election, the PPPP abstained from voting instead of joining the opposition parties led by the PML-N and the MMA by resigning from Parliament in protest. Prior to the vote, the Supreme Court had ruled that the victor would be declared only after a judicial decision on opposition petitions against the legality of the election. With the legality of the NRO also under challenge in the Supreme Court, Musharraf's hold on power looked more fragile than ever.

In the immediate aftermath of 9/11, Musharraf had cleverly navigated Pakistan caught in a minefield of regional and international politics. Over time, the duplicity of his regime in its approach to America's "war on terror" became increasingly untenable. Occasional summits with Indian leaders and more sustained back-channel diplomacy did not yield any break-through in India–Pakistan relations. Domestically, Musharraf blundered in dealing with a newly assertive judiciary, a compromised but vibrant media, and a civil society that was using new technologies to communicate and disseminate information in order to overcome the historic disadvantages in mobilizing effectively against an authoritarian state. Even more worrying for the future was his alienation of Balochistan. The murder of Akbar Bugti would continue to plague the general in the future. Yet in late 2007, as fresh elections approached, the spotlight was on how Musharraf would negotiate the challenge posed by Benazir Bhutto's return to Pakistan.

TEN

ENTANGLED ENDGAMES

ONCE THE EXPECTATIONS ABOUT HER impending return became overwhelming, Benazir Bhutto had to make the most momentous decision of her life. Not returning to Pakistan would mean retiring from active politics, an unthinkable proposition for a politician keen to set the record straight by gaining another term in office. But in choosing to go home before reaching a definitive agreement with Musharraf, she placed herself at grave personal risk. Questions were raised whether she was fully aware of just how much Pakistan had changed during the past eight years of her self-imposed exile. When Benazir asked whether the Americans had made it clear that her safety was his responsibility, Musharraf tartly told her: "Your security is based on the state of our relationship."[1] With the validity of his election dependent on a judicial verdict, Musharraf was afraid that the PPP leader's return might further tilt the balance of popular opinion against him. So he instructed her to come after the 2008 elections, indicating that he could not guarantee the security of the former prime minister, as there were credible reports of suicide squads being dispatched from FATA to assassinate her.[2] Press reports of unknown origin claimed that Baitullah Mehsud, the leader of the Tehrik-i-Taliban Pakistan (TTP), formed in December 2007, was sending dozens of suicide bombers to kill Benazir on her arrival in Karachi. Sources close to Baitullah denied he had made any such threat, adding "we don't strike women."[3] Benazir disclosed that "a sympathetic Muslim foreign government" had provided her with a list of the designated assassins, who she had reason to believe were working at the behest of certain high-ranking individuals in the government.[4] She named three people—Pervez Elahi, the PML-Q chief minister of Punjab; General Hamid Gul, the former DG of the ISI and a Taliban sympathizer; and Brigadier Ejaz Shah, the head of IB and Musharraf's long-standing associate.

Ignoring Musharraf's warnings as dictatorial balderdash and asserting that "the time of life is written and the time of death is written," a remarkably calm Benazir landed in Karachi on October 18, 2007, to an adoring welcome by hundreds of thousands of supporters. Upon emerging from the plane, she raised her hands to the skies and tearfully said a prayer. She had just received a message from the general's men to cancel the planned procession from the airport to Jinnah's mausoleum, where she was scheduled to address a rally. Undeterred by the report of a security threat, Benazir proceeded with her plan. Millions watched across the globe, as she stood exposed on an open roof truck designed to withstand bomb attacks while the cavalcade moved at a snail's pace through the streets of Karachi. As night set in, the streetlights suddenly started to flicker and go off. The procession was blanketed in darkness before a deadly bomb blast set the scene ablaze, leaving 139 dead and 290 injured. Benazir herself was unharmed. After the incident, she alleged that the attacks could not have taken place without the complicity of top officials in the security and intelligence services. She told a leading Pakistani journalist: "You can name Musharraf my assassin if I am killed." Benazir specifically pointed an accusing finger at Brigadier Ejaz Shah. A former provincial chief of the ISI in Punjab, Shah had been the handler of Sheikh Omar Saeed, the convicted murderer of Daniel Pearl.[5]

Well aware of what was at stake, Benazir did not make her suspicions public but conveyed them in an e-mail to her lobbyist in Washington, Mark Siegel. Expecting the Americans to come to her assistance was naive. The Bush administration was solidly behind Musharraf. However, by late October the general was convinced that the court ruling on his continuation in the office of president would go against him. Assured of his indispensability to the Americans, he decided to preempt the judicial decision. On November 3, 2007, in a rambling and incoherent speech, Musharraf declared a state of emergency and suspended the constitution. In a burst of awkwardly phrased utterances that led one insolent commentator to liken him to a self-important drunken uncle, he catalogued the reasons for the extraconstitutional coup: "extremism has become too extreme"; "nobody is scared of us anymore"; "Islamabad is full of extremists"; "there

Benazir Bhutto on her arrival in Karachi on October 18, 2007. *The White Star Photo Pvt. Ltd. Archive.*

is a government within government"; and "officials are being insulted by the judiciary."[6] This was effectively an indictment of his regime's failures. In a series of measures bordering on the egregious to the absurd, Justice Chaudhry was dismissed and Abdul Hameed Dogar appointed as the new chief justice. Police raids led to the imprisonment and house arrest of prominent lawyers, opposition politicians, human rights activists, and even academicians who participated in meetings to protest against the imposition of the emergency. Special powers were conferred on the police to clamp down on the demonstrations. Harsh steps were taken against the media, and the broadcasting of private and international channels was suspended.

It was a pathetic display of political judgment. The opposition to the emergency was widespread, with the Internet and social media outwitting the regime's crackdown on the freedom of expression. The better educated chanted, "Give us back our country," while the more popular cries were "Go, Musharraf, Go" and "restore the judiciary." In mid-November, Benazir, who had also been put under house arrest, broke off negotiations with the government and called for Musharraf's resignation as president and army chief. She indicated her willingness to form a coalition government with opposition parties. The general was faced with an even bigger crisis than the one he had tried to avert. So he was forced to make some conciliatory gestures. Elections were announced for January 8, 2008. The existing assemblies were dissolved, and an interim government was set up under the chairman of the Senate, Mohammad Mian Soomro. After the Supreme Court dismissed the last legal challenge to his reelection as president, Musharraf on November 28 finally resigned as chief of army staff. His close aide and DG of the ISI, Lieutenant General Ashfaq Parvez Kayani, became the new army chief. Long in coming, this marked the beginning of the end for the general-turned-politician. In a major blow to his hopes of the PML-Q doing well in the general elections, the Saudi king personally intervened to ensure Nawaz Sharif's return to Pakistan in late November.

On December 15, 2007, Musharraf lifted the emergency after taking all the necessary steps to safeguard the changes he had made to the judiciary. Curbs on the media were relaxed, but there was no end to demonstrations demanding the restoration of the preemergency judiciary. As the politicians took to the campaign trail with a vengeance, their harangues against

Change of command: Generals Musharraf and Kayani. *The White Star Photo Pvt. Ltd. Archive.*

the regime meshed uneasily with fears about their security. On December 27, with the country in the heat of the election campaign, Benazir was killed in a suicide bomb attack after inveighing against extremism at a PPP rally in Rawalpindi. Vital evidence was lost once the police suspiciously washed down the assassination scene. In another critical lapse, no autopsy was carried out, with the result that Benazir's death has remained a subject of open speculation. Members of her family, who saw the corpse, maintained that she had been shot in the neck, contradicting the government claim that the death occurred as a result of her head hitting the handle of the vehicle's sunroof. Others believed she had perished in the bomb explosion that killed twenty others.

The all-important question of responsibility for her murder was consigned to Pakistan's library of unsolved political murder mysteries. A deal between the state's intelligence operatives and militants associated with the Taliban to eliminate Benazir seemed more than likely.[7] But there were Pakistanis who suspected Asif Zardari's hand in his wife's murder. In another characteristically Pakistani twist, a flawed politician had fallen prematurely only to become an unassailable martyr-saint, a larger-than-life Benazir—the mystical Shaheed Rani (martyred princess). Once shock and disbelief made way for outbursts of popular grief, there was looting and burning in several cities, notably in Sindh, resulting in the death of forty-five people. Sharply criticized for not making adequate security arrangements for Benazir, Musharraf declared three days of mourning and strongly countered suspicions that his intelligence agencies and officials were linked with the perpetrators of the crime. On December 30, Zardari presented to the PPP central executive committee Benazir's handwritten will, in which she had named him as the interim leader of the party in case anything happened to her. Conscious of his negative persona, he announced that their nineteen-year-old son, Bilawal Bhutto Zardari, would succeed Benazir as PPP leader once he had finished studies at Oxford. It was a needless gesture in an electoral atmosphere imbued with symbolism. Benazir's assassination had removed the only politician openly committed to combating extremism as Pakistan's own war. Her tragic elimination from the political scene united a divided people for the moment, giving the PPP a distinctive edge in the elections that were postponed until February 2008 to allow for the mandatory forty-day period of mourning.

The PPP's Return to Power

On February 18, 2008, security fears and an election boycott by smaller parties led to a low voter turnout of 44 percent, producing a hung Parliament. With 31 percent of the popular vote, the PPP secured 121 general and reserved seats in the national assembly. The PML-N came second with ninety-one seats. Musharraf's party, the PML-Q, won just fifty-four seats, a sharp drop of over 50 percent from its tally in the 2002 elections. In the provincial assembly elections, the PML-Q lost everywhere except Balochistan, while the PPP swept Sindh, and the PML-N and the Awami National Party (ANP) won the most seats in Punjab and the NWFP, respectively. This put paid to Musharraf's dreams of becoming Pakistan's longest surviving ruler. The PPP and the PML-N agreed to form a coalition government and restore the judges dismissed in November 2007. An agreement was also struck with the ANP and the JUI-F (Maulana Fazlur Rahman's faction) of the NWFP. On March 31, the coalition was sworn into office with the PPP's Yousaf Raza Gilani as prime minister.

One of the first steps taken by the new government was to release several judges arrested during the emergency. The deposed chief justice's rulings

Nawaz Sharif being welcomed at Zardari House in Islamabad by Bilawal Bhutto Zardari and Asif Zardari. *The White Star Photo Pvt. Ltd. Archive.*

in cases involving terror suspects had piqued not only the ISI but also the Americans. After detailed briefings by the military, the PPP-led coalition in a major policy decision took political ownership of military operations against insurgent strongholds in both FATA and the settled areas of the NWFP. This exposed the government to charges of fighting America's war against its own people. Apprehensive of American policies in Afghanistan, the PML-N leadership had to be persuaded to support the operations in FATA. Contrary to its reassurances to the PML-N, the PPP began dragging its feet on the restoration of the judges. The reason was all too apparent. Reinstating Justice Iftikhar Chaudhry threatened to scuttle the NRO, dubbed the "greatest laundering and dry-cleaning act known to the sub-continent."[8] In mid-May, Nawaz Sharif used the nonimplementation of the judges' restoration to withdraw his ministers from the cabinet. Needing the PPP's numbers in Parliament to turf Musharraf out of office, the PML-N leader announced his party's continuing support for the government.

More behind-the-scenes negotiations paved the way for the PPP and the PML-N to bring impeachment proceedings against Musharraf, who on August 18, 2008, opted to resign rather than face humiliation. In a clear sign of continuity in their thinking on civil–military affairs, the new army chief, General Kayani, made sure that Musharraf was given the Pakistani Army's guard of honor as he left the president's office for the last time to live in Rawalpindi's Army House. A discredited civilian president would never have been given anything like the ceremony that surrounded Musharraf's departure from the Pakistani political scene. People across the country celebrated the end of an era that had seen them losing all sense of security and hope as a military regime parading as a democratic government pursued a policy of alignment with America whose strategic interests in the region clashed with those of the Pakistani Army command. Having achieved its main purpose, the PML-N formally withdrew from the coalition, citing the ongoing dispute over the judges' issue. Since the PPP had put forward Zardari as its presidential candidate, the PML-N nominated the former chief justice of the Supreme Court Saeeduzzaman Siddiqui. On September 6, Zardari won a comfortable majority and was sworn in as president three days later.

In yet another bizarre turn in the history of the Islamic Republic of Pakistan, one of the most vilified individuals in the country had assumed presidential office. This miracle would never have occurred if Benazir had been alive. Zardari had his detractors within the PPP, especially in Sindh, and it was widely known that his late wife had wanted to keep him not just out of politics but also out of Pakistan. To his credit, Zardari handled the difficult transition after Benazir's death with surprising skill, indicating he was a political operator who knew when and how far to compromise. This was to serve President Zardari well in managing coalition government politics while he and his government tried navigating a minefield of contradictory pressures from America and the army high command.

In February 2009, tensions between the PPP and the PML-N were inflamed after a Supreme Court verdict barring Nawaz and his brother, Shahbaz, the chief minister of Punjab, from holding elected office. Punjab was placed under the rule of the governor, Salman Taseer, a PPP loyalist. An infuriated Nawaz Sharif blamed Zardari's machinations for this sudden change and reiterated his demand for the restoration of the judges. In mid-March, agitation by the lawyers and PML-N activists threatened a "long march" to Islamabad just as militancy in the northwest was gathering momentum. This worried Washington sufficiently to warrant General Kayani's personal intervention, resulting in the reinstatement of Chaudhry as the chief justice. In another conciliatory move, the governor's rule was lifted in Punjab and the Supreme Court restored Shahbaz Sharif as chief minister of Punjab. The judiciary's role in settling questions that were appropriately debated in Parliament lent a wholly new tinge to Pakistani politics. On July 31, the Supreme Court ruled Musharraf's November 2007 emergency order unconstitutional. Acclaimed as a victory for democracy, the shift to a more independent judiciary was a tribute to the perseverance of the lawyers' movement. Once back in office, Justice Chaudhry acquired extensive powers for appointing and dismissing judges, as well as vetoing laws and constitutional amendments. Although this was a welcome change from the past, judicial activism threatened to pit the honorable judges against not only a long domineering executive but also a weak and fragmented Parliament.

These institutional tussles were taking place against the backdrop of growing instability and violence. Pakistan was at war with itself. FATA was the epicenter, with the NWFP serving as the primary target of retaliatory militant bombings. But links between the TTP and Punjabi militants made certain that no part of Pakistan was safe. In January 2008, a suicide bombing had killed twenty-four at the Lahore High Court on the day of a scheduled protest by the lawyers demanding the restoration of the judges. The militants grew bolder by the day, attacking a munitions factory near the capital, massively bombing the Marriott Hotel in Islamabad in September, before attacking the visiting Sri Lankan cricket team in Lahore the following March. The Sri Lankans escaped unharmed, but the driver, who heroically steered the bus to safety, and six policemen died. This marked the end for hopes of international teams returning to the cricket-mad country and raised serious questions about the logic of the PPP-led coalition's policy on extremism.

Though reiterating his government's commitment to eliminating extremism, Prime Minister Gilani had offered to negotiate with militants who laid down their arms, a contradiction in terms for the Pathan tribesmen fighting the army in FATA and parts of NWFP like Swat. The government's olive branch was an opportunity for the militants to drive home their advantage on the ground, just what the Americans feared the most. With news of suicide bombings pouring out of Pakistan, there was international dismay over an agreement in May 2008 between the ANP government in the NWFP and pro-Taliban militants in Swat. Calling themselves the Tehrik-i-Nifaz-i-Shariat-i-Muhammadi (TNSM), literally the movement for the enforcement of the sharia, the Swat militants were led by Sufi Muhammad, who had landed in prison after trying to wage a jihad against America in Afghanistan. Sufi's son-in-law Fazlullah took control of the movement in his absence. Known as "Radio Mullah" for his radio broadcasts against the government and diatribes against women's emancipation, Fazlullah was running a lucrative timber trade, deforesting the paradisiacal Swat valley in the name of implementing the Islamic sharia. His men had bombed several girls' schools in the former princely state of Swat. In an attempt to get Fazlullah to moderate his stance, the government released Sufi Muhammad. But there was no end to militant attacks on government forces and educational institutions for girls even after the peace agreement. In February 2009, the NWFP government signed a further cease-fire agreement with the TNSM and agreed to allow the adoption of the sharia in large parts of the NWFP's Malakand Division, which included the Swat valley, Lower Dir, and Buner.

Billed by the Western media as a "capitulation" and abject surrender by Pakistan to the militants, the deal was aimed at expediting the provision of speedy justice in Swat and its adjoining areas rather than relegating them to the writ of the Taliban. There was no question of permitting laws contrary to the provisions of the constitution. What the deal signposted was the army's reluctance to enforce the writ of the state in Swat without popular support. This was provided by the furor over an amateur video showing a seventeen-year-old girl being lashed for an alleged liaison with a man that was telecast extensively and was accessible on the Internet. Spontaneous street protests by Pakistan's small but active civil society signaled a change in attitude. The outrage against Taliban excesses was real. Once the Swat Taliban overplayed their hand by spreading southwest into Buner, just 100 kilometers from Islamabad, alarm bells rang across the globe. Washington under the newly elected administration of President Barack Obama led the international charge against Pakistan's failure to combat extremism. As the peace agreement collapsed and thousands of civilians fled the violence in Swat, there was growing support for decisive military action. In mid-May 2009, most political parties signed a joint declaration of support for the army action. Encouraged by the swing in the public mood, the Pakistani Army conducted a second operation and regained control over Swat at the request of an elected government. The carefully choreographed operation was tainted by allegations of human rights violations as the Taliban used young boys as shields against the advancing Pakistani Army. But there was no repeat of the media's cartwheel in the aftermath of the Lal Masjid siege.

This was partly due to a virtual media blackout on the military operations in FATA. The focus of the reporting was on the heroism and sacrifice of Pakistani soldiers, which contributed to a hardening of anti-Taliban sentiments. However, there was no corresponding decline in anti-Americanism. The sharp increase in drone attacks against militants in FATA after the Obama administration took office increased public animosity toward America. Government spokesmen routinely condemned the attacks for causing collateral damage to civilians while demanding that the United States let the Pakistani military carry out the drone strikes. US State Department cables released by WikiLeaks, however, suggest that what the spokesmen were saying publicly differed dramatically from the reality behind the scenes. General Kayani not only gave his tacit agreement to the drone campaign against militants in FATA but also asked for round-the-clock surveillance of the conflict areas.[9] It was well known that some of the drones were actually flown from bases within Pakistan.

Meanwhile, relations with India were beset by a new crisis. On November 26, 2008, just as the army was poised to commence a major operation in South Waziristan, Pakistani-based militants linked to the Lashkar-i-Tayyiba carried out a deadly attack in Mumbai. The assault on India's financial capital was designed to start a war between the two nuclear-armed neighbors. This would force the Pakistani Army to redeploy its units from the northwestern tribal areas to the eastern border, relieving pressure on militants in South Waziristan and Swat. Rooted in battles under way in Afghanistan, FATA, and Kashmir, the attack on Mumbai left 166 people dead and some 300 injured. Pakistan's foreign minister, Shah Mahmood Qureshi, was in New Delhi at the time of the Mumbai carnage. Kayani sent his personal plane to bring the minister home. Criticizing India for jumping to conclusions, the army chief strongly denied Pakistan's responsibility for the attacks. Indians were outraged by the refusal of the Pakistani authorities to hand over or convict the leader of the Lashkar-i-Tayyiba, Hafiz Muhammad Saeed, who they believed had masterminded the carnage in Mumbai. The sole serving assassin, Ajmal Kasab, said during interrogation that the mission was supported by the ISI. He was convicted and sent to the gallows four years later.

The Mumbai killings deeply strained relations between the new American administration and the Pakistani military leadership. Once President Obama had announced a withdrawal date from Afghanistan, initially set for 2011 but later extended to 2014, the army high command and the ISI had even less reason to sever ties with the Afghan Taliban. By playing for time, they could try and achieve their objectives in Afghanistan after the US withdrawal just as they had done after the Soviets pulled out. In March 2009, following a "head to toe, soup to nuts" review of US foreign policy toward Afghanistan and Pakistan, Obama unfurled the "Af-Pak" strategy.[10] The exclusion of India, a key player in Afghanistan, was open to criticism on both conceptual and operational grounds. Sustainable peace in Afghanistan required addressing the India–Pakistan angle and recognizing its inherent connection with Kashmir. At New Delhi's insistence, the Obama administration de-hyphenated American policy toward India and Pakistan. This was consistent with US interest in forging an economic and strategic relationship with India. But a fragmented approach to the problem in Afghanistan, particularly the unwillingness to push India on Kashmir, was hazardous to the cause of peace. It was the US military's continued need for operational cooperation with its Pakistani counterpart that prevented an open rupture between the two estranged allies.

On August 5, 2009, an American drone attack killed Baitullah Mehsud, throwing the TTP into a vicious leadership crisis and raising expectations of an army action against militants holed up in South Waziristan. General Kayani and his commanders had been taking their time to start the "mother of all battles," raising eyebrows across the globe as well as at home about the army's commitment to take on "terrorism central." Taking advantage of the delay, the militants laid mines in the territory the army would have to cross to reach their well-protected redoubts. Meanwhile, FATA's suicide factories continued producing an endless flow of human weapons to strike at will anywhere in the country. In a staggering display of nerve, militants on October 10, 2009, attacked army headquarters in Rawalpindi, killing six army personnel. Five days later there were simultaneous attacks on two police training centers and the regional headquarters of the Federal Investigation Agency in Lahore. Meant to dissuade the army from launching the "Rah-i-Najat" (path of salvation) in South Waziristan, the effect was diametrically different. Threats to girls' schools in Lahore were the last straw that broke public resistance to a war nobody really wanted. A major ground and air offensive involving an estimated

30,000 Pakistani soldiers started on October 17 against approximately 10,000 militants, including foreigners from Central Asia. But there were lingering doubts about the Pakistani Army's commitment to take the campaign to its logical conclusion into North Waziristan, thereby easing America and NATO's difficulties in the Afghanistan quagmire.

With a death toll close to the cumulative fatalities between 2003 and 2008, 2009 was the bloodiest year for Pakistan. It was also the year of decision. By persisting in choosing their targets at will and terrorizing the populace, the militants made the mistake of expecting the state to abandon all pretense at governing as had happened in the tribal areas. But Pakistan's urban centers were a world apart from FATA, where the local population had been left with no choice but to seek protection from the militants. Islamist parties like the Jamaat-i-Islami and sections of the electronic media blamed the attacks on America, India, and even Israel. But more and more people had come to accept that the war against the militants, although linked with the US-led occupation of Afghanistan, was a war Pakistan had to fight in its own interests.

This fortuitous development was a potential turning point in Pakistan's entanglement with extremism. However, it required an efficient government that placed performance before personal profit to overcome formidable roadblocks on several fronts. The economy remained a primary cause for disquiet. Foreign investments declined as a crippling national energy crisis reared its ugly head. The problem was rooted in a political economy of corruption in which stealing electricity and bribing linesmen instead of paying bills was the norm. The cantankerous debate on the construction of the Kalabagh dam between Punjab and the non-Punjabi provinces was another major reason for the energy shortages. In December 2004, Musharraf had publicly confirmed that the dam would be built in the larger interests of Pakistan. This provoked an acrimonious debate in Sindh and the NWFP against what was seen as a Punjabi project that would inundate their best agricultural land. The dam was never built, and in May 2008 the PPP-led government announced that it had been consigned to the archives of interprovincial dead heats. By the spring of 2008, the demand for electricity was outstripping supply by nearly 4,000 megawatts, resulting in long hours of load shedding and state-induced conservation measures that hit the livelihoods of millions and pushed the economy deeper into a slump.

To match words with deeds, the PPP government needed to somehow get down to the business of governing Pakistan. Governance had not been a strong suit of the party ever since Benazir's first government. The military operations in the northwest had restored the army's public image, badly tainted during the final phase of Musharraf's government. With the ISI still operating as a state within a state, the PPP government's capacity to project strong leadership far less redress the imbalance in civil–military relations was severely constrained. Zardari's tactic of displaying Benazir's photograph while speaking in public, both at home and abroad, and parroting her favorite line, "democracy is the best revenge," failed to win him sympathy. His ill-conceived attempts to assert civilian authority drew the scorn of the intelligentsia and incensed the army chief to a point where there was talk of a military intervention.

Zardari backed down gracefully, letting the army high command rule the roost on foreign and defense policy. The army chief's behind-the-scenes involvement was instrumental in the uproar created over the Kerry-Lugar Bill, which made US development aid to Pakistan conditional on evidence of progress in establishing civilian control over the ISI. Kayani's hands were further strengthened in November 2009, when the Supreme Court under Justice Chaudhry revoked the NRO. Zardari and the PPP's interior minister, Rehman Malik, were the main beneficiaries of Musharraf's notorious NRO. The opposition parties kicked up a storm, demanding Zardari's resignation. To avert the crisis, another intercession by the top khaki occurred, after which the president agreed to transfer control over the nuclear command structure to the prime minister. Primarily concerned with perpetuating his immunity from criminal proceedings as president and firmly in control of the PPP, Zardari was not averse to whittling down his powers in favor of Gilani, who was beholden to him for the prime ministerial office.

On April 8, 2010, in a historic leap in the direction of democracy based on an appreciation of the limitations of power by all the main political parties, Parliament unanimously approved the Eighteenth Amendment. This reversed a long process of transferring power from the prime minister to the president in an ostensibly parliamentary form of government that had been in place since the time of Zia-ul-Haq, whose name was suitably removed from the constitution. Under the amendment, the president could no longer dismiss governments or dissolve assemblies and had to take prime ministerial advice in appointing service chiefs and provincial governors. In a boost for provincial autonomy, the concurrent list of subjects was abolished. The two-term bar on a prime minister and a chief

Map of Pakistan, post-1971. Azad Jammu and Kashmir are to the left of the Line of Control.

minister was also removed. Seen as restoring Pakistan's long-suffering parliamentary form of government, these provisions were welcomed by a cross section of political opinion. But there were contentious ones as well including the new method of appointing judges through a judicial commission and changing the name of the NWFP to Khyber Pakhtunkhwa (KPK) in response to the ANP's long-standing demand. Skillful negotiations and tactical compromises averted a derailment of the agreement between the PPP, the PML-N, and the ANP. A few days later, Zardari signed the Eighteenth Amendment, becoming the first president in Pakistan's history to voluntarily reduce his powers in the interest of strengthening both parliamentary democracy and the federation.

Earlier in a major step toward interprovincial cooperation, the nineteen-year dispute over the NFC award on the distribution of financial resources was solved through mutual agreement by the four provinces. In a rare display of national unity, Punjab agreed to multiple criteria for determining allocations. Population, revenue, backwardness, and the principle of giving more to less populated areas were now to provide the basis for apportioning resources between the federal center and the constituent units. Except for Punjab, where the PPP was in a tense coalition with the PML-N, relations between the federal and the provincial governments remained relatively free of enmity. Zardari's deft political diplomacy brought the MQM into the coalition at the center and in Sindh, easing Karachi's miseries for twenty months, before a deadly sectarian bombing in late December 2009 shattered the peace of the city. Pakistan was clearly no closer to prevailing over extremism. But there was a rare glimmer of hope. The consensus on the NFC award and the Eighteenth Amendment was a milestone in the history of the state of martial rule. Parliament, the prime minister, the judiciary, and the provincial governments had more autonomy than ever in a military-dominated state. They now needed to capitalize on the opportunity and work within the limits of their institutional power, a vague conception in a country where repeated interruptions of the political process had seen military and quasi-military rulers toss and turn constitutions at will with the approval of the judiciary.

Justice Chaudhry fired the first volley in the battle between the different branches of government by asserting that the much-touted restoration of parliamentary sovereignty was not inviolable. Parliament could legislate only within the strict parameters set out by the constitution. In an astounding display of priorities given the multiple challenges, ranging from bankruptcy, a debilitating energy shortage, tribal insurgency, and urban terrorism, Pakistanis became engrossed in the educational qualifications of some of their elected members. In mid-2010 a number of legislators were discovered holding fake academic degrees, infringing a law in force at the time of the 2008 elections requiring candidates to hold a bachelor's degree or its equivalent. Introduced by Musharraf, the requirement was repealed by the Supreme Court in April 2008 as an infringement of fundamental rights. Scrapping the requirement did not absolve the elected representatives from the charge of having lied about their qualifications to the Election Commission. Zardari was alleged to have also misreported his academic qualifications at the time of filing his candidacy.

These political maneuverings coupled with the Supreme Court's activism were a sword of Damocles for Zardari and Gilani. So they sought to neutralize any possible move by the army chief to cut short the PPP government's term in office. In an unparalleled move by a civilian government, Kayani's term as army chief was extended for another three years. This was assailed in the press and seen by some quarters as evidence of the government pandering to American interests. Once the decision was made public in July 2010, the four main pillars of the Pakistani state—the president, the cabinet headed by a prime minister, the chief justice, and the army chief—had confirmed tenures in office until 2013. It was an ideal arrangement for a country submerged in difficulties and where no elected civilian government had completed a term in office since 1977.

As if to prove an oracle on Pakistan's persisting bad luck, catastrophic floods in mid-August 2010 inundated a fifth of the country, affecting more than 15 million people and killing several hundreds. The United Nations reported that the floods created more havoc than the Asian tsunami of 2004 and the earthquake that hit northern Pakistan in 2005. In a comment on the lingering imbalances between the civilian and military institutions, the government's relief efforts were hopelessly inadequate. While this gave the army an opportunity to burnish its public image by leading the relief effort, the possibility of militants resurfacing in the badly hit Khyber Pakhtunkhwa remained a source of deep concern. There were fears of popular rage over escalating food prices merging with militant activities to strain an already perilous internal security situation. Without some semblance of law and order, Pakistan's democratic spring could only end in tears.

The year 2011 began catastrophically for Pakistan. On January 4, the governor of the Punjab Salman Taseer was shot and killed by one of his own security guards in Islamabad. A businessman, politician, and a media magnate with a liberal disposition, Taseer had locked horns with the PML-N, which was the PPP's partner in an uneasy coalition in the province. He firmly stood his ground against the rising trend to target minorities under the controversial blasphemy law. In late 2010, the religious right condemned Taseer to hellfire for visiting an illiterate Christian mother of five who had been sentenced to death for slandering the

Prophet. A television anchor mischievously drove Taseer into saying that while he respected the Prophet, the blasphemy law needed to be amended. The assassin, Malik Mumtaz Hussain Qadri, said he had killed the governor for opposing the blasphemy law. Though he claimed to have acted alone, investigations revealed that other members of the security guard were aware of his intentions but did nothing to stop him. A follower of a Sunni Barelvi group, Dawat-i-Islam (Invitation to Islam), Qadri had been motivated by a cleric who advocated death for anyone charged with blasphemy.

In an apparent somersault that left liberal opinion shuddering, some of the lawyers' groups who had fought for an independent judiciary hailed Qadri as a hero. Fearing for his security, the official cleric refused to lead Taseer's funeral prayer. In an unthinkable breach of protocol, senior civil officials stayed away from a serving governor's last rites. It was a dismal display of the state's surrender to the street power of the clerics who had turned the blasphemy law into an instrument to legitimate murder. Originating in the colonial Penal Code of the 1860s, the provision delimited the freedom of expression to protect religious sensibilities against undue provocation. A secular law was turned into an instrument of "Islamization" during the Zia era and in 1986 blasphemy under article 295 (c) of the constitution was made punishable by death. There were hardly any cases registered under the blasphemy law in Pakistan until then. By the time of Taseer's assassination, there were hundreds of cases of blasphemy, mainly against Ahmadis and Muslims. A law to protect Muslim sentiments had become a ploy to eliminate individuals in the name of Islam. The judiciary's delay in booking Qadri and the media's extensive coverage of his triumphant statement in court extolling his action as "following Islam" galvanized human rights groups, who used the new information technologies effectively to coalesce segments of urban society. Qadri was formally indicted on February 11, 2011, and sentenced to death on October 1 by an Anti-Terrorist Court in Rawalpindi. A group of lawyers created pandemonium in the court against the judgment. Qadri's lawyers appealed the decision, calling it illegal, as no one had been terrorized and in fact "people heaved a sigh of relief after the killing of the blasphemer."[11]

Taseer's death was a setback to hopes of building a more liberal society, graphically symbolizing the dangers of religious extremism in everyday life. If his own security guard could riddle the governor of the most powerful province of the country with twenty-six bullets, no one was safe in Pakistan. The sense of insecurity and disillusionment with the state's ability to tackle the economic, political, and security challenges grew exponentially. Between 2003 and 2010, more than 30,000 terror-related casualties were reported, while security expenditure ballooned to almost three times the assistance Pakistan was receiving from Washington. Military operations in FATA displaced hundreds of thousands of people, raising fears of fleeing militants mingling with sectarian outfits and criminal mafias operating in the cities. The floods had left the economy in tatters and drawn a disappointing response from the international community. Business confidence was crushed by an endless spree of politically motivated killings, rising crime rates, and a growing shortage of electricity and gas.

Most disquieting was Karachi's return to anarchic violence after the December 2009 bombing of a Shia procession of mourners on the occasion of Ashura, the martyrdom of the Prophet's grandson Hussain, at Karbala. The city was wracked by sectarian violence, random suicide bombings, and targeted killings of both ANP and MQM supporters, threatening political disruption in Sindh and also at the center. Dependent on the support of both parties, the PPP government could not afford to break with the MQM in Sindh. Pakistan's largest and most cosmopolitan city, Karachi was by now a teeming metropolis of over 20 million. The demographics in the MQM's political base had shifted against Urdu speakers, giving Pathans and Punjabis an overall edge. Karachi is a prized asset in the Pakistani political matrix. From the security of his exile in London, the MQM leader Altaf Hussain ranted against the moderate and secular ANP for allegedly harboring Taliban militants. The MQM chief was right up to a point. Taliban nestled with internally displaced persons fleeing military operations in Swat and South Waziristan settled in the outskirts of Karachi between 2010 and 2011. In time they had gained enough clout in parts of the city to set up their own courts. But Altaf Hussain was wrong to blame the ANP. Looking to establish control over Karachi's Pathan localities that they had coerced into submission, the Taliban went on a killing spree against ANP leaders. A poorly armed police has been no match against heavily armed militants belonging to the Mehsud tribe, who linked up with the city's land mafia and criminal networks and began collecting funds through kidnappings, bank robberies, and extortion for their brethren battling the Pakistani Army in the tribal areas. The MQM's attempt to cash in on anti-Taliban sentiments in anticipation of national elections scheduled for 2013 marked the beginning of a vicious and bloody battle for the control of Karachi.

No government at the center could feel secure with the economy and the country's main financial center hurtling toward endgames of their own before the American endgame in Afghanistan that was consuming the attention of the military high command. In the months following General Kayani's extension, relations with Washington dipped to an all-time low. On January 27, 2011, an American CIA undercover agent, using the alias Raymond Davis, shot dead two persons in Lahore who were suspected to be ISI agents. A car coming to rescue Davis killed another person. A hyperactive media used the incident to whip up public fury against the tribulations of Pakistan's relationship with the United States. There were impassioned calls for Davis's trial in Pakistan, with the TTP chipping in by threatening retaliation if the American agent was released. Media reports in the United States suggested that the agent was part of a covert CIA-led team engaged in surveillance on militant groups suspected of seeking access to Pakistan's nuclear arsenal. Later it emerged that Davis was a private contractor hired by the CIA after the Mumbai attacks of November 2008 to spy on the Lashkar-i-Tayyiba, which was suspected of plotting audacious attacks globally. This put the CIA on a collision course with the ISI, which considered the Lashkar-i-Tayyiba a strategic asset for its purposes in Kashmir.[12] While initially rejecting American demands for the repatriation of their national, the Pakistani government with the ISI's approval released Davis after the families of the two victims were paid "blood money" under Pakistan's Islamic laws. No relief was provided to the third victim's families, a clear sign of the ISI's partiality toward the two men killed by Davis. It later emerged that a local tycoon and not the Americans provided the money for the transaction. The Raymond Davis incident incensed Pakistanis and was blamed on the PPP government's policy of appeasing America.

The sharp deterioration in US–Pakistani relations over the Davis episode led to a suspension of intelligence sharing between the two countries. Pakistan pulled out of talks on the Afghanistan war to protest the continuation of drone attacks.[13] The real reason was more complex. In June 2010 there was a botched bombing attempt of New York's Times Square by a Pakistani-born American linked with the Taliban in FATA. This reinforced fears that the next terror attack on America might emanate from Pakistan's northwestern tribal areas. Special efforts were already in place to improve US human intelligence capabilities in Pakistan. To escape the ISI's shadowing of their personnel, the Americans had created their own intelligence networks consisting of hundreds of private US citizens and Pakistanis, infuriating the army high command. Things were heading toward a showdown between the army and the civilian government over the Pakistani ambassador to Washington, Hussain Haqqani, who General Kayani accused of acting on American direction and granting visas to US nationals in contravention of GHQ's explicit orders.[14]

The climax came on May 2, 2011, with the discovery of Osama bin Laden in the garrison town of Abbottabad following a covert US mission. Pakistanis were stunned to find their military napping while five US helicopters penetrated the national airspace and killed bin Laden despite repeated official denials of his presence in the country. Preferring the charge of incompetence to complicity with America, Kayani denied any prior knowledge of the operation. This provoked unprecedented criticism of the military in Pakistan and further soured attitudes toward its main international patron. On May 22, twenty militants infiltrated a high-security naval base in Karachi, killing thirteen people, injuring sixteen, and blowing up two military aircraft. The Pakistani Taliban claimed the attack as revenge for the killing of the Al Qaeda leader. An independent journalist, Syed Saleem Shahzad, investigating the incident found links between Al Qaeda and senior naval officers. He was allegedly tortured and murdered by ISI operatives.

There was an explosion of public rage against both the army and the ISI. Combined with the domestic fallout of the Abbottabad operation, the murder of a journalist who was simply doing his job made the ISI a target of disdain. This presented a rare opportunity to redress the imbalance in civil–military relations. In a surprise visit to Pakistan in late May 2011, US Secretary of State Hillary Clinton praised Pakistan for being a good partner in the fight against terrorism but conceded differences between the two countries on how to conduct the campaign. Joint intelligence sharing was resumed between Pakistan and the United States as a first step to restoring trust. These confidence-building measures did not alter the existing situation. Taliban militants regularly torched Pakistani trucks carrying war supplies for American and NATO troops in Afghanistan. With the endgame in Afghanistan in its final phase, the army was determined to resist any American-backed attempt to enhance civilian control over the ISI.

An opinion piece in the *Financial Times* of London by a controversial Pakistani American businessman, Mansoor Ijaz, placed the civilian government at loggerheads with the army and the ISI. Known for his acerbic attacks on the ISI, Ijaz claimed that a week after the raid on bin Laden's hideout, a senior Pakistani diplomat asked him to pass Zardari's message to the Americans that the military was planning to intervene.[15] The undated and unsigned memo sent to Admiral Mike Mullen, the top US military officer at the time, was later released to the press. It spoke of "a unique window of opportunity" for the "civilians to gain the upper hand over army and intelligence directorates due to their complicity" in the bin Laden affair. In return for American assistance in strengthening its hands, according to the memo, the civilian government would revamp Pakistan's security policy, curb the ISI's support to the Jalaluddin Haqqani group in North Waziristan that was attacking American forces in Afghanistan, and place the nuclear arsenal under a more transparent regime.[16] Ijaz subsequently named the Pakistani ambassador in Washington as the source of the memo. General Shuja Pasha, the head of the ISI, dashed off to London to meet Ijaz without seeking clearance from the civilian government.

In the ensuing months, Pakistan was riveted by the "Memogate" scandal. Haqqani resigned but denied writing the memo or contacting Ijaz.[17] In what appeared to be a concerted counterattack by the ISI, Blackberry messages exchanged between the two men were released to the press. The air was rife with speculation about the involvement of the nation's favorite punching bag in President House. After his meeting with the ISI chief, Ijaz changed his stripes, accusing the Zardari-led government for the deceitful campaign against Kayani and Pasha that led to a worsening of the US–Pakistani relationship.[18] Haqqani was tried for high treason after the PML-N filed a petition aimed squarely at Zardari. Generals Kayani and Pasha went to court to record their testimonies in what was an open declaration of war against the PPP government. Prime Minister Gilani called their affidavits "unconstitutional and illegal." This elicited a strongly worded retort from the military warning against such serious allegations against

the army chief and the ISI spymaster that could lead to "very serious ramifications with potentially grievous consequences for the country."[19]

Unsubstantiated chatter about the civilian government dismissing
Kayani and Pasha was now replaced by renewed talk of the army maneuvering to remove Zardari through judicial action. Within a week of the
military's rebuke of the prime minister, the Supreme Court issued a notice
to Gilani, chastising him for disobeying its ruling on the NRO case by not
asking the Swiss authorities to reopen the money laundering case against
Zardari dating back to the 1990s. The prime minister maintained that he
could not write the letter in view of the president's immunity. This failed
to deter a judiciary that was now exceeding the limits of its jurisdiction to
evict Zardari from office on either treason or corruption charges. Opposition parties welcomed the judicial intervention in the political process.
Imran Khan, the leader of the PTI, which like the Jamaat-i-Islami had
boycotted the 2008 elections, led a blitzkrieg against Zardari on the basis
of his alleged corruption. The PPP was set to gain control of the Senate in
elections scheduled for the spring of 2012. If the Supreme Court disqualified Zardari, the entire political setup could be brought down, requiring a
fresh reference to the people before the Senate elections.

Despite gratuitous rumors in the Indian media of a military coup in
Pakistan, the Senate elections went ahead on schedule. Instead of his boss,
Gilani took the fall after the Supreme Court convicted him in April of
contempt of court and, in what was Pakistan's first judicial coup, disqualified him from holding prime ministerial office. Raja Pervez Ashraf of
Punjab, who was being investigated for fraud, took over as prime minister
while the PPP considered ways of writing itself out of the judicial soap
opera to complete its term in office. This was ammunition for Pakistan's
wits behind a glut of comedy shows on television deriding politicians but,
significantly enough, not the army or the judiciary. The new prime minister was promptly nicknamed "Raja rental" because of his involvement in
the rental power plant business. A popular comedy program, *Hum Sab
Ummed Saay Hain* (We Are All Hoping for Something), on GEO TV has
look-alike actors for the entire political spectrum, including Musharraf,
who are made fun of along with foreign leaders like Prime Minister Manmohan Singh and President Obama. The ability to momentarily laugh
oneself to tears amid the gloom and doom of everyday life in Pakistan is

evidence of both inner resilience and the existence of a robust popular culture that has always thrived on humor, particularly political satire.

A pulverized country found cause to rally around the banner of state sovereignty after US-led NATO forces killed twenty-four Pakistani soldiers at a checkpoint along the Afghan border on November 26, 2011. Islamabad suspended NATO supply lines, leading to eight months of rancorous exchanges with Washington that snapped the few remaining fragments of trust between the two allies. In a display of national bravado that raised questions about their sincerity, civilian and military leaders outdid one another in demanding an apology from the US president along with an assurance that similar incidents would never again take place. Both the Americans and the Afghan government claimed that the operation was conducted in response to firing from Pakistan. The delay in reaching an understanding with Washington had less to do with US imperiousness than with the dysfunctional character of civil–military relations in Pakistan, demonstrating the disjunction between national rhetoric and the realities of power. With high stakes in post-2014 Afghanistan, the military command in a rare departure from the norm on security matters left the decision on the supply routes in the hands of a fractious and emotionally charged Parliament. The delay in Parliament arriving at a decision weakened Pakistan's case for an apology. The ultimate miscalculation was in appreciating the lengths to which the United States was prepared to go to secure its strategic interests in Afghanistan, paying billions of dollars more to the Central Asian republics than the millions given to Pakistan to keep critical military supplies flowing.

On July 3, 2012, after a guarded apology by the US secretary of state, Pakistan reopened the NATO supply lines. It was a belated exercise in damage control that had served only to strengthen the military's claim to make strategic policy decisions. None of the Pakistani demands were conceded. The agreement eased the operational concerns of US-led NATO forces in Afghanistan but left all the contentious issues unaddressed. Topping the list of Pakistan's resentments toward the United States have been the ongoing drone attacks in FATA and the interference of American intelligence and private security agencies in its internal affairs. Pakistan's negative profiling in the American media as an "ally from hell" and a "failed state" that uses nuclear blackmail and harbors terrorists has given rise to the perception that India can better serve US interests in post-2014

Afghanistan. This perspective overlooks the ineffaceable realities of geography. As several American officials have been hard-pressed to admit, Pakistan remains a difficult but crucial ally in the war against the Taliban in Afghanistan. While criticizing the links between the ISI and the Afghan Taliban, Americans have not recoiled from relying on Pakistani intelligence connections to start talks with Taliban willing to disavow ties with Al Qaeda.

The double talk by both sides points to greater stresses in the Pakistani–US relationship as the endgame in Afghanistan draws closer. This is unavoidable so long as the army high command makes key strategic decisions, leaving the civilian government little scope to redefine the national security model to account for emerging geostrategic realities. Secretary of State Hillary Clinton went out of her way to stress that American interests in Pakistan are not limited to securing the military's short-term operational assistance. The Kerry-Lugar Bill authorizing $7.5 billion in nonmilitary aid to Pakistan aimed at establishing civilian control over the military, and specifically the intelligence agencies, has been a provocation for the military. Fears of misappropriation prevented most of the Kerry-Lugar funding from being utilized for development projects that could strengthen civil society and democratic processes in Pakistan, a missed opportunity at a time of mounting popular anger over the barrage of American drone attacks on FATA under the Obama administration. Hinting at US disinterest, if not formal disengagement, this kept the focus of the imperiled alliance on securing operational cooperation from Pakistan's military, an institution whose interests are seen to pose the biggest threat to American purposes in Afghanistan. Whether the United States has the option of abandoning a nuclearized and politically unstable Pakistan is a delicate and multifaceted question that can be viewed through the distorting prism of an impending military withdrawal from Afghanistan only at great peril for regional as well as global security.

A complete rupture in US–Pakistani relations is unlikely, but a major shift has already taken place. Public anger in Pakistan at the surge in drone attacks has made support for the alliance with America a liability for political parties. The dissolution of the "special relationship" with the United States will have a profound bearing on the future of civil–military relations in Pakistan. Even as they appear to be crashing under the weight of their own contradictions, Pakistanis have shown extraordinary resilience in bearing the human and material costs of a withering war in Afghanistan that they mostly blame on American imperial overreach. Many see the loosening of ties with the United States under the Obama administration as an opportunity to decrease dependence on an ally whose surges of beneficence have perpetuated military dominance and brought destruction rather than democracy or development. In recognition of the changed relationship with Washington, the PPP government in its final days in office handed control over the strategic Gwadar Port to China. Risking US economic sanctions, President Asif Ali Zardari signed a $7.5 billion gas pipeline deal with Iranian president Ahmadinejad to help Pakistan cope with a grave energy crisis. Historic relations with Turkey have also been fortified. A rising economic power, Turkey under the Justice and Development Party has been one of the few countries willing to invest in a Pakistan ravaged by militant violence. Since the "Arab Spring," Saudi Arabia and the Gulf monarchies have been more interested than ever in the stability of a Sunni-majority country with nuclear capability.

Support from Muslim countries will be important but not a panacea for what is still an America-dependent Pakistani security state. The drying up of US military and economic assistance will increase ties with China but also force Pakistan to rethink its relations with India. This has become more imperative than ever as militant violence keeps foreign investors away and the energy crisis cripples the national economy. India's growing economic muscle has compelled Pakistan to reassess ties with its premier enemy. Any breakthrough in relations between the two countries will have to overcome the constraints of India's domestic politics and the reservations of Pakistan's powerful military. Relations between the two countries have been in the doldrums since the 2008 attack on Mumbai. It will require a skillful balancing of trade incentives and diplomatic initiatives by Islamabad to appease Indian sentiments outraged by the savagery of the attack on India's financial heart by Pakistani militants linked with the ISI-backed Lashkar-i-Tayyiba. New Delhi, too, has to ease the Pakistani military's concerns about growing Indian influence in Afghanistan. An Indo-Pakistan peace dividend in the form of enhanced economic ties between the two regional rivals may well prove to be the most valuable outcome of the American withdrawal from Afghanistan.

Divided and damaged by an alliance of convenience with America, Pakistan is not altogether without options as it ponders the end of its dependence on the United States. Proactive diplomacy and greater trading ties with neighbors can revive the economy and serve as a precursor to peace in the region. If the politicians can somehow avoid letting their differences open the trap door to allow the military back in, Pakistan may well succeed in crossing the fading red lines of an entrenched authoritarianism and become a functioning federal democracy. This historically elusive goal seemed to be within reach once the elected governments at the center and the provinces completed their constitutional terms without a judicial or military intervention. It was a memorable achievement for a country waiting to break the jinx against constitutionally managed democratic transitions. There were the usual alarms and excursions. Media outlets outdid one another with their voracious appetite for sensationalism; there was ample opportunity for high drama in an insurgency-wracked country. In October 2012, a fifteen-year-old schoolgirl, Malala Yusufzai, survived a targeted attack by the Taliban in Swat. An avid blogger, she had gained international attention with her bold advocacy for girls' education in defiance of the Taliban ban and bombing of girls' schools. There was uproar against the Taliban both internationally and also within Pakistan. The staggering spread of militant violence fueled speculations of a derailment of the electoral process. A Pakistani-Canadian cleric, Tahir-ul-Qadri, upped the ante by leading a "long march" to Islamabad demanding electoral transparency and the disqualification of tax evaders and those charged with corruption or criminal activity.

Amid the usual fare of conspiracy theories, Pakistan reached a historic milestone on March 15, 2013, when the national assembly completed its term. Under the provisions of the Twentieth Amendment ratified by the outgoing Parliament, caretaker governments were established at the center and the four provinces. They were to work under an independent Election Commission consisting of members of the judiciary chosen by the ruling alliance in consultation with the main opposition party, the PML-N. Tahir-ul-Qadri filed a writ petition requiring a scrutiny of candidates to ensure that they met the moral criteria laid out in articles 62 and 63 of the constitution. An array of politicians under investigation for various infringements of the law were loath to see their electoral chances ruined by this unwarranted interference from a Pakistani-Canadian national. The media's extensive coverage of Qadri's drive for accountability before elections won some public approbation but also elicited considerable skepticism about the cleric's real intentions. The Election Commission could disqualify only candidates who had already been convicted. To establish a candidate's eligibility under the terms of the constitution required the Election Commission to solicit information from several other government departments, an onerous bureaucratic exercise that would delay the elections and generate political controversy. It was only after the Supreme Court rejected Qadri's petition that the date for the elections was formally announced.

A Landmark Election

With elections scheduled for May 11, 2013, fears of a military intervention or some improbable twist in the political saga gave way to a growing realization of just how much Pakistan had changed. A casualty of an ill-advised national security policy justified in the name of Islam since the early 1980s, the state had no monopoly over the instruments of violence or ideology. Instead of the presidency or the military and its intelligence agencies conniving to manipulate the electoral process, it was the outlawed TTP that set the tone of the campaign by declaring democracy un-Islamic. Pamphlets articulating the Taliban viewpoint warned citizens against participating in the elections. Dubbing the outgoing ruling alliance "secular," the TTP selectively targeted the PPP, the ANP, and the MQM as revenge for their support of the military operations in FATA and KPK. Though the ANP was worst hit, the offices, rallies, and candidates of the PPP and MQM were attacked in KPK, Sindh, and Balochistan, resulting in over 130 deaths before polling day. By contrast, "pro-Taliban parties" like the PML-N, Imran Khan's PTI, the JUI-F, and the Jamaat-i-Islami, who proposed talking to the TTP, were permitted to campaign freely in Punjab as well as the other three provinces that were awash with the blood of so-called secular parties.

Playing strictly by the rules in the most exceptional of times, the Election Commission, headed by the revered retired octogenarian justice Fakhruddin G. Ebrahim, withdrew the security cover for ministers and high-ranking officials of the former governments, both at the center and in the provinces. The unwillingness, if not inability, of the caretaker governments to extend protection to PPP, ANP, and MQM candidates made for an uneven playing field. Qamar Zaman Kaira, the former federal minister for information, complained that while even nominal security had been withdrawn from the two former PPP prime ministers, the degree of protocol being extended to the Sharif brothers during the campaign was putting the legitimacy of the elections into question. He appealed to the caretaker chief minister of Punjab, Najam Sethi, to take notice of the situation as it was creating the impression that the Sharifs were still ruling the province.[20] A reshuffle of senior civil servants was ordered, but there was nothing to prevent the middle and lower ranks of the provincial administration from supporting the PML-N. In a tense electoral atmosphere, an unexceptional statement by the caretaker federal interior minister that Nawaz Sharif was a national leader whose security was vital for the credibility of the electoral exercise elicited protests from other political parties and confirmed suspicions of the PML-N being the favored party.

Regardless of the systemic biases against the PPP and its allied parties, they were responsible for the anti-incumbency groundswell building up against them. Zardari's legendary corruption matched by the PPP's appalling record of governance made a huge dent in the party's support base. Anti-PPP sentiment was strongest in Punjab, where a massive energy crisis blamed on the federal government had badly hurt the economy. Terrorist threats to Bilawal Zardari Bhutto, who was not eligible to seek election until he turned twenty-five, left the PPP without a face to match the PML-N's Nawaz Sharif and the PTI's Imran Khan. With Zardari constitutionally debarred from playing a role in the elections, the PPP responded to security fears by abandoning all pretense of being in the fray in Punjab and concentrated attention on winning in Sindh. The PPP, the ANP, and MQM protested the lack of security made available to them in the face of deadly Taliban attacks but in a clear recognition of their historical significance for the democratic process did not boycott the elections. The oddity of only the right of the political spectrum being in a position to trawl for votes in a historic election highlighted Pakistan's transformation from a onetime moderate haven into a breeding ground of right-wing conservatism in tacit sympathy with proponents of extremist ideologies.

As a banned outfit waging war against the state, the TTP's ability to influence the outcome of an election they damned as un-Islamic by indiscriminate violence queered the pitch of the electoral campaign. The All Pakistan Ulema Council tried countering the Taliban's intrusion into the

domain of Islamic discourse with a fatwa endorsed by clerics from different schools of Islamic thought. They declared that elections, far from being un-Islamic, were a religious obligation for all Muslims.[21] This did not
stop the Taliban's murderous rampage through Karachi and KPK, trau-
matizing the local populace and spreading fear and despondency across
the country. Analysts despaired at the prospect of a low voter turnout.
Even the usual festivities associated with elections were missing. Security concerns led the Election Commission to restrict the size of election
hoardings and banners to prevent parties from putting up larger-than-life
portraits of their leaders, taking away some of the color and spectacle typical of elections in Pakistan. With no history of the Election Commission
ever enforcing the law on electoral expenses, candidates found other ways
of spending money to win votes without risking disqualification.[22] Despite the pain and suffering caused by the Taliban's endless carnage, people showed no lack of resolve in wanting to cast their votes. For all the
brickbats thrown at them, often with some justification, the media played
an invigorating role in creating an election atmosphere that was conspicuously missing from the streets and alleys of urban Pakistan as well as the
rural hinterlands. Instead of an open debate among equal contestants at
the national level, only the leading candidates of parties not on the Taliban's hit list were able to directly engage with the electorate.

A third-time contender for prime ministerial office, a wiser and more
mature Nawaz Sharif led his PML-N from the front, elating supporters
with reminders of his past achievements; promises of economic renewal
by solving the energy crisis and making peace with India; and resolutions
of putting an end to American drone attacks in FATA and initiating negotiations with the Taliban. The swing in the PML-N's favor in Punjab was
unmistakable. A faceless PPP burdened by incumbency was destined for
one of its worst routs in Pakistan's largest province, pitting the PML-N
against the PTI. Imran Khan's star power and, to quote a veteran journalist, "exaggerated sense of personal invincibility" had seen the PTI emerge
as a potent new force on the Pakistani political horizon.[23] Paid advertisements calling for a "new Pakistan" and extensive media coverage of Khan's
election rallies created momentum for the PTI in the urban areas. Some
television channels showed footage of the 1992 World Cup final won by
the team captained by Imran Khan. If a partial media tipped the scales in
the PTI's favor for avid cricket fans, other heads roiled on seeing the

Imran Khan leading an anti–US drone "peace caravan" to South Waziristan, October 7, 2012. *The White Star Photo Pvt. Ltd. Archive.*

quintessential antipolitician hero in the improbable role of politician. His self-righteous condemnation of political rivals and vows to end corruption within ninety days of coming into office were easy to dismiss as electoral rhetoric. However, his emotional video message upholding anti-Ahmadi clauses of the constitution created a stir. He denied ever soliciting the Ahmadi vote, alarming PTI's liberal supporters, who had mistaken the party's modernity, if not Khan's earlier life as a playboy lionized in the Western media, as evidence of a "secular" ideology. Imran's statement on the Ahmadis seemed the more egregious in light of his invocations of Jinnah's Pakistan. Even confirmed cynics were riled.

No less controversial was the cricketing legend's take on relations with the United States and the Taliban. The claim that a PTI government would shoot down American drones and open talks with the Taliban led the more astute to wonder about Imran Khan's sense of geopolitical realities. Lack of precision on how to go about addressing key problems and a catchall slogan for a "new Pakistan" proved less than convincing for an electorate looking for concrete solutions to their problems. Despite his charisma, Imran Khan was unable to give the PTI the look of a party set to make a real difference. For all the talk about the youth bulge, the party's upper echelons consisted mainly of the same old faces that had been tried and tested before. The message of change appealed to the urban, educated upper and middle classes, but Pakistan's electoral arithmetic was weighted in favor of rural constituencies where the PTI was organizationally weak or nonexistent. The biggest stumbling block was in Punjab's rural constituencies, where the landed classes had earned windfall profits from record food crops in 2010–11 they attributed to the PML-N government's agricultural policies but which in fact were a result of the PPP government's pro-agrarian pricing policies. An economic study claimed that Punjab's overall growth rate lagged behind other parts of Pakistan in the four years up to 2011, leading to criticism of Shahbaz Sharif's Lahore-centric development priorities.[24] But Punjab was still relatively better governed than the other provinces. Most voters in the province were inclined to want more of the same, cutting Imran Khan's slogan of "change" down to size. Voting the PML-N into office at the center and the province seemed to be the most rational and effective way of putting an end to electricity shortages, unemployment, and inflation.

Unmistakable signs of a pro-PML-N wave in Punjab did not deter Imran Khan from predicting a PTI victory. Encouraged by the addition of 36 million new voters, he dreamt that the PTI had swept the polls and hoped that as in the past this dream would also come true.[25] His indefatigable romp across Pakistan created a surge that led the PTI's most ardent supporters—educated youth addicted to social media in the main—to presume they were winning. Imran Khan's narrative on corruption and reputation for integrity elicited unprecedented enthusiasm among the very rich and well-off in Lahore, Karachi, Peshawar, Rawalpindi, and other key cities. The urban elite's newfound interest in politics, however, was no indicator of it being better placed to understand the complexity of the problems bedeviling Pakistan. The educated youth factor certainly gave the PTI's campaign added vigor, as did throngs of fashionable women from upmarket urban residential areas. But as many, if not more, Punjabi youth and women backed the PML-N. Three days before polling date, Imran Khan fell headfirst to the ground fifteen feet below from a makeshift lift taking him onto a stage to address a rally in Lahore. The cricket superstar's unlucky fall elicited widespread concern and sympathy. Ignoring the PTI chairman's brash references to him at public rallies, Nawaz Sharif prayed for Khan's health and suspended his campaign for a day. Others

less forgiving interpreted the hero's fall in his hometown as divine intervention to teach him some humility. The campaign ended with Nawaz
Sharif addressing a massive rally in Lahore and Imran Khan speaking
through a televised videoconference link from his hospital bed.

There was relief and cautious rejoicing. The Taliban had failed to stop
the elections. Pakistan's much vaunted democratic transition was now
unstoppable. With 600,000 security personnel protecting sensitive polling stations, there was a surprisingly high voter turnout on May 11, 2013,
in defiance of Taliban death squads and their controversial edict on Islam
and democracy. Despite security fears, 55 percent of the electorate voted,
compared with 44 percent in the 2008 elections, in a strong endorsement
of representative government. An early-morning attack in Karachi killing
thirteen people did not stop voters in the city from lining up for hours
outside polling stations. Tightened security arrangements in Punjab, including a welcome clampdown on the public display of weapons, resulted
in a 60 percent turnout. Voters in the Federal Capital Area topped the
turnout rates with 64 percent. Sindh was not too far behind at 54 percent.
Violence stricken KPK registered a 45 percent turnout while Taliban in-
fested FATA with 36 percent had the lowest turnout with almost no women
voting in some constituencies. In insurgency-torn Balochistan, a 43 percent turnout was an improvement on 31 percent in 2008. But the increase
was in Pathan dominated areas. There was virtually no voting in the
Baloch constituencies, a matter of great concern since the participation of
Baloch nationalists led by Sardar Akhtar Mengal in electoral politics had
raised hopes of addressing the province's grievances against the center.

By the evening of May 11, early returns showed the PML-N leading in
more than 112 seats with about thirty each for the PPP and the PTI. The
scale of the PML-N victory belied predictions that Pakistan was headed
for a hung Parliament. On the streets of Lahore, bands of youth wildly
celebrating a PTI victory a few hours earlier had been replaced by ecstatic
young supporters of the PML-N carrying banners, blaring music, and
screaming "shair" (lion)—the party's electoral symbol. There was stunned
silence at the PPP's reverse landslide, though few outside the party circles
were prepared to lament the result or question the legitimacy of the PML-N
mandate. Relief at the end of the PPP's corrupt and nonperforming government matched surprise at the extent of the PML-N victory. There was
quiet satisfaction at the success of the democratic process, however flawed

and in need of reform it may be. Who won mattered less than the fact of an ordered transition from one civilian government to another. Far from being a reductive stance toward landmark elections, this view held by intellectuals, lawyers, and the educated elite represented a firm belief in the imperative of the rule of law for a country that had suffered irreparable damage from repeated military interventions and quasi-military constitutional coups in its history. An emphasis on the importance of the continuity of the political process did not mean overlooking key issues associated with the credibility of the elections.

Nawaz Sharif's emergence at the helm of the largest single party in the national assembly was largely anticipated. But the extent of the victory surprised even die-hard PML-N supporters. As in the past, the PML-N won a higher percentage of the national assembly seats (129 out of 272, or 47.4 percent) than votes (32 percent). On the eve of a famous victory, Nawaz Sharif had given a clear message to the electorate when he said during a television interview that a split mandate would make the next five years far worse than the previous five. Leaving other parties far behind in a federal system, however, was not without disadvantages. The PML-N power base was in Punjab, from where it won 120 of the province's 148 national seats. Six seats from KPK, two from FATA, one each from Sindh and Balochistan, and the addition of nineteen independents and forty-one reserved seats for women and minorities gave the PML-N a simple majority with 189 seats in a national assembly that had a total strength of 342 seats. Despite a spirited campaign, the PTI failed to prevent the PML-N's flight to victory. While getting the second highest vote share in the country with just under 17 percent of the popular vote, the PTI bagged twenty-eight seats (10.2 percent) in the national assembly, making it the third largest party after the PPP, which won thirty-six seats with around 15 percent of the vote.[26] Province-wise the biggest upset was in KPK, where the ANP was wiped out by the PTI. Asfandyar Wali, the ANP leader, gracefully accepted defeat but tellingly blamed the result on the absence of a secure and even contest. "We thought CEC Fakhruddin G. Ibrahim would adjudicate the electoral contest," he said regretfully, but "the real referee was Hakimullah Mehsud," the TTP leader.[27]

The PPP's media experts called the results "manipulated" but accepted them in the interest of democracy. Party circles had a difficult time explaining an electoral defeat in which their supporters had not just stayed home in disgust at the PPP government's mismanagement but opted for either the PML-N or the PTI. PPP loyalists might try taking comfort in the party's ability to rise from the ashes. But the hard truth was that the left-of-center party they had supported since 1970 had not only lost its leftist orientation and urban base but was now a "feudal" party completely out of touch with the people. A dynastic fiefdom rather than a modern party with internal democracy, the PPP held out no hope for political aspirants from the rising middle classes in an urbanizing country. The theme of martyrdom for the sake of democracy still had some resonance in Pakistan. But without a clear vision of how to improve a dismal and fast-changing present, the use of the Bhutto name to advance the interests of the Zardari clan had few takers. The PPP was confined to its base in rural Sindh, losing its traditional stronghold in southern Punjab—the political base of former Prime Minister Gilani—where it had failed to deliver on the promise of a separate province, free from the dominance of Lahore. This left the PPP with just two national assembly seats from Punjab, a dismal showing for a party that had secured over fifty seats from the province in 2008.

Accusations of rigging and related electoral malpractices had poured in from all over Pakistan on polling day. There were reports of fraudulent stamping and defacement of votes as well as burning of ballot boxes in some constituencies. Booth captures by MQM workers and threats to the polling staff delayed voting in some polling stations in Karachi. But the MQM's stranglehold over the city had visibly weakened. The media headlined protests by the PTI's educated upper- and middle-class supporters against the MQM's electoral malpractices. There were similar charges in Lahore, where the PTI alleged ballot rigging in two constituencies. One of these was Imran Khan's home constituency, where he lost to the PML-N candidate. The PTI leader demanded a recount in twenty-five constituencies. Continued street protests against ballot rigging threatened to discredit a significant step in Pakistan's democratic odyssey. According to a member of the Human Rights Commission of Pakistan, candidates manipulated votes with the help of the police and returning officials in one hundred polling stations.[28] A recount in the affected constituencies would not have made a difference to the overall result given the huge margin of the PML-N victory. A sense of urgency dictated that the election controversy be set aside to let the newly elected government get on with the business of resolving the problems of power outages and militancy to end years of economic stagnation. Without an economic revival and better governance, the future of the democratic process would remain uncertain. Once saner counsels prevailed, the more dubious aspects of the election process were left in the hands of the courts and election tribunals set up by the Election Commission to hear the complaints. But the brouhaha over rigging refused to die down. Questioning the credibility of the courts and the Election Commission's tribunals based on their past record, Imran Khan swore he would upon recovery lead street protests if investigations of poll rigging lacked transparency.[29]

Elections in Pakistan have hardly ever been free of administrative manipulation even if the "establishment" has occasionally failed to deliver the desired results, as happened in 1970 and to a lesser extent in 2002. The idea of a free and fair election, therefore, can be meaningfully addressed only with reference to the nature of the state and Pakistani political culture. Charges of electoral rigging refer to irregularities in the voting process on Election Day. Systemic rigging prior to the polls, however, has typically been the more prominent aspect of manipulated election results in Pakistan. This takes a variety of forms, including changes in electoral laws; reshuffling the administrative bureaucracy to ensure "positive" results; unfair use of government resources, including the media, to the advantage of the official favorite; delimitation of constituencies to suit candidates supported by state agencies like the ISI; and, most important, a malleable chief election commissioner. Elections are not necessarily rigged with the active support of the chief election commissioner or the Election Commission, who for the most part are unaware of what is happening in far-flung constituencies.

The unenforceability and misuse of election laws has much to do with the administrative bureaucracy's entanglements with Pakistani society and politics.[30] Far from being the representatives of an impersonal and rule-bound state, local government officials and the police are often beholden to influential political families who control the local patronage networks. In the absence of organized machineries, party tickets in Pakistan are given to so-called electables, who more often than not are scions of influential political clans. In a rapidly urbanizing setting, however, politicians belonging to the same family are no longer drawn exclusively from the landed classes. An obvious case in point is the House of Sharifs.

According to one estimate, over the last three decades a mere 400 families have shaped policies, programs, and legislation affecting the lives of a 180 million Pakistanis. Between 1985 and 2008, two-thirds of the elected legislators and about half of the top three contestants in the national assembly elections in Punjab belonged to established political families. Instead of being limited to the upper echelons of political parties, "dynasticism" is deeply embedded in constituency politics.[31] The monetization of politics since the Zia era transformed the character of elections in Pakistan. Those with local influence and access to state patronage and control over development funds have the wherewithal and clout to get themselves elected. Rigging at polling stations occurs when an established candidate's main support groups, who are often old hands in the art of "choreographing" elections, cast bogus votes with the collusion of the police, the local bureaucracy, and polling staff drawn mainly from government schoolteachers and lower judicial officials. Other extralegal methods include an excessive use of money to pressure and entice voters; the provision of transport to voters on polling day; use of strong-arm tactics against rival candidates' polling agents; intimidation of voters to prevent them from going to polling stations; and tampering with ballots and getting away with fixing the result.[32]

Winning an election in Pakistan in effect means foiling attempts by rival candidates to engineer the result. Lacking well-oiled party machineries capable of thwarting electoral fraud, only candidates with political muscle and deep pockets can expect to carry the day. The Election Commission has a poor record of booking candidates for any serious electoral irregularities. Since 1985 there has been a growing trend among candidates to spend astronomical sums of money to win elections, well in excess of the legal limit. Political parties and candidates are required under the election laws to submit their accounts for audit and also report their election expenses. The information, if supplied, is incomplete, as neither parties nor candidates honor the law on electoral expenditure. But no one has been charged, far less disqualified. While the institutional weaknesses of the Election Commission of Pakistan have much to answer for this, political parties have also allowed statutory provisions on election expenditure to lapse in their quest to preserve their numbers in Parliament.[33]

Against the backdrop of a depressing electoral history, there were high expectations of a free and fair election in 2013. Breaking the barrier seemed possible given the perceived impartiality of the Election Commission, consisting of five retired judges, an independent-minded judiciary, a watchful media, and by and large neutral caretaker governments. There was at least no visible involvement of the ISI and the military, nor were there any "election cells" in the presidency as in the past. The fresh preparation of electoral rolls and the elimination of bogus voters also lent greater credibility to the elections. However, a deeply politicized and openly partisan police and administrative bureaucracy could still improve the chances of candidates and parties to the detriment of opponents without coming under the scrutiny of the law. The pervasiveness of systemic bias for or against a political party makes it impossible to blame any single individual, group, or institution for electoral wrongdoing. Pervasive police and bureaucratic connections with candidates in local constituencies makes the anonymity of responsibility in systemic rigging a bigger challenge for the managers of the electoral process than bogus ballots in certain constituencies. The PTI's insistence on electoral transparency would be more meaningful if instead of simply ballot rigging it broadened the discourse on electoral malpractices to the larger and more pressing question of ensuring the political neutrality of state officials responsible for conducting the elections.

To what extent were the 2013 elections free and fair? They were as free and fair as the structural and existential realities of Pakistan permitted. The displacement of merit in recruitment, placement, and promotion has led to a precipitous decline in service standards in the police and the civil bureaucracy. Instead of serving the state, police and civil officials seek patrons in ruling parties or parties-in-waiting to advance their career prospects. So long as there is an all too close interface between state officials and politicians, a completely free and fair election in Pakistan will remain an aspiration. Conducted under the democratically superfluous framework of caretaker governments to accommodate fears of partisanship by an incumbent government, the 2013 elections nevertheless are an important landmark in the realization of that elusive objective. The endorsement of democracy in the face of Taliban terror by the largest voter turnout in four decades is perhaps the most encouraging sign of all. Equally hopeful has been the smooth transition from one civilian government to another and the establishment of governments at the center and the provinces without the usual political rancor. Mian Nawaz Sharif has got a solid mandate and after fourteen years made history with an unprecedented third stint as prime minister. His task in an unenviable one and will test the new government to the utmost as it moves on multiple fronts to pull Pakistan out of its current morass. Only time will tell whether the geostrategic situation that surfaces after the American endgame in Afghanistan will give Pakistan a reasonable chance to deal with the swarm of political, economic, social, and environmental challenges that have weighed it down for so long.

EPILOGUE

Overcoming Terror

EVER SINCE ITS BLOOD-STAINED ADVENT on the global scene in 1947, there has been unceasing speculation about Pakistan's imminent collapse. Such dreary forecasts have not been entirely improbable even if they have not come to fruition. Far from disintegrating soon after its creation, as had been widely anticipated, Pakistan endured a difficult postcolonial transition and the severe demands of an international system shaped by Cold War rivalries. Survival, however, was achieved at the cost of weakening democratic processes, intrinsic to maintaining a fragile federal equation, and coming under bureaucratic control and military dominance within the first few years of independence. A disputed border with Afghanistan on the west and the Kashmir conflict with India on the east combined with domestic political discord between diverse and far-flung regions to foster a massive insecurity complex that more often than not erased the distinction between perceptions of external and internal threats to the country's existence.

Fears of Afghan and Indian intervention in the NWFP, Balochistan, and, prior to 1971, also in the eastern wing inspired a feverish narrative of security in which defending the national borders justified ruthless suppression of political dissent. Pakistan's willingness to join US-sponsored security pacts aimed at staving off India had a decisive bearing on the military's ascent to power. An insecurity complex based on fears of Indian hegemony facilitated the military's dominance over civilian institutions and has been the main reason for Pakistan's faltering struggle to constitute a viable federal system consistent with the democratic aspirations of its different regions.

The uncertainties of the geostrategic environment that unfolds in the wake of the US withdrawal from Afghanistan in 2014 evoke the worries of another departing military power from the region more than six and a half decades ago. As they debated their withdrawal from India, the British chiefs of staff had questioned the logic of creating a new country out of the northwestern and northeastern extremities of the subcontinent—Pakistan—that would cost as much to defend as undivided India but with less than a quarter of its economic resource base. Left with a staggering defense burden, accentuated by the Kashmir dispute with India, Pakistan under the direction of a pro-Western clique of senior bureaucrats and military officials actively solicited the patronage of the United States, which was looking for allies in the Cold War. Pakistan's pro-Western tilt was confirmed by the signing of military pacts with the Americans in the 1950s. Significantly, this rattled the left wing in the country even more than the socially conservative right wing, which paraded as the monitors of the Islamic pulse of the people. Opposition to Pakistan's security treaties with the United States, especially in the eastern wing, was one factor prompting the first military coup in 1958. In the 1960s, stronger ties between Ayub Khan's military regime and Washington led to a crackdown on left-wing parties and an embryonic labor and peasant movement. Although the 1965 war jolted relations with the United States, it was only after the breakaway of Bangladesh in 1971 and the Soviet invasion of Afghanistan in 1979 that the concordance of interests between an American-backed Pakistani military regime and right-wing parties using religion came into its own.

America's funding of Islamist groups of varying stripes and colors against the Soviet Union gave the Afghan "jihad" a global character, with Pakistan's northwestern tribal areas serving as the main staging ground. Muslim radicals from the Middle East, Central Asia, Europe, and North America flocked to Pakistan where, along with over 3 million Afghan refugees, they were welcomed by General Zia-ul-Haq's military regime. Arab ideologues frustrated with the repressive nature of the regimes in their home countries found a ready outlet in Pakistan of the 1980s. While easing political pressures on authoritarian regimes in the Gulf region, the infusion of money from Saudi Arabia promoted a heady doctrine of

Wahabi-Salafist Islam in an overwhelmingly Sunni Barelvi Pakistan. The American CIA for its part assisted the ISI's makeover into the most powerful institution of the Pakistani state with deep pockets and interests in practically all sectors of the national economy. Once the Soviet withdrawal led to a loss of American interest in Afghanistan, the ISI crafted the Taliban in 1996 to avoid losing a skirmish after winning the war.

During the next five years, concrete material and political advantages accrued to a highly select group of senior military officials and their clients, who made a killing through arms procurement, drug cartels, and urban land mafias. The ensuing violence, corruption, and crime fueled by involvement in the Afghan war thoroughly destabilized Pakistan. Rivalries between Saudi Arabia and Iran for regional supremacy and also between Tehran and Baghdad during the Iran–Iraq War were played out on Pakistani soil with devastating effects on the local sectarian balance. With the military and its intelligence agencies actively taking sides in the Shia–Sunni conflict, no part of the country remained immune from terror in the name of Islam, perpetrated by Muslims against fellow Muslims in the main. The situation has been especially fraught in KPK, FATA, and Balochistan, provinces whose proximity to Afghanistan has made them particularly vulnerable to the collateral damage of the US-led wars against the Soviet Army and Al Qaeda.

The paradox of the much-vaunted homeland for the subcontinent's Muslims becoming a veritable killing field of Islam is attributable in the first instance to the strategic and economic consequences of India's partition. No less critical have been the ties of dependency Pakistan forged with the United States since the early 1950s. Despite mutual distrust and a clear divergence of interests, US–Pakistani interdependency increased exponentially during the American-sanctioned "jihad" against ungodly communism in the 1980s; following a ten-year rupture in the early 1990s, this interdependency was formally revived in September 2001. Barring concerns specific to the conclusion of American military engagement in Afghanistan, namely, nuclear proliferation and terrorism, the recent strategic and economic partnership between the United States and India has made Pakistan largely redundant in Washington's scheme of things.

An unraveling of the US–Pakistani relationship, if pushed to its logical conclusion, will have untold consequences for not just South Asia but also Saudi–Iranian competition for dominance in the Persian Gulf and the

Middle East. Even as Saudi-funded Sunni groups have been indiscriminately targeting the Shia minority community in parts of Pakistan, neighboring Iran has been seeking to end its international isolation by capitalizing on the strains in Islamabad's relations with the Americans. So far the bond of Sunnism and the attractions of Arab petro dollars, to say nothing of US pressure and the approaching endgame in Afghanistan, have deterred Pakistan from reviving relations with Iran to a point where the sectarian conflict can be neutralized. The choice may not be as simple and clear-cut for Islamabad now that the Arab Spring's promises of freedom, justice, and democracy have made way for what portends to be a long, bitter, and deadly fall under military dictatorship and other variants of authoritarian rule.

Two US-sponsored wars in Afghanistan in three decades together with the impact of the contemporary phase of globalization have strengthened historical linkages between the Middle East and South Asia to such an extent that trends originating in one region are often a precursor to what could happen in the other. A breakdown in US–Pakistani relations due to differences over Indian involvement and the political denouement in post-2014 Afghanistan could lead Islamabad to openly oppose American geostrategic ambitions in South Asia and add immeasurably to Washington's mounting woes in the Middle East. The one silver lining in the clouds from the US point of view has been Pakistan's close dealings with Saudi Arabia, which despite being the purveyor of a rigid Salafist worldview that is inimical to the American way of thinking remains an important ally of Washington on account of its vast oil wealth and strategic location in the Gulf. So long as Islamabad and Riyadh are on the same page over Iran, Washington may well have no real cause for concern.

This could change as Pakistan, economically enfeebled by the blowback of the war in Afghanistan, looks to stretch its network of friends and supporters to offset the cooling of relations with the United States. The global implications of a reversion to authoritarianism in Egypt—where the military has ousted the country's first democratically elected president, Mohammad Morsi of the Muslim Brotherhood, with the backing of Saudi Arabia and the acquiescence of the United States—may turn out to be a test case. Remembering his own predicament at the hands of the military in 1999, Prime Minister Nawaz Sharif joined Turkey and Qatar in opposing the military's crackdown on the Muslim Brotherhood in Egypt in contravention of the stance taken by the Saudi government. With Washington and Riyadh pursuing a narrowly focused anti-Iran agenda in the Middle East, especially in Syria and Iraq, and not recoiling from welcoming the military back into politics in Egypt, the PML-N government in Islamabad may find it difficult to sustain the warmth of its old contacts with the Saudi royal family, much less trust Pakistan's already estranged American patrons. Unlike in Egypt, the long history of movements for democracy in Pakistan will ensure that its people will not allow their aspirations to be reduced to a stark and unenviable choice between religious majoritarianism and military dictatorship.

The 2013 elections, marking the first ever democratic transition from one civilian government to another in more than six decades of independence, is a potential opening for Pakistan to make a break with recurrent spells of direct military rule. This will require a deepening of democracy and building of appropriate mechanisms for political mobilization and transparency, thereby forcing a readjustment in the existing skewed balance of power between civil and military institutions. The opportunity comes at a time when decades of failed attempts at centralization and controlled politics have resulted in a disturbing fragmentation of state institutions, organized crime kindled by a growing informal economy, and the rising specter of an ungovernable nuclear country. The decline in state authority has been evident in escalating violence along political, sectarian, and criminal gang lines. Institutional disarray, corruption, and maladministration pervade all walks of life, governmental and private. Yet for all the talk about Pakistan being a failing or failed state, its citizens are not altogether without hope and, despite evidence to the contrary, eagerly want the state to start delivering. The demand for a state may be in inverse proportion to its extant capacities but is a sure sign of the desire among Pakistanis for a modicum of efficient governance. This was the sentiment that brought out voters in droves in the elections of May 2013 despite the extreme violence that attended the campaign and the threat of further attacks by the Pakistani Taliban on polling day. The PPP government's inability to address elementary aspects of governance resulted in the party's rout in Punjab. But the extent of the PPP's defeat was also a warning to the winning parties that a similar fate awaited them unless they addressed the pressing problems facing a terrorized and economically moribund country.

Against the backdrop of a global economic downturn, Pakistanis share many of the same anxieties that brought people out into the streets of Tunisia, Egypt, Bahrain, Syria, and, for different reasons, also in Turkey. But these similarities cannot detract from key differences in historical and geopolitical context. The future course of democracy in Pakistan is inextricably linked with its capacity for overcoming terror, both conceptually and existentially. A great deal hinges on the capacity of Nawaz Sharif's government to begin undoing the effects of decades of military dominance and the undermining of the rule of law so that Pakistan can play its part as a responsible and valued member of the international community. Improving relations with India through trade expansion and agreement on outstanding issues like Kashmir and the sharing of the Indus River water were high on Sharif's agenda when he took office. But although the PPP-led government had committed itself to giving India most favored nation status in trade, this was postponed indefinitely by the new dispensation in Islamabad after a series of firing incidents along the LOC killed military personnel on both sides. The setback points to the continuing ability of the Pakistani Army to scuttle, if not actually veto, any peace moves with India that do not serve its purposes.

For all its litany of woes, Pakistan is not going to disappear from the map of the world in a hurry. Although there are innumerable challenges, internal and external, the situation has not altogether gone off the rails. Power equations have changed, and Pakistan's state of martial rule is no longer in a position to exercise power without some combination of political parties to legitimize the arrangement. With the military authoritarian postcolonial state now needing to accommodate rather than distort or control the political process, there are ample opportunities for renegotiating the dialectic between the state and the political process. These reflect key shifts in the political economy, where the commercialization of production and exchange has been paralleled by the increasing monetization of politics. These historical developments account for the complexity and ferocity of social conflicts in Pakistan today. But they also contain the threads of hope for a dramatic break with old and tired policies of confrontation with regional neighbors in the interest of shared peace and prosperity.

The prospects of such a fresh start in the region remain hostage to the familiar scenario of Pakistan alternating between being a victim and a springboard of the terror networks that have spanned the interregnum between the war against the Soviets and the post-2001 American-led military operations in Afghanistan. Popular belief that Pakistan has been fighting America's war for money has sorely hindered the campaign against the militants. Pakistani Army personnel have been fighting battle-hardened militants from Central Asia, the Middle East, and other parts of the world in FATA, suffering heavy casualties and causing the displacement of millions. International suspicions have remained, however, about the Pakistani Army's commitment to bringing the campaign to its logical conclusion and helping ease American and NATO difficulties in pulling out of the Afghanistan quagmire. Drone attacks in FATA have taken out key militants but also stirred anti-Americanism and made it trickier for the Pakistani Army to fight against the insurgents without alienating its own rank and file. The death and mayhem unleashed by suicide bombers in Pakistani cities as vengeance for the military operations in their territory indicates that the Taliban retain the capability of hitting back hard.

The threats and challenges facing Pakistan sixty-seven years after its birth appear to offer little scope for a smooth and immediate resolution. However, the prognosis is not altogether hopeless. Unlike Middle Eastern dictators who used outright coercion to completely marginalize the political opposition and rule for decades on end, no military ruler in Pakistan has survived in power for more than eleven years. A long history of political activism has seen Pakistani opposition parties overcoming their divisions and organizational limitations to dislodge military regimes that had lost popular support. Another reason why Pakistan may be relatively better positioned than Egypt to avoid a military takeover is the very different correlation of regional and international factors in their domestic politics. A critical pillar in America's Israel-centered policy toward the Middle East, Egypt has a history of bitter contention between a nationalist army and Islamist parties like the Muslim Brotherhood. By contrast, the relationship between the military and the Islamists has been an ambivalent one in Pakistan, posing a very different set of challenges.

The US-supported Pakistani military allied with the Jamaat-i-Islami and also with the Deobandi-oriented JUI in KPK not for religious reasons but for political and strategic ones. The ISI's sponsorship of the Taliban and associated militant organizations in pursuit of tactical gains in Afghanistan and Kashmir produced a large network of retainers, many of

them linked to criminals and murderers, who could be used in the flourishing heroin trade. Controlled by the military's own National Logistics
Cell, the drug trade and the siphoning off of weapons earmarked for the
war in Afghanistan transformed Pakistan into a place out of hell, where
mafia dons backed by politicians and the army rubbed shoulders with
those labeled terrorists.

The military's huge stake in the country might on the face of it seem to
make Pakistan an ideal candidate for a takeover by the defense forces. But
Pakistan's history reveals the dangers of ruling provinces of vastly uneven
political and economic resources with a thwack of the military whip. Unlike the short-lived Arab Spring of 2012, there have been several Pakistani
springs fired by the emotive force of regionalism that have all too easily
been dismissed as secessionist and delegitimized in the state-sponsored
national narratives. If the political mainstream had accommodated regional demands, not manipulated them to suit the purposes of the incumbent government, the curbs on military rule would have been far more
effective than they proved to be. The steps taken to consolidate the federation under the Eighteenth Amendment and, more consequentially, in the
NFC award increasing the share of the provinces require an uninterrupted
and autonomous political process to improve relations between the center
and the provinces. Another military intervention at a time when parts of
the country are already in the control of insurgents and criminal militias
with links to serving and retired operatives of the state's intelligence agencies could bring the whole edifice crumbling down. However, the military
is unlikely to want to take charge of a precariously placed national economy. Confining itself to the role of ultimate arbitrator may be the better
choice for an army that has seen its prestige decline in direct proportion
to the ground it has lost to civilian militias created by its own intelligence
agencies.

The primary lesson to emerge from Pakistan's history is that democratic transitions after a period of military rule are inherently messy and
reversible. A constitutional change from one civilian government to another is a necessary but insufficient condition to bring about a decisive
shift in the civil–military equation. The army continues to shape foreign
and defense policies and has the ultimate say in internal security matters.
A great deal depends on just how well Nawaz Sharif has learned from past
oversights and whether he can strengthen democratic institutions and

improve his own room to maneuver on both the domestic and the foreign policy fronts without provoking an army takeover. The ability to prevent a military coup does not imply civilian supremacy. It will take decades of an unbroken process of democratic politics in which governments are voted in and out of office before civilians can match the clout of their military counterparts. If the prime minister's hefty mandate at the center and in Punjab, together with opposition governments in the non-Punjabi provinces, does not lure him into amassing power unduly—an occupational hazard that led to his downfall in 1999—Nawaz Sharif's elected government may succeed in leading Pakistan away from decades of martial rule.

There are other encouraging signs. Civil society in Pakistan remained badly disorganized because of consistent disruptions of the political process, a long history of weak political parties, and the absence of any rule of law. The lawyers' movement in the spring of 2007 for the reinstatement of a chief justice, unceremoniously removed from office by a military dictator, raised hopes that the supremacy of the law would be upheld. Though the lawyers' movement did not live up to expectations, this had nothing to with Pakistan's surrender to Islamist radicalism but was a by-product of the lingering infirmities of civil and political society in a military authoritarian state. In contrast to the past, when the judicial arms of the state typically toed the line of the executive, whether military or civilian, Pakistan now has an assertive and independent-minded judiciary that has shown signs of activism that were unthinkable in the earlier decades. Instead of a state-controlled media that could easily be cowed into submission, the technologically driven phase of contemporary globalization has revolutionized communications and led to the setting up of several privately owned television channels. For the first time in Pakistan's postcolonial history, the third nonelective institution of the state and the fourth estate have got a rare opportunity to side with a vocal, if fractured, civil society that will oppose any unconstitutional move by the army. This can usher in a significant shift in the political landscape as the people of Pakistan join their counterparts in the Middle East to demand better governance as well as social and economic opportunities.

Disenchantment with religious extremism is finding expression through a variety of mediums. More and more Pakistanis, not just those with access to the new social media, are questioning the role of the military in politics and want control of their affairs to be vested in the hands of a

Parliament they can elect and hold accountable. There is admiration for Turkey, whose blending of Islamic belief and practice with a cosmopolitan and democratic outlook under the Justice and Democratic Party is held up as a role model Pakistan should emulate in its efforts to move beyond military rule. There is growing recognition by Pakistanis that the military in alliance with select elites and religio-political groupings has been using Islam to achieve its security goals rather than any virtuous religious purpose. The surge in suicide bombings of heavily populated urban areas has underscored the extent to which the ethical meaning of jihad as striving for a noble endeavor has been lost in the temporal maelstroms of Pakistan's power politics. With the state sinking under the weight of its own contradictions, seemingly unable to control militant groups flaunting Islam to justify perpetrating violence against fellow Muslims and non-Muslim minorities alike, Pakistanis are not only asking questions but have been displaying extraordinary innovation, skill, and dynamism in a variety of fields, including the creative arts.

The burgeoning of a popular culture in the midst of state-sponsored Islamization and terrorism is a remarkable feat for Pakistan. It draws on rich and vibrant poetic, musical, and artistic traditions that are well manifested in the country's diverse regional and subregional settings. Resistance themes inspired by regional folklore and culture have always been intrinsic to the dialogue between the rulers and the ruled, both imaginary and real. Decades of authoritarianism and state-sponsored nationalism have only strengthened the appeal of regional counter-narratives in artistic productions. Creative engagements with the regional and transnational realms of cultural and intellectual production, facilitated by the new technologies, are producing rich and innovative forms of artistic expression. Among the more noteworthy achievements in recent times has been the spectacular success of the extensively telecast "Coke Studio" sessions, where talented Pakistani musicians, such as Atif Aslam, Shafqat Amanat Ali, Abida Parveen, and Arif Lohar, are sponsored by the soft drink US multinational to render scintillating new fusions of some of Pakistan's greatest folk and popular songs. There is a rich tradition of musical and artistic creativity in Pakistan that has actively engaged with transnational trends, resulting in innovative blending and fresh departures. Before his tragically early death in 1997, Ustad Nusrat Fateh Ali Khan regaled audiences at home and globally with his enrapturing *qawwalis* (a form of Sufi devotional music) for hours on end. The globalization of Pakistani music has been accompanied by a remarkable leap in the transnational reach of the creative arts. Building on the works of Shakir Ali, Zubeida Agha, Sadequain, Zahoorul Akhlaque, and many others who pioneered the modernist phase in Pakistani painting in the earlier decades, a younger generation of painters are making creative uses of new ideas and technologies to both access and influence a diverse and dynamic transnational artistic scene. The dazzling array of new directions in the contemporary art, literature, and music of Pakistan displays an ongoing tussle between an officially constructed ideology of nationalism and relatively autonomous social and cultural processes in the construction of a "national culture." Although Pakistan cannot match the output of India's performing arts and robust commercial film industry, a number of its independent artists, musicians, and writers have been in the vanguard of creativity in the subcontinent as a whole.

The contrast between collective failure and individual success is not a novel occurrence in an authoritarian state. It is the lack of acknowledgment of this cultural renewal based on individual creativity that has consigned Pakistan to the ignoble status of the instigator of global terror. Pakistanis have much to answer for in this distorted image, but the course ahead will partly depend on the openness of the international community to their considerable cultural achievements. While the intensification of religious extremism has certainly left deep psychological scars, it has not been a one-dimensional process leading to the inevitable "Talibanization," as is often projected in the international media. Violence in the name of religion has also prompted counternarratives. There are many Pakistanis who object to the state's projection of an imported Saudi variant of Islam that together with the military high command's strategic security paradigm has converted their country into a source of extremism. This is amply evident in the musical, artistic, literary, and dramatic productions coming out of Pakistan, reflecting the politicization of the personal that invariably accompanies the depoliticization of the public arena under authoritarian and semiauthoritarian regimes. If military dictatorships have not stunted the creative impulse, the unending waves of terror and counterterror are being resisted through imaginative recourse to local, regional, as well as transnational idioms of a cosmopolitan humanism that celebrates rather than eliminates the fact of difference.

These countervailing trends evoking peace and accommodation may appear inconsequential in comparison with the aggressive and exclusionary narratives on jihad and Muslim identity that have enjoyed state support for over three decades. But the misery and human degradation that has sprung from the effects of external wars on Pakistani soil have been an equally powerful factor in the rising popular interest in the rich cultural repertoire of the mystical traditions of the country. These conflicting dynamics of moderation versus extremism signify the battle for the soul of Pakistan that continues to be waged on several fronts, imperceptibly and inconclusively. If Pakistanis continue conflating the teachings of Islam with the methods and ideology of the militants and turn a blind eye to the threat the Taliban pose to individual and collective security, overcoming terror will remain an unrealizable dream. Yet that dream exists and is being expressed in Pakistan's literature, music, and the arts.

No elected government in Pakistan can afford to be complacent about handling the threat of militancy given a dangerously fluid geostrategic situation along the western border with Afghanistan. Renewed civil war in Afghanistan after the withdrawal of the US-led forces will bring another torrent of refugees into Pakistan's restive northwestern tribal areas, KPK and Balochistan, imposing unbearable strains on their already faltering provincial administrations. Suing for peace in Afghanistan and taking steps to eliminate terror networks, with at least the tacit consent of the military, is the ideal option for an elected government in Islamabad. Without brokering an agreement among the warring groups in Afghanistan and bringing the military on board to rein in homegrown militants, the tide of violence that will erupt could throw the entire region into chaos, with unimaginable consequences for nuclear Pakistan.

The sobering fact is that the magnitude and range of problems besieging Pakistan are so enormous that even the best efforts on the part of a competent elected government may not be enough to steady the course. Learning to live with the shortcomings of their chosen representatives without losing faith in the democratic process will not come easily to a divided and frustrated people who have been ruled by the military and fed negative narratives about politics and politicians. If there is one thing Pakistan needs to take from Egypt's experience since 2011, it is that there is a world of difference between an ineffective government that can at least be voted out of office and the abject failure of democratic processes, which military interventions unvaryingly signify. Understanding that subtle but crucial distinction may hold the key to Pakistan's release from interminable cycles of military authoritarianism and trigger the beginnings of a long but arduous journey toward a functioning democracy. After eluding Pakistan for over six decades, democracy is coming to be recognized by a cross section of society in all the different provinces as the one remaining salve that can relieve the extreme stresses caused by aborted political processes and military authoritarianism. It is a hope that has to be seized upon so that Pakistan can provide its long-suffering people with a reasonable chance to realize their thwarted aspirations. In the process, they might begin laying the foundation for a new and more robust federal union based on mutual respect and accommodation among the different constituent units. Being played out in the vortex of global politics, the battle for the soul of Pakistan does not yet have a clear winner. The citizens of Jinnah's Muslim homeland have a voice still in determining its future.

NOTES

GLOSSARY

ACKNOWLEDGMENTS

INDEX

NOTES

Prologue

1. Begum Liaquat Ali Khan to Governor-General of Pakistan, August 12, 1952, No. 2685-GG/52, PMS/52 Correspondence with the Governor General of Pakistan, National Documentation Center, Islamabad, Pakistan (henceforth NDC).

2. Benazir Bhutto, *Reconciliation: Islam, Democracy and the West* (London: Simon and Schuster, 2008), p. 8.

3. *Report of the United Nations Commission of Inquiry into the facts and circumstances of the assassination of former Pakistani Prime Minister Mohtarma Benazir Bhutto,* http://www.un.org/News/dh/infocus/Pakistan/UN_Bhutto_Report_15April2010.pdf, p. 4.

4. Alan Campbell-Johnson, *Mission with Mountbatten,* 2nd ed. (London: R. Hale, 1972), p. 87.

5. This has invited protest from the few historians Pakistan possesses. See, for example, K. K. Aziz, *The Murder of History in Pakistan: A Critique of History Textbooks Used in Pakistan* (Lahore: Vanguard Publications, 1993), and Mubarak Ali, *In the Shadow of History* (Lahore: Progressive Publishers, 1993).

6. Faiz Ahmad Faiz, "Bol" (Speak), *Poems by Faiz,* trans. Victor Kiernan (1971; reprint, Lahore: Vanguard Books, 2009), pp. 86–89.

1. From Minority to Nation

1. Mohammad Ali Jinnah's speech at the Aligarh Muslim University Union, March 10, 1941, in *Speeches, Statements & Messages of the Quaid-e-Azam,* ed. K. A. K. Yusufi (Lahore: Bazm-i-Iqbal, 1996), 2:1348–1349.

2. A misleading analogy between the demand for Pakistan and the creation of Israel informs the work of some scholars. See, for example, Faisal Devji, *Muslim Zion* (Cambridge, MA: Harvard University Press, 2013).

3. *The Times* (London), September 12, 1959, p. 4.

4. See Ayesha Jalal, "Conjuring Pakistan: History as Official Imagining," *International Journal of Middle East Studies* 27, no. 1 (February 1995): 73–89.

5. Cited in Ayesha Jalal, *The Sole Spokesman: Jinnah, the Muslim League, and the Demand for Pakistan* (Cambridge: Cambridge University Press, 1985), p. 7.

6. Ibid., p. 71.

7. Muhammad Iqbal's presidential address to AIML in December 1930, in *Foundations of Pakistan, All-India Muslim League Documents: 1906–1947,* ed. Sharifuddin Pirzada (Karachi: National Publishing House, 1970), 2:159.

8. Ibid., p. 160.

9. Ibid., pp. 309–310.

10. Choudhary Rahmat Ali, *Pakistan: The Fatherland of the Pak Nation* (Cambridge: Foister and Jagg, 1947), pp. 228–229.

11. M. R. Afzal, ed., *Speeches and Statements of the Quaid-i-Azam Mohammad Ali Jinnah, [1911–34 and 1947–48]* (Lahore: Research Society of Pakistan, 1980), p. 42.

12. Yusufi, *Speeches, Statements & Messages,* 1:3–4, 8, 14.

13. Ibid, pp. 5, 10.

14. Ibid., pp. 73–74.

15. Cited in Beverley Nicols, *Verdict on India* (London: Jonathan Cape, 1944), p. 193.

16. Sayyid Ahmad Khan's speeches at Patna, January 27, 1883, and Gurdaspur, January 27, 1884, in *Writing and Speeches of Sir Sayyid Ahmad Khan,* ed. Shan Mohammad (Bombay: Nachiketa Publications, 1972), pp. 159–160, 266–267.

17. Jawaharlal Nehru, ed., *A Bunch of Old Letters Written Mostly to Jawaharlal Nehru and Some Written by Him* (London: Asia Publication House, 1960), p. 278.

18. For a discussion of these Muslim schemes, see Ayesha Jalal, *Self and Sovereignty: Individual and Community in South Asian Islam since 1850* (London: Routledge, 2000), ch. 8.

19. Jinnah's interview to representatives of Punjab Muslim Student's Federation, Lahore, August 5, 1944, in Yusufi, *Speeches, Statements & Messages,* 3:1938.

20. Jinnah's address to the AIML at Lahore, July 30, 1944, in Pirzada, *Foundations of Pakistan,* 2:493–495.

21. Yusufi, *Speeches, Statements & Messages,* 2:1348–1350.

22. Jalal, *Sole Spokesman,* p. 70.

2. Truncated State, Divided Nation

1. Faiz Ahmad Faiz, "Freedom's Dawn (August 1947)," *Poems by Faiz,* trans. Victor Kiernan (1971; reprint, Lahore: Vanguard Books, 2009), pp. 123–126.

2. Ayesha Jalal, *Self and Sovereignty: Individual and Community in South Asian Islam since 1850* (London: Routledge, 2000), ch. 9.

3. See Ayesha Jalal, *The Pity of Partition: Manto's Life, Times, and Work across the India-Pakistan Divide* (Princeton, NJ: Princeton University Press, 2013).

4. All references to Manto's partition short stories here are from *Bitter Harvest: The Very Best of Saadat Hasan Manto,* ed. and trans. Khalid Hasan (New Delhi: Penguin, 2008), pp. 9–20, 39–48.

5. Manto, "Yaum-i-Istiqlal" [Independence Day], *Manto Rama* (Lahore: Sang-e-Meel, 1990), pp. 351–353.

6. Saadat Hasan Manto, "Toba Tek Singh," *Manto Nama* (Lahore: Sang-e-Meel, 1990), pp. 11–18. For an English translation see Khalid Hasan, *Wet Afternoon* (Lahore: Alhamra, 2001), pp. 44–51.

7. Beverley Nichols, *Verdict on India* (London: Jonathan Cape, 1944), pp. 189–190.

8. Jinnah's interview with Reuters correspondent Duncan Hooper, October 25, 1947, in *Selected Speeches and Statements of the Quaid-i-Azam Mohammad Ali Jinnah (1911–34 and 1947–48),* ed. M. Rafique Afzal, 4th ed. (Lahore: Research Society of Pakistan, 1980), p. 439.

9. Ibid.

10. Ibid., pp. 456–457.

11. Abdullah Malik, *Purani Mehfilain Yaad Aa Rahi Hein (Aap Beeti)* (Lahore: Takhle-eqat, 2002), p. 396.

12. A. Hameed, *Lahore Lahore Aye* (Lahore: Vanguard Books, 2008), pp. 21–24, 36.

13. *Speeches, Statements and Messages of the Quaid-e-Azam,* ed. K. A. K. Yusufi (Lahore: Bazm-i-Iqbal, 1996), 4:2604–2605.

14. Afzal, *Speeches and Statements,* p. 440.

15. *Quaid-i-Azam Mohammed Ali Jinnah: Speeches and Statements as Governor-General of Pakistan, 1947–48* (Islamabad: Directorate of Films and Publications, Ministry of Information, Government of Pakistan, 1989), pp. 131, 155.

16. Ralph Waldo Emerson, "Uses of Great Men," in *The Works of Ralph Waldo Emerson* (New York: Black's Readers Service, 1965), p. 424.

17. Muhammad Iqbal, *Bal-i-Jabrial,* in *Kulliyat-i-Iqbal* (Karachi: Al Muslim Publishers, 1994), pp. 17, 28.

18. Muhammad Iqbal, *The Reconstruction of Religious Thought in Islam* (1934; reprint, Lahore: Sang-e-Meel, 1996), pp. 136, 157.

19. Jinnah's address to the Karachi Bar Association, January 25, 1948, in Afzal, *Speeches and Statements,* p. 455.

20. *Report of the Court of Inquiry Constituted under Punjab Act II of 1954 to Enquire into the Punjab Disturbances of 1953* (Lahore: Superintendent Government Printing Press, 1954), pp. 182, 200.

21. Ibid., p. 218.

3. A Sprawling Military Barrack

1. See, for instance, Stephen Cohen, *The Idea of Pakistan* (Washington, DC: Brookings Institution, 2004); and Hassan Abbas, *Pakistan's Drift into Extremism: Allah, the Army, and America's War on Terror* (Armonk, NY: M. E. Sharpe, 2005).

2. Ayesha Jalal, "Inheriting the Raj: Jinnah and the Governor-Generalship Issue," *Modern Asian Studies* 19 (1985): 29–53.

3. See Sugata Bose, "Instruments and Idioms of Colonial and National Development," in *International Development and the Social Sciences: Essays on the History and Politics of Knowledge,* ed. Frederick Cooper and Randall Packard (Berkeley: University of California Pres, 1998), pp. 45–63.

4. Cited in Ayesha Jalal, *The State of Martial Rule: The Origins of Pakistan's Political Economy of Defence* (Cambridge: Cambridge University Press, 1990), pp. 51–52.

5. Extract from note by B. Cookram (CRO) to UK embassy, Washington, DC, August 23, 1948, British Foreign Office records, DO 133/81, Adam Matthew Digital Archives (henceforth AMDA), p. 19.

6. *The Times* (London), December 27, 1947.

7. *The Times* (London), April 19, 1948.

8. Memo on "North West Tribal Areas and Afghanistan," DO 134/19, AMDA, p. 4.

9. Nehru to Clement Attlee, November 23, 1947, DO 133/68, AMDA, pp. 3–5.

10. Liaquat to Attlee, November 24, 1947, DO 133/69, AMDA, p. 8.

11. Note by Paul Grey, November 26, 1947, DO 133/69, AMDA, p. 13.

12. A. H. Reed (UK High Commission, Pakistan) to Stephenson (CRO), March 3, 1948, DO 134/1, AMDA, p. 7.

13. Extract from note by B. Cookram (CRO) to UK embassy, Washington, DC, August 23, 1948, AMDA, p. 45. For an account of the Faqir of Ipi's activities, see Sana Haroon, *Frontier of Faith: Islam in the Indo-Afghan Borderland* (New York: Columbia University Press, 2007), ch. 6.

14. See William A. Brown, *The Gilgit Rebellion* (Bethesda, MD: IBEX, 1998), and Martin Sokefeld, "From Colonialism to Postcolonial Colonialism: Changing Modes of Domination in the Northern Areas of Pakistan," *Journal of Asian Studies* 64, no. 4 (November 2005): 939–973.

15. Formulated by Khalid Bin Sayeed in *Pakistan: The Formative Phase* (Karachi: Pakistan Publishing House, 1960), the concept of the "viceregal system" has been adopted by a succession of scholars and has passed into the domain of popular political culture.

16. Jinnah's press conference in Sibi, Balochistan, February 15, 1948, in *Selected Speeches and Statements of the Quaid-i-Azam Mohammad Ali Jinnah (1911–34 and 1947–48),* ed. M. Rafique Afzal, 4th ed. (Lahore: Research Society of Pakistan, 1980), p. 457.

17. On the "overdeveloped" nature of the postcolonial state, see Hamza Alavi, "The State in Post-Colonial Societies: Pakistan and Bangladesh," *New Left Review* 1, no. 74 (July–August 1972).

18. Francis Mudie to Liaquat Ali Khan, February 13, 1948, Correspondence of the Prime Minister with the Governor of West Punjab, 2(2)-PMS/48, National Documentation Center (NDC), Islamabad.

19. Cited in Jalal, *The State of Martial Rule,* p. 117.

20. Report I, Dated 15/6/1951, File no. 23(34), PMS/53, Judgment in the Rawalpindi Conspiracy Case), NDC.

21. Faiz Ahmad Faiz, *Dast-i-Saba,* in *Nuskha-i-Wafa* (Lahore: Maktaba-i-Karavan, n.d.), pp. 107–190.

22. Cited in Farooq Naseem Bajwa, *Pakistan and the West: The First Decade, 1947–1957* (Karachi: Oxford University Press, 1996), p. 18.

23. Cited in Jalal, *The State of Martial Rule,* p. 128.

24. Cited in ibid., p. 132.

25. Ibid., pp. 133–135.

26. Current Intelligence Bulletin, Office of Current Intelligence, Central Intelligence Agency, October 17, 1951, http://www.icdc.com/~paulwolf/pakistan/liaquat17oct1951 .htm.

27. Correspondence between American diplomats in Pakistan and Department of State, 1951–1954, in ibid.

28. Dhaka was spelled as Dacca in the period before 1971. However, I have chosen to use the current spelling, which is much closer to the Bengali pronunciation of the name.

29. Feroz Khan Noon to Liaquat Ali Khan, correspondence with the Governor of East Bengal, 2(1)-PMS/52, February 28, 1952, NDC.

30. Fazlur Rahman to Liaquat Ali Khan, September 14, 1949, F.No. 14-313/49-Est, correspondence with the Minister for Commerce and Education, 3(4)-PMS/50, NDC.

31. Raziur Rahman (secretary to governor) to Ali Asghar (private secretary to prime minister), correspondence with the Governor of East Bengal, 2(1)-PMS/52, June 14, 1952, NDC.

32. Manto, letter no. 1, December 16, 1951, in *Bitter Fruits: The Very Best of Saadat Hasan Manto* trans. Khalid Hasan (New Delhi: Penguin, 2008), pp. 612–613.

33. Manto, letter no. 4, February 21, 1954, in ibid., p. 624.

34. "Serious Economic Crisis: Policy of Drift," *The Times* (London), April 18, 1953.

35. John K. Emmerson (Charge d'Affaires, American Embassy, Karachi) to Department of State, September 25, 1954, http://www.icdc.com/~paulwolf/pakistan/karachi25s ept1954.htm.

36. Iqbal Akhund, *Trial and Error: The Advent and Eclipse of Benazir Bhutto* (Karachi: Oxford University Press, 2000), p. 68.

37. See Ayesha Jalal, "Towards the Baghdad Pact: South Asia and Middle East Defence in the Cold War," *International History Review* 11, no. 3 (August 1989).

38. See Qudrutullah Shahab, *Shahabnama* (Lahore: Sang-e-Meel Publications, 1987), chapter on Ghulam Mohammad, pp. 642–645.

39. Cited in Hamid Ali Khan, *Constitutional and Political History of Pakistan* (Karachi: Oxford University Press, 2005), p. 88.

40. According to Kelsen's theory, a successful revolution established its own legality. See Hans Kelsen, *Pure Theory of Law,* trans. from the second revised and enlarged German edition by Max Knight (Berkeley: University of California Press, 1978).

41. Gul Hassan Khan, *Memoirs of Lt. Gen. Gul Hassan Khan* (Karachi: Oxford University Press, 1993), pp. 133-135.

4. Pitfalls of Martial Rule

1. "Martial Law Set up in Pakistan Crisis," *New York Times,* October 8, 1958.

2. "Pakistan Leader Defends Change," *New York Times,* October 9, 1958.

3. For an endorsement of the new regime, see Herbert Feldman, *Revolution in Pakistan: A Study of the Martial Law Administration* (London: Oxford University Press, 1967).

4. Alexander Symon (UK High Commissioner [HC], Karachi, to Foreign Office [FO]), October 24, 1958, DO 134/26, Foreign Office Collection of Files on India, Pakistan and Afghanistan, 1947–80, Adam Matthew Digital Archives (henceforth AMDA), pp. 89, 93, 95.

5. "Life in Pakistan Changes Sharply," *New York Times,* October 12, 1958.

6. Symon to FO, October 24, 1958, DO 134/26, AMDA, pp. 5–6.

7. Faiz Ahmad Faiz, *Dast-i-Saba,* in *Nuskha-i-Wafa* (Lahore: Maktaba-i-Karavan, n.d.), p. 329.

8. W. Mallory-Browne, Counselor, American Embassy Karachi, to Department of State, July 16, 1959, NND 867414, RG 59, Box 3873, National Archives of the United States of America.

9. Land Reforms Commission—Draft Martial Law Regulation on Land Reforms, File No. 630/CF/58-I, National Documentation Center (henceforth NDC), Islamabad, pp. 29–31.

10. N. J. Barrington (UK High Commission, Rawalpindi) to FO, February 27, 1967, FCO 37/184, AMDA, p. 36.

11. "Pakistan Regime Ending First Year," *New York Times,* October 25, 1959.

12. For the correspondence between Ayub Khan and Muhammad Ibrahim, see Sufia Ahmed, ed., *Diaries of Justice Muhammad Ibrahim (1960–1966)* (Dhaka: Academic Press and Publishers Library, 2011), pp. 222–258.

13. "Pakistan to Have a Presidential Form of Government," *The Times* (London), March 2, 1962.

14. N. J. Barrington (UK High Commission, Rawalpindi) to Stratton, August 12, 1966, DO 134/31, AMDA, p. 21.

15. Barrington's meeting with Khizar Hayat Tiwana, no date, DO 134/31, AMDA, p. 5.

16. Ayub's diary entry, January 22, 1967, in *Diaries of Field Marshal Mohammad Ayub Khan, 1966–1972,* ed. Craig Baxter (Karachi: Oxford University Press, 2007), p. 52.

17. Meeting of the Pakistan Federal Cabinet in Rawalpindi, Monday, December 22, 1958, author's archive.

18. Meeting of the Pakistan Federal Cabinet, Wednesday, December 24, 1958, author's archive.

19. Ayub's diary entry, September 6, 1966, in *Diaries of Field Marshal Mohammad Ayub Khan*, p. 5.

20. Record of UK HC's conversation with Law Minister Muhammad Munir, August 12, 1962, DO 134/29, AMDA, p. 3.

21. Press clipping from *Daily Jang* (Karachi), July 12, 1962, DO 134/29, AMDA, pp. 17–18.

22. Ayub's diary entry, September 4, 1966, in *Diaries of Field Marshal Mohammad Ayub Khan*, p. 4.

23. See Rashid Amjad, *Private Industrial Investment in Pakistan: 1960–1970* (Cambridge: Cambridge University Press, 1982).

24. Thomas L. Hughes, "Pakistan: Economic Disparity and Political Discontent," US State Department research memorandum, March 12, 1969, FCO 37/471, AMDA, p. 12.

25. "President Ayub Firmly in Power in Pakistan," *The Times* (London), February 25, 1965.

26. Ayub's diary entry, April 11, 1967, in *Diaries of Field Marshal Mohammad Ayub Khan*, p. 79.

27. Hamid Khan, *Constitutional and Political History of Pakistan* (2001; reprint, Karachi: Oxford University Press, 2007), pp. 174–175.

28. Bhutto to Ayub Khan, May 12, 1965, author's archive.

29. General Mohammed Musa to Bhutto, May 21, 1965, author's archive.

30. Bhutto to Ayub Khan, May 12, 1965, author's archive.

31. Bhutto's unsigned memos to Ayub Khan, n.d., author's archive.

32. Ibid.

33. Bhutto to Ayub Khan, August 5, 1965, author's archive.

34. Note by D. Connelly, August 17, 1965, DO 133/173, AMDA, p. 22.

35. P. M. Shaw's reports on two visits to Kashmir, DO 133/177, AMDA, p. 247.

36. Cited in Mumtaz Mufti's autobiography, *Alaf Nagri*. For the English translation, see http://www.defenceblog.org/2011/11/miracles-in-1965-indo-pak-war.html.

37. Minute by D. K. Timms (British FO), October 5, 1965, FO 371/180963, AMDA, pp. 180–181.

38. Telegram from US Embassy in Pakistan to the Department of State, Rawalpindi, September 10, 1965, *Foreign Relations of the United States, 1964–1968*, vol. 25, *South Asia* (Washington, DC: Department of State, 1999), #200, http://history.state.gov/historical documents/frus1964-68v25/d200.

39. Telegram from US Embassy in Pakistan to the Department of State, Rawalpindi, September 19, 1965, ibid., #215, http://history.state.gov/historicaldocuments/frus1964 -68v25/d215.

40. Johnson's conversation with US ambassador to the UN, Arthur Goldberg, September 18, 1965, editorial note, ibid., #213, http://history.state.gov/historicaldocuments /frus1964-68v25/d213.

41. Memorandum from the President's Deputy Special Assistant for National Security Affairs (Komer) to the President's Special Assistant for National Security Affairs (Bundy), Washington, October 7, 1965, ibid., #235, http://history.state.gov/historicaldocuments /frus1964-68v25/d235.

42. "President's Visit to the United States," n.d., Bhutto notes, author's archive.

43. Memorandum of Telephone Conversation between President Johnson and the Under Secretary of State (Ball), Washington, December 14, 1965, *Foreign Relations of the United States, 1964–1968*, vol. 25, *South Asia* (Washington, DC: Department of State, 1999), #264, http://history.state.gov/historicaldocuments/frus1964-68v25/d264.

44. Record of Johnson's meeting with Ayub, December 15, 1965, ibid., #267, http:// history.state.gov/historicaldocuments/frus1964-68v25/d267.

45. President's Visit to the United States," n.d., pp. 27–28, author's archive.

46. N. J. Barrington (UK High Commission, Rawalpindi) to Stratton, August 12, 1966, DO 134/31, AMDA, p. 21.

47. Rounaq Jahan, *Pakistan: Failure in National Integration* (New York: Columbia University Press, 1972).

48. N. J. Barrington's note "Mr. Nurul Amin and the President" based on conversation with Amin's private secretary Shamsuddin, July 7, 1967, FCO 37/178, AMDA, pp. 4–5.

49. Ayub's diary entry, May 24, 1967, in *Diaries of Field Marshal Mohammad Ayub Khan*, p. 100.

50. Bhutto's speech at the Rawalpindi Bar Association, April 24, 1967, DO/134/31, AMDA, pp. 34–61.

51. Pickard (UK HC, Rawalpindi) to Michael Stewart, UK MP, "Disturbances in West Pakistan," n.d., FCO 37/466, AMDA, p. 106.

52. Zulfikar Ali Bhutto's affidavit to the West Pakistan High Court, writ petition No. 1794 of 1968, author's archive.

53. Ayub's diary entry, November 13 and December 20, 1968, and February 21, 1969, in *Diaries of Field Marshal Mohammad Ayub Khan,* pp. 283, 291, 301.

54. UK High Commission (Rawalpindi) to FO, telegram, February 11, 1969, FCO/37 468, AMDA, p. 184.

55. See, for instance, UK Deputy High Commission (Dhaka) to FO, telegram, March 5, 1969, FCO 37/469, AMDA, p. 207.

56. Ayub's letter to Yahya Khan, March 26, 1969, in Altaf Gauhar, *Pakistan's First Military Ruler* (Lahore: Sang-e-Meel, 1993), http://www.therepublicofrumi.com/archives /69ayub24.htm.

57. Pickard to FO, telegram, April 9, 1969, FCO 37/471, AMDA, p. 150.

58. Pickard to FO, March 26, 1969, FCO 37/470, AMDA, p. 114.

59. Ayub's diary entry, November 1, 1969, in *Diaries of Field Marshal Mohammad Ayub Khan*, p. 337.

60. See Shuja Nawaz, *Crossed Swords: Pakistan, Its Army, and the Wars Within* (Karachi: Oxford University Press, 2008), pp. 50–251, 258–260.

5. Toward the Watershed of 1971

1. PPP's brief submitted to the Hamoodur Rahman Commission of Inquiry into the 1971 War appointed by the Central Government of Pakistan, prepared by Rafi Raza (special assistant to Bhutto), in author's archive (henceforth *PPP to HRC*), December 26, 1971, pp. 4–6; and *Dawn* (Karachi), October 31, 1968.

2. Z. A. Bhutto's "Brief Memorandum on the Current Situation," April 14, 1971, *PPP to HRC*, appendix 57.

3. Z. A. Bhutto, *The Great Tragedy* (Karachi: Vision Publications, 1971), pp. 27, 73–74.

4. Jinnah's speech in Dhaka, March 21, 1948, in *Quaid-i-Azam Mohammad Ali Jinnah Speeches as Governor-General of Pakistan, 1947–1948* (Lahore: Sang-e-Meel, 1989), pp. 97, 101.

5. Habib Jalib, "Khatrey Mein Islam Nahin" (Islam Is Not in Danger), in *Charoon Janab Sunata* (Lahore: Al Ahmad Publications, 1994), p. 133.

6. There is a vast body of literature on the displacement and resettlement of populations after 1947. See, for instance, Tai Yong Tan and Gyanesh Kudasiya, *The Aftermath of Partition in South Asia* (London: Routledge, 2000); Ian Talbot, *Divided Cities: Partition and Its Aftermath in Lahore and Amritsar, 1947–1957* (Karachi: Oxford University Press, 2006); and also Ian Talbot and Shinder Thandi, eds., *People on the Move: Punjabi Colonial, and Post-Colonial Migrations* (Karachi: Oxford University Press, 2004). For a study of the impact of the mass migrations on two cities in Pakistani Punjab, Gujranwala, and Sialkot, see Ilyas Chatta, *Partition and Locality: Violence, Migration, and Development in Gujranwala and Sialkot, 1947–1961* (Karachi: Oxford University Press, 2011).

7. See Vazira Fazila-Yacoobali Zamindar, *The Long Partition and the Making of Modern South Asia: Refugees, Boundaries, Histories* (New York, Columbia University Press, 2007), chs. 1–3; and Sarah Ansari, *Life after Partition: Migration, Community and Strife in Sindh, 1947–1962* (Karachi: Oxford University Press, 2005), chs. 3–4.

8. Farina Mir, *The Social Space of Language: Vernacular Culture in British Colonial Punjab* (Berkeley: University of California Press, 2010).

9. Saadia Toor, *The State of Islam: Culture and Cold War Politics in Pakistan* (London: Pluto Press, 2011), ch. 3.

10. Hussain Haqqani's *Pakistan: Between Mosque and Military* (Lahore: Vanguard, 2005) attributes the close nexus between the military and the mosque after the 1980s to the early years of Pakistan. Inattention to the nuances of the argument can efface the qualitative differences in the relationship between religion and the state in the first twenty-five years and the post-1979 political and international geostrategic context.

11. For an in-depth analysis of Mawdudi's thought and politics, see Vali Nasr, *Mawdudi and the Making of Islamic Revivalism* (New York: Oxford University Press, 1996).

12. Ayub's diary entry, April 4, 1967, in *Diaries of Field Marshal Mohammad Ayub Khan, 1966-1972*, ed. Craig Baxter (Karachi: Oxford University Press, 2007), p. 79.

13. Ayub's diary entry, December 5, 1970, to January 1, 1971, ibid., pp. 417-435.

14. Ayub's diary entry, December 10, 1970, and 1 January 1971, ibid., pp. 421, 436.

15. *The Report of the Hamoodur Rahman Commission of Inquiry into the 1971 War (as Declassified by the Government of Pakistan)* (Lahore: Vanguard, n.d.), pp. 77-78 (henceforth *Hamoodur Rahman Commission*).

16. Anthony Mascarenhas, *The Rape of Bangladesh* (Delhi: Vikas, 1971), pp. 70-71.

17. *PPP to HRC*, p. 20.

18. Mascarenhas, *The Rape of Bangladesh*, p. 74.

19. Brigadier A. R. Siddiqi, *East Pakistan, the End Game: An Onlooker's Journal, 1969-1971* (Karachi: Oxford University Press, 2004), p. 58.

20. Admiral S. M. Ahsan's testimony to the Hamoodur Rahman Commission, reproduced in Brigadier (retd.) A. R. Siddiqi, "The Admiral's Dilemma," *The Nation* (Lahore), December 17, 1996.

21. Admiral S. M. Ahsan's testimony to the Hamoodur Rahman Commission, reproduced in Brigadier (retd.) A. R. Siddiqi, "The Die Is Cast," *The Nation* (Lahore), December 19, 1996.

22. Siddiqi, *East Pakistan, the End Game*, p. 50.

23. Gul Hassan Khan, *Memoirs of Lt. Gen. Gul Hassan Khan* (Karachi: Oxford University Press), 1993, p. 256.

24. Siddiqi, *East Pakistan, the End Game*, p. 51.

25. *PPP to HRC*, p. 18.

26. Ibid., p. 22, and "Adjustment on Trade, Currency, Taxation—Bhutto's Terms for Cooperation: Crisis Discussed with President," *Pakistan Times*, February 20, 1971.

27. *Hamoodur Rahman Commission*, pp. 81-82.

28. Ibid., p. 88.

29. Cited in Rafi Raza, *Zulfikar Ali Bhutto and Pakistan, 1967-1977* (Karachi: Oxford University Press, 1997), p. 67.

30. Ibid., p. 87.

31. Bhutto, *The Great Tragedy*, p. 43.

32. The associated included, most notably, General Abdul Hamid Khan, Lt. General S. G. M. M. Pirzada, Lt. General Gul Hassan, Major General Umar, and Major General Mitha.

33. "Transfer Power to Majority Parties- Bhutto Stresses General Accord: Strong Plea for One Pakistan," *Pakistan Times*, March 15, 1971.

34. Telegram from Consulate General in Dhaka to Department of State, April 6, 1971, *Foreign Relations of the United States, 1969-1976*, vol. 11, *South Asian Crisis* (Washington,

DC: Department of State, 2005), #19, http://history.state.gov/historicaldocuments/frus 1969-76v11/d19.

35. For a critical account of the support given by Nixon and Kissinger to Yahya Khan's regime during the civil war in East Pakistan, see Gary J. Bass, *The Blood Telegram: Nixon, Kissinger, and a Forgotten Genocide* (New York: Alfred A. Knopf, 2013).

36. Roedad Khan, *Pakistan—A Dream Gone Sour* (Karachi: Oxford University Press, 1997), pp. 29–30.

37. Lt. Gen. A. A. K. Niazi, *The Betrayal of East Pakistan* (Karachi: Oxford University Press, 1998), pp. xxvi, 274–275.

38. Habib Jalib, "Baghiya Lahoo Lahan" (The Garden Is a Bloody Mess), http://www .revolutionarydemocracy.org/rdv9n1/jalibpoems.htm.

39. Faiz Ahmad Faiz, "Dhaka saay Waapsi" (1974), from *Shaam-i-Shahir-i-Yaran*, in *Nuskh-i-Wafa* (Lahore: Maktaba-i-Karavan, n.d.), p. 527.

6. The Rise and Fall of Populism

1. Z. A. Bhutto, *The Great Tragedy* (Karachi: Vision Publications, 1971), pp. 74–75.

2. *President of Pakistan Zulfikar Ali Bhutto's Speeches and Statements, December 20, 1971–March 31, 1972* (Karachi: Department of Films and Publications, Government of Pakistan, 1972), p. 3.

3. Ibid., pp. 3–4, 7, 15–16.

4. Feroz H. Khan, *Eating Grass: The Making of the Pakistani Bomb* (Stanford, CA: Stanford University Press, 2012), chs. 3 and 4.

5. Bhutto's message on Jinnah's birth anniversary, December 25, 1971, *Speeches and Statements*, pp. 20–21.

6. Bhutto's address to the nation, January 2, 1972, ibid., p. 34.

7. Gul Hassan Khan, *Memoirs of Lt. Gen. Gul Hassan Khan* (Karachi: Oxford University Press, 1993), pp. 364, 380–381.

8. Rafi Raza, *Zulfikar Ali Bhutto and Pakistan, 1967–1977* (Karachi: Oxford University Press, 1997), pp. 149–150.

9. Kamran Asdar Ali, "The Strength of the Street Meets the Strength of the State," *International Journal of Middle East Studies* 37 (2005): 99–100.

10. Dispatch by P. D. McEntee, UK Consul General in Karachi, on his first impressions after four months of his appointment, January 25, 1973, FCO 37/1338, Adam Matthew Digital Archives (henceforth AMDA), pp. 102–103.

11. Record of conversation between A. F. Dingle (Australian Chargé d'Affaires, Islamabad) and Wali Khan in Peshawar, April 3, 1972, FCO 37/1138, AMDA, pp. 111–112.

12. Note of conversation between Amin Jan, an employee of the British Information Service, and Wali Khan, December 3, 1972, FCO 37/1138, AMDA, p. 6.

13. Memorandum by Henry Kissinger (Advisor National Security Affairs) to President Nixon, March 7, 1973, *Foreign Relations of the United States, 1969–1976*, vol. E-8,

Documents on South Asia, 1973–1976 (Washington, DC: Department of State, 2007), #112, http://history.state.gov/historicaldocuments/frus1969-76ve08/ch4.

14. Z. A. Bhutto, *My Pakistan* (Lahore: Bhutto Legacy Foundation, 2011), pp. 31–32, www.bhutto.org.

15. "Pakistan under Civilian Rule," July 1973, *Foreign Relations of The United States, 1969–1976*, vol. E-8, *Documents on South Asia, 1973–1976*, #138, http://history.state.gov/historicaldocuments/frus1969-76ve08/d138.

16. Bhutto's address to the nation, March 3, 1972, *Speeches and Statements*, pp. 110–111.

17. Cited in Raza, *Zulfikar Ali Bhutto and Pakistan*, p. 161.

18. Ayesha Siddiqa, *Military Inc.: Inside Pakistan's Military Economy* (London: Pluto Press, 2007), p. 80.

19. Minutes of the Special Cabinet Meeting, February 12, 1973, Rawalpindi, 40/CF/73, National Documentation Center, Islamabad, pp. 3–4, 8.

20. Mubashir Hasan, *The Mirage of Power: An Inquiry into the Bhutto Years, 1971–1977* (Karachi: Oxford University Press, 2000), pp. 202–208.

21. Cited in UK HC (Islamabad) to FO, telegram, December 2, 1972, FCO 37/1138, AMDA, p. 9.

22. British Embassy (Islamabad) to FO, April 3, 1974, FCO 37/1408, AMDA, p. 52.

23. *PPP Manifesto, 1970*, http://www.ppp.org.pk/manifestos/1970.html#p4.

24. Commonwealth Secretariat Coordination Department note on the deputy secretary general Azim Hussain's comments, March 25, 1974, FCO 37/1408, AMDA, p. 55.

25. They included some of the most prominent journalists in Pakistan today, notably Najam Sethi, editor of the *Friday Times* and former editor of the *Daily Times;* Ahmed Rashid, correspondent of the *Far Eastern Review* and author of several popular books on Afghanistan and Central Asia; and the journalist Rashid Rahman, editor of the *Daily Times.*

26. Agha Shorish Kashmiri's letter sent to the British Ambassador, June 14, 1973 Lahore, FCO 37/1338, AMDA, pp. 7–8.

27. Bhutto to Masud Mufti, deputy commissioner of Larkana, September 12, 1969, author's archive.

28. Cited in Gordon Fraser, *Cosmic Anger: Abdus Salam—The First Muslim Nobel Scientist* (New York: Oxford University Press, 2008), location 4934 Kindle edition.

29. For instance, one such charge was made by Shahid Javed Burki, *Pakistan under Bhutto, 1971–1977* (New York: St. Martin's Press, 1980), chs. 6 and 7.

30. The six parties included the Muslim League, the Tehrik-i-Istiqlal, the Pakistan Democratic party, the National Democratic Party, the Khaksar Tehrik, and the Muslim Conference.

31. Smaller agriculturalists did not have to pay income tax on less than twenty-five acres of irrigated land. The tax rate was lowered from an upper limit of 60 percent to 50 percent. Corporate tax was reduced from 30 percent to 20 percent. Civil and military

pensions were increased and a great deal made of Iqbal's centenary celebrations in a clear attempt to stoke Punjabi pride. Raza, *Zulfikar Ali Bhutto and Pakistan*, pp. 317–318.

32. Ibid., pp. 326–333.

33. Ibid., p. 343.

34. Memorandum of Conversation between Bhutto and Kissinger, February 5, 1975, *Foreign Relations of the United States, 1969–1976*, vol. E-8, *Documents on South Asia, 1973–1976*, #189, http://history.state.gov/historicaldocuments/frus1969-76ve08/d189.

35. Memorandum of Conversation between Kissinger and Pakistani ambassador Yaqub Khan, December 17, 1976, ibid., #239, http://history.state.gov/historicaldocuments/frus1969-76ve08/d239.

36. Khalid Mahmud Arif, *Working with Zia: Pakistan's Power Politics, 1977–1988* (Karachi: Oxford University Press, 1995), p. 52.

37. "Bhutto Says Americans Aid Critics," *New York Times,* April 29, 1977.

38. Cited in Robert Wigg, "Mr. Bhutto Accuses US of Financing Pakistani Opposition," *The Times* (London), April 29, 1977.

39. Zulfikar Ali Bhutto, *If I Am Assassinated* (New Delhi: Vikas, 1979), p. 22, www.bhutto.org.

40. Shuja Nawaz, *Crossed Swords: Pakistan, Its Army, and the Wars Within* (Karachi: Oxford University Press, 2008), p. 337.

7. Martial Rule in Islamic Garb

1. Richard Wigg, "Mr. Bhutto Voices Fear of a Coup as MPs Demand His Resignation," *The Times* (London), April 18, 1977.

2. "You can forget elections" was a comment General Zia-ul-Haq made at a meeting with newspaper editors. Cited in A. P. Fabian to FO, September 9, 1980, FCO 37/2358, Adam Matthew Digital Archives (henceforth AMDA), p. 31.

3. Roedad Khan, *Pakistan—A Dream Gone Sour* (Karachi: Oxford University Press, 1997), p. 84.

4. Hussain Haqqani, *Pakistan: Between Mosque and Military* (Lahore: Vanguard, 2005), p. 127.

5. Khan, *Pakistan—A Dream Gone Sour,* pp. 87–88.

6. Z. A. Bhutto to Justice Anwar-ul-Haq, May 7, 1978, http://www.bhutto.org/trial.htm.

7. *White Paper on the Performance of the Bhutto Regime,* 4 vols. (Islamabad: Government of Pakistan, 1979).

8. Shuja Nawaz, *Crossed Swords: Pakistan, Its Army, and the Wars Within* (Karachi: Oxford University Press, 2008), p. 364.

9. Cited in Zulfikar Ali Bhutto, *My Dearest Daughter: A Letter from the Death Cell* (Lahore: Classic, 1994), p. 7, www.bhutto.org.

10. Asma Jahangir and Hina Jilani, *Hudood Ordinances: A Divine Sanction? A Research Study of the Hudood Ordinances and Their Effect on the Disadvantaged Sections of Pakistan Society* (Lahore: Sang-e-Meel Publications, 2003).

11. American Embassy (Islamabad) to Secretary of State, July 11, 1979, *Documents from the US Espionage Den (45): US Interventions in Islamic Countries—Pakistan—I* (Tehran: Muslim Students Following the Line of the Imam), p. 102.

12. British Ambassador (Islamabad) to Secretary of State, FO, January 5, 1979, FCO 37/2190, AMDA, pp. 17–18.

13. For a detailed account of the attack on the US embassy in Islamabad which mirrors the information available in the British Foreign Office papers used in this chapter, see Steve Coll, *Ghost Wars: The Secret History of the CIA, Afghanistan, and bin Laden, from the Soviet Invasion to September 10, 2001* (New York: Penguin Books, 2004), pp. 21–37.

14. Foreign Broadcasting Information Service (FBIS) Daily Reports, Karachi Domestic Service, November 21, 1979.

15. British Embassy (Islamabad) to FO, telegram, November 29, 1979, FCO 37/2192, AMDA, p. 7.

16. British Embassy (Islamabad) to FO, telegram, January 8, 1980, FCO 37/2358, AMDA, p. 250.

17. See Yaroslav Trofimov, *The Siege of Mecca: The 1979 Uprising at Islam's Holiest Shrine* (New York: Doubleday, 2007).

18. For a work exclusively pursuing this line of argument, see Frederic Grare, *Pakistan and the Afghan Conflict, 1979–1985: With an Afterword Covering Events from 1985–2001* (Karachi: Oxford University Press, 2003), intro. and ch. 1.

19. Telegram from the US Mission in Geneva to the Department of State and the American Embassy in Pakistan, April 27, 1973, *Foreign Relations of the United States, 1969–1976*, vol. E-8, *Documents on South Asia, 1973–1976* (Washington, DC: Department of State, 2007), #125, http://history.state.gov/historicaldocuments/frus1969-76ve08/d125.

20. Robert M. Gates, *From the Shadows: The Ultimate Insider's Story of Five Presidents and How They Won the Cold War* (New York: Touchstone, 1996), p. 146.

21. Cited in "Pakistan Drops Election Idea and Names Advisory Panel," *New York Times*, December 26, 1981.

22. Cited in a letter from Pakistanis for Democracy to US Senator Frank Church, circa February 1980, FCO 37/ 2358, AMDA, p. 231.

23. "Rebels against the Bhutto Women," *The Economist*, April 19, 1980, pp. 41–42.

24. Frank J. Prial, "Pakistan Keeps Bhutto Family behind Barbed Wire", *New York Times*, November 15, 1980.

25. For a detailed account of the hijacking and Murtaza's role, see Raja Anwar, *Terrorist Prince: The Life and Death of Murtaza Bhutto* (London: Verso, 1997), chs. 8–10.

26. Stuart Auerbach, "Pakistani Denounces Hijacking as Foreign-Linked Conspiracy," March 15, 1981, Islamabad, Washington Post Foreign Service.

27. Hamid Khan, *Constitutional and Political History of Pakistan,* 3rd ed. (Karachi: Oxford University Press, 2007), p. 368.

28. "Thousands Clash during Protests against Government in Pakistan," *New York Times,* August 15, 1983.

29. "Protestors Said to Stone Zia's Motorcade," *New York Times,* September 11, 1983.

30. "Zia Is a Dog," September 13, 1983, United Press International.

31. "Mrs. Bhutto Asks Army to Overthrow Zia," *New York Times,* September 27, 1983.

32. "Lawyers Demonstrate in Lahore," *Washington Post,* October 7, 1983.

33. Cited in Adrian Levy and Catherine Scott-Clark, *Deception: Pakistan, the United States, and the Secret Trade in Nuclear Weapons* (New York: Walker and Company, 2007), p. 44.

34. For a Pakistani military perspective on the nuclear program, see Feroz H. Khan, *Eating Grass: The Making of the Pakistani Bomb* (Stanford, CA: Stanford University Press, 2012).

35. Richard M. Weintraub, "Pakistan, Long a Source and Conduit of Drugs, Becomes Major Consumer," *Washington Post,* December 21, 1987.

36. Williams K. Stevens, "Pakistan Tightens Curbs on Dissent," *New York Times,* May 20, 1984.

37. Bhutto, *If I Am Assassinated* (Delhi: Vikas, 1979) pp. 171–172, www.bhutto.org.

38. Khan, *Constitutional and Political History of Pakistan,* p. 374.

39. Habib Jalib, *Ise Shehar-i-Kharabi Mein* (reprint, Karachi: Danyal, 2001), p. 93.

40. Pakistanis for Democracy to US Senator Frank Church, circa February 1980, FCO 37/ 2358, ADMA, pp. 232–233.

41. Ahmad Faraz, *Shayher-i-Sukhan Arista Hae: Kulliyat* (Islamabad: Dost Publications, 2004), pp. 914–916.

42. Mazhar Ali Khan, *Viewpoint* (Lahore), editorial, June 15, 1980, in *Pakistan: The Barren Years: The Viewpoint Editorials and Columns of Mazhar Ali Khan, 1975–1992,* comp. Mahir Ali (Karachi: Oxford University Press, 1998), p. 230.

43. Mushtaq Gazdar, *Pakistan Cinema, 1947–1997* (Karachi: Oxford University Press, 1997), pp. 163–166.

44. Ibid., p. 175.

45. Barry Renfrew, "Pakistani Government Assailed through TV Reviews," Associated Press, October 22, 1985. The sentiment echoes a popular barb against state television during the Zia era. A frustrated viewer called the managing director of PTV and told him to fix his television set. When the startled official told him to get a technician, the viewer replied: "a technician can't solve the problem; a mullah has got into my set and only you can take him out!"

46. Khan, *Constitutional and Political History of Pakistan,* p. 362.

47. Saeeda Gazdar, "Twelfth February, 1983," in *Beyond Belief: Contemporary Feminist Urdu Poetry,* trans. Rukhsana Ahmad (Lahore: Asr Publications, 1990), pp. 18–21.

48. Cited in *Quaid-i-Azam and Muslim Women,* National Centenary for Birth Celebrations of Quaid-i-Azam Mohammad Ali Jinnah (Islamabad: Ministry of Education, Government of Pakistan, 1976), pp. v–vi.

49. Barry Renfrew, "Opposition Stages Nationwide Anti-Government Protests," Associated Press, January 5, 1986.

50. Jamsheed Marker, *Quiet Diplomacy: Memoirs of an Ambassador of Pakistan* (Karachi: Oxford University Press, 2010), pp. 344–346.

51. Sherbaz Mazari, *A Journey of Disillusionment,* 3rd ed. (Karachi: Oxford University Press, 2006), p. 588.

52. Marker, *Quiet Diplomacy,* p. 345.

53. Mazari, *A Journey of Disillusionment,* pp. 586–588.

54. The precise cause of the crash that killed Zia was never conclusively determined. One of the more popular conspiracy theories in Pakistan was that there was a bomb in the cases of mangoes that were placed on board the plane at the last minute. For a fictional account of the story, see Mohammad Hanif, *A Case of Exploding Mangoes* (New York: Vintage Books, 2009).

55. Faiz Ahmad Faiz, "Hum Bhi Dekhain Gae," from *Dast-i-Sabha,* in *Nuskh-i-Wafa* (Lahore: Maktaba-i-Karavan, n.d.), pp. 130–131.

8. Democracy Restored?

1. Benazir Bhutto, *Daughter of the East: An Autobiography,* 2nd ed. (New York: Simon and Schuster, 2007), pp. 350, 353.

2. Ian Buruma, "A Nation Divided," *New York Times,* January 15, 1989.

3. Isabel Maloney, "Benazir Bhutto: Her Real Life Greek Tragedy Reaches a Climax," *Sydney Morning Herald* (Australia), October 15, 1988.

4. Bhutto, *Daughter of the East,* p. 380.

5. Roedad Khan, *Pakistan—A Dream Gone Sour* (Karachi: Oxford University Press, 1997) p. 108.

6. Maloney, "Benazir Bhutto."

7. Buruma, "A Nation Divided."

8. Mazhar Ali Khan, November 10, 1988, in *Pakistan: The Barren Years: The Viewpoint Editorials and Columns of Mazhar Ali Khan, 1975–1992,* comp. Mahir Ali (Karachi: Oxford University Press, 1998), p. 427.

9. Shuja Nawaz, *Crossed Swords: Pakistan, Its Army, and the Wars Within* (Karachi: Oxford University Press, 2008), p. 415.

10. Bhutto, *Daughter of the East,* p. 393.

11. Mushahid Hussain, "Pakistan: Benazir Blends Khaki with Mufti," Inter Press Service, April 13, 1990.

12. Bhutto, *Daughter of the East,* pp. 388, 393.

13. "Bhutto Must Achieve Reform," *Financial Times,* November 9, 1989.

14. Mazhar Ali Khan, September 21, 1989, *Pakistan: The Barren Years,* pp. 447–448.

15. Nawaz, *Crossed Swords,* pp. 425–426.

16. Habib Jalib, *Ise Shahir-i-Kharabi Mein,* 3rd ed. (Karachi: Maktaba-i-Danyal, 2001), p. 100 [my translation of the Urdu].

17. Jamsheed Marker, *Quiet Diplomacy: Memoirs of an Ambassador of Pakistan* (Karachi: Oxford University Press, 2010), pp. 359–360.

18. Ibid., p. 360.

19. "Bhutto Says She Favors Pact With India to Bar Atom Arms," *New York Times,* July 10, 1989.

20. Bhutto, *Daughter of the East,* p. 396.

21. Mazhar Ali Khan, November 16, 1989, *Pakistan: The Barren Years,* p. 455.

22. Cited in Iqbal Akhund, *Trial and Error: The Advent and Eclipse of Benazir Bhutto* (Karachi: Oxford University Press, 2000), p. 55.

23. Mazhar Ali Khan, June 28, 1990, *Pakistan: The Barren Years,* pp. 465–466.

24. Roedad Khan, *Pakistan—A Dream Gone Sour,* p. 109.

25. Lawrence Ziring, "Pakistan in 1990: The Fall of Benazir Bhutto," *Asian Survey* 31, no. 2 (February 1991): 115–116, 119.

26. Thomas P. Thornton, "The New Phase in U.S.-Pakistani Relations," *Foreign Affairs* 68, no. 3 (Summer 1989): 142–143, 148–149, 152.

27. Nawaz, *Crossed Swords,* p. 442.

28. "Sharif on the Run," *The Economist,* July 21, 1991.

29. Benazir Bhutto, *The Plunder of Pakistan* (Karachi: People's Democratic Alliance, 1991).

30. Ayesha Siddiqa, *Military Inc.: Inside Pakistan's Military Economy* (London: Pluto Press, 2007), pp. 144–150, 183–193.

31. Nawaz, *Crossed Swords,* p. 450.

32. See Chapter 7.

33. Russell Watson, "'Dynasty' Meets 'Family Feud,'" *Newsweek,* January 24, 1994, http://www.newsweek.com/dynasty-meets-family-feud-187370.

34. Ihtasham ul Haque, "Public Pressure Mounts for Recovery of Loans," *Dawn* (Karachi), September 4, 1996.

35. Fatima Bhutto, *Songs of Blood and Sword* (New Delhi: Penguin Viking, 2010), pp. 259, 416–417, 420.

36. "Bhutto's Mother Terms Slaying of Son 'Conspiracy' against Family," Deutsche Presse-Agentur, September 22, 1996.

37. "Nobody has a Right to Get Rid of Me: PM" (Benazir Bhutto's Interview with Imtiaz Alam), *The News* (Karachi), October 19, 1996.

38. Ayaz Amir, "Who Is Conspiring against Whom?," *Dawn,* October 7, 1996.

39. Ayaz Amir, "The Mood of the Sovereign Awam," *Dawn,* November 25, 1996.

40. "Benazir Wants Leghari to Quit," *Dawn,* November 7, 1996.

41. Nasir Abbas Mirza, "The NDRP: Fortune Favours the Corrupt," *The Nation* (Lahore), March 25, 1997.

42. M. Ziauddin, "More Bonds to Be Issued," *Dawn,* October 20, 1997; Sabihuddin Ghausi, "Foreign Loan Payments May Exceed $5bn," *Dawn,* October 21, 1997; M. Aftab, "Taxes! Who Cares, and Who Pays?," *Dawn,* March 25, 1997; "Debt Root-Cause of Sagging Economy," *Dawn,* March 31, 1997.

43. Nawaz, *Crossed Swords,* p. 493.

44. John F. Burns, "Nuclear Anxiety: The Overview; Pakistan, Answering India, Carries out Nuclear Tests; Clinton's Appeal Rejected," *New York Times,* May 29, 1998, http://www.nytimes.com/1998/05/29/world/nuclear-anxiety-overview-pakistan-answering-india-carries-nuclear-tests-clinton.html?pagewanted=all&src=pm.

45. Nawaz, *Crossed Swords,* p. 500.

46. Apart from Musharraf, the six other core planners of the operation were the chief of general staff, General Aziz Khan; the commander of the Tenth Corps, Lieutenant General Mahmud Ahmad; the force commander of the Northern Areas, Brigadier Javed Hasan; the commander of the Eightieth Brigade, Brigadier Masood Aslam; director-general of military operations, Lieutenant General Tauqir Zia; and director of military operations, Brigadier Nadeem Ahmad. This information comes from Nasim Zehra, *From Kargil to the* Coup, unpublished manuscript on the Kargil war, p. 6. I am indebted to Zehra for letting me see her work in progress on the inside story of the Kargil operation from the perspective of its main planners.

47. Ibid., p. 8.

48. Seymour M. Hersh, "A Reporter at Large: On the Nuclear Edge," *New Yorker,* March 29, 1993.

49. Zehra, *From Kargil to the* Coup, pp. 121–122.

9. A Geostrategic Riddle

1. "Oh Pakistan," *The Economist,* October 16, 1999, pp. 19–20.

2. "Dangerous Coup in Pakistan," editorial, *New York Times,* October 13, 1999.

3. Kamran Khan, "What Does the US Expect from Pakistan," *The News* (Karachi), September 23, 1999; Steve Coll, *Ghost Wars: The Secret History of the CIA, Afghanistan, and Bin Laden, from the Soviet Invasion to September 10, 2001* (New York: Penguin Press, 2004), pp. 440–445.

4. Nasim Zehra, "A Self-Written Obituary," *The News,* October 16, 1999.

5. Ayaz Amir, "What Now," *The News,* October 15, 1999.

6. Celia W. Dugger, "Country Is Calm," *New York Times,* October 13, 1999.

7. "Spotlight on Pakistan's Taliban Connection," *The News,* October 15, 1999.

8. Khan, "What Does the US Expect from Pakistan," *The News,* September 23, 1999.

9. Cited in "Musharraf Always Keeps His Commitments: Time," *The News*, October 25, 1999.

10. Dugger, "Country Is Calm."

11. Mir Jamilur Rahman, "Tough Decisions Ahead," *The News*, October 16, 1999.

12. Pervez Musharraf, *In the Line of Fire: A Memoir* (London: Simon and Schuster, 2006), pp. 135–138.

13. Celia W. Dugger, "Treason Charge against Ousted Prime Minister," *New York Times*, November 11, 1999.

14. Hassan Abbas, *Pakistan's Drift into Extremism: Allah, the Army, and America's War on Terror* (Armonk, NY: M. E. Sharpe, 2005), p. 192.

15. Celia W. Dugger, "Exile Deal Leaves Pakistanis Feeling Betrayed," *New York Times*, December 17, 2000.

16. Amit Baruah, "Hijackers, Militants Quetta-Bound: Taliban," *The Hindu*, January 2, 2000.

17. "All 3 Militants Freed by India Entered Pakistan: Azhar," *The News*, January 6, 2000.

18. Selig Harrison, Senior Fellow of the Century Foundation, cited in "Musharraf Faces Coup Threat from Junta, Washington," *Hindustan Times*, January 25, 2000.

19. Jane Parlez, "Pakistanis Lost Control of the Militants, US Hints," *New York Times*, January 26, 2000.

20. M. Ziauddin and Ihtasham ul Haque, "National Accountability Bureau Set Up; Cases against Nawaz being Investigated; Press to Remain Free; Peaceful Co-existence with India; Musharraf Hints at Referendum," (Karachi), November 2, 1999.

21. "US Warned against Coddling Pak Military Regime," *Hindustan Times*, January 24, 2000.

22. Cited in L. K. Sharma, "UK Media Unimpressed with Clinton Talk," *Times of India*, March 28, 2000.

23. Ayesha Jalal, "On the Wrong Side of History" and "New American Agenda in the Region," *Dawn*, May 2 and 3, 2000.

24. Bruce Reidel, *Deadly Embrace: Pakistan, America, and the Future of the Global Jihad* (Washington, DC: Brookings Institution Press, 2011), pp. 60–61.

25. Judith Miller, "South Asia Called Major Terror Hub in a Survey by US," *New York Times*, April 30, 2000.

26. Abbas, *Pakistan's Drift into Extremism*, p. 194.

27. Nasir Malick, "Reshuffle in Army Command in the Offing," *The News*, August 31, 2000.

28. Ayesha Jalal, *The Pity of Partition: Manto's Life, Times, and Work across the India-Pakistan Divide* (Princeton, NJ: Princeton University Press, 2013), p. 187.

29. Musharraf, *In the Line of Fire*, p. 201.

30. "Armitage Refutes Musharraf's Claim," CBS News, February 11, 2009, http://www.cbsnews.com/2100-224_162-2035633.html.

31. Musharraf, *In the Line of Fire*, pp. 201–204.

32. The sense of betrayal was well understood by Steven R. Weisman, who covered Pakistan in the 1980s. See his "On the Front Lines of the Global War on Terror," *New York Times*, September 21, 2001.

33. Shireen Mazari, "The Flaw in Pak-US Ties," *The News*, September 13, 2001.

34. "Indian Media Tries to Implicate Pakistan," *The News*, September 13, 2001.

35. Manoj Joshi, "India Helped FBI Trace ISI-Terrorist Links," *Times of India*, October 9, 2001.

36. James Risen and Judith Miller, "A Nation Challenged: The Spies; Pakistani Intelligence Had Ties to Al Qaida, US Officials Say," *New York Times*, October 29, 2001, http://www.nytimes.com/2001/10/29/world/nation-challenged-spies-pakistani-intelligence-had-ties-al-qaeda-us-officials.html.

37. Ahmed Rashid, *Descent into Chaos: The US and the Failure of Nation Building in Pakistan, Afghanistan, and Central Asia* (New York: Viking, 2008), ch. 13.

38. Nicholas D. Kristof, "U.S Interests Trump Hypocrisy on Pakistan," *New York Times*, December 21, 2001.

39. "Pakistan's Musharraf Launches Referendum Campaign", *The Daily News* (Lahore), April 10, 2002.

40. Jim Hoagland, "Nuclear Enabler," *Washington Post*, October 24, 2002.

41. http://ecp.gov.pk/GE/2002/PartiesPostionNA.aspx.

42. Glenn Kessler, "Musharraf Denies Rape Comments; Recording Shows *Post* Article Correctly Quoted Pakistani President," *Washington Post*, September 19, 2005.

43. Syed Irfan Raza, "'Sharia Guidelines' Issued," *Dawn*, May 12, 2007.

10. Entangled Endgames

1. Ron Suskind, *The Way of the World: A Story of Truth and Hope in an Age of Extremism* (New York: HarperCollins, 2008), p. 268.

2. Benazir Bhutto, *Reconciliation: Islam, Democracy, and the West* (London: Simon and Schuster, 2008), pp. 5–8.

3. "Attack on Ms. Bhutto Was Foretold," editorial, *Daily Times* (Lahore), October 20, 2007; "Baitullah Mehsud Denies Killing Benazir," http://www.andhranews.net/Intl/2007/December/29/Baitullah-Mehsud-denies-27769.asp.

4. Bhutto, *Reconciliation*, pp. 8–9.

5. Amir Mir, *The Bhutto Murder Trail: From Waziristan to GHQ* (New Delhi: Tranquebar Press, 2010), Kindle edition, locations 337–347, 427.

6. Mohammed Hanif, "Musharraf and the Drunk Uncle," *Counterpunch*, November 9–11, 2007, http://www.counterpunch.org/2007/11/09/musharraf-and-the-drunk-uncle/.

7. See Owen Bennett-Jones, "Questions Concerning the Murder of Benazir Bhutto," *London Review of Books*, December 6, 2012.

8. Ayaz Amir, "Why It's Hard to Believe These Napoleons," *The News* (Karachi), August 8, 2008.

9. Chris Allbritton, "Pakistani Army Chief Sought More Drone Coverage in '08: WikiLeaks," Reuters, May 20, 2011, http://www.reuters.com/article/2011/05/20/us-pakistan-wikileaks-idUSTRE74J3UV20110520.

10. Cited in "Time Now to Refocus on Pakistan, Afghanistan: Obama," *Dawn* (Karachi), March 1, 2009.

11. Obaid Abbasi, "Murder Case: Taseer's Assassin Appeals Death Sentence," *Express Tribune* (Karachi), October 7, 2011.

12. Mark Mazzeti, "How a Single Spy Helped Turn Pakistan against the United States," *New York Times,* April 9, 2013.

13. For an insider account of Washington's view of the situation, see Vali Nasr, *The Dispensable Nation: American Foreign Policy in Retreat* (New York: Doubleday, 2013), ch. 3.

14. Hussain Haqqani, *Magnificent Delusions: Pakistan, the United States, and an Epic History of Misunderstanding* (New York: Public Affairs, 2013), p. 342.

15. Mansoor Ijaz, "Time to Take on Pakistan's Jihadist Spies," *Financial Times* (London), October 10, 2011.

16. Confidential Memorandum Briefing for Admiral Mike Mullen, Chairman, Joint Chiefs of Staff, http://www.foreignpolicy.com/files/fp_uploaded_documents/111117_Ijaz percent20memopercent20Foreignpercent20Policy.PDF.

17. Haqqani, *Magnificent Delusions,* pp. 348–349.

18. Fasih Ahmed, "When Mansoor Ijaz Met Shuja Pasha," *Newsweek* (Pakistan), November 20, 2011, http://newsweekpakistan.com/scope/591.

19. Saeed Shah, "Pakistan Army Steps up Confrontation with Government," *The Guardian* (London), January 11, 2012.

20. "Sharif's Protocol Despite ECP Orders Unfair: Kaira," *Pakistan Today,* April 20, 2013.

21. "Pakistani Clerics Proclaim Voting Is 'Islamic Duty,'" *Dawn,* April 25, 2013.

22. Hasan Muhammad, *General Elections in Pakistan: Some Untold Stories and Personal Experiences* (Lahore: Mavra Publishers, 2012), pp. 236–237, 380–382.

23. M. Ziauddin, "Media Wrong, Once Again," *Express Tribune,* May 14, 2013.

24. Sartaj Aziz et al., "The State of the Economy: The Punjab Story," fifth annual report of the Institute of Public Policy, Lahore, 2012, http://ippbnu.org/AR/5AR.pdf.

25. Zahid Hussain, "Imran Khan's Dream," *Dawn,* April 9, 2013.

26. Election Commission of Pakistan, Party Position (National Assembly), http://ecp.gov.pk/overallpartyposition.pdf.

27. "ANP's Mandate Snatched through Terrorism, Says Asfandyar," *Dawn,* May 16, 2013.

28. I. A. Rahman, "More Sweet than Sour," *Dawn,* May 16, 2013.

29. "Imran Khan Threatens Protests against Rigging," *Dawn*, June 11, 2013.

30. For a perceptive study of the workings of Pakistan's postcolonial bureaucracy, see Matthew Hull, *Government of Paper: The Materiality of Bureaucracy in Urban Pakistan* (Berkeley: University of California Press, 2012).

31. Ali Cheema, Hassan Javid, and Muhammad Farooq Naseer, "The Paradox of Dynastic Politics: Facts and Myths about Political Dynasties in Punjab and Their Implications," *Herald* (Karachi), *Political Dynasties*, Elections 2013 special issue, May 2013.

32. Muhammad, *General Elections in Pakistan*, pp. 169–170, 318.

33. Ibid., pp. 512–522.

GLOSSARY

awam	people
batwara	division
chadar	a large wrap
char diwari	four walls of the home
lotas	turncoats
maliks	tribal elders
muhajir	refugee
panchayats	local governments
qawwali	a genre of Sufi devotional music
qiamat	Day of Judgment
rajm	death by stoning
razakars	volunteer militias
zakat	Muslim alms tax
zameen	land
zan	woman
zar	wealth
zina	adultery

ACKNOWLEDGMENTS

I was fortunate to have institutional backing and the encouragement of several individuals. Tufts University provided consistent support over the years and generously granted me time off from teaching to complete the research and writing of this book. My colleagues at the History Department and the Fletcher School have been accommodative of my intellectual pursuits. I am especially grateful to Annette Lazzara, the department administrator, for her exemplary competence, thoughtfulness, and humanity. Students taking my "Contemporary South Asia" course at Fletcher were among the first to hear some of the arguments advanced in this book. Over the years I have benefited from discussions about Pakistan and its role in global politics with several individuals, not all of whom can be mentioned by name. A special thanks is due to Amartya Sen for asking difficult questions about Pakistan that helped me clarify some of my own ideas better. I have had lively discussions on Pakistan with Farina Mir, Neeti Nair, Lata Parwani, and Mridu Rai. I gained insights through my conversations with many people in Pakistan of whom I would particularly like to mention Durre Ahmed, Khalid Ahmed, Abida Hussain, Asma Jahangir, I. A. Rahman, Najam Sethi, and Nasim Zehra.

Ideas and insights alone could not have brought this project to fruition. I owe a posthumous debt to my late father, who left behind a stash of papers, some of which I have used and referred to as "author's archive" after duly accounting for the thirty-year rule. The application of the official Secrecy Act in Pakistan, however, is highly uneven, and most government departments have yet to declassify the documents and make them available to the public. I was able to access the holdings of the National

Documentation Center in Islamabad with the help of my doctoral student Shayan Rajani, to whom special thanks is due. Bilal Baloch, Nida Piracha, and James Schmidt assisted me in getting relevant materials for the book from the Tufts and Harvard Libraries. I want to thank Hameed Haroon of the Dawn Media group for granting me permission to reproduce images from their digital archive as well as Arif Mahmood and Niloufer Patel for facilitating the process. The team at *Newsweek Pakistan* went out of their way to get me a map of contemporary Pakistan at very short notice. Isabelle Lewis drew the maps that appear in the book.

I have presented parts of the book at the Forman Christian College in Lahore and at Amherst College in Massachusetts. The comments of two anonymous readers for Harvard University Press were immensely helpful in making the final revisions and refinements. I was fortunate to have an excellent editor in Joyce Seltzer, who read the entire manuscript and made valuable suggestions for improvement. Her gentle prodding and encouragement gave me the incentive to complete this book in a timely fashion.

I have been blessed with a wonderful and caring mother who has always provided unconditional love and support. My siblings and their families have been understanding and accommodative of my scholarly endeavors. Naazish Ataullah, Nita Nazir, and Amber Sami applauded my efforts while reminding me of the lighter side of things. Sugata Bose was solid in his support and a great sounding board. He has seen yet another of my projects from inception to conclusion and read innumerable drafts of the manuscript. His critical comments and counsel have done much to improve the quality of the book. I am wholly responsible for any blemishes that remain.

INDEX